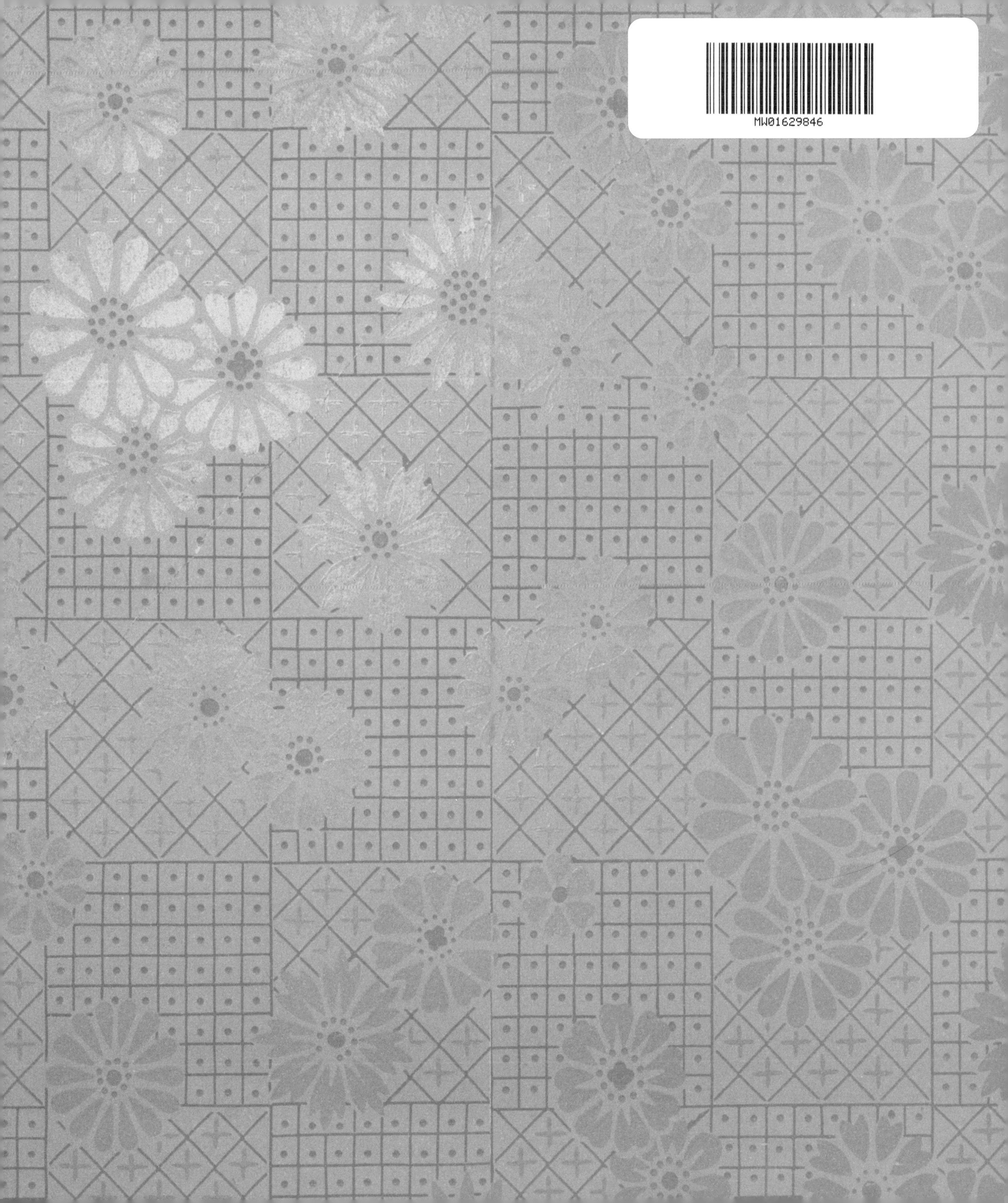

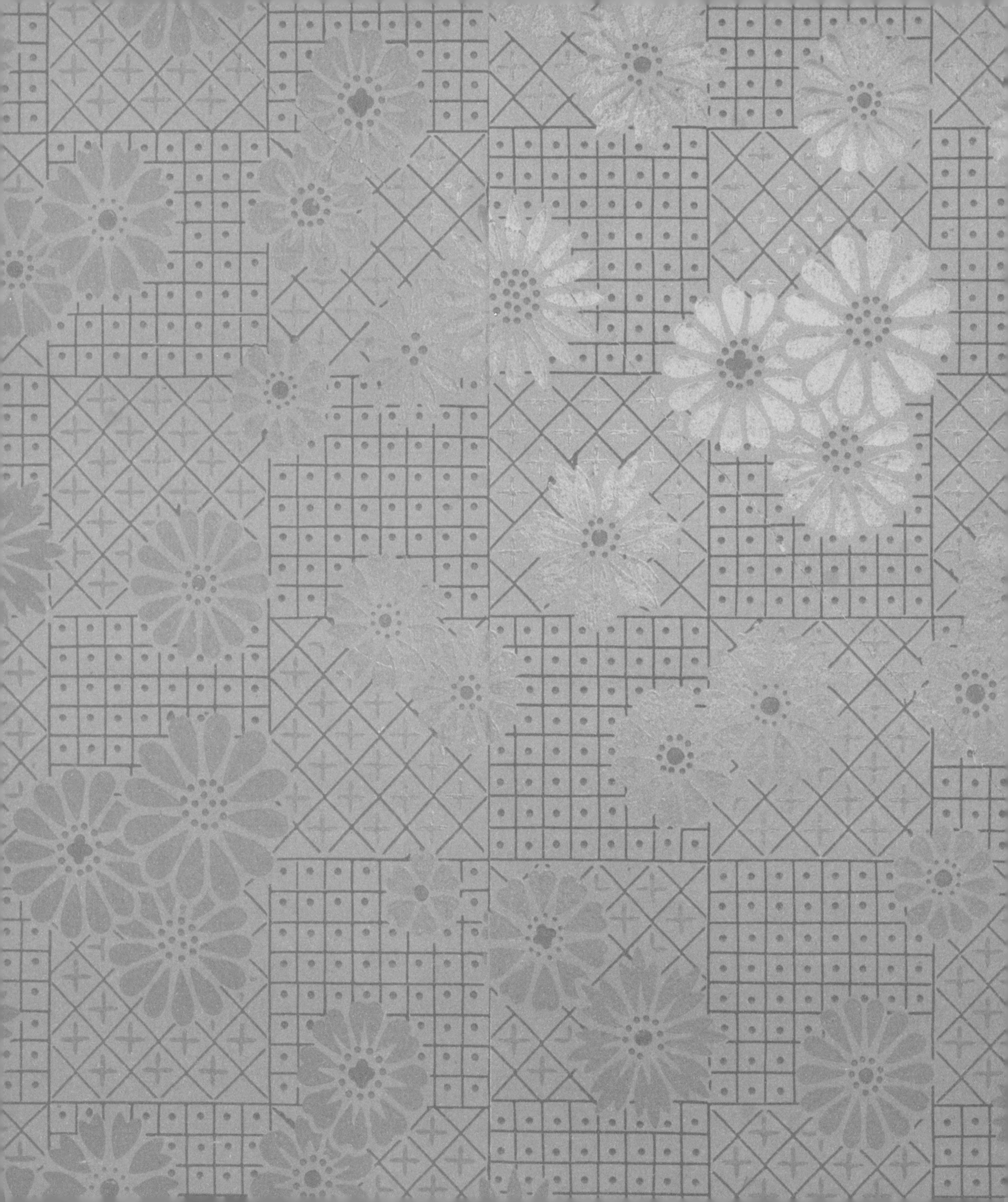

The Influence of Japanese Art on Design

The Influence of Japanese Art on Design

Hannah Sigur

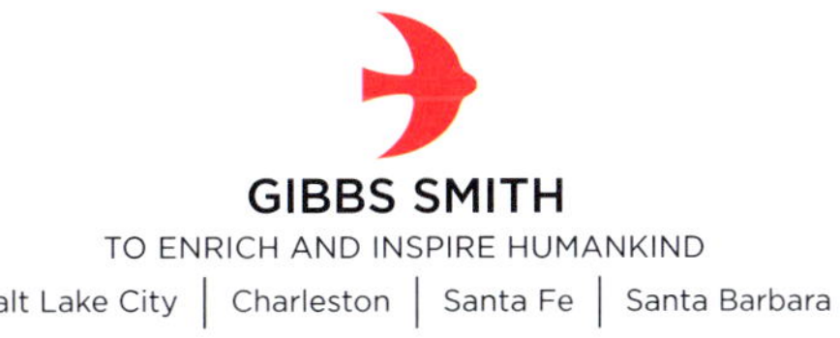

For Susan Jean Zemsky

First Edition
12 11 10 09 08 5 4 3 2 1

Published by
Gibbs Smith
P.O. Box 667
Layton, Utah 84041

Orders: 1.800.835.4993
www.gibbs-smith.com

Designed and produced by Ron Stucki
Printed and bound in Hong Kong
Gibbs Smith books are printed on either recycled 100% post-consumer waste or FSC-certified papers.

Library of Congress Cataloging-in-Publication Data

Sigur, Hannah.
The influence of Japanese art on design / Hannah Sigur. — 1st ed.
p. cm.
Includes bibliographical references and index.
ISBN-13: 978-1-58685-749-3
ISBN-10: 1-58685-749-5
1. Decorative arts—United States—Japanese influences. 2. Decorative arts—United States—History—19th century. 3. Art, Japanese—Influence. I. Title.
NK807.S48 2008
709.73'09034—dc22

2008020741

Contents

Acknowledgments

This book began with a lecture for the 2001 San Francisco Fall Antique Fair. The journey from that initial research has traversed a continent of marvelous people who have widened my vistas with generous gifts of knowledge, time, opportunity, encouragement, sharing, and, above all, infectious joy in a fascinating and pivotal era in both American and Japanese history and the beautiful objects it produced. I especially would like to thank the following individuals:

Hank Dunlop, California College of the Arts, and Cohen-Bray House, Oakland, California;

Dr. Laurence Ruggiero (Director), Donna Climenhage (Curator), Jennifer Thalheimer (Collections Manager), Betsy Peters (Curator of Education), and April Brown, The Charles Hosmer Morse Museum of American Art, Winter Park, Florida;

Anne Mallek (Curator), Gamble House, Pasadena, California;

Dale Wheary (Director of Historical Collections and Programs), Maymont House Museum, Richmond, Virginia;

Rebecca M. Warda (Collections Manager), Widener University Art Gallery & Collection, Chester, Pennsylvania;

Dr. Emily Sano (former director), Asian Art Museum of San Francisco;

Dr. Lisa Koenigsberg, Initiatives in Art and Culture, New York, New York;

Dr. Charles Brownell, Virginia Commonwealth University, Richmond, Virginia;

Dr. Diana Strazdes, University of California–Davis;

Dr. Whitney Chadwick and Irene Anderson, San Francisco State University;

Michael Weller, Argentum Antiques, San Francisco, California;

Allen Michaan, Auctions by the Bay, Alameda, California;

Helga Fleishman, Imari, Inc., Sausalito, California;

Ben Macklowe, Macklowe Gallery, New York, New York;

Kuwabara Kazuo, Scott Konishi, Oriental Treasure Box, San Diego, California;

Edward Forcum, Rosebud Gallery, Berkeley, California;

and to Enterprise for High School Students, San Francisco, California; Ian Berke, Vicky Berol, Len and Patti Blumen, Jackie Colman, Dr. Thomas C. Folk, Gloria S. Garaventa, Stephen Glaser, Monmohan

Grover & Barbara Yates, William P. Hood Jr., Dr. Janet Leja, Barry Lubman, Meher McArthur, Stephen McMaster, Colleen Murphy and Erv Shindell, Richard D. Reutlinger, Steve Sanders and Joyce Davis, Julie L. Sloan, Alan Steele, Kristine A. Steensma, Richard Tuck, Marybeth Welch, Virginia Wrenn, Norman & Nancy Zinner, and Dr. Karen Zukowski and David Diamond.

This book owes much to the support, skills, patience, generous spirit, good will, and good humor of staff—especially Elizabeth Broman—of the library of The Cooper-Hewitt National Design Museum, Smithsonian Institution—and research librarians, permissions administrators, and curators at the Bancroft, Environmental Design, and Asian Studies libraries of University of California–Berkeley; the Chicago Historical Society, the Grolier Club; the Huntington Library, the Mark Twain House; the Freer Gallery of Art/Arthur M. Sackler Gallery, Smithsonian Institution; the Library of Congress, Prints and Photographs Division; The Philadelphia Free Library; the Museum of Fine Arts, Boston; the Jane Voorhees Zimmerli Art Museum, Rutgers University; and the University of Buffalo Archive. You have not only my heartfelt gratitude but also my admiration for the work that you do so selflessly.

And I am more than grateful to my daughter, Margot, who had to endure a childhood completely framed by Japan and Japanese art. Finally, none of this would ever have happened were it not for my husband, Chris, who originally turned my attention to Japan—its dimensions past and present, positive and negative—living, ever-changing, and altogether real. Having done so, he shared my fascination as the unique vital role of the art of Japan revealed itself—in a transformational era in world history, in Japanese-American relations, and in America's vision of itself.

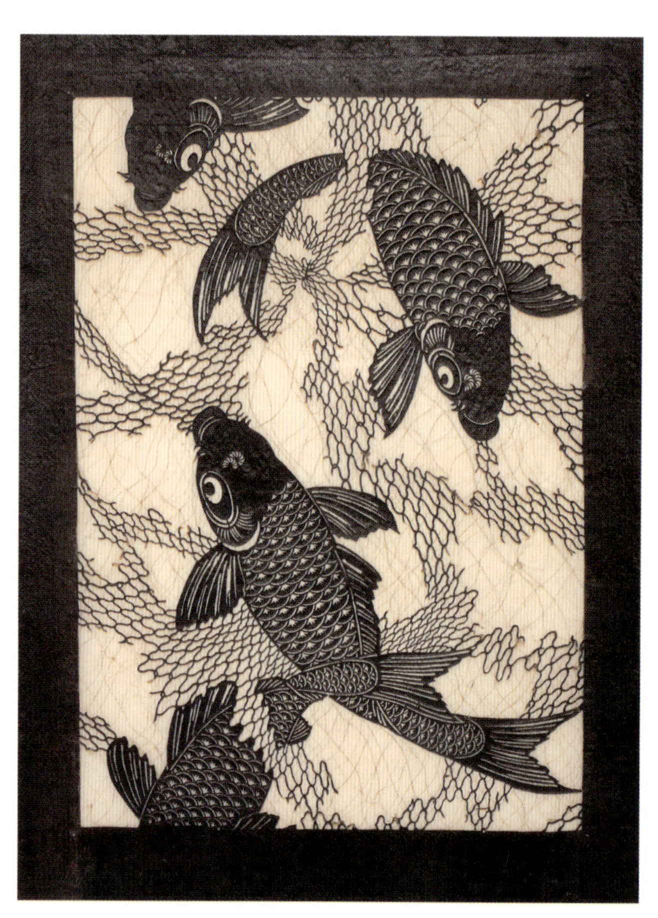

Prologue

The actual people who live in Japan are not unlike the general run of English people—that is to say, they are extremely commonplace, and have nothing curious or extraordinary about them. In fact, the whole of Japan is a pure invention. —OSCAR WILDE[1]

During the vibrant, energetic, and flamboyant era of radical transformation dubbed by Mark Twain as the "Gilded Age," a phenomenon popularly called the "Japan Craze" swept the West. In the United States, it spread from coast to coast, enticed everyone from robber barons to street vendors with its allure, and touched every aspect of life from patent medicines to wallpaper. And, in an era that idealized domesticity, its greatest and most lasting impact occurred in and around the home: dining utensils, dishes, objects, furnishings, and concepts of interior design that defined the very spaces by which people of the time most defined themselves. In short, the Japan Craze typified its own era and initiated almost every direction that modern standards of domestic aesthetics have taken. In having done so, it set the stage for the everyday world we now inhabit.

Japanese art was not alone among non-Western traditions in leaving a mark on Western design, but its effects were by far the deepest. There were two reasons. One was aesthetic: an extraordinary way of reaching beyond the divisive specifics of culture to communicate eloquently for itself alone. Americans of the time found in it every design language: modernism or tradition, abstraction or realism, technical virtuosity or unfettered naturalism, craft or art, romance or functionalism. The other was timing. The story of Japanese influence on American ceramics, metals, textiles, furniture, glass, and interiors is also one of a newly technological and newly international world in which disparate societies mingled in awkward tandem, each pursuing its ambitions and seeking to remake itself in the face of rapid radical change. On this single emerging stage, some saw in the ordinary objects of a vanishing old Japan a fresh model for the American future. It is also a tale of Japanese and American talent, ambition, and vision; and finally, it is a romance of charming fantasy—an American daydream that the Japanese actively fomented, fueled on both sides by the lighter and darker aspects of human nature. So successful was the result that by the time the Craze had spent itself around World War I, Japanese aesthetic ideas had been assimilated to the point of invisibility, having permanently altered the home and, with it, our worldview. To tell that story is the aim of this book.

1. Wilde 1889.

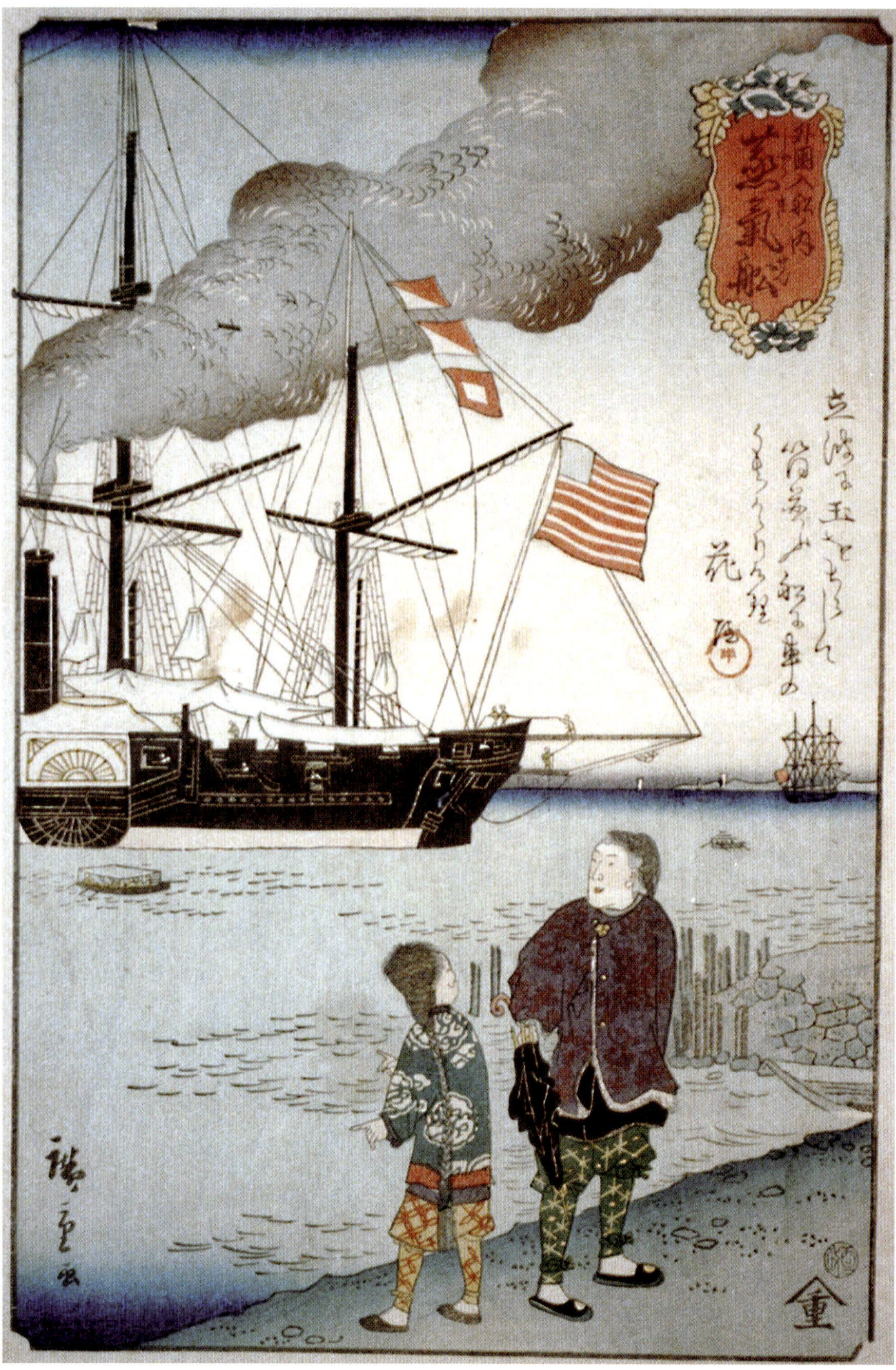

HIROSHIGE II OR HIROSHIGE III. *GAIKOKUJIN SEN NO UCHI: JŌKISEN (FOREIGNER'S SHIP: STEAMSHIP);* UKIYO-E WOODBLOCK PRINT: 1861; 13.58 x 9.06 INCHES. In Yokohama, newly internationalized by Perry's forced opening, a Chinese man and boy stand on the harbor shore near an American sidewheel steamer much like Commodore Perry's own "black ships."

1

STRANGE DREAMS AND STRANGE AWAKENINGS

The Great Face to Face

The story of Rip van Winkle is, like so many other things, reversed in Japan, where it is the country that has gone to sleep and the visitor that is up to date.[1]

—HENRY T. FINCK

One hot and muggy July day, Commodore Matthew Calbraith Perry of the United States Navy sailed four black ships into Uraga Bay near the Shogun's capital city of Edo, forcibly terminating nearly 250 years of Japanese self-imposed semi-isolation. His bold entry was not entirely unexpected. The shogunal government had observed the activities of Western nations in the region for years, already crossed paths with several American representatives, and viewed the intensions of all foreigners with increasing alarm. Yet, if at first unbalanced by the rude intrusion, the Japanese were not passive from the outset in what ensued. Looking from Perry's steamships and cannon (state of the art 1853) to their own armor, matchlocks, and swords (state of the art 1553), they quickly understood that only a policy of *realpolitik* would preserve Japan's mastery of its destiny. What that would entail remained as unnervingly mysterious as the figure of Perry himself.

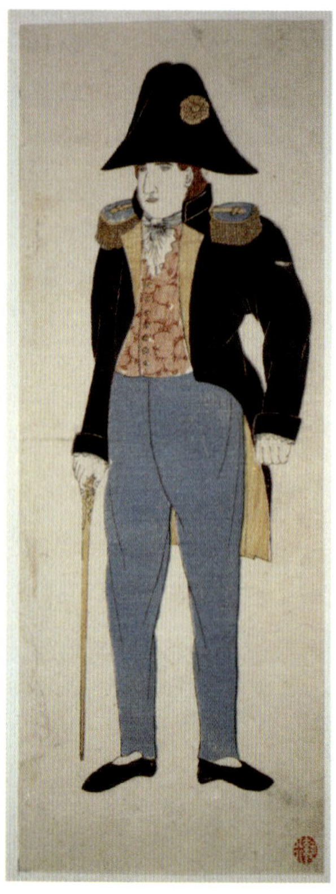

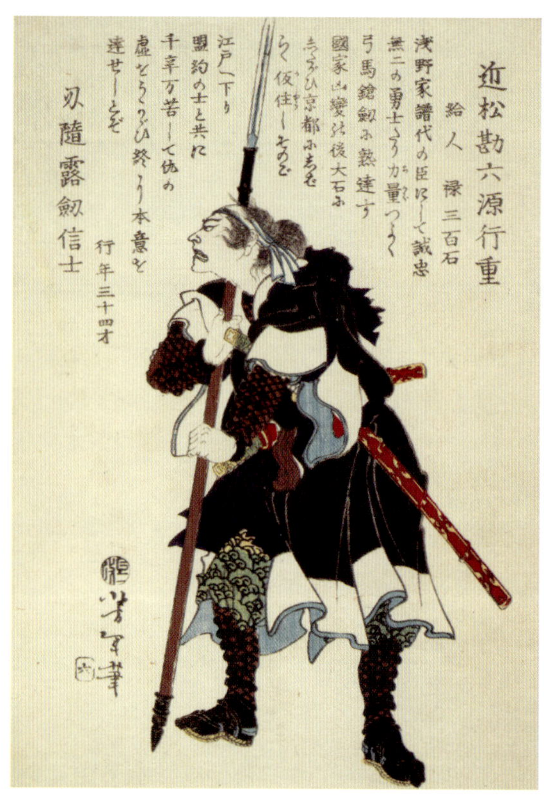

Above: Unknown artist. *Commodore Matthew Calbraith Perry in Japan;* Nagasaki woodblock print; ca. 1850–1900; 16.02 x 5.91 inches.

Above, Right: Taiso Yoshitoshi, *Ronin;* ukiyo-e woodblock print; 1869; from *Seichū gishi meimei gaden.* A "masterless samurai" grimaces fiercely as he leans on his lance.

For all its centuries of isolation, Japan was not wholly unknown to the West. In Perry's time, an educated person with a taste for exotic histories might recall "Zipangu," the mysterious island nation rescued from Mongol invasion by a miraculous windstorm, as described in the thirteenth-century accounts of the Venetian explorer Marco Polo. Late sixteenth-century Portuguese and Spanish forays certainly would have come to mind: their proselytizing of Christianity (the religion of the "civilized," in the West's view) was what prompted Japan not only to abruptly and violently terminate their brief relationship but also to slam shut her doors to most of the outside world ("barbarian," in their view). He then might have marveled at the thought of the single-minded, determined Dutch who followed. Their willingness to leave Japanese souls to their own devices in favor of trade prompted the Japanese to privilege them with an exclusive relationship that lasted two hundred years down to Perry's day. But, for this highly lucrative prize, the handful permitted in the country endured virtual imprisonment on a tiny artificial island off the southern port city of Nagasaki; the Japanese paradoxically accorded their chief representative the honors of a noble on his single yearly trip off the island, a progress to pay respects to the shogun.

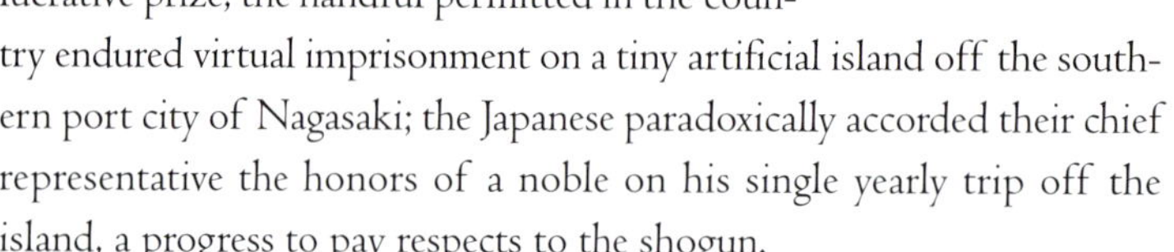

The informed American of Perry's time might have possessed a few mental images had he seen English translations of the seventeenth-century *Atlas Japanensis* or the eighteenth-century *Das Heutige Japan,* both compiled by notable Dutch East India Company employees. But these pictures and descriptions reflected the draconian restrictions imposed by the Japanese government that barred all but a very few select citizens from direct contact and permitted the Dutch only their single, closely monitored annual excursion to the capital. These vague impressions might have been slightly clarified by a visit to the museum in Leiden, established by the early nineteenth-century employee Philip Franz von Siebold to house the collection of lacquer, ceramics, paintings, prints, and plant and animal specimens he assembled before his expulsion from Japan for attempting to

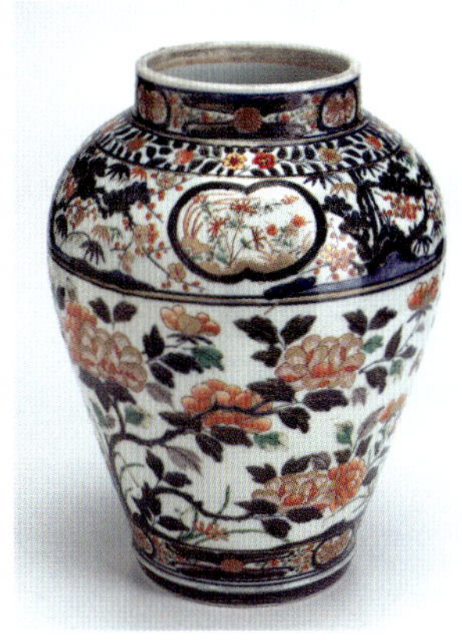

Above: Jar; late seventeenth century; porcelain with underglaze blue and overglaze enamels and gold; 16.25 inches high. An early export Imari jar has floral and *shochikubai* ("pine, bamboo and plum") motifs, its brilliant colors and dense ornamentation a Japanese interpretation of Chinese taste; lid not extant.

Below: John Stalker and George Parker. Fantasy image of Japan; 1688; from *A Treatise of Japanning and Varnishing.*

acquire maps of the country. In general, by Perry's day, an unusual state of affairs had persisted for over two centuries, leaving Japan and its people glossed with an aura of the distant, the exotic, the dangerous, and the odd.

Over the course of this time, a few Japanese arts had made a small but indelible imprint in European minds. Vogues for porcelain from Imari and opulent lacquered cabinetry both began in the seventeenth century and lasted nearly a hundred years. Their pattern of creation, reception, and influence in many ways anticipated what was to come: Designed almost exclusively for export to the West, the ceramics included objects specified by Dutch traders, who encouraged the Japanese to incorporate Chinese-style motifs. Pagodas, gardens, maidens in Japanese kimono or Chinese robes, bearded mountain sages or warriors in strange armor, palaces, huts, bamboo, lotus blossoms, and fans presented a jewel-like, thematically scrambled fantasy world that created misperceptions regarding not only authenticity and Japanese taste but also Japan itself.

Lacquered woodwork of lustrous black or red and elaborately decorated with gold, silver, and mother-of-pearl also captured European imaginations. With few who could distinguish Japanese examples from contemporary Chinese and Indian products also on the market, "Japanese" became a byword for high quality of a certain look. Cabinets, book stands, tobacco boxes, and other objects, already inauthentic, fascinated European craftsmen, who often dismantled them to incorporate the parts into Western cabinets and desks. Their efforts to replicate the lacquer technique itself came to be called "japanning." In his detailed treatise on the subject, the seventeenth-century English cabinetmaker John Stalker enthused, his flights of fancy extending to the distant mysterious source:

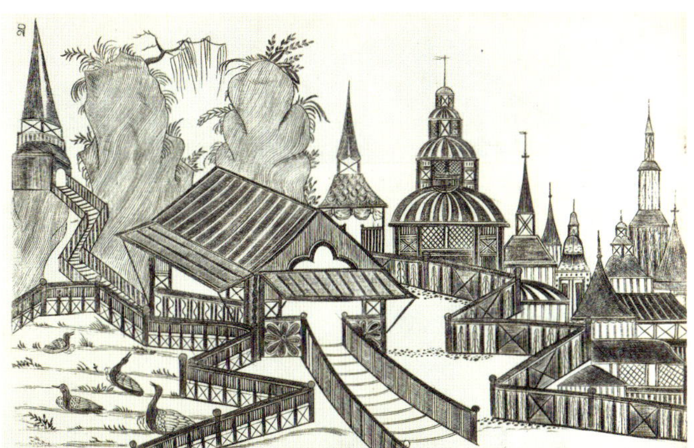

> *. . . Rome must now give place: the glory of one country Japan alone, has exceeded in beauty and magnificence all the pride of the Vatican at this time. . . . Japan can please you with a more noble prospect, not only whole towns, but cities too are there adorned with as rich a covering, so bright and radiant are their buildings, that when the sun darts for his luster upon their Golden roofs, they enjoy a double day by the reflection of his dreams . . .*[2]

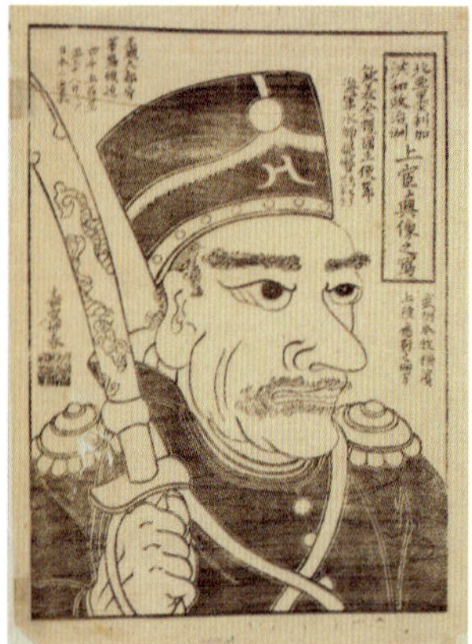

Anonymous artist. *Kita-Amerika kyōwa seiji-shū jōkan shinzō no utsushi* (Accurate picture of commanding officer from the republic of North America); woodblock print; ca. 1854; 12.52 x 9.21 inches. Done at the time of Commodore Perry's reception at Yokohama, this image is thought to depict Captain Henry Adams, a senior officer of Perry's crew.

In this complicated way, mongrel porcelain and lacquer objects appeared exotic to both sides. Erroneously perceived by most Westerners as authentically Japanese, their appeal to Europeans lay in being "foreign" versions of familiar useful forms. Un-Japanese to their creators, they provided a design template based upon discriminate borrowing and revealed a genius for both meeting and shaping the desires of a foreign market. They also produced a vision of hidden Shangri-La that carried forward to the moment of Perry's encounter and persisted even afterwards in the minds of many.

Mid-nineteenth-century America was a rising maritime power in an era when, aided by technological advances and abetted by an ingrained sense of moral justification, Western nations unhesitatingly advanced their economic and political ambitions. After more than two centuries of Dutch monopoly, what Commodore Perry wanted was simple and straightforward: the lucrative market of backward, weak Japan on terms dictated by the United States. In 1854 Perry repeated his bold intrusion, impelling the Japanese to accept a treaty giving the United States access to major ports. Its doors unbolted on one outsider's terms, Japan now had to open them to all comers. Ensuing treaties exploited the gross imbalance of power that favored the West and opened a Pandora's box of troubles for the Japanese: unequal partner on its own territory and stripped of nearly all control or profit from trade, the government also had no authority over nonnationals. Barbarians—large, smelly, uncouth, and hairy Americans, Englishmen, Germans, Frenchmen, Dutchmen, and Russians—now disrespectfully swaggered with impunity around the impoverished but still-proud nation, its mire of self-inflicted antiquation blatant to all. The shogun's government dispatched a fact-finding mission abroad to better acquaint itself with the new challenge, but it accomplished nothing except to aggravate the sense of embarrassment and inadequacy. The ill-prepared and clueless delegation, convinced of a venture into a black hole of barbarism, traveled with its own rice and oil lamps; and though honored with red carpet treatment in the United States, its intimidated senior members rarely ventured from their hotel rooms, while its junior-most member abandoned all dignity and gallivanted about as the darling pet of tittering society ladies. Frustration, anger, humiliation, factionalism, and social pressures erupted to violence.

In 1868, fifteen years after Perry's audacious incursion, the 250-year-old Tokugawa shogunate collapsed.

The usurpers, samurai like the Tokugawa themselves, legitimized their coup by claiming to act on behalf of the emperor. This was callow sixteen-year-old Mutsuhito (1852–1912). In 1868, less than a year on the throne, he was but the latest link in an unbroken chain of shadowy remote figures claiming to extend their divine dynasty back two thousand years to the Sun Goddess, Amaterasu Omikami. During his reign, the Japanese referred to him as *tennō;* the Western press adopted the exotic term *Mikado,* and after his death, he and his era would be posthumously named *Meiji.*

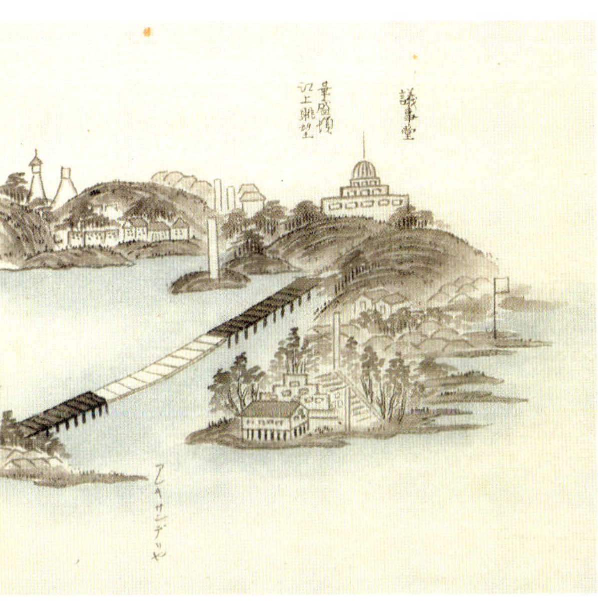

Unknown artist. From *Meriken kōkai nikki ryakuzu.* The unfinished Washington Monument and the Capitol, Washington, D.C.; not before 1860; ink and watercolor; copied from a sketch made by a member of the first Japanese delegation to the United States.

For most of this history, his ancestors had reigned but not ruled. Various factions maintained a firm grip upon the practical realities and pleasures of power. In the new order that did not change, the tennō presided as a figurehead. But, in one of the complex paradoxes that Westerners would come to view as characteristic of "Japaneseness," this embodiment of the country's most ancient and conservative traditions, completely unlettered in the ways of the West, was transformed into an image of progressive, dignified modernity. Soon after ascending the throne, he adopted a Western military-style uniform embellished with fringe, brass buttons, epaulettes, and a sash bedecked with medals. He never appeared in public dressed otherwise. His empress carried out her public life corseted and bustled in the latest European fashion. With this ingenious maneuver, the governing coterie galvanized the country to the gargantuan task of modernization while giving the West a public face it could relate to. Avid American press commentaries on the day-to-day activities and milestones of the Japanese royals, related in the same adulating tone as for their European counterparts, testify to this public relations success.

Meanwhile, with unparalleled speed and intensity, the powers behind the throne set upon a project of unimaginable scope, ambition, and expense: to restore national integrity and impel respect within Japan and before the new Western-dominated world in which the nation now found itself. Being poor in natural resources, the country decided upon

Near Right: H.I.M. The "Mikado."

Far Right: H.I.M. The Empress of Japan.

Facing, Upper: Prince Iwakura of Japan; ca. 1860–1875.

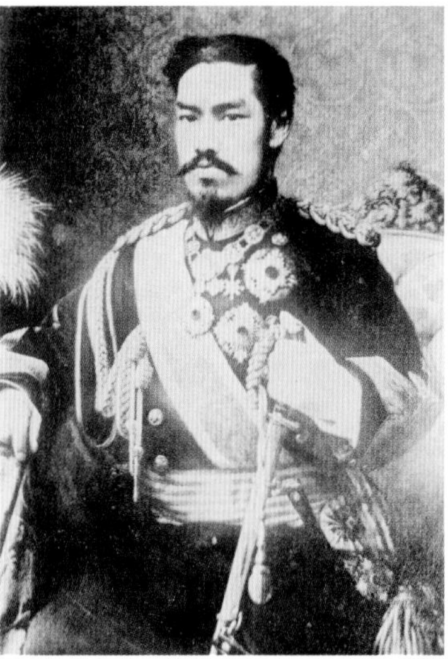

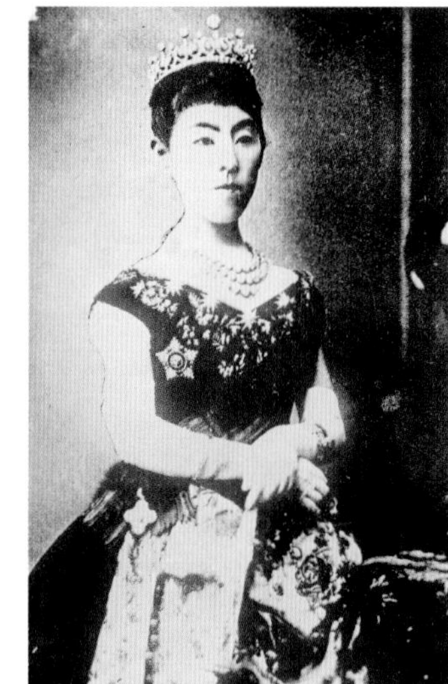

Western-style commerce and industry to fund and to symbolize the new order. This had to be built from the ground up, upon the foundation of a completely restructured society. To this end, in 1871 the government dispatched to Europe and America its first of many major research and diplomatic missions. Under the direction of Prince Iwakura Tomomi,[3] it traveled for eighteen months. The Iwakura Mission was, for most of its members and hosts alike, the first direct encounter with a strange world. For Westerners, it must have presented a puzzling mixed message: some photos show Iwakura exotically turned out in topknot and elegant traditional garb, surrounded by barbered subordinates in beautifully tailored Western suits; others show accompanying wives in kimono while the husbands appear in Western dress; still others show all members in traditional finery. Powerful figures in Western business and government received them with enthusiasm.

The Mission sought to educate itself about business and manufacturing models and to renegotiate trade terms. They did not succeed in the latter, which became an ongoing spur in the Japanese quest to compel international respect. But their tours of vital industrial, municipal, and educational systems provided the foundation for the radical transformation necessary to launch a new Japan and, by doing so, to earn the regard they sought. Among the most adaptable and ultimately successful discoveries were modern textile manufacturing methods, observed in Philadelphia, in Boston, and in English cities. These innovations found

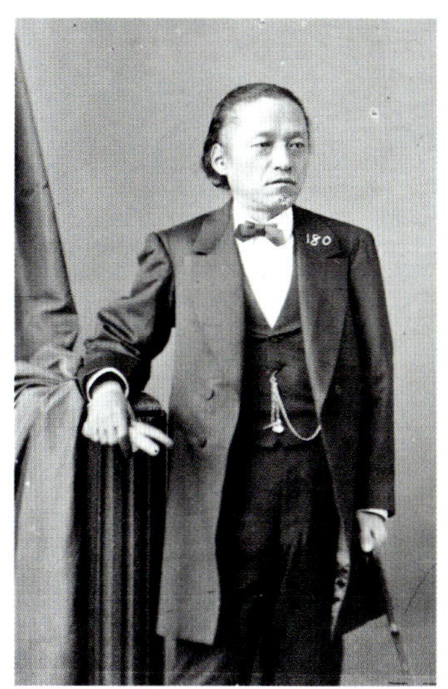

a natural home in Japan, with its centuries-old, highly developed, and traditionally admired textile traditions that encompassed everything from one-of-a-kind brocades and embroideries to stenciled prints. Within a few years, the melding of Japanese design sensibilities to mass production techniques resulted in affordable silk and cotton batistes, chintzes, and crepes, as well as gauzes, linens, embroideries, drapery fabrics, bedspreads, laces, rugs, and floor matting fresh with novel patterns and colors. These coincided with a Western decorating vogue for festooning interiors with textiles. In the United States, advertisements from the new, mainstream department stores such as B. Altman's in New York and John Wanamaker in Philadelphia, and from numerous articles on home décor in *Art Amateur, Godey's Lady's Book, Ladies' Home Journal,* and other publications testify to the ubiquitous presence and influence of these designs in the American home. By 1903, 1,649 factories and 302,367 private family enterprises in Japan were churning out modern textiles for the Western market, from mass-produced to the highest quality.[4] By Meiji's death in 1912, Japan led the world, having perfectly met the demands of the American pocketbook and the American vision of the ideal interior—that vision in many respects altered by ideas (some genuine, some not) garnered from Japan itself.

BELOW: ADVERTISEMENT FOR JAPANESE LEATHER PAPERS; AS PUBLISHED IN *DECORATOR AND FURNISHER* (JULY 1885): 125. Along with textiles, "leather papers" for wall coverings were one of the most popular of Japanese mass-manufactured exports.

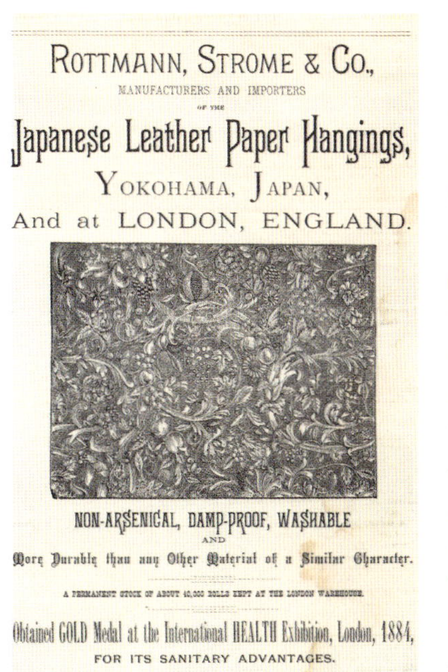

In this success, Japanese ingenuity had tapped a well of receptiveness. The opening of their nation coincided with a time of rapid profound change in the American economic and social fabric with the Civil War and its aftermath—the very moment of the coup that brought Meiji to titular power. Even as Japan leapt to catch up, the Industrial Revolution was entering a second accelerated phase that between 1870 and 1900 would completely alter Americans' perceptions of their daily world and their identity within it. New industries and technologies were luring farmhands, European emigrants, and even women to jobs in cities. There, under the stern eye of a new type of overseer, the white collar manager, they dedicated themselves to making a rapid succession of new products that transformed daily life—canned foods, central heating systems, mass-produced furniture, telephones and electronics, motion picture cameras, automobiles, and ready-made garments, to name a few.

This changing economy spurred the emergence of a new middle class. According to the ideals of the era, it dedicated its increasing leisure time, prosperity, and education to attaining social recognition. Desire for material proof of success was intense, even a subject of satire. Among its chief symbols was home ownership, which expressed social and financial arrival as nothing else could. Their aspirations were matched by a massive building boom of single-family homes in new suburbs, made possible and affordable by new construction techniques, expanding public transportation and utilities, and financial incentives. Enticed by popular house plan books such as *American Cottage Homes* (1878) and *Artistic Modern Homes of Low Cost* (1881), and prefabricated "instant home" models sold by catalogue at Sears, Roebuck and Co., Montgomery Ward, Aladin Homes, and Radford Company, people of almost every economic level willingly endured enormous sacrifice in order to achieve the goal of ownership.

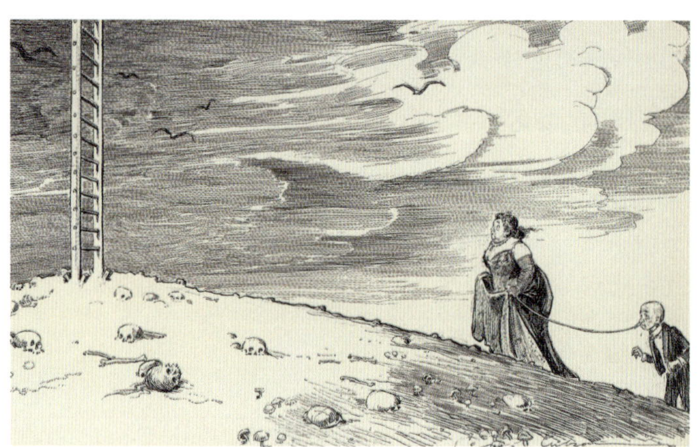

Charles Dana Gibson. Frontispiece from *The Social Ladder*. Gibson depicts a determined matron leading her milquetoast husband on a leash through the nose towards the ladder of aspirations, across a bleak landscape littered with the skulls of those who have failed in the quest, oblivious to the circling vultures.

The changed living patterns that emerged from evolving social ideals, family economics, and domestic commerce sparked a major transformation inside the home: room size, function, and interior organization—all altered from the past. This meant that the arts of the home—architecture, décor, and furnishings—became a natural extension of attention. "In these days, when the correct furnishing of our homes is a matter of careful study and reflection; when true art principles are beginning to prevail and attention is paying to the fitness of means to ends; people are making search for good and beautiful forms in the most ordinary appliances as well as in the more permanent objects, called fixtures,"[5] said a prominent commentator. The most dramatic changes occurred between 1876 and 1915, not coincidentally the peak years of the Japan Craze. Japan represented much more than a turn of fashion.

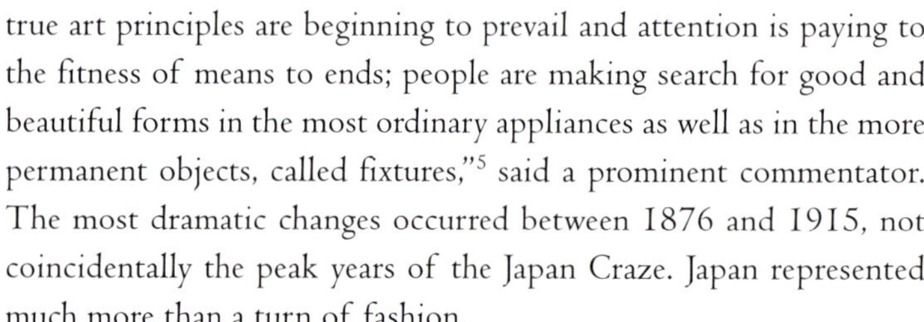

Though not all were sufficiently affordable or immediately accessible to everyone, these newly manufactured products that Americans themselves created, the transformed communications and transportation they enjoyed, and the new conditions in which they toiled, while offering manifold benefits, also disrupted the comfortable patterns of relationships, occupations, and domesticity that had sustained every class

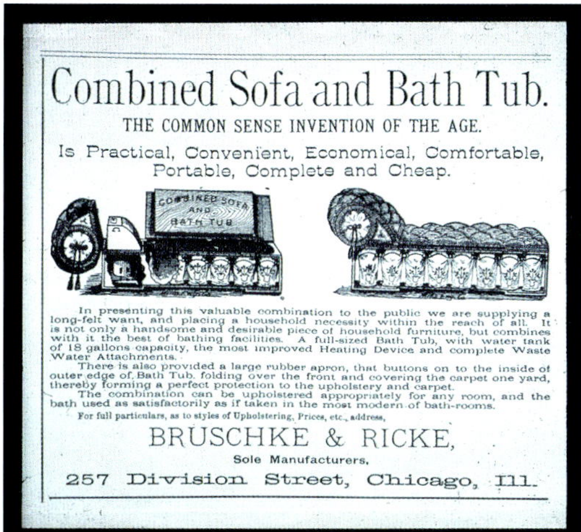

ADVERTISEMENT, AS PUBLISHED IN *DECORATOR AND FURNISHER* (MARCH 1884): 230. Products of the day reflected upwardly mobile Americans' delight in the novel, the inventive, and the practical, sometimes with bizarre results.

for generations. Local governments struggled to manage cities swollen with the poor and uneducated assembled from unfamiliar places, now thrown together to endure arduous living and labor conditions; a boom and bust economy left even the growing middle class vulnerable. People sought refuge and clarity in utopian communities, religion, and even the occult. Uncertainty left many yearning, romanticizing the life of the past as a purer, more civilized existence than that of the present.

In the ensuing furor over the condition of domestic life, "home" as a comforting nest presided over by a nurturing wife and mother became an ideal. Intellects of the day, most notably the British cultural titan John Ruskin, declared that a society's art and architecture directly reflected the morals and values of the people who dwelt in and used its buildings. A host of other major and minor minds on both sides of the Atlantic echoed his sentiments. For advice on how to meet this challenge, people hungrily consulted the scores of domestic manuals written by British and American authorities of interior décor and household management, and produced by the now-booming publishing industry. But the new products available to them did not meet the test. As cheaply made as they were affordable, machine-made traditional designs became stiff, formal, and academic.[6] Homogeneity replaced individualism. Furnishings and essential household items cycled in and out with fads. In a market flooded with mass-produced commodities, shoddiness flew in the face of emerging values.

In such a climate, decorative arts became a matter of serious debate. People looked with nostalgia toward the vanished craftsman, now idealized as a paragon whose skill and spiritual connection to his chosen medium resulted in objects of inevitable beauty, and naturally infused everyday life of the past with moral uplift. In the contemporary machine-made replacements, intellects of the day saw not mere ugliness. To them, flimsiness, sameness, and lack of appeal meant social alienation, a loss of pride in community and in one's work. Ordinary people were dismayed by the uninviting, the uncomfortable, and the inefficient. And so, critics and pundits bewailed a society "destitute of sound aesthetic taste" and ranted about artists as a "mercenary, egotistical class largely

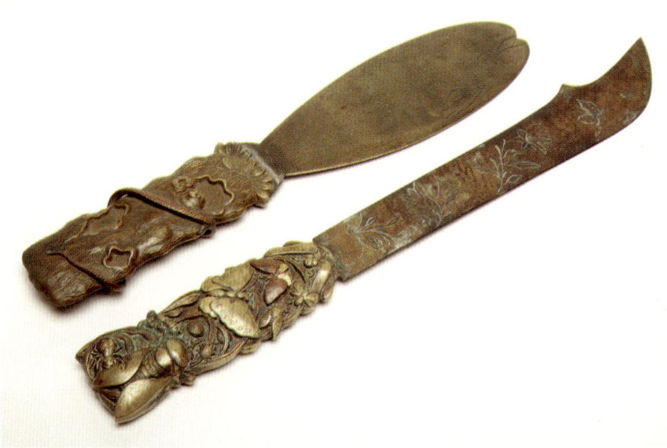

ignorant of culture . . . [whose] highest ambition [is] to get rich,"[7] and commented grimly on carpets emblazoned with blushingly coy maidens courted by bashful shepherds. For their part, artists declared patrons had tired of absurdities, one ridiculing a public announcement depicting nightgown-clad young ladies presenting a player piano to the city of New York. Decorative arts stood front and center of society's most thorny dilemma. Unanimous opinion held they were in a crisis. Without drastic change, they were doomed to extinction,[8] and with them, civilization itself.

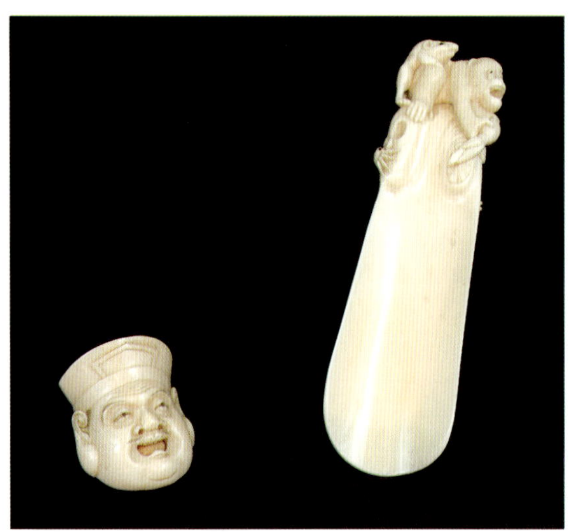

Above, Upper: Desk appointments; ca. 1880–1890; bronze and mixed metals; spatula, 9.75 inches; letter opener, 11.75 inches. Elegant utensils for the well-appointed desk were among the familiar objects "exoticised" by Japanese workshops for export.

Above, Lower: Export pieces; late nineteenth century; ivory. Pictured are a shoehorn (with a grip in the form of a monkey and a rat fighting over a piece of fruit) and a miniature mask (in the form of Daikoku, the God of Wealth, from a set of the Seven Lucky Gods).

At this moment of flux in American life, Japan appeared with exquisite timing and an agenda paradoxically at odds with the ideal cultivated by their intended market: At the very moment that the West was grappling with industrialized modernity as an evil, the Japanese recognized it as the key to survival in a new world and prepared to utilize anything and everything as a tool towards attaining it. That meant following and even anticipating the whims and winds blowing across Western markets in order to meet every conceivable desire. But that presented a challenge, for what Westerners, especially Americans, saw in "Japan" varied because their images arose from within the American spirit in a time of stress and in an era in which Americans strove for "authenticity," linking it to ideas about art and its social role and the home as the moral underpinning of modern life. In the midst of this confusing and uncertain swirl, an unfamiliar exotic culture had thrust itself before their view. American desires were tea leaves that the Japanese had to learn to read.

For some, "Japan" simply meant inexpensive commodities. To the factory worker renting a cold-water city flat or the newly middle-class professional buying a suburban home, their mass-produced textiles, wallpapers, and other machine-made household goods offered availability, quality, novelty, and charm affordable to almost everyone. For others, "Japan" meant the manifestation of any one of several ideals as envisioned by images and materialized in products. This propelled exports to the West in disparate directions. Consequently, even as new manufactured goods from an increasingly dynamic and modern nation came to dominate the American market, a decidedly mixed image of Japan itself was emerging in American minds, in the creation of which the Japanese themselves colluded.

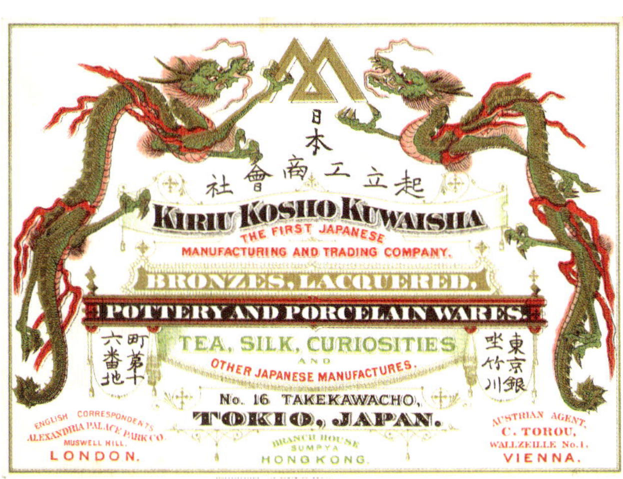

Trade card; chromolithograph; ca. 1876; 11 × 14 inches. The trade card for Kiritsu Kosho Kaisha First Japanese Manufacturing and Trading Company uses an early style of transliteration.

Japanese business and government interests likewise were recognized in high-quality decorative arts, ironically produced by old-fashioned, labor-intensive methods. They introduced beautifully crafted bronzes, enamels, art embroideries, carved ivory figurines, and furniture to the Western marketplace. These products served a dual purpose: In Japan, they provided employment to legions of talented craftsmen from families who for generations had made the traditional objects required by the wealthy of the old regime and now displaced by a modern world that had no need; abroad, they met the desires of the market and created a positive public image.

Both mass-produced and high-end manufactures benefited from sophisticated research initiatives undertaken by delegations sent abroad for the purpose, a mission accomplished with unabashed pride. For a time, the best were sold mostly through a government-established private export company called Kiritsu Kosho Kaisha. Founded in 1873, it had offices in Japan and abroad, including one in Philadelphia, which introduced the Western public to objects made by a variety of artisanal concerns in Japan. Immensely expensive for Meiji's fledgling government to run, Kiritsu Kosho Kaisha closed in 1891, never having succeeded in weaning the American public from its desire for the cheap "oriental" gewgaws that constituted the most direct encounter with "Japan" for the vast majority of Americans.

Yamanaka & Company found a more successful formula of sales and products as purveyor of antiques and new high-end furniture, which it

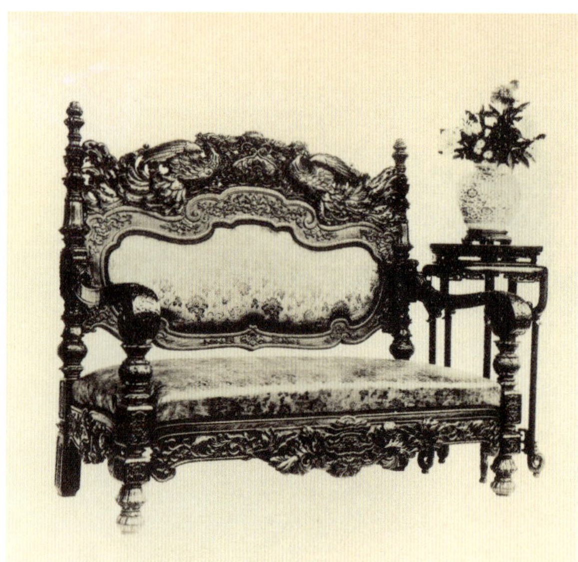

YAMANAKA & COMPANY. CATALOG PHOTO; 1905. The company proudly made this sofa the opening offering of their "Horiuji" line of furniture, which debuted in its *Catalogue of Room Decorations and Artistic Furniture*.

nevertheless approached in a similarly adaptive fashion. Its sales catalogue of 1905 proclaimed the following:

> *We have also sent our own experts on a road to investigate general requirements and tastes of our foreign customers; on the other hand, so as to give every convenience and facility to our customers, many qualified designers have been sent out and stationed in each of our foreign branches, so that they are always able to receive orders for our manufactures, and thus to enable our customers in foreign countries to place an order in close contact with our factory.*[9]

But the market demanded "authentic," and Yamanaka intended to meet its desires, as its catalogue introduction continued:

> *Besides it has been our aim to place before our customers pure Japanese fine arts in the strictest sense of words. . . . As to the designs adapted, we may say that they are all taken from the well known State Treasures, as well as from the rare articles kept in old temples and Shrines, and many other different sources, in which Japan alone in this world is still renowned.*

Yamanaka followed through on these mutually exclusive promises with a line of exquisitely made furniture encrusted with ornament derived from family crests, temples, shrines, and other sources, reassuringly familiar and completely appropriate for a Western interior, their pièce de résistence an upholstered and carved extravaganza in high Western style but sporting motifs garnered from a famous temple dating to the sixth century.

Meanwhile, an affordable and suitably exotic destination, Japan itself beckoned the curious and intrepid. "With $1,200 a New Yorker [could] travel to and spend three months in Japan and return with enough left over for an expensive dinner."[10] Many returned with stories of a charming old-fashioned old world, a "land of miniatures," and a happy, humorous, clean, self-reliant, and artistic society in which "there is not a beggar or a man unable to read, not even a boor, drunkard or a ruffian. The women are beautiful, the men are robust and energetic, there is no trouble about fashions; education is universal, books are plentiful . . . ."[11] The journalist Henry T. Finck declared, "The story of Rip van Winkle

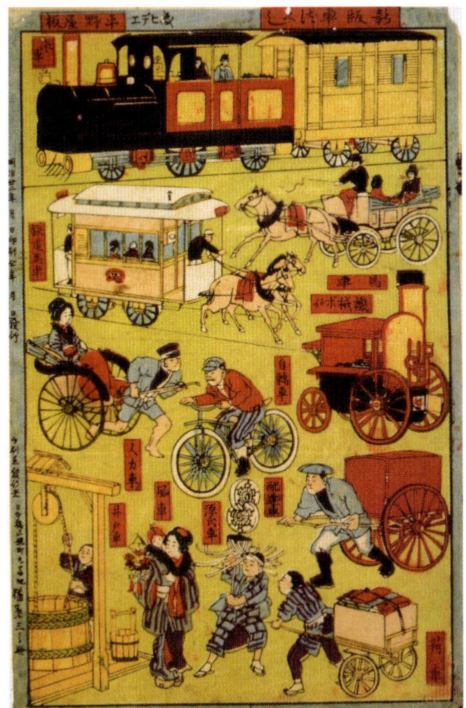

is, like so many other things, reversed in Japan, where it is the country that has gone to sleep and the visitor that is up to date,"[12] adding that he aimed to show ". . . the principal points in which Japanese civilization is superior to our own," and concluding that "Japanese civilization is based on altruism, ours on egotism."[13] Enthusing on his first encounter, another journalist exclaimed, "If this is barbarism, save me from civilization."[14] Extolled a third, "Heathen they are indeed, but barbarians they are not," and went on to declare, "Contrasted with the Chinese—pigtailed, pig-eyed, and pig-headed—the Japanese seemed almost of another sphere."[15]

While visiting Americans delighted themselves with quaint temples, exotic castles, exquisite gardens, and dainty maidens mincing pigeon-toed in kimono, Japan itself was going through a transition that made changes in the West seem tame, its contemporary life a flat-out race to modernity with few parallels in history. What Europe absorbed over two centuries, Japan desired to swallow in a single gulp. Not even Buddhist temples escaped upheaval. New government. New social classes. New education. New occupations. New clothes. New entertainments. New architecture. Gas and electricity. By 1904 the short rail line laid between Tokyo and Yokohama in 1872 had ballooned to 4,250 miles of track with 1,700 locomotives, 800 of them from the United States, and the one-wire telegraph service set up in 1871 encompassed 31,170 miles of line.

Above: Unknown artist. *Kuruma Zukushi (Melange of Vehicles)*; woodblock print; 1870; 14.37 x 9.25 inches. This vibrant image captures the newfound energy of daily life in the cities of Meiji Japan, especially the capital, which had recently been renamed Tokyo.

Right: Ladies with parasols; stereoview; 1902. Depicted are ladies with parasols, who daintily make their way across a quaint bridge in the famous garden of Hikone—typical subjects for stereoscopes that replicated in imagery the accounts of early visitors to Japan.

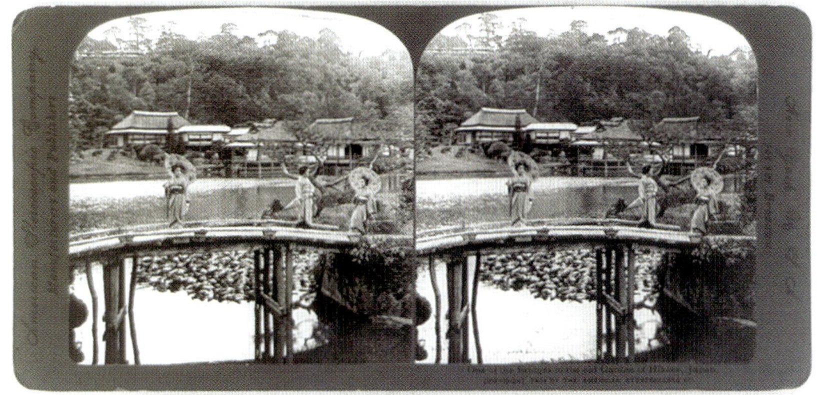

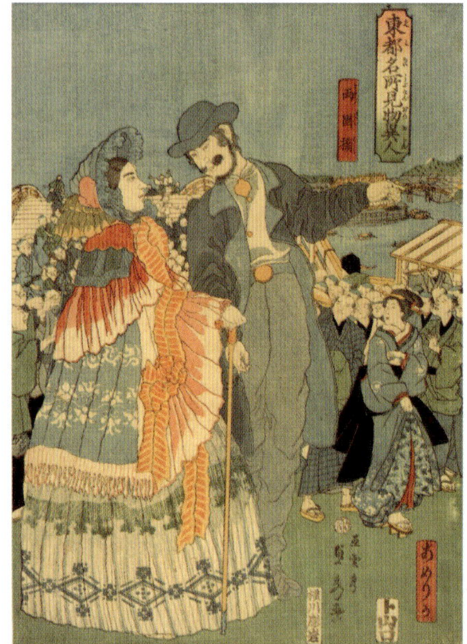

The postal service established about 1870 was handling well over 900 million pieces by 1903.

The waning Tokugawa government had allowed the establishment of bazaars, which accomplished the trick of transforming the outmoded and ordinary of Japanese life into new curios for foreigners. The upheaval of the Meiji restoration only increased a sense of urgency: within Japan, it focused on aggressive assimilation of anything deemed useful from Western civilization and on rejection of anything bearing the taint of Japan's backward recent past. Most visitors took advantage of this to shop like mad, craving exactly what the frantically modernizing Japanese were all too happy to get rid of. Accessories, clothing, art, and other objects were pointless detritus of a feudal past to one while tantalizingly novel and attractive to the other.

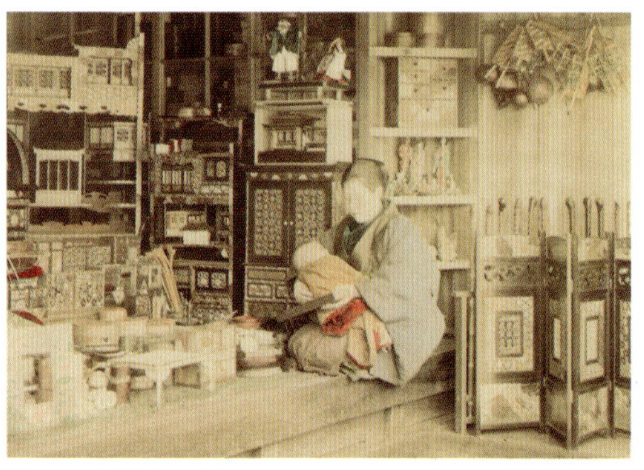

But, while almost anything had an anxious seller and a willing buyer, the gap between the real Japan and the entrancingly quaint, exotic, and peaceful idylls gracing the inauthentic export items proved to be an insurmountable barrier. Even in the heat of voracious acquisition, a distinction in Western minds between Japanese art and the reality of Japan itself often came through. As one diarist put it,

> *In those days Japan was a treasure trove of art objects to be had at bargain prices. The streets of its cities were lined with shops of curios, textiles and pawn goods. Throngs of trades people would gather at one's door at dawn . . . their goods in carts. There were even passers-by who would quite willingly sell the netsuke from their obi. This barrage of offers was so incessant that one was almost overwhelmed by . . . a distaste for buying.*[16]

Above, Upper: Utagawa Sadahide. *Tōto meishō kenbutsu ijin—Ryōgokubashi (Foreign sightseers in famous spots of Edo—Ryōgoku Bridge)*; woodblock print; 1861; 14.72 x 10.16 inches.

Above, Lower: "Nursing Woman at the Curio Store"; hand-colored albumen print; late nineteenth–early twentieth century.

The acerbic Henry Adams, an avid and knowledgeable collector of Japanese art who bought in quantity while on an extended tour of the country, wrote of his distaste for the food ("inedible"), the tea ("nauseating"), the climate ("beastly"), and the odor ("the excrement of many generations").[17]

But, for American sensibilities unmoored or discomfited by contemporary life, Japan's *ersatz* packaging of old and new decorative arts in the

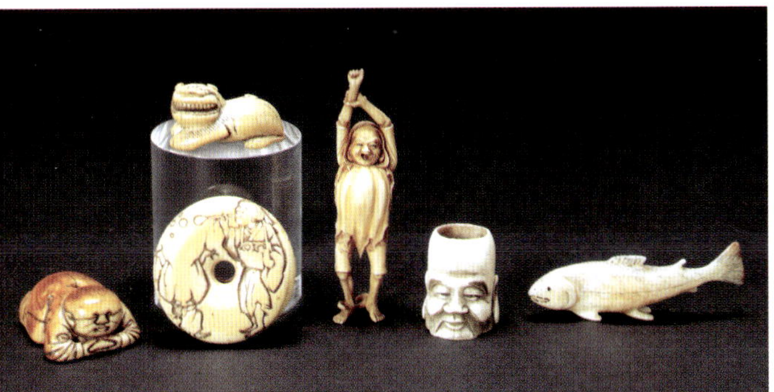

wrappings of its discarded past presented a vision of a world defined by the ideals lost to modern society. The myth proved persistent and resilient despite the diplomats, missionaries, businessmen, and travelers who ventured to Japan and came to know the Japanese—twenty years after Meiji ascended the throne, Siegfried Bing would write the following:

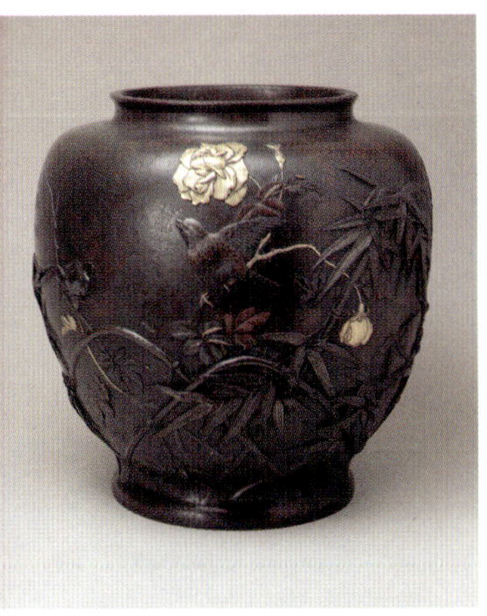

> *. . . for whilst strict limits have been placed . . . to the bounds within which our imagination has been permitted to wander, and whilst our industrial arts have in consequence assumed a stiff and conventional character destructive to the boldness of originality, Japan appears to have indulged in freedom from and laxity of rules and method. Not that the Japanese artist emancipates himself from all rule, or ever lets his fancy wander at haphazard. Far from this; the constant guide whose indications he follows is called "nature". . .*[18]

Many Japanese chafed at this simplistic, confining, not to mention often inaccurate characterization, but a conscious decision was made to exploit it, with the result that as Japan itself surged forward, American visions of the country largely remained fueled by assumptions not vastly different from those of John Stalker two hundred years before. Neither newspaper images of the Mikado greeting foreign dignitaries in a sartorial style in keeping with Japan's stunning westward transformation, nor proof of her developing military prowess as the era progressed ever completely displaced this impression.

ABOVE, UPPER: NETSUKE; EIGHTEENTH–NINETEENTH CENTURY; IVORY; APPROXIMATELY 1 TO 3 INCHES HIGH. Though Meiji-period Japanese regarded *netsuke* as old-fashioned, the miniature size, intricate carving, and exotically whimsical themes made this type of artwork among the most appealing of objects to Westerners.

ABOVE, LOWER: UNKNOWN CRAFTSMAN, FOR KIRITSU KOSHO KAISHA. BAS-RELIEF VASE; CA. 1874–1890; BRONZE AND MIXED METALS; 14 INCHES HIGH; MARKED WITH THE COMPANY'S NAME AND DOUBLE-MOUNTAIN LOGO ON THE UNDERSIDE. The immediacy of a flitting sparrow perching upon a rose entangled with bamboo, windblown across the sides of a baluster vase, epitomized the Japanese aesthetic of vivid realism applied to decorative arts as championed by Siegfried Bing.

1. Finck 1895, viii.
2. Stalker and Parker 1688.
3. Japanese names are given in Japanese fashion, with surname first.
4. Francis 1913, 316.
5. Smith 1875, 44.
6. Hosley 1990, 117.
7. Ibid.
8. Put 2000, 10.
9. Yamanaka 1905.
10. Finck 1895, ix.
11. *Arthur's Home Magazine*, September 1868.
12. Finck 1895, viii.
13. Ibid., ix.
14. *Putnam's Magazine*, May 1868.
15. *Hours at Home*, November 1867.
16. Put 2000, 43.
17. Quotes excerpted from Benfey 2003, 144, 145.
18. Bing 1888, 5.

2

Arts and Agendas on the Public Stage

The World's Fairs

The crowds, some like sheep, run here, run there. One man starts, one thousand follow. Nobody can see anything; nobody can do anything. All rush, push, tear, shout, make plenty noise, say "damn great" many times, get very tired, and go home.[1]

The quaint little people with their shambling gait, their eyes set awry in their head and their . . . grave and gentle ways, how can it be in them . . . to make such wonderful things?[2]

Despite the uncertainties brought by change, Westerners of the late nineteenth century considered themselves at the threshold of a breathtaking and beautiful horizon. To most, the Industrial Revolution's ongoing transformation of daily life was for the better, especially in the realms of transportation and communication. These breached barriers of geography and even time that had daunted humanity for millennia. Nowhere was this new vista more vast, confusing, and exciting than in the United States. Beckoned by financial and social opportunity, throngs of poor European emigrants disembarked from steamships at American ports; boarded the world's most extensive, rapid, and efficient railways; and, according to regular schedules set by newly standardized time, seeded the entire United

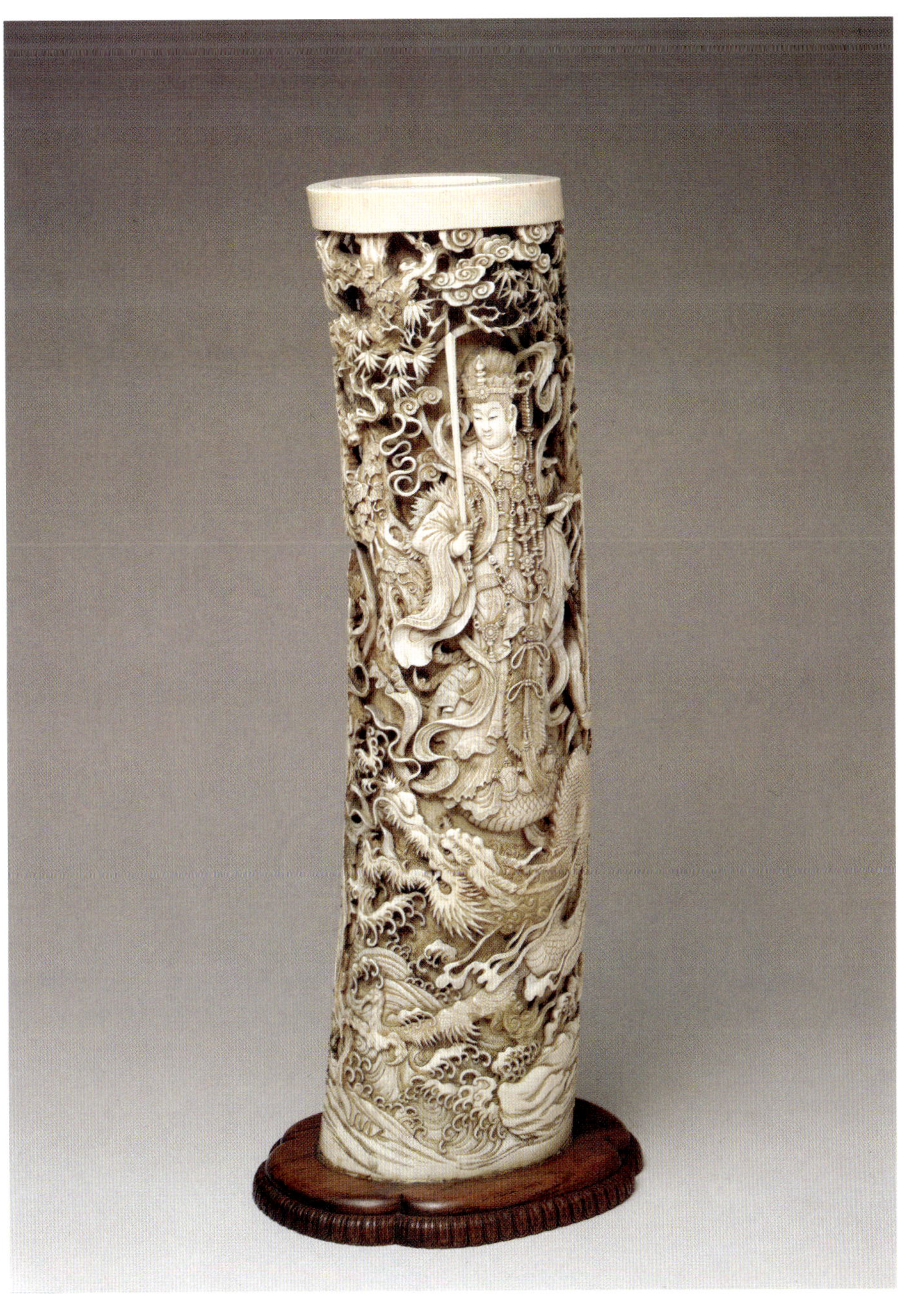

Brush pot; ca. 1876–1880; ivory; 17.75 inches high; signed "dai Nihon teikoku Sekine Harumichi" ("made by Seikine Harumichi [of] great imperial Japan"). Created to awe, this extravagant version of a traditional desk accoutrement is one of a pair made from a large section of elephant tusk, with exceptionally fine work in undercut relief. Such ivories enjoyed prominent display at expositions, as they never failed to excite commentary. Yet despite the Japanese goddess Benzaiten among the otherwise Buddhist deities gracing its sides, its style, technique, and material replicated Chinese taste at its most excessive, making this piece a contributor to American confusion over Japanese and Chinese arts.

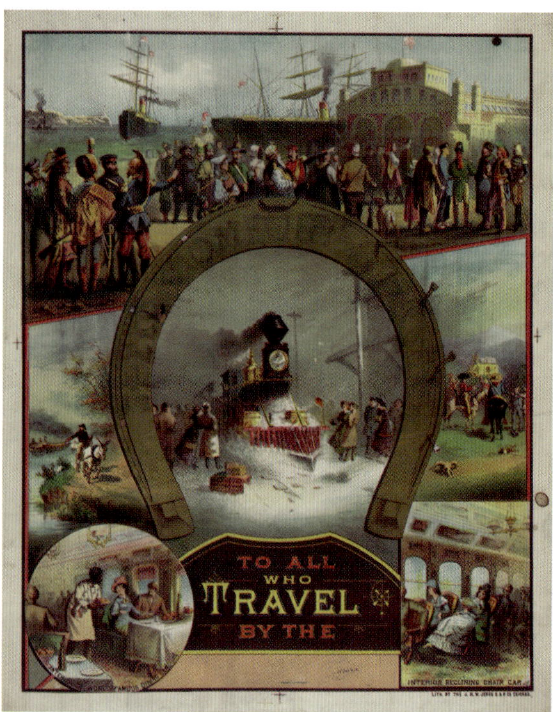

J. M. W. Jones S. & P. Co. "To all who travel"; chromolithograph; ca. 1882.

States with their customs, foods, and languages. The completion of the transcontinental railroad in 1869 only accelerated their momentum and brought even Chinese and Japanese to the farthest-flung hinterlands of the American continent. The inevitable hostility bred by this unfamiliar mingling could be worked to advantage by those with initiative. In California, legislation beginning in 1882 that excluded Chinese labor opened an opportunity to impoverished Japanese. Their swelling numbers included not just farm labor but also skilled craftsmen, many of whom would come to leave their marks on American domestic arts.

Meanwhile, the tightening web of railway tracks and telephone lines gradually consolidated national unity and, with it, encouraged a sense of "general public." This population was more sophisticated than in any previous generation, thanks to widening cultural mingling and also to expanding literacy. Increasingly, thanks to the spread of gas and, ultimately, electric lighting, readers could indulge their every literary whim into the night, enthusiastically catered to by a booming publications industry that made the most of "lightning" presses, vastly improved graphics, photographs, falling postal costs, and, lastly, the transatlantic telegraph. Introduced in 1858, only five years after Commodore Perry thrust Japan and the West into each other's consciousness, the telegraph presented the country with a new cornucopia of information, global in content.

From this point onward, newspapers, periodicals, and journals increasingly embraced Japan, with feature articles expounding on its foreign policy, economics, current events, traditional culture, and modern life, many in the form of travelogues, stories, and analyses by "experts," resident or visitor. Like the recounts of travelers to the bazaars of Yokohama and Kobe, these revealed a deep vein of ambivalence, the two sentiments reflected in descriptive language ranging from awestruck adulation of exotic allure . . .

Life in Great Cities III: Yedo

No squalid misery of accumulations of filth encumbers the well-cared-for-streets, and a beggar is rarely seen. . . . [E]verywhere is visible a busy, industrious,

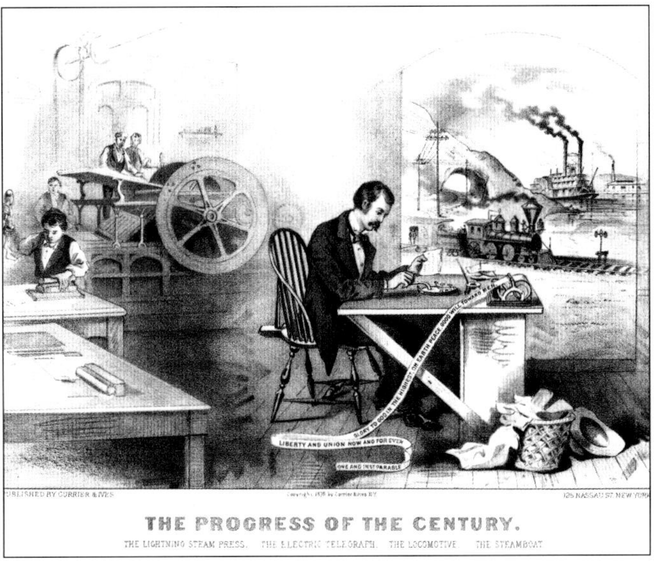

CURRIER AND IVES. "THE PROGRESS OF THE CENTURY—THE LIGHTNING STEAM PRESS, THE ELECTRIC TELEGRAPH, THE LOCOMOTIVE, THE STEAMBOAT"; LITHOGRAPH; CA. 1876.

good-humored, and seemingly contented people. Life is simple and natural, food is healthful and cheap; the manners of the people are distinguished for politeness and kindness. Everyone can read and most can write. They have a religion which they value. One man marries one woman, the same as with us; the love between parents and children is strong and universal. [The ladies] . . . have a natural grace . . . the most fascinating, elegant ladies that I ever saw in any country in the world. The Japanese gentleman is . . . of pleasing address and most polished manners."[3]

. . . to condescending recounts of ordinary Japanese customs seemingly odd or even prurient to Americans, such as "Shame and modesty are words unknown to Jap vocabulary"[4] and employing belittling, feminizing adjectives such as "dainty," "small," and "delicate" even to descriptions of men. Americans summed up their bemusement in the impression that the best way to understand Japan was to interpret it as the inversion of everything familiar:

Queer If True

Japan is a country of paradoxes and anomalies. They write from top to bottom, from right to left, in perpendicular instead of horizontal lines. Their books begin where ours end. Their locks turn from left to right. . . . Shops go to customers. People sit on their heels. Horses' heads are where their tails would *be in an English stable. . . . [O]ld men fly kites where the children gravely look on. . . . Ladies black their teeth instead of keeping them white . . . their anti-crinoline tendencies are carried to the point of interfering . . . with all locomotion. . . . Top-spinning is followed as a profession. . . . Their pocket is their sleeve. . . . Their music is without melody; their landscapes without prospective [*sic*], light or shade; their figures without drawing—mere crude colors and grotesque forms dancing in mid-air. . . . They have bank notes of the value of a farthing. They have long understood the utilization of sewerage and the manufacture of paper, not from rags but from the bark of trees. . . . They use no milk or animal food; they have no sheep nor pigs, the flowers have no scent, the birds no song, and their fruits and vegetables no flavor.*[5]

Awkwardness with Japan and other newly acquainted societies did not dispel a universally shared sense that the entire globe lay revealed as never before, bathed in a vibrant climate of commercial opportunity, social exchange, and cultural invitation. The ultimate celebrations of this emergent "worldview" were the international expositions. Even in their own day, people recognized them as definitive events of the era, a pundit commenting with only slight hyperbole: "Of all events in recent history, only wars have had more dramatic influence than World Expositions upon the expression of civilization."[6]

The international exposition movement began before Japan had even surfaced in Western popular consciousness: in 1851 London was the location of the Great Exhibition of the Works of Industry of all Nations, also called The Crystal Palace Exhibition. The brainchild of Queen Victoria's husband, Prince Albert, and the industrial design innovator Sir Henry Cole, it aimed to highlight British technological, mercantile, and imperial superiority by showing off its best against the best of other countries. Its huge success inspired a movement whose momentum only flagged in 1915, when the outbreak of World War I brought its heyday to a close, to resume with waning importance to the pale reflections of the present day. In that assertive and gregarious age, any country aspiring to recognition in the world community joined in these extravaganzas of genial competition and curiosity, and, if possible, hosted at least one of its own. Heads of state presided over the openings of the grandest. Expositions cropped up all over: London again in 1862 and 1910, Paris in 1867, 1878, and 1900, Vienna in 1873, Philadelphia in 1876, Amsterdam in 1883, New Orleans and

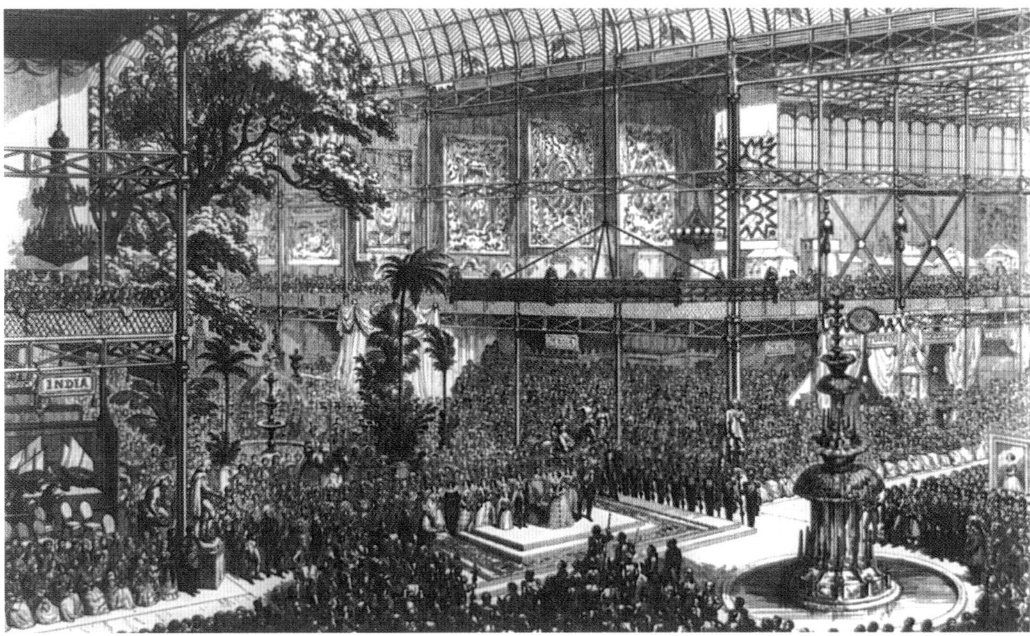

GEORGE CRUIKSHANK. "OPENING OF THE GREAT INDUSTRIAL EXHIBITION OF ALL NATIONS, BY HER MOST GRACIOUS MAJESTY QUEEN VICTORIA AND HIS ROYAL HIGHNESS PRINCE ALBERT, ON THE 1ST OF MAY, 1851, TAKEN ON THE SPOT"; ENGRAVING; 1851.

Nuremberg in 1885, Barcelona in 1888, Chicago in 1893, St. Louis in 1904, San Francisco in 1894 and 1915, and numerous smaller versions in Europe's regional cities and in other U.S. cities, including Nashville, Boston, Buffalo, Denver, Atlanta, New Orleans, Omaha, Seattle, San Diego, Cincinnati, Norfolk, Portland, and Louisville.

The expositions were open to everyone, and official records suggest such stratospheric numbers as eight million to the London International Exhibition of 1862, over nine million to the U.S. Centennial International Exhibition of 1876 in Philadelphia, nineteen million to the Louisiana Purchase International Exposition of 1904 in St. Louis, and more than ten million to the Exposition Universelle et Internationale of 1910 in Brussels. The tallies for the World's Columbian Exhibition of 1893 in Chicago topped them all at a staggering twenty-seven and a half million, which would have accounted for 25 percent of the United States population at the time. These figures, now considered the result of inaccurate counting methods,[7] were unsurprising in light of the organizers' harried delight at the spectacle of fairways undeniably clogged with breathless gawking throngs. Journalists from all over the world mingled in the mobs, wiring descriptions of sights, sounds, and highlights to their papers and magazines; the fairways' thrilling energy and exotic transient air became the backdrops for stories serialized in periodicals and in novels of all sorts. For people of prominence, the expositions were a must—their arrival, tours, and impressions of the sights and sounds duly recorded in the society pages. In short, the fairs consumed everyone's attention, and that only enhanced the impression that the whole world had gathered in their carefully laid out, landscaped precincts. Henry Adams—sniffing, "I did not detect a single refined-looking being . . . but there may have been one or two who, like ourselves, had drifted there by accident or necessity"[8]—considered the fairs themselves a "religion" necessary to understanding the rapidly changing world in which people now lived and to counterbalancing the increasingly impersonal quality of American life. Japan came to exploit this impression more adroitly than any other country.

Promoters sought to celebrate a global community connected as never before, thanks to the machine age. Exhibitions were unabashedly idealistic and didactic. Consensus held that by assembling nations, each presenting itself at its best, mutual respect would inevitably flower and would ultimately bear in the near future an international utopia of peace and technological advancement as its fruit. This required winning enthusiastic public attention, so learning had to be enticing, fun, and readily grasped. Organizers arranged the world's achievements—industry, manufacturing, society, and instructional tableaus based on the latest anthropological theories—in elaborate complexes of grand palaces set in huge, elegantly landscaped gardens. Individual nations beguiled visitors with idealized "quintessential" national buildings. The Meiji government recognized that this presented an opportunity. In 1871 it established a special Exhibition Bureau with broad authority and financial power, through which it poured resources into manufacturing an enchanting public image.

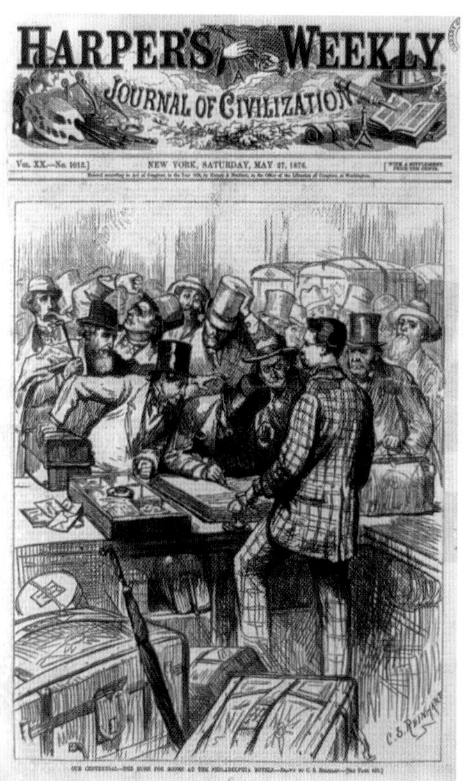
HARPER'S WEEKLY
JOURNAL OF CIVILIZATION
Vol. XX.—No. 1012.] NEW YORK, SATURDAY, MAY 27, 1876.

C. S. Reinhart, "Our Centennial—the Rush for Rooms at the Philadelphia Hotels"; wood engraving; as published in *Harper's Weekly*, May 27, 1876.

Its first official venture took place at the Weltausstellung in Vienna in 1873, only five years after Meiji ascended the throne. It included a village set in a faithfully re-created bucolic countryside of hills, a lake with bridges and a waterfall, and a shrine. It was a charming image utterly at odds with Japan's ongoing reinvention of itself as a modern nation. Indeed, with the fairs as the resource par excellence for that challenge, the government had included with its delegation a committee of sixty-six engineers. The ninety-six-volume report they produced on the West's proudly flaunted cutting-edge technologies provided the basis the government sought, but the huge success of the village installation assured that the very impression most Japanese wanted to dispel would in fact define "Japan" at every exposition to come: a perfect romantic vision of a rural and primitive past—all the more alluring for its exotic air.

Of course, this image was no more artificial than the rest of the "world in microcosm" that fairgoers encountered. Each nation made sure of the best possible impression; no bustled, parasoled, and hatted

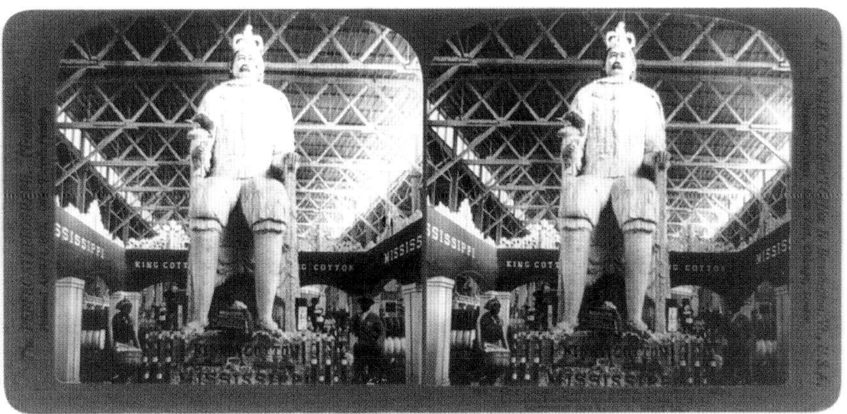

H. C. White Co. "King Cotton"; stereoview; ca. 1904; as viewed at the Mississippi exhibit in the Agricultural Building, Louisiana Purchase International Exposition, St. Louis.

matron would have her sense of propriety rattled. Her equilibrium was another matter. In the vast halls dedicated to highlights of science, technology, and production, she wandered awestruck amid steam generators, automated looms, and automobiles; through pavilions displaying coffins and shoes; past towering giants constructed from tons of cotton or mammoth donkeys made of dried fruit. In enormous exhibition buildings and mingled among the popcorn stands, cigar pavilions, and beer gardens on the park grounds, the installations of culturally and geographically disparate nations appeared in sometimes-bizarre juxtapositions: in one instance, Japan found itself next to Sweden, in another next to Morocco. The hodgepodge resulted partly from political maneuvering for advantageous locations, but, above all, it was the unintentional and unrecognized outcome of the latest educational theories asserting the idea that people learned best by passive absorption. The inviting displays appeared almost free of explanation.

The goal, an abridged almanac of world civilization, was a grand scheme clouded by fantasy, tinted by rosy-hued romanticism, and warped by overconfident, unwitting cultural hubris. The new social science of anthropology captivated progressives with its optimistic view of all humanity as inexorably moving forward, but it misguidedly catalogued individual societies according to a rigid pyramid of progress in an order increasingly dark-complexioned as it descended. Japan's aggressive pace of modernization, untainted traditional culture, and uncompromising sense of dignity and social values—paradoxically maintained by its successful avoidance of Western colonization—ranked it at the top among the "yellow" races in this "scientific" index. Perhaps the most bizarre explanation for Japan's uniqueness among Asian societies was a theory accepted by many in Japan, Europe, and America, identifying the population as one of the Lost Tribes of Israel,[9] Jews themselves already widely identified as "oriental" outsiders of threatening genius. While the second-tier assessment rankled, the drive to win over the West convinced the Japanese to give the public what it wanted, and this assured the fairyland vision presented at Vienna would continue. Westerners responded with approval:

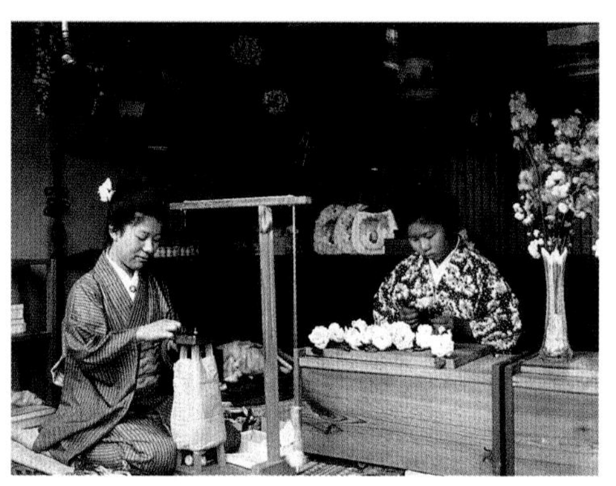

Living tableau of Japanese ladies making souvenirs; photograph; 1904; as viewed at the Louisiana Purchase International Exposition, St. Louis.

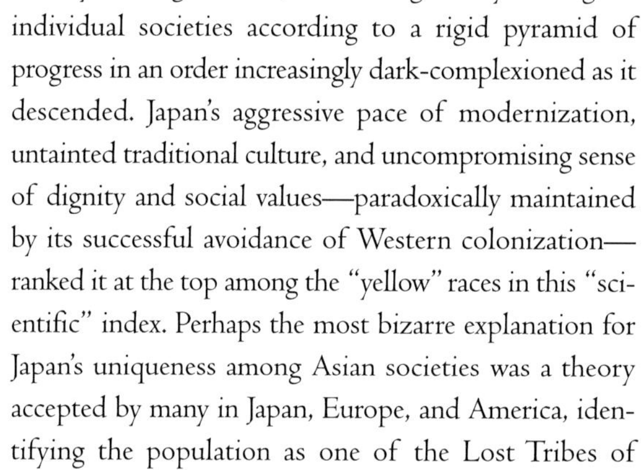

We went into the Japanese Village, under a high arch, all fixed off with towers, and wreaths and swords—dretful ornamental. There wuz more than a hundred natives here. Their housen are back in the inclusure, and their workshops in front, and in these shops and porticos are carried on right before your eyes every trade known in Japan, and jest as they do it at home—carvers, carpenters, spinners, weavers, dyers, musicians, etc., etc. The colrin' they do is a sight to see, and takes almost a lifetime to learn.

The housen of this village are mostly made of bamboo—not a nail used in place. Why, sometimes one hull side of their housen would be made of a mat of braided bamboo. . . . Their housen wuz made in Japan and brung over here and set up by native workment. They have thatched ruffs and kinder open-work sides, dretful curious-lookin' and on the wide porticos of these housen, little native wimmen set and embroider, and wind skeins of gay-colored cotton, and play with their little brown black-eyed babies.[10]

The colossal expense the fairs incurred drove participating nations to moneymaking methods in order to recoup and, even better, to turn a profit. So, edification found itself the organizing principle for a vast bazaar. The new middle class encountered its first taste of a world beyond the familiar confines of the towns and regions in which they lived. But, with even the department store so novel that few had ever actually experienced one, the exhibition buildings' vast interiors—endless aisles crammed with objects strange and familiar, large and small, in vitrines or stacked in tall pyramids, a barrage of brilliant color, a cacophony of blaring bands, crushing crowds, and wafting smells from food concessions, all absent of context or explanation—amounted to a disorienting sensory jumble of noise, sight, scent, and quantity. Many were simply overwhelmed, sometimes to the point of panic but more often to delighted phantasmagoria. It is not too much to say that the international exposition brought the world into the average home. But it is equally fair to say the image was piecemeal, boxed for consumption, sanitized, and confused. Japanese arts and crafts became a creative spark, thanks in part to an environment that encouraged ad hoc mixing.

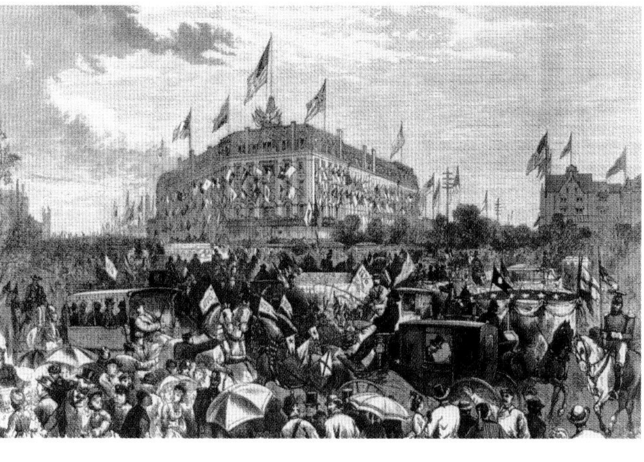

"THE CRUSH ON OPENING DAY OF THE CENTENNIAL AT THE INTERSECTION OF ELM AND BELMONT AVENUES, PHILADELPHIA, 1876"; WOOD ENGRAVING; FROM A DRAWING BY SCHELL AND HOGAN; AS PUBLISHED IN *HARPER'S WEEKLY*, JUNE 3, 1876.

The strange pairing of condescension and adulation in the West's view of Japan emerged even before Meiji's ascension, inseparable from the exposition movement itself, with definitive impact upon Japanese initiatives in matters of taste. After the sharply unpleasant wake-up alarm from Perry in 1853 came a happier one at the hands of Sir Rutherford Alcock (1809–1897) in 1862, recently returned from service as Britain's first consul to Japan. In its dangerously antiforeign environment, he had been the most fearless and forward-thinking of envoys, among the very few to venture beyond the relatively safe enclaves of the shogunal capital Edo and the

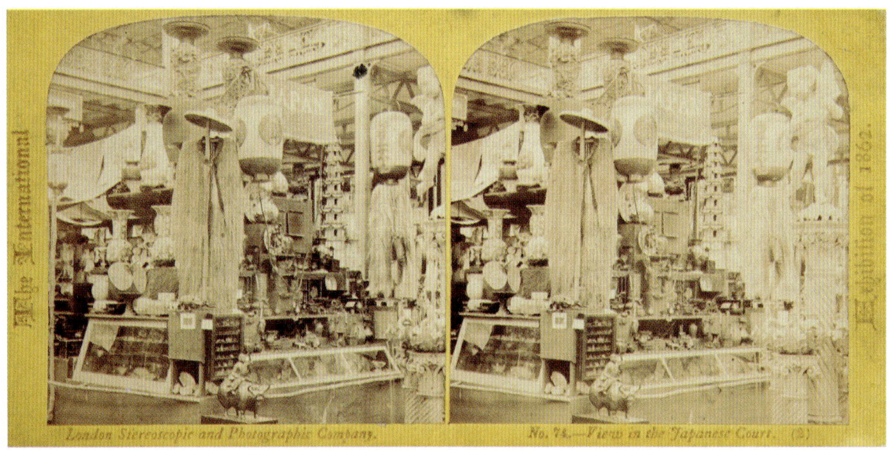

"Rutherford Alcock's Japanese Court at the Great London Exposition"; stereoview; 1862.

nearby port city Yokohama. For the London International Exhibition on Industry and Art of that year, the British government requested that he set up a small Japanese Court. There, crammed into glass cases, hanging from the ceiling, stacked atop one another, and piled on the floor, Alcock introduced to the public nearly one thousand paintings, textiles, decorated papers, porcelains, lacquers, carvings, baskets, maps, toys, paper lanterns, umbrellas, wooden pillows, baskets, straw raincoats, rope shoes, gaudy ceramics, ornate bronzes, prints, and illustrated books. The assemblage consisted mostly of ordinary household objects along with items from workshops catering to foreign taste of the past or newly directing themselves to the desires of Japan's nascent expatriate community. No Japanese had been consulted. All had appealed to Alcock's perspective as a European with an untutored eye regarding Japanese standards of aesthetics and quality. The six million Europeans and Americans said to have explored the Japanese Court found them incendiary to their imaginations. To those few Japanese present, they were lamentable embarrassments epitomizing everything Japan sought to leave behind and were the very depths of taste. Their dismay at the message conveyed proved well-founded. But some, if taken aback, were delighted at the explosive fervor unleashed by an initiative with which they had little to do. Alcock had revealed the prestige and reach of exhibitions and Japanese art crafts as undeniable assets in the drive to confront the world community.

This induced the most powerful domain leaders to participate in the international arena in the international way—at the Exposition Universelle of 1867 in Paris. At that fair, jockeying among the Tokugawa and

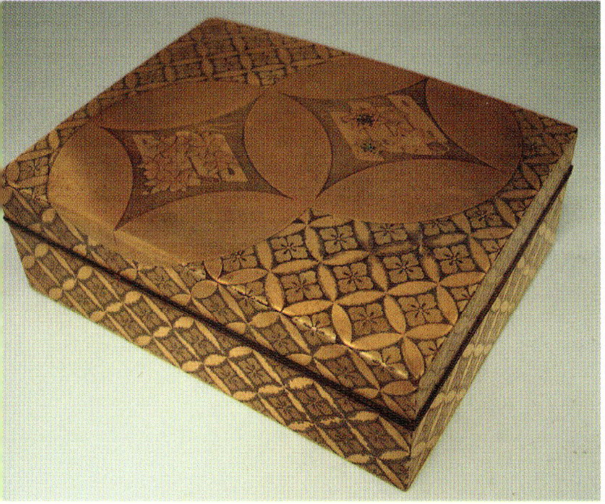

BOX; GOLD LAQUER; EDO PERIOD; 1.75 x 5.5 x 4.25 INCHES. Dating to the period of the Paris exposition of 1867, this box—ornamented with an elegant geometric pattern of overlapping circles, floral rhombuses, maple leaves, and cherry blossoms—is the sort that might have been exhibited there. A traditional opulence rather than the export style that would come to dominate expositions after the establishment of the Meiji regime, it displays much of what dazzled Westerners from their first encounters—exotic technique superbly executed, precious materials, and skill in dynamically asymmetrical, two-dimensional design.

their enemies left organizers completely confused as to who exactly ruled Japan, but altogether they made a huge impact: one thousand two hundred and sixty-nine containers, the majority containing ceramics but also lacquers, gold work, paintings, prints, paper, weapons, and textiles. Paris—since the mid-1850s under the sway of the woodblock prints and books that had revolutionized everything from ceramic decoration to the works of avant-garde artists like Manet and Degas—fell deeper under the spell. These same *daimyō* (feudal lords), from regions with long experience with export ceramic production and Western trade, were later prominent among the aggressively dynamic, reformist oligarchs who brought down the Tokugawa shortly after the fair.

The world might be as patronizing as it was stunned, but Japan was galvanized. The Victorian emphasis on the morally uplifting power of art meant that exhibitions and competitions of decorative art crafts were major events at the expositions. International acclaim had made clear the nation's preeminence in this one area. Regardless of the dubious eye with which they were regarded at home, the detritus of the old regime and export-driven ceramics, bronzes, lacquers, ivories, textiles, and even cheap fans and souvenirs were now recognized as vital tools in a crucial initiative to refashion the image of Japan as a modern kingdom "worthy of full fellowship in the family of nations,"[11] as Meiji's ambassador to Washington later put it. Building a market for these items would also contribute to a second major goal to develop manufacturing, the foundations for which were laid by the findings of the Iwakura Mission. As Japan energetically pursued this goal, a parallel transformation in American domestic style would evolve at the intersection of the fairs, where the pots, ivories, paintings, embroideries, teahouses, gardens, and other artistic delights that Japan presented to the public met the changes in American society.

Despite harsh economic pressures, primitive industries, and intense need among a poor populace, the Meiji government instituted an official policy of supporting fine and decorative arts directed by the official Exhibition Bureau. Expenditures were always among the largest of the participating nations—and Japan participated in them all. At subsequent fairs it negotiated tens of millions of feet of exhibition space, and

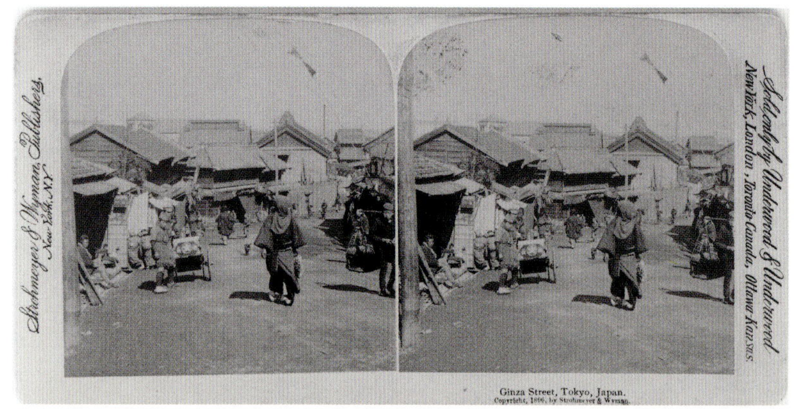

Right: Tokyo Ginza District; stereoview; ca. 1896. The Japanese government carefully apportioned its resources as it brought the country out of the feudal era and into the industrial age. Transportation, communication, and education were paramount. But the unpaved streets and ramshackle buildings of this image show that twenty-five years after a devastating 1871 fire, Tokyo's Ginza district, central to the economy and national pride since the seventeenth century as the location of the shogun's silver mint, had yet to see the resources suitable to its new role as the budding banking center of modern Meiji Japan.

often had the grandest displays of any country. The World's Columbian Exhibition of 1893 in Chicago displayed 1,750 tons of Japanese crafts spread out over 82,850 square feet in three locations. The California Midwinter International Exposition of 1894 in San Francisco, a much smaller affair overall, had even more. Greater still was the Louisiana Purchase Exposition of 1904 in St. Louis, with 150,000 square feet. In themselves and in the motifs that adorned them, Japanese arts and crafts conveyed the desired message with powerful effect, especially when "packaged" with the proper atmosphere of lovely gardens nestling quaintly exotic shrines, rural village buildings, and elegant teahouses presided over by delicate kimono-clad damsels.

America's love affair with Japan began with a splashy debut at the U.S. Centennial International Exhibition of 1876 in Philadelphia, where it plummeted into American consciousness as if "... from another planet [with] ... a display so novel and attractive as to be an unfailing source of interest to all visitors of whatever other nationality."[12] The Meiji government could not have chosen a more opportune moment to electrify the American consciousness than this grand hundredth-anniversary celebration of the founding of the United States. Proclaimed the "... greatest exhibition the world

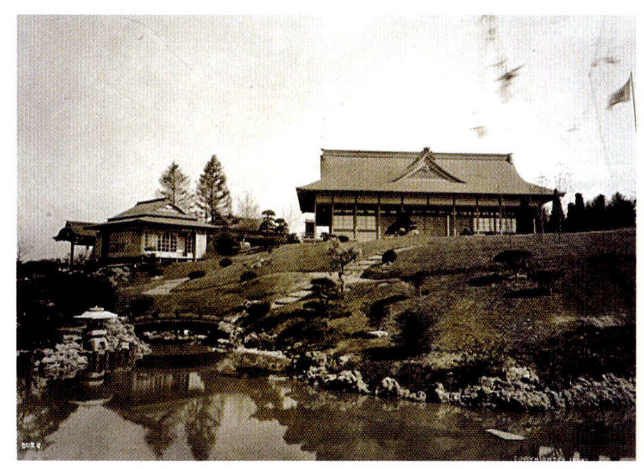

Below: Imperial Japanese Pavilion and Cottage; photograph; 1904; as viewed at the Louisiana Purchase International Exposition, St. Louis. Noting the powerful impact of Japanese gardens upon Westerners, the government's exhibition committees spared no expense in presenting exquisite designs complete with elegant buildings constructed to the last detail in traditional materials and techniques.

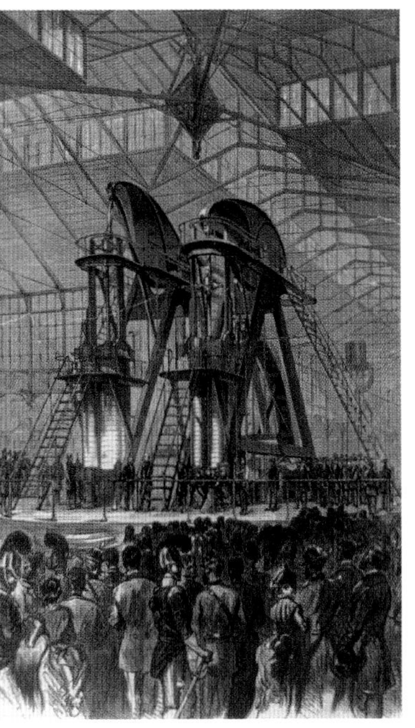

"OUR CENTENNIAL—PRESIDENT GRANT AND DOM PEDRO STARTING THE CORLISS ENGINE"; WOOD ENGRAVING; AS PUBLISHED IN *HARPER'S WEEKLY*, MAY 27, 1876. Before a huge crowd, the United States head of state and the emperor of Brazil start the engine, officially opening the fair.

has ever seen"[13] and the "eighth wonder of the world,"[14] the Centennial exhibition was considered by every patriotic American as the seminal event of the decade at the very least, the country's proud assertion that it had ascended to its destiny among the globe's preeminent nations.

The fair occasioned undeniable proof of American technological superiority—ruefully acknowledged by a European press awestruck at the engineering of the fair's gargantuan Main Building at 21.47 acres in area, "the largest in the world"[15]—with groundbreaking communications innovations displayed in Machinery Hall that included the first commercially viable typewriter by Christopher Latham Sholes of Wisconsin and the Telephonic Telegraphic Receiver by Alexander Graham Bell, who was born a Scot but had lately moved to Boston and was now claimed as America's own. Industrial preeminence in the form of all manner of laborsaving products was paraded before a fascinated public, among them the Line-Wolf Ammonia Compressor for refrigeration and ice-making, the Otis Brothers & Co. Steam Elevator Machine, and the gigantic but miraculously noiseless Corliss Centennial Steam Engine that powered the entire fair. Of less self-evident value were refinements to better edify the masses wending their way around the precincts, such as the novelty of tableaus—model rooms illustrating furnishings, occupations, and social customs of the world; the appropriately posed mannequins providing narrative enhancement were sometimes replaced by real people engaging in the activity concerned.

But in one all-important benchmark, that of cultural and intellectual matters, the fine and applied arts exhibits made clear that Americans still had some catching up to do. An undercurrent of defensiveness flowed beneath the patriotic bombast; commentators paired a recognition that American art and technological schools had yet to produce top-notch results with pained attempts to prove as hackneyed the prevailing European attitude that Americans were too materialistic to pay attention to beauty. Irate over exhibitors who had "misjudged the average American art-knowledge"[16] and offered inferior goods, one pundit declared:

> *One of the most interesting and instructive features of the Exhibition is the evidence it affords of how our young republic . . . has thrown off the simplicity of living necessary in its early days when existence was a long struggle with poverty, and with increasing wealth and prosperity is gathering to itself the most*

> *costly and elegant appliances for making life not only comfortable but luxurious, which money can buy. In every quarter of the world the invention of the artist and sculptor and artisan is taxed to supply the demand . . . to give us of the best that can be produced . . . and our own workmen, though lacking the facilities for study and self-education to be had on the Continent, are so constantly receiving into their ranks foreign artisans of the best class, that their joint work, which may fairly be called productions of American industry, compare favorably with European examples. . . . The time is coming . . . when our art-workmen will be peers of any anywhere. It must have been gratifying to every one visiting the Centennial, who was interested in the welfare and progress of this country, to observe how many choice and beautiful objects of art of foreign manufacture were purchased by Americans. . . . [T]heir benefit to the community in cultivating a correct taste and a higher standard of excellence is simply incalculable."*[17]

Not unlike the Japanese themselves, a competitiveness based upon prevailing national anxiety that characterized American dealings with the world made the Centennial exhibition a milestone. It inspired the establishment of art schools and societies nationwide, the founding of museums, and the travels of Americans to study abroad—all part of a reform movement dedicated to the transformation of American taste and standards away from the shoddy and tacky towards quality and beauty. Moral uplift and subsequent refinement in the country's international profile would inevitably follow. Japan's aesthetic perfection appeared with perfect timing, an opportunity to reveal discernment and sophistication, and an alternative to the European model in developing an elegant, new "American style." This was one reason why journalists dedicated a great deal of space to the Japanese presence.

A second reason was that Japan's Exhibition Bureau had planned meticulously and grandly to assure a debut that would captivate. It appointed thirty of the country's most prominent figures, including a foreigner—Gottfried Wagener, a German residing in Japan as an industrial consultant, whose expertise and foreign taste made him invaluable to the lucrative export arts. With a budget of over $600,000 (roughly $10 million today), this commission had combed the empire for a cornucopia of appropriate products. Above all, it underwrote the expenses of the best craftsmen in Japan so that they could exhibit.

Their work left the American public slack-jawed. Particular effort had gone into bronzes, the most highly esteemed applied art of the day.

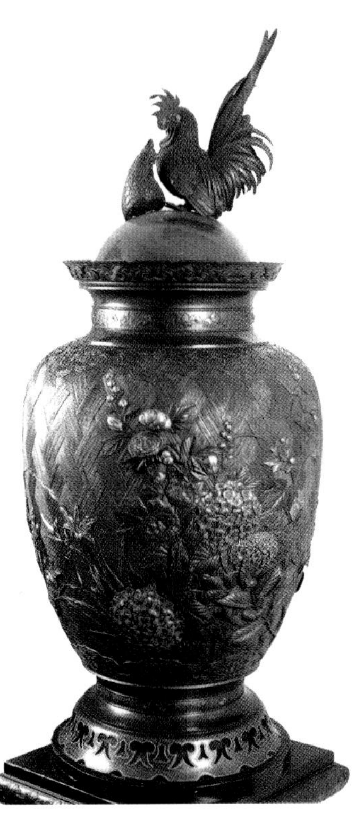

SUGIURA SEITARO. BALUSTER VASE; CA. 1874–1876; CAST BRONZE INLAID WITH GOLD, SILVER, AND PRECIOUS METAL ALLOYS; 46 INCHES HIGH; SIGNED ON THE BOTTOM WITH SUGIURA'S STUDIO NAME "YUKINARI SEN" ("CARVED BY YUKINARI"); MARKED WITH KIRITSU KOSHO KAISHA'S DOUBLE-MOUNTAIN LOGO. Kiritsu Kosho Kaisha enjoined one of the most renowned metalsmiths of the day to make this baluster vase depicting an all-over design of butterflies flitting amidst branches of peony, chrysanthemum, lily, lilac, magnolia, and aster around a basket capped with a lid on which perch a life-sized bantam rooster and hen. Reputedly, it was made for the Japanese Pavilion at the Centennial exhibition. Wealthy Pennsylvania industrialist and art collector Alfred O. Deshong, among the many dazzled by its colossal size and tour-de-force technique, purchased it for his important and substantial art collection.

Brilliantly conceived to appeal to Western ideas of quality and novelty, their elaborate "Asianesque" forms, ornate embellishments, and narrative elements from Japanese and Chinese folktales took their stylistic cues from the ponderously intricate French bronzes and ceramics considered the world's best. In the minds of many, Japan had surpassed them. Critics rhapsodized over their beautiful color, "we do not remember to have seen surpassed by any other specimen of like material,"[18] their feat of coupling huge size with dazzling refinement, of minute detail employed with powerful and economic effect "without triviality"—mixed metals in an array of unfamiliar techniques, astonishingly life-like realism, and, above all, the application of both to "the wonderful observation . . . in their study of natural objects . . . coupled with that subtle desire to give a grotesque turn to the work. . . ."[19] Highlights included a candelabra of a heron on one foot, holding a branch with places for candles, standing upon a crawling tortoise; another in the form of a confidently striding stork that, along with the just-caught eel writhing in its beak, also snatched a lotus stalk artfully worked into the lamp base rising from its head; and a four-foot-tall vase embellished with undulating dragon-shaped handles and panels damascened in silver and gold. But such never-before-seen originality of design and technical skill had to be understood as strange to be comprehensible: This was "labor such as only oriental workmen practice . . . as no Christian people can afford the time to emulate."[20]

These and the rest of the plenitude offered by Japan not only mingled with the offerings of other nations in the Centennial's six enormous halls but, more importantly, resided by itself in a national architectural installation as well. Capitalizing on their recent success in Vienna, Meiji's financially strapped government had taken on the huge expense in order to create a public image of Japan as among a small elite of eleven nations able to afford such an undertaking and, even more, as the sole Asian nation capable of doing so and therefore the only one of international significance. The gamble paid off resoundingly. According to *Harper's Weekly,* one of the preeminent publications of the era, no other structures on the fairgrounds had "excited more interest."[21]

The complex included an official residence large enough to house sixty persons, a teahouse nestled in the very first Japanese garden in the United States, and a bazaar. All would leave a far-reaching impact on American architecture, landscape, and interior design. The buildings had

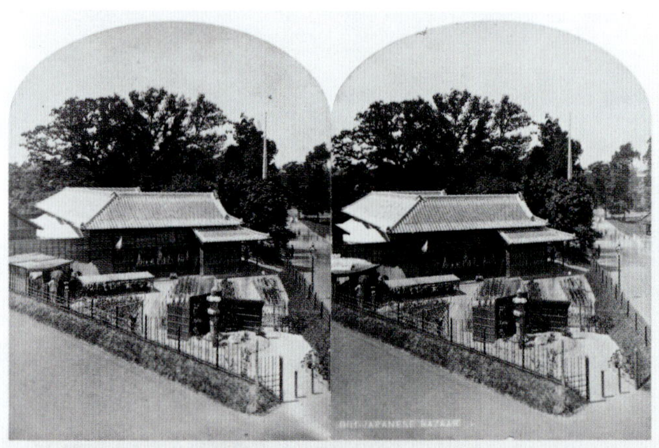

Above: Japanese bazaar; stereoview; 1876; as viewed at the Centennial exhibition, Philadelphia.

Below, Right: Japanese dwelling; chromolithograph; 1876; as viewed at the Centennial exhibition, Philadelphia. Noting that the dwelling constructed by Japan to house its exhibition officers excited more interest than any other building at the fair, reports of the time detailed its unusual and exacting construction methods, beautiful materials, novel layout, and components—its light and air-controlling sliding panels on the upper storey, the black tile roof, the carved birds and flowers ornamenting the entry, and the exotically patterned carpets of the interior.

been constructed in Japan and then dismantled for shipment to the United States, where even their arrival offered a moment of theater: delivery by train to Philadelphia filled nineteen boxcar loads. Reassembly on the fairgrounds created such a sensation that the laborers had to be shielded from the crowds. In the newspapers, commentators extolled the eschewing of nails, the complexity of mechanical puzzles, and the artisanal precision of the finest cabinetmakers. "They have not learned the ways of civilized house-builders as yet, and innocently suppose that doors and windows are intended to open and shut with ease, and without catching or binding or sagging. We might learn many things in mechanics from these Oriental workmen."[22]

Of the completed complex, a journalist wrote, "'we follow the multitudes inside the little bamboo fence."[23] His words make evident the number of visitors and hint at the dreamlike wonder awakened when fairgoers, their life experiences confined to ordinary American cities, towns, and farms, crossed into the dainty and picturesque world of the garden. There, for a moment, fantasy was real. Under the exquisitely courteous

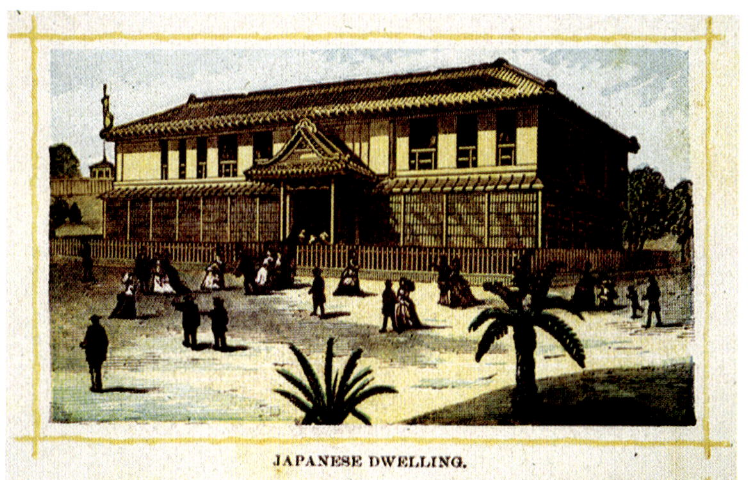
JAPANESE DWELLING.

attentions of strangely small, bizarrely attired men ("to us they seem all wrong: men arrayed in such garments, and hair in such a way, we are half inclined to doubt the manhood"[24]) and petite women in "monstrous" dress, visitors could indulge in an exotic flight of the imagination, visiting the teahouse to sample "peculiar" food and treating themselves to a bit of alien treasure from the bazaar.

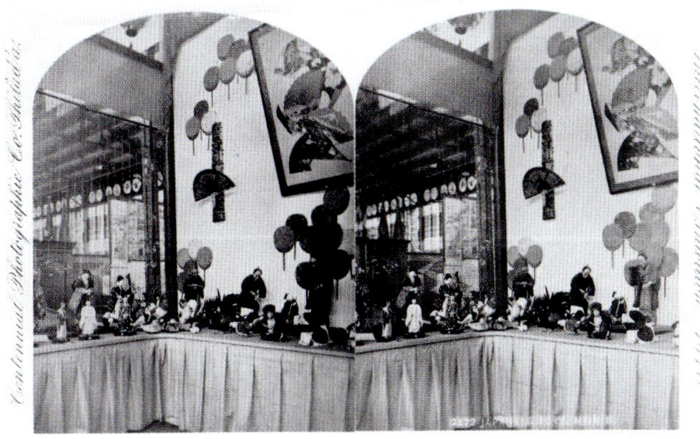

ABOVE: JAPANESE SOUVENIRS; STEREOVIEW; 1876; AS VIEWED AT THE CENTENNIAL EXHIBITION, PHILADELPHIA.

And such treasure! With the experience of several European fairs behind them, the Exhibition Bureau and its suppliers of art wares—among them Kiritsu Kosho Kaisha, M. Marunaka & Company, Yamanaka & Company, Minoda, and the preeminent dealer and urbane Paris resident Hayashi Tadamasa—had honed a fine eye for what would attract Americans: a careful selection of flotsam of the past that, along with the garden and buildings themselves, bespoke the image that Westerners found so romantic: armor, horse fittings, bows, arrows and spears, old sets of porcelain, lacquer boxes and personal items such as inro, bronzes, cunningly carved ivory *netsuke* (toggles carved as miniature sculptures), a model of a pleasure boat—mingled with new things of a very precise nature. To American eyes this all qualified as "bric-a-brac," an important category of production designated "social goods," or affordable objects for the home.

The careful display of bric-a-brac allowed people of the era not only to personalize their homes but also to project a certain character with

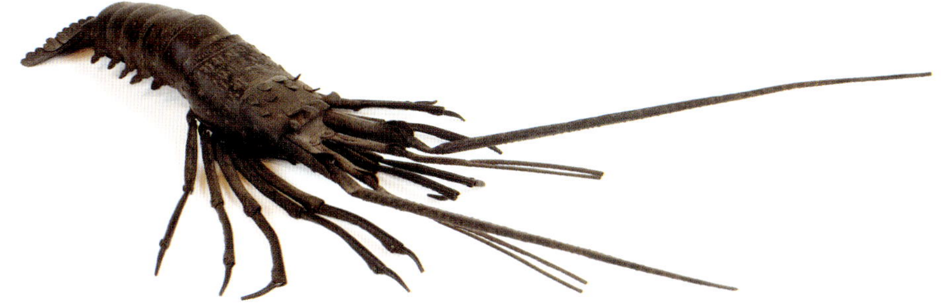

BELOW: IRON CRAWFISH; 11 INCHES LONG. This item is typical of the Japanese-made bric-a-brac that entranced the public at the 1876 Centennial exhibition and afterwards. Crustaceans, bugs, and other creatures, whose movable body parts in precise anatomical detail created an astonishing realism, were cunningly crafted by Japanese smiths to astonish and delight Westerners.

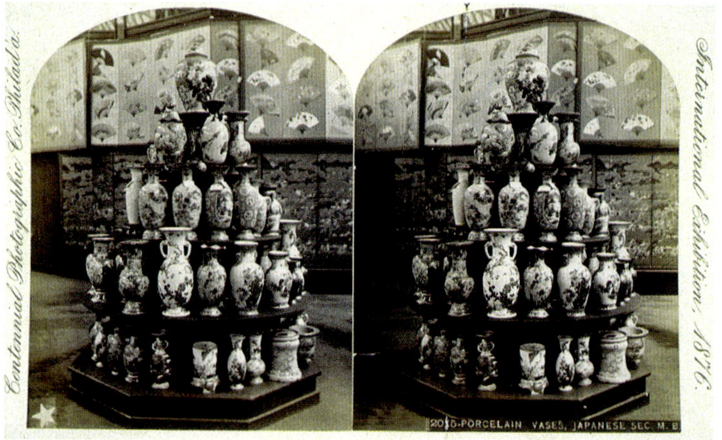

Right: Inexpensive vases; stereoview; 1876; as viewed at the Centennial exhibition, Philadelphia.

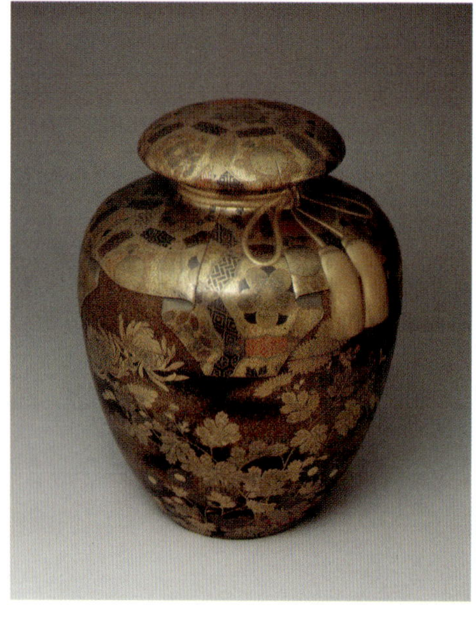

Above: Lidded jar; gold and black lacquer; ca. 1875–1890. This container, in the form of a lidded tea presentation jar sealed with a cloth secured by a knotted cord, enticed and thrilled Americans not only for the opulent surface effects of its textile and floral patterns but mostly for its clever trompe l'oeil, a technique in which Japanese artist craftsmen in many media excelled and American craftsmen emulated with enthusiasm.

respect to education, spirituality, sophistication, and other concerns. Fairs gave even those with no means or inclination for a direct experience of foreign places the opportunity to accumulate collections of exotic provenance for display. These eclectic groupings would indicate owners as persons of refinement and culture according to the tenets of the Aesthetic movement that dominated the decades of the 1870s and 1880s, in which Japanese art would play an immensely influential role. Among its many elements, the Aesthetic movement linked spiritual uplift to preindustrial craftsmanship and cosmopolitanism but also demanded a "harmonious" atmosphere. "The trouble with these strange forms is that it is hard to make them harmonious with the other appointments of the room. . . . [A] Japanese banner, on a Chinese paper, with a French ceiling, a Turkish rug, and American furniture, is too much of a mongrel to be endorsed by good taste."[25] Harmoniousness required that such exotica be confined to a defined space referred to as an "art corner," where they would be displayed with other carefully selected objects on a display chest or special shelf known as a whatnot. The art corner was essential to the décor of a parlor or library in the well-appointed home.

The bric-a-brac of the whatnot shelf addressed the desires of middle-class people to replicate the uplifting elegance of the grand items presented for delectation at Memorial Hall on a small scale in their own

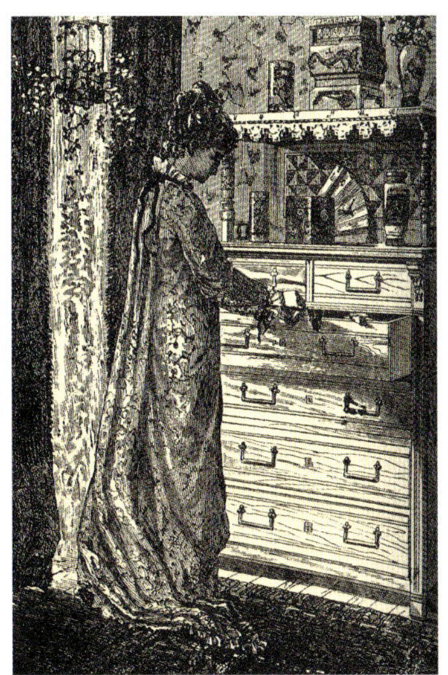

"A PEEP AT ELEGANCE"; ILLUSTRATION; AS PUBLISHED IN *THE HOUSEWIFE'S LIBRARY: MANY VOLUMES IN ONE* (1883), 458. An up-to-date young wife is busy at a chest and whatnot shelf displaying a Japanese fan, vases, and other exotic items. Author and prominent taste pundit George A. Peltz opined, "Antique forms are much in demand, and the very ruins of the world have been scoured to furnish suggestions for modern decoration. The trouble with these strange forms is that it is hard to make them harmonious with the other appointments of the room. If there is an Egyptian or Chinese or Japanese room wherein the peculiarities of these nations are the dominating motive, then you have an harmonious effect. Such a result is artistic. But a Japanese banner, on a Chinese paper, with a French ceiling, a Turkish rug, and American furniture, is too much of a mongrel to be endorsed by good taste."

homes. The colossal cost of those pieces, some of which took multiple master craftsmen more than a year to create, made them available only to the fantastically wealthy. Whether grand or modest, in some way all met criteria the public had come to expect from Japan: technical virtuosity, a rich mix of materials, and elaborately executed decoration of "curious, grotesque shapes mingled with strikingly faithful reproductions of leaves, vines and other forms of nature,"[26] applied to a functionality suitable for American life. The wide range of prices made almost anyone able to afford something. Lacquer cabinets, boxes, and trays ranged from 50 cents to $1,000, equivalent to between $7 and $15,000 today. Of lacquer, many pundits uttered what was to become a standard complaint of the future—that quality had declined since the old days. By way of example, one cited a piece supposedly three hundred and fifty years old that could be had for $5,000, or approximately $75,000 today. This supposed deterioration did not deter many talented and discerning individuals in the art world of the time: Edward C. Moore, the chief silver designer of Tiffany & Company, purchased a lacquer writing box for $300 to add to what was to become a noted collection of Japanese art.

The Centennial exhibition ended with Japan having achieved an effect both electrifying and jarring to American sensibilities in arts and culture, areas of enormous importance in the minds of the time. Critical commentary echoed the patronizing incredulity of European pundits. "It is as one of the great surprises of the fair: we have been accustomed to regard that country as uncivilized or half-civilized at best, but we found here abundant evidences that it outshines the most cultivated nations of Europe in arts which are their pride and glory, and which are regarded among the proudest tokens of their high civilization."[27] If oblivious to the massive changes underway in the first eight years under Meiji's reign and increasingly out of sync with real Japan, it was an image deliberately cultivated by the Japanese themselves. They did not accept the grating insult of being judged "heathen" by barbarians. Rather, in dire need of a new model for their transforming society, they accepted the spirit of the prevailing "scientific" view, and even its Euro-centric coloration, while embracing the fairs as arenas for a complicated game of internationalism at which they came to excel. Winning meant giving the West what it found attractive and positive about Japan while using its ambivalence to advantage. Literally gathering a representative sampling of its national offerings under such a roof as the exhibition's Japanese Bazaar, they consolidated,

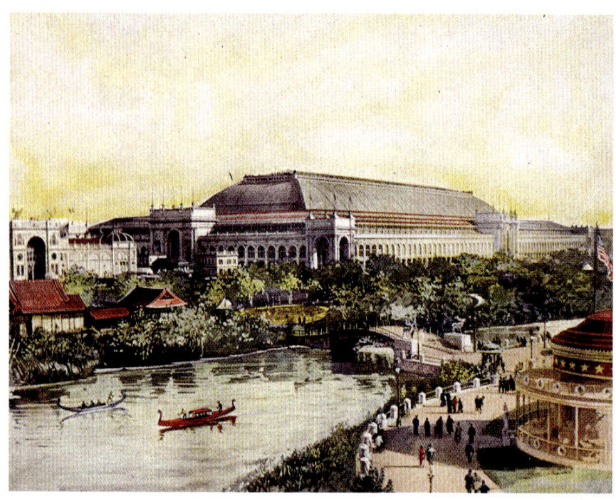

THE HŌŌDEN; CHROMOLITHOGRAPH; 1893; AS VIEWED AT THE WORLD'S COLUMBIAN EXHIBITION, CHICAGO. Strollers cross the bridge to the Hōōden as gondoliers glide by the Wooded Isle.

defined, and, to their minds, controlled their public image.

The 1893 World's Columbian Exhibition was a cusp in the cultural and economic landscape of the United States. The fair's Director of Works declared it the third greatest event in American history,[28] superseded only by national independence in 1776 and the outbreak of the Civil War in 1861. Antonin Dvorak composed the *New World Symphony* in its honor. Long after its concessions closed, its exhibits dismantled, its thousands of dazzling incandescent lights switched off, and the milling thousands gone their separate ways, this four-hundredth anniversary commemoration of the discovery of the New World lived on as the impetus to an unfolding transformation in American everyday life. Japan's conspicuous presence at the fair made it integral to this process in ways that paralleled a growing maturation in the relationship between the two countries in the forty years since Perry. This included an increased sophistication on the part of Americans with respect to Japanese arts both in their own right and in the possibilities they presented to creative American minds.

The Columbian exhibition's impact lay in its grand-scale, forward-thinking organizational plan, its locale, and, above all, its timing. The clarion of the new century a mere seven years in the future, it was hosted by a city appropriately vibrant and young, a place emblematic of the dynamic adolescent nation. Only sixty years old, Chicago had arisen from the ashes of a catastrophic fire as a major and growing metropolis, the continent's transportation hub, a manufacturing powerhouse, and boasting a skyline punctuated by that signature American architectural hallmark of modernity, the skyscraper. Equally appropriate in its way was the revealing light this gleaming surface cast upon the flimsy supporting apparatus of contemporary American life: cities rampant with corruption, filthy streets, open sewage, ethnic and racial tension, burgeoning populations crammed into crime- and disease-ridden slums and sweatshops, industrial and agricultural volatility, and a tottering banking system, all barely clinging together under the rapacious gaze and enthrallingly conspicuous splendor of robber barons. Such a fragile scaffold could not hold: The fair coincidentally opened as if on cue at the very moment of its inevitable implosion in the worst financial panic in United States history. Six hundred banks failed and thousands of factories and businesses closed, throwing more than two and a half million out of work. An unemployment rate of more than 10 percent would persist for seven unrelenting years. But, incredibly, people came to the Columbian exhibition in the hundreds of thousands. Fifty cents opened a gracefully landscaped, model urban precinct of two hundred buildings known as the White City. There, a casual ramble through the fourteen elegant Beaux-Arts Great Buildings promised a future more convenient, tasty, and fun in exhibits of such new products as Cream of Wheat, Aunt Jemima Pancake Mix, Postum, Juicy Fruit gum, and Shredded Wheat, technologically propelled and eased by the electrical marvels of the lightbulb, moving sidewalks, launches, and elevated trains—not to mention more entertaining, thanks to Thomas Edison's motion picture camera. After a refreshing Pabst Blue Ribbon Beer, visitors could indulge themselves in a mile of delightful distraction on the Midway Plaisance, on the gigantic engineering wonder known as the Ferris Wheel or myriad other rides, at sideshow ethnological displays of "primitive" cultures, at wild-animal acts, and in the exotically colorful and fragrant bazaars of "Egypt," "Turkey," and "Japan."

And thousands strolled across a low bridge over a mirror-like lagoon to the bucolic Wooded Isle at its center. There, set in its own garden, a jewel in the very heart of the White City, Japan's exquisite Hōōden serenely presided over the surrounding bustle. To secure this premier spot, the Japanese Royal Commissioner had moved with decisiveness and sophistication at the fair's earliest planning stages, rushing from his headquarters in New York to Chicago, where his arrival aroused great excitement. Clothed in superbly tailored Western suits and exuding urbane ease, he wined and dined at the most exclusive clubs and society homes, promoting his country's suit to dazzled hosts and an approving press. These included the irresistible enticement that this beautiful building would become a grand gift to the city at the fair's end. It was a brilliant stroke not lost on rivals: the Commissioner had succeeded in making this graceful structure not only Japan's national centerpiece but literally that of the entire event.

Japan repaid the public with a building perfectly suited to the times. It epitomized the didactic concept prevailing at expositions that emphasized learning through passive encounter and was as beautiful as it was educational. The Hōōden, or "Phoenix Hall," approximated the exterior form and organization of a celebrated eleventh-century Buddhist sanctuary whose name it borrowed in slightly altered form. Inside, visitors encountered three distinct spaces, an overview of the major milestones of Japan's aristocratic and imperial architectural history, each resplendent according to its times—its wall paintings of tree peonies, wild ducks and reeds, mountain summits and pines—all the work of the faculty and students of Japan's premier art academy. The complex offered further educational and aesthetic rewards in gorgeous unfamiliar materials as well as the quality and novelty of the "curious" construction methods of its coffered ceilings, its lacquer and gold embellishments, its hand-carved native hardwoods with metal ornaments, and its figured nail heads. Many considered it the architectural triumph of the fair. As a magnet for Charles and Henry Greene, a young Frank Lloyd Wright who came scores of times over the fifty years the building stood, and numerous lesser lights, the exquisite Hōōden was one of the most influential buildings of its time.

Its cost of approximately $100,000 was the hugely expensive capstone of an extravagant presence "said to be the handsomest and costliest ever made by the Empire."[29] The Japanese financial commitment was the third largest after Germany and France, vastly outstripping Denmark, Norway, Greece, Italy, Spain, and even England. It garnered nearly three

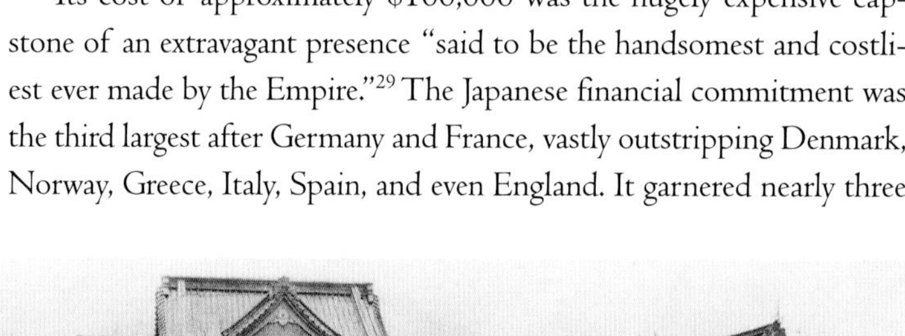

The Hōōden; photograph; 1893; as viewed at the World's Columbian Exhibition, Chicago. Courtesy of the Chicago History Museum.

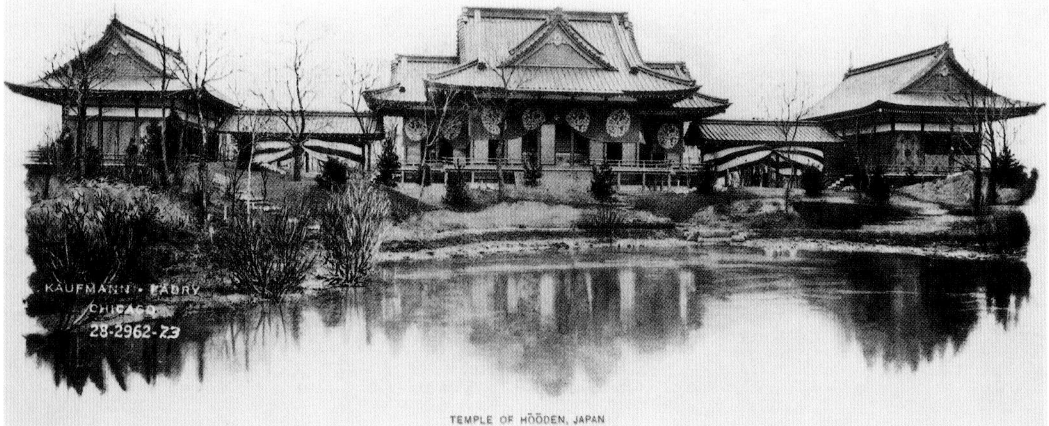

acres of accumulated exhibition space, almost 10 percent of the total fair, in addition to extensive allotments for buildings—a scale that had caught everyone off guard: "of all the countries that will exhibit . . . the plans outlined by Japan are now attracting the greatest interest. . . . The appropriation by . . . the Flowery Kingdom was a genuine surprise . . . ."[30] The jewel in the very heart of the White City, Japan's Hōōden was complemented on the grounds by a teahouse on the lake, a bazaar on the Midway Plaisance, a botanical garden, a portion of a home interior in the Women's Building, and a pavilion in the Manufactures Building. The building itself contained a collection of relics, carvings, and other art treasures loaned from the private imperial collection, from the national museum, as well as from industrial implements, and was presided over by a staff of attendants, guards, and gardeners sent from Japan to Chicago. "In short, a small section of Japan will be shown at the Fair,"[31] not as a mere showcase but as a nation of stature, depth, sophistication, and breadth of achievement—a contender to eclipse the charisma of any other foreign power. Both the Japanese government and the business community had enthusiastically involved themselves. There was much more than national prestige at stake.

Ever since Alcock's revelation at the 1862 London fair, Japan had made arts and art crafts the tools of conflicting agendas dedicated to a common aim: a place among the ranks of preeminent nations in the international galaxy. This was a matter of pride and necessity. But the Western gravitational pull inevitably placed Japan in a reactive position, unable to control the path and position of its orbit. Contemporary arts and art crafts thus evolved according to two very different purposes: one concerned with virtuoso technique because the West so admired it, the other with achieving regard in the vague realm of "pure" artistic expression because the West valued it above all else as the indicator of a civilized society. Always a delicate cross-cultural process to which prominent thinkers, politicians, business people, and a group of influential resident Westerners all contributed, the challenge only grew as a transforming Japan dealt with entrenched American social attitudes and an evolving market, taste, and sophistication. By the 1890s, "authentic or inauthentic" had come to preoccupy art pundits who, in the style of the day, unhesitatingly made a weapon of it in withering criticism. Some in Japan viewed these developments with alarm, discerning a growing loss of control over their own image in a way that threatened cultural integrity and appeal for their arts. "If we remain indifferent to this and continue in the conventional way, they will make the merits of our art entirely their own and there will no longer be a market for Japanese arts and crafts. This is certainly a very real danger."[32] The grand presence in Chicago was designed to reassert a legitimate claim over its own and at the same time attain success in the final step toward parity with the West. But rather than resolving these issues, the exhibition brought Japan's awkward position into the glaring light of day.

The quest for economic power and recognition had given rise to an array of ceramics, metals, textiles, ornamental printing and bookbinding, furniture, upholstery, paperhangings and papier-mâché, jewelry, and glass. According to the definitions of the day, these exemplified "art crafts" and "industrial arts," utilitarian objects embellished with ". . . such ornamentation as makes it lovely or pleasing to look upon, attractive to the eye, ministering to the wants of the mind . . . ."[33] Their appeal rested on exotic decorativeness responding to popular Western notions of "Japanese" applied to Western functionality and on their quality. Critics placed Japanese applied art products at the pinnacle. Commenting on the Chicago exhibition, the *New York Times* asserted that Japanese embroidery craftsmen had "elevated their standard to a height that . . . probably marks the limit of human attainment," praising originality of conception, color harmonies, clearness and precision of design, and, "of utmost essential importance, patience and loving devotion in execution." Other critics concurred, and added accolades for Japanese metalwork. The *New York Times* commented, "The world will be supplied with metal masterpieces as exquisite in design and manipulation as any of the treasures of the Middle Ages."[34]

But despite such paeans, Japan had stumbled. On the one hand, Westerners simply were not willing and, of late, no longer able to pay for the astonishing technical virtuosity they so admired, preferring to bemoan its inevitable demise as Japan's modernizing society resulted in fewer craftsmen and prohibitive costs. Kiritsu Kosho Kaisha, conspicuous at the 1876 Centennial exhibition, had already gone out of business. But Japanese manufacturers had erred as well. They had not anticipated American taste's growing move away from ornate Aestheticism toward the simplicity of Arts and Crafts—ironically due in part to increasing appreciation of traditional Japanese aesthetics and design alternatives in a time of changing lifestyles. They also had failed to foresee competition.

Western manufacturers now understood the nature of Japanese appeal in decorative arts. As the acknowledged benchmark, Japan faced a formidable challenge. The Danish display at Chicago had favorably "surprised" the influential *Art Amateur* with blue-and-white wares whose "quality of paste and glaze, purity of form and distinction of design recalled the best of old Japan." Meanwhile, Japanese submissions fared unevenly: the mass-produced housewares crowding the national display at the Manufactures Building earned nods as products to be reckoned with in the burgeoning and highly competitive new world of products for the home. Yet, while pronouncing some ceramics "not out of the race" in their "novel and agreeable effects,"[35] pundits excoriated others, declaring that "deterioration" in quality demanded they "be shattered into fragments."[36] More tellingly, even in noting complicity by the American market in the sorry state of Japanese art crafts overall, critics bludgeoned only Japan with blame, as if to imply that in responding to that temptation, the nation had revealed a kind of moral weakness. The denunciation made clear that genuine welcome to the international fraternity continued to be blocked by a lurking Western desire that Japan remain an idealized—and malleable and inferior—avatar of the past:

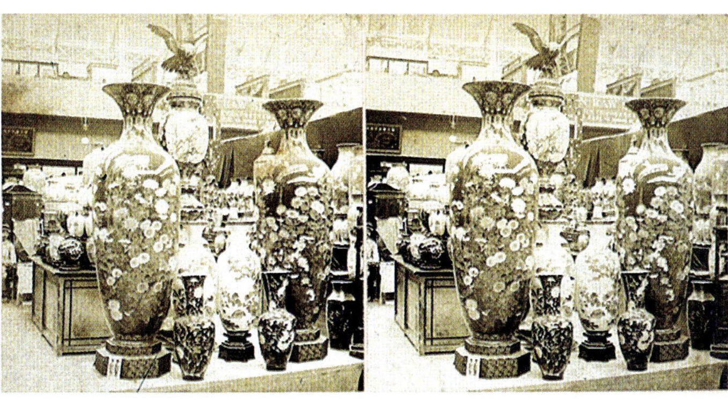

CLOISONNÉ ENAMEL OR CERAMIC VASES; STEREOVIEW; 1893; AS VIEWED AT THE WORLD'S COLUMBIAN EXHIBITION, CHICAGO. Japan's vases awed visitors with their tour-de-force size and equally outsized cost.

> *Everyone knows that since the opening of the empire a quarter of a century ago, an entirely false direction has been given to many of the higher Japanese industries, in obedience to a demoralized . . . commercial instinct which for a while threatened to entirely obscure the lofty traditional ideals. The readiness of European and American purchasers to accept an inferior style tempted the manufacturers too sorely and they were recreant to the faith the nation had professed for centuries.*[37]

This made the second challenge all the more important: success in the lofty realm of "fine art." In the hyper-idealized sentiments of the day, this was the apex of human achievement, born only from a society of spiritual, moral, and intellectual superiority. *Fine art* was defined in vague yet elevated terms: "the expression of something not taught by nature, the presentation of that ideal, the mere conception of which raises man above the level of savagery."[38] In visual realms, it meant architecture, sculpture, painting, and the related arts of etching and engraving. These enjoyed pride of place at the exhibitions, accorded a separate building in a prime location. Artists competed at home to represent their nations and again for the juried prizes that would rank them as the best of the best. In fine art, Japan had met only rebuke. Her distinctive pictorial art styles were not comprehensible to judges who neither understood nor respected a tradition not based upon verisimilitude. The areas at which they excelled to universal acclaim were relegated to the categories of "applied" and "industrial" arts, deemed lesser because their intent was not pure moral uplift but utility, their technical virtuosity and visual appeal in service to practical function. The Japanese chafed in the second and third tiers, lauded for being the best of the second best.

From the Japanese perspective, it all made little sense. The term *fine art* itself had become known to them only in 1873 at the Vienna exposition, when it was translated from German. Vague definition aside, Japan had no such overarching concept. Over the course of two millennia, its visual culture had emerged a multifaceted and nuanced thing. Lacquers were lacquers; tea bowls were tea bowls; sword fittings were sword fittings; temple carvings were temple carvings. "Paintings" were variously folding or sliding screens, scrolls, or album leaves. Each possessed its own criteria of excellence and roster of masters, most regarded as artisans rather than individuals of genius. Articles made for export were just that—export—outside this ancient standard because none played any role in Japanese life.

Epitomizing the disconnect between East and West were opposing perspectives on the woodblock prints called ukiyo-e. In Japan, they were cheap broadsides outside the canon of valued things, and their beauty, technical virtuosity, and the talent of their masters went unrecognized. But as pictures in the West, they met the criteria for fine art and were regarded with awe for originality of color, composition, style, motif, and superlative technique. This sparked a collecting frenzy from the time of their introduction in the mid-1850s. In short, what the West valued from Japan, Japan did not value for itself; what Japan valued did not accord with Western ideas of worth. In fine art as with everything else, Japan had found itself confronted with a criterion that suited its own rich, ancient, and venerated heritage no better than an ill-fitting shoe.

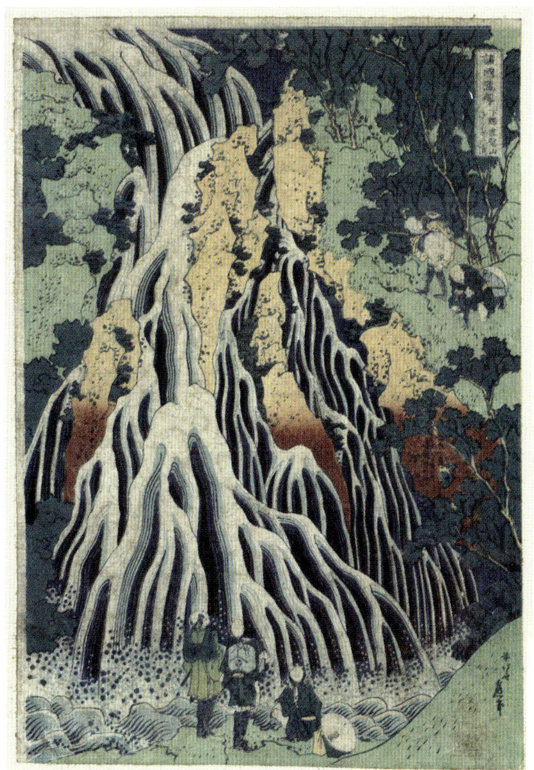

KATSUSHIKA HOKUSAI. *SHIMOTSUKE KUROKAMI-YAMA KURIFURI NO TAKI (KURIFURI FALLS AT MOUNT KUROKAMI IN SHIMOSUKE)*; UKIYO-E WOODBLOCK PRINT; FROM THE SERIES *SHOKOKU TAKI MEGURI (VISITING FAMOUS WATERFALLS OF JAPAN)*; PRINTED LATER, CA. 1833.

Success in the realm of fine art had long been an ambition for the Meiji government as the means by which Japan could claim to deserve the status to which it aspired. At home the debate to resolve it would spill into the aisles of the diet, impact the educational system, and create unrest among revered figures from traditional aesthetic and intellectual circles who found themselves devalued. To succeed at home and abroad, Western standards had to be met, to which they were compelled to adapt. In Chicago they finally attained what at first blush appeared a breakthrough with an ingenious redefinition: Japanese tradition might not *identify* "fine art," but in light of Japan's universally acknowledged high aesthetic standards in all media across its history, *everything* was "fine art" and had been all along. Given the vague nature of the concept anyway, judges accepted the semantics with outward equanimity, opining, "In the case of Japan, the usual classification of painting, sculpture, architecture and engraving had to be abandoned. Her art is too unlike our own to be listed in the same manner."[39] In outward deference a new, supposedly impartial system of judgment assessed a work by a numerical scale of quality. Those earning below a certain number were automatically "applied art"; those above were "fine art." Japan could now submit a variety of creations for competition—paintings on silk, lacquers, bronzes and other metals, ivories, woodcarvings and inlays, and ceramics—none pre-categorized as "fine art" or "applied art." In achieving this, they sparked a cross-cultural discussion that swirled for years, inadvertently giving impetus and energy to Western decorative arts. For as one influential pundit declared with respect to the distinction, ". . . we should not forget that with us it is largely artificial . . . ."[40]

This apparent victory constituted only half the goal. The second aim was unassailable recognition as a modern nation, which necessitated Japanese "fine art" stand according to the conventional Western-defined standard. Signs were positive: Western pundits by now conceded, some more willingly than others, that Japanese tradition included works that

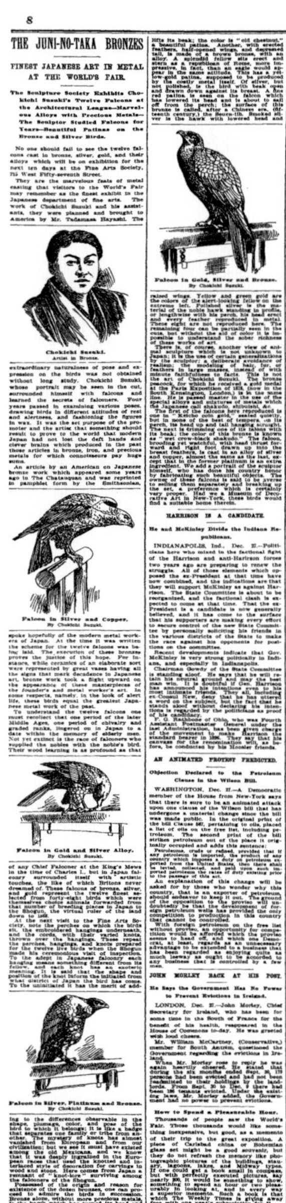
8

THE JUNI-NO-TAKA BRONZES

FINEST JAPANESE ART IN METAL AT THE WORLD'S FAIR.

The Sculpture Society Exhibits Chokichi Suzuki's Twelve Falcons at the Architectural League—Marvelous Alloys with Precious Metals—The Sculptor Studied Falcons for Years—Beautiful Patinas on the Bronze and Silver Birds.

No one should fail to see the twelve falcons cast in bronze, silver, gold, and their alloys which will be on exhibition for the next ten days at the Fine Arts Society, 215 West Fifty-seventh Street.

They are the marvelous feats of metal casting that visitors to the World's Fair may remember as the finest exhibit in the Japanese department of fine arts. The work of Chokichi Suzuki and his assistants, they were planned and brought to America by Mr. Tadamasa Hayashi. The

Suzuki Chokichi. *Juni-no-Taka* (*Twelve Falcons*); as they appeared in the *New York Times*, December 28, 1893.

met the criteria for fine art in showing "... little trace of any mere utilitarian." Some went so far as to admit that "we should lay aside our notion that Japanese art is merely amusing, or that, if it has a serious side, it is one that need not concern us."[41] Moreover, in modernizing the education system, Japan had established a fine arts academy whose curriculum incorporated Western methodologies, media, and concepts, including the fostering of the independent "artist." The Chicago exhibition became its moment of debut: for the first time Japan placed chosen works of living artists in direct competition with those of America and Europe.

The government turned to Japan's best to produce fine art the whole world would consider world class. The pressure was intense. The burden of letting down the emperor and the nation led to towering anxiety and propelled some artists to extremes of effort. One became so overwhelmed from endlessly reworking the painting of a tiger, which failed his own standard of perfection each time, that he had a breakdown and ended up in an asylum, "by no means assured that he will ever be able to resume his career."[42] But it was almost all for naught. The competition results at Chicago revealed the boundary of Western acceptance: In a move that must have stung, the judges rejected the oil paintings and most watercolors and drawings entered by the Japanese as below the numerical minimum, admonishing, "... they too often wander beyond their limitations and aim at rivalry of Western methods. The error is disastrous in exact proportion to the length to which it is pursued. Its evil consequences are evident ...." They excoriated many sculpture submissions for disregard of anatomical precision. Even worse, they equated these failures to the "impossibility" of making traditional Japanese drama interesting to an American, thereby the inevitable result of an essential incompatibility, and concluded, "Until a proper awakening to this highest of artistic needs is brought about, Japan will always lag behind the Western world and fail to command such serious attention as she longs to win."[43]

Not even art crafts escaped unscathed. In a reflection of changing tastes, judges once dazzled by the huge elaborate vases now rated them as "having all the signs that mark decadence in Japanese art ...."[44] But a spectacular set entitled *Juni-no-Taka* (*Twelve Falcons*)—cast in bronze, gold, and silver by the master Suzuki Chokichi (1848–1919)—was a telling exception to this sorry state of affairs. It was meant to awe. "It

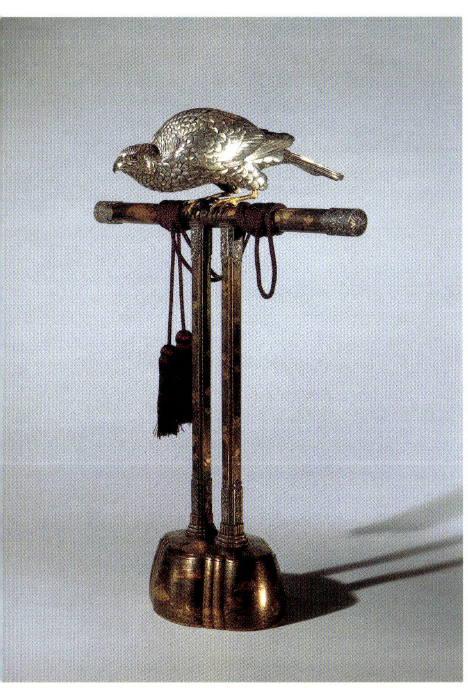

SANO TAKACHIKA. INCENSE BURNER; CA. 1893–1894; 27 INCHES HIGH OVERALL; SIGNED "TAKACHIKA"; SEALED "ZO." Suzuki Chokichi's famous *Twelve Falcons*, which created such a furor at the Columbia exhibition in Chicago, looked much like the work of other skilled metalsmiths of the time, who similarly interpreted well-loved themes from Japanese feudal times in three dimensions and precious materials. The incense burner is executed in silver with gold and shakudo; the lacquer stand is mounted in silver. Courtesy of the Nasser D. Khalili Collection of Japanese Art, London, England.

was the set purpose of the promoter and the artist that something should result to prove to the world that modern Japan had not lost the deft hands and clever brains which produced in the past those articles in bronze, iron and precious metals for which connoisseurs pay huge sums."[45] Already internationally recognized as a craftsman for magnificent vases, incense burners, and the like—"applied art" all—Suzuki had gone about this project as any Western artist of the time would, by nature study, a task that took four years. Lauded as one of the highlights of the entire exhibition, critics remarked upon the astonishing verisimilitude he achieved. However, what most captivated them beyond breathtaking technical expertise was the link of his theme with the feudal sport of falconry as practiced by the shoguns. In short, while Suzuki alone achieved the success sought by his government, the accolades came in precisely those areas that they always had—art crafts—and in themes that called to mind a romantic but defunct era, as made clear in the comments of one critic that "these birds equal the greatest Japanese metal work of the past." In the end, the attitudes they sought to undo simply reasserted themselves in another guise, so that little actually changed for Japan.

From Japan's point of view, the status quo must have appeared as incomprehensible as it was insulting. Western society prided itself as leading a march toward a golden age, paraded at the international expositions. Japan found this justifiable and worthy in light of undeniable, as yet unmatched, technological and economic advances and resulting political power. How could the values of the past—a past emphatically left behind—support the parallel claim that their absence left Western civilization teetering on the brink of chaos? If the West really had lost a sense of beauty, pride in one's work, authenticity, quality, and a moral foundation for creativity, how could it then be the arbiter of those very things? And why should Japan be thrust on an artificial pedestal as the image of those values, her own right to articulate what she supposedly represented denied? Public opinion grew increasingly irritable as the twentieth century dawned, fanned by encounters of Japanese residing abroad with the saccharine and demeaning public

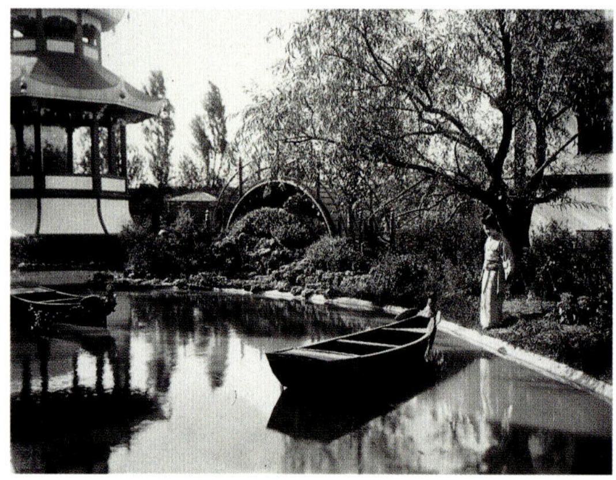

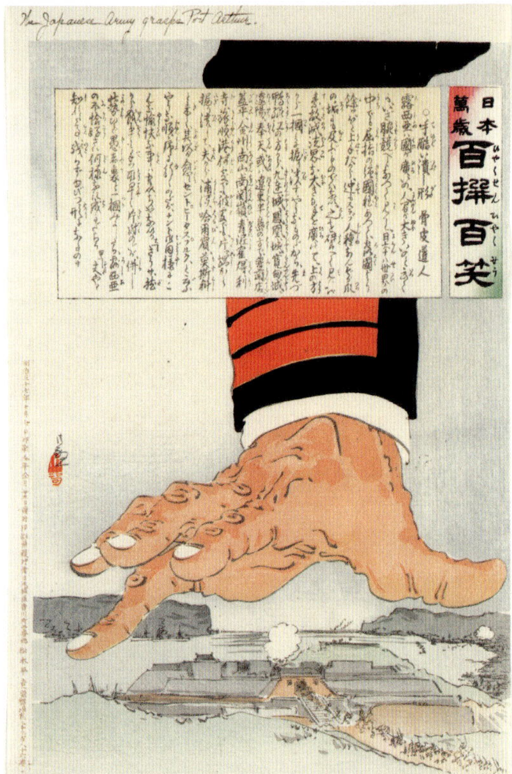

image, their indignation all the stronger for pride in their nation's new international stature. One described the Japanese Village constructed for a major London horticultural exhibition in 1910 as "a sketch of the lowest class of peasants . . . a sight which must fill Japanese gentlemen with nothing but displeasure and shame."[46]

Yet, their own government bankrolled many of these very projects, for there were advantages. Japan's growing modernity and power had been met with suspicion and anxiety rather than acceptance. With its extravagant antiquarian installation for the 1904 Louisiana Purchase International Exposition in St. Louis, the Meiji government couched its ambitions with a bowdlerized ideal to which few in the West and virtually no one in Japan sincerely aspired. The cheerful, gorgeous yet dainty, reassuringly romantic image counterbalanced an accompanying presentation of a spectrum of frontline achievements in hydraulic electric power, state-of-the-art railway, mail and telegraph systems, infectious disease control, telephone transmitters, and an educational system that now "had to be seen to be credited."[47] More broadly, it cast a softening veil over a tough aggressiveness: almost concurrently with the opening of the fair, Japan had entered into war with Russia, the superpower of the era—a war it shortly would win, upending a long-standing status quo and decisively inserting itself into the ranks of nations to be reckoned with. The installation in St. Louis was a highly successful ploy. Even as Japanese militarism rattled nerves on both sides of the Atlantic, commentators could barely contain their delight at the vision offered up at the fair; only Italy rivaled Japan for depth of attention. The American public devoured the experience.

Appropriately opened by larger-than-life President Theodore Roosevelt, the St. Louis exhibition was huge, larger in area than the Centennial exhibition, the Columbian exhibition, and the Pan-American

FACING, UPPER: DAMSEL BY THE POND IN THE JAPANESE GARDEN; PHOTOGRAPH; 1904; AS VIEWED AT THE LOUISIANA PURCHASE INTERNATIONAL EXPOSITION, ST. LOUIS. At the international expositions, Japan took great pains to present a charming public image, such as this one.

FACING, LOWER: KOBAYASHI KIYOCHIKA. *TEHIDOI TSUBUSHIGATA (PRESSURE FROM A HEAVY HAND)*; UKIYO-E WOODBLOCK PRINT; CA. 1904; 14.41 × 9.69 INCHES; FROM THE SERIES *NIHON BANZAI HYAKUSEN HYAKUSHI (LONG LIVE JAPAN: ONE HUNDRED VICTORIES, ONE HUNDRED LAUGHS)*. Public opinion at home regarding Japan's growing international presence was fanned to patriotic pride, shown by a large Japanese hand crushing Port Arthur, the battle that sealed Japan's victory in the Russo-Japanese War of 1904–1905.

Exhibition of 1901 in Buffalo combined. People described it in almost cosmic terms: "So thoroughly did it represent the world's civilization that if all man's other works were by some unspeakable catastrophe blotted out, the records established at this Exposition by the assembled nations would afford the necessary standards for the rebuilding of our entire civilization."[48]

With the panache acquired from the experience of twenty-six previous exhibitions, Japan emphasized its importance in its choice of representative for the opening ceremonies: His Royal Highness Lieutenant General Prince Fushimi Sadanaru (1858–1923), first cousin and officially adopted brother of the emperor himself. A public relations triumph, St. Louis fell all over itself to impress this "notable representative of Japanese culture and manliness,"[49] sending the exposition's Committees on Foreign Relations, Receptions, and Entertainment, the mayor, and the commanding general of the northern division of the United States Army to greet his arrival and whisk him off to receptions, banquets, dress reviews, and ladies' teas.

Japan had seized the moment. Its second major war in ten years had brought the "little kingdom of the Pacific"[50] to the forefront of peoples' attention. While hostilities had made finances tight, it spent a million dollars on the exposition. Its magnificent installation opened with a gala hosted by the Japanese ambassador to Washington, Baron Kogoro Takahira, for two thousand guests, including Roosevelt's

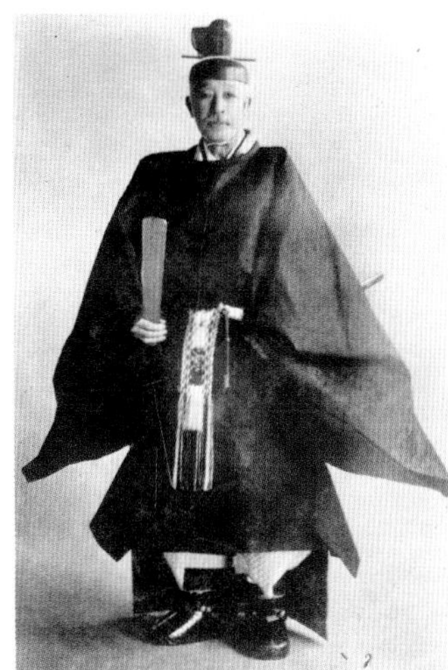

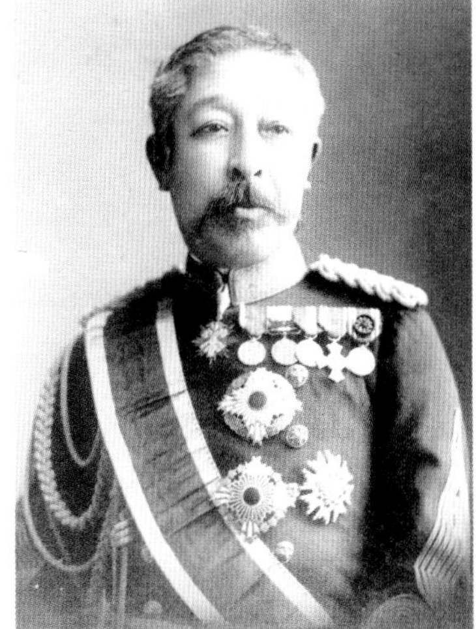

NEAR RIGHT: Prince Fushimi Sadanaru, in his regalia for the Japanese Imperial Court.

FAR RIGHT: The prince, in the general's uniform he undoubtedly wore for many of his public engagements with the Western elite.

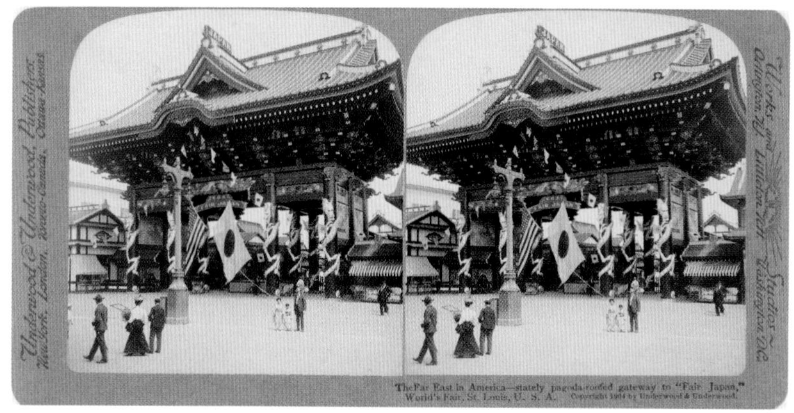

The Yomeimon Gate; stereoview; 1904; as viewed at the Louisiana Purchase International Exposition, St. Louis. The gate was described as "The Far East in America—stately pagoda-roofed gateway to 'Fair Japan,' World's Fair, St. Louis, U.S.A."

glamorous daughter Alice, the darling of the society pages. Its eight buildings cost $80,000—the sixth largest of the fair after the far more prosperous United States, Germany, France, Brazil, and Great Britain. Described as "a picture of real Japan," with a bazaar and shops selling "odd wares," its highlights included replicas of the most iconic structures of Japan's imperial and martial past: the Nikko Yomeimon Gate, the Shishinden imperial audience hall, the Kinkakuji retreat, and the Nio-mon Gate—forty-two feet high, forty feet wide, and eighty feet deep, of gold lacquer overlaid with silver "gleaming like the mellow gold of kings' treasures" and "not a nail . . . used in its construction."[51] In the vast gardens and along the international entertainment road called the Pike, Buddhist priests carried out daily rites amidst hundreds of religious images; acrobats performed on tall poles, little girls wove rugs, a man carved single beans into minuscule sculptures, fortune-tellers waved the tools of their trade, a military band and a troupe of girls entertained with "strange music," roosters "with tails twenty feet long" strutted, and jinrikishas provided novel transportation. President Roosevelt rode in one when he visited the gardens. There, amid imported 200-year-old pines, ". . . their winding walks and rustic bridges, their flower beds and grassy hillsides, their little mountain stream and water-fall and lake, and their quaint-looking pagodas and teahouses . . . suggestive of fairy land," forty "dainty maidens in native costume" served him tea with "waxen hands" while he enjoyed the antiquated spectacle of samurai fencing bouts with swords and spears. At the end of the fair, the Japanese government sold their entire garden and buildings for $500.

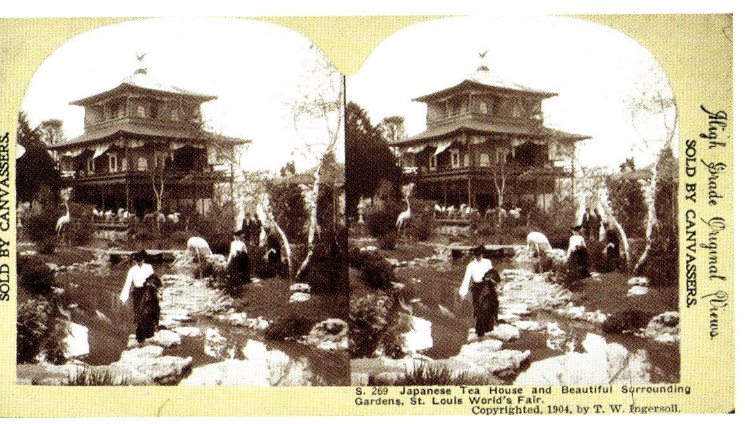

Replica of Kyoto's famous Kinkakuji Pavilion and Gardens at the Louisiana Purchase International Exposition, St. Louis; stereoview; 1904.

A lesson had been learned from the lackluster response to its art in Chicago. This time, no stone was left unturned in reaffirming Japan's great strength in the eyes of the West: "art as applied to the trades and industries."[52] At a cost of approximately $1 million and square footage three times that of Chicago, twenty thousand individuals and firms laid eighty thousand exhibits before the public in prominent locations all over the fair. The art crafts in the Palace of Varied Industries rivaled exhibits in the Palace of Fine Arts. Entered through the magnificent replica of the Yomeimon Gate of Nikko, it covered an area of 54,737 square feet. Inside, the visitors feasted their eyes on elegantly arranged displays of the phenomenally expensive to the very affordable: fine bronze statues, ceramics of every variety ranging from six-foot vases to delicate porcelain figures of almost microscopic detail, ivory carvings, cloisonné, silver work, furniture, embroideries, jewelry, lacquer, textiles of all sorts, and a host of toys, umbrellas, and hats. Critics marveled at a cabinet and two five-foot-tall vases, "the largest . . . ever manufactured,"[53] all of cloisonné; a huge ivory tusk carved into a chain of ever-shrinking elephants; and an opulent reproduction of a cabinet owned by the emperor: four tiers of drawers, doors, and mirrors decorated with every conceivable hue available in lacquer. One rather new art craft of special note were pictures executed in cut velvet.

To capitalize on the enthusiasm and to further infuse the public with their art products, cunning little souvenirs were proffered as gifts at receptions, and representatives negotiated permanent business arrangements with American firms. And, in a decisive swipe, exhibitors made an art historical point by a comparative display of delftware to emphasize their Arita blue-and-white porcelains as the inspiration for the better-known and much-loved Dutch ceramics.[54] The voluble press burst into paragraph after paragraph of florid praise, one writer concluding, "On all sides, it was conceded that no finer exhibit could have been made."[55] The enraptured public purchased with such energy that stocks had to be refreshed only two months after the fair opened.[56]

Perhaps reflecting Japan's rising prestige as much as it did improvements in its art academy training in the eleven years since Chicago, fine arts likewise enjoyed high praise. With only the barest hint of condescension, judges rated Japanese efforts in Western techniques in portraiture and landscape as indicative of the "innate artistic sense of the Japanese people, and demonstrated, moreover, how well they were learning to handle European materials and methods."[57] Of greater importance, they further expanded the revised definition of "fine art," first redefined in Chicago. To correct "certain unjust conditions which have grown up in the art world,"[58] the distinction between "fine art," and "industrial art" was completely erased, and all work, regardless of medium, ". . . in which the artist-producer had worked with conviction and knowledge—was recognized as equally deserving of respect in proportion as it was worthy from the standpoints of inspiration and technique."[59] To that end, for the first time, it honored the craftsmen who actually produced the magnificent tour-de-force works as artists and not the companies and designers they worked for. Moreover, "it was desired that the art of Japan, admittedly one of the most potent influences in directing the trend of Western art expression, should be given a place commensurate with the position of strength and dignity which it has attained in the schools of the world."[60] And in a gesture in the best spirit of didacticism, Japanese planners were invited to present to the American public examples of what the greatest authorities in Japan considered the most exemplary and the most "purely national in character." This resulted in an exhibition of two hundred forty-seven works of ivory, bronze and other metals, terra-cotta, wood, lacquer, and painting occupying seven galleries from which even Western-influenced Japanese works were excluded. So significant was this achievement regarded in Japan that the entire collection also enjoyed a private invitational exhibition for three thousand prominent art world figures in Tokyo.

The success of the St. Louis exposition was perhaps the high point among major initiatives by the Japanese government in its use of art and art crafts as diplomatic means. Times were changing. Japan was now a recognized international presence, having shown itself as a political powerhouse through military and economic might, and in the moral, intellectual, and spiritual arenas that the era deemed so essential as represented by the arts. Even more, this had been accomplished largely on Japanese terms, "seeing how Japan [had] absorbed the best from every nation in the world and turned it into a system of her own."[61] For their part, Americans had emerged from the unrest-riddled economic depression following the crash of 1893 to an altered environment of reduced expectations. By 1904 women presided over smaller households with fewer servants than their mothers had enjoyed. This strongly impacted lifestyle, encouraging a move away from the eclectic cluttered amplitude of the Aesthetic movement towards the restrained and simple ideals of Arts and Crafts. Japan would prove to be a model as ideas, designs, media, and attitudes—generated authentically or not—were assimilated into American visual culture. Interestingly, for all the measures of acceptance, Americans still clung to the ideal they had thrust upon the Japanese, who had found it so useful a tool.

1. As quoted in Allwood 1977, 57.
2. Rydell 1984: "All the World's a Fair," 30.
3. *Putnam's Magazine,* April 1868.
4. *Los Angeles Times,* June 8, 1902.
5. *Arthur's Illustrated Home Magazine,* September 1868, 27.
6. Wilson 1876.
7. From conversations with Dr. James Gilbert, Distinguished University Professor, History Department, University of Maryland.
8. As quoted in Allwood 1977, 43.
9. *New York Times,* February 11, 1906.
10. Holley 1893, 593.
11. As quoted in Checkland 2002, 26.
12. Smith 1875, 129.
13. *Arthur's Illustrated Home Magazine,* January 1876, 44.1.
14. McCabe 1876, 5.
15. Ibid., 332.
16. Smith 1875, 186.
17. Ibid., 59, 185.
18. *Saturday Evening Post,* July 15, 1876.
19. Smith 1875, 323.
20. Ibid., 131.
21. *Harper's Weekly,* August 26, 1876.
22. Ibid.
23. *Saturday Evening Post,* July 15, 1876.
24. Smith 1875, 266.
25. Peltz 1883, 434.
26. *Harper's Weekly,* August 12, 1876.
27. McCabe 1876, 417.
28. As quoted in Schlereth 1991, 174.
29. Flinn 1893, 97.
30. *Arthur's Home Magazine,* May 1892, 62.
31. Ibid., 401.
32. As read in Croissant 1987, 52–75.
33. Smith 1875, 4.
34. *New York Times,* April 23, 1893.
35. *Art Amateur,* December 1893.
36. Ibid.
37. *New York Times,* April 23, 1893.
38. Smith 1875, 3.
39. Flinn 1893, 64
40. *Art Amateur,* August 1893.
41. Ibid.
42. *New York Times,* December 28, 1893.
43. *New York Times,* April 23, 1893.
44. *New York Times,* December 28, 1893.
45. Ibid.
46. Elliott 1986, 133.
47. Francis 1913, 329.
48. Ibid., vi.
49. Ibid., 218.
50. Halstead 1904, 438.
51. Ibid., 438–440.
52. Francis 1913, 329.
53. Ibid., 398.
54. Ibid., 316.
55. Bennitt and Stockbridge 1905, 303.
56. Ibid., 304.
57. Francis 1913, 343.
58. Ibid.
59. Ibid., 345.
60. Ibid., 358.
61. Bennitt and Stockbridge 1905, 303.

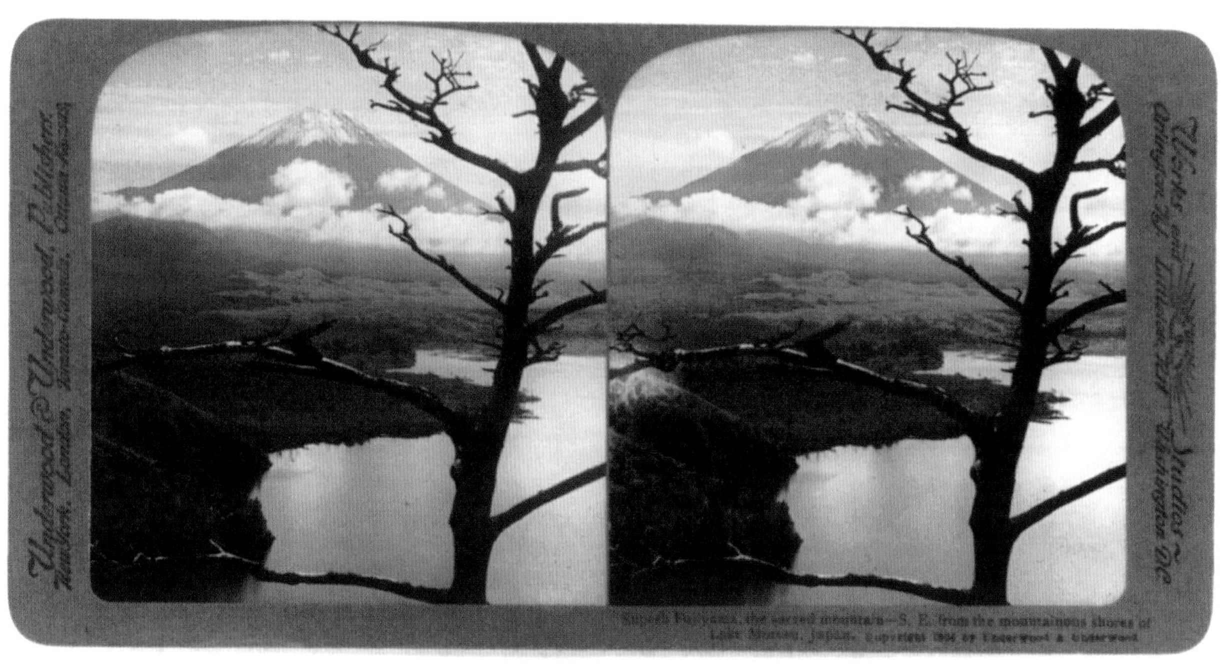

"Superb Fujiyama, the sacred mountain—S.E. from the mountainous shores of Lake Motosu, Japan"; stereoview; 1904.

3

International Comings and Goings

The Crafting of an Artful Market

Fifteen years more . . . and we shall get the news from Yeddo daily at our breakfast tables as a thing of course.[1]

"The Japan Craze" was much more than a pas de deux of admiring but wary partners from either side of the Pacific. The size, energy, and groundbreaking sophistication of the Meiji government's initiative at the expositions was only a partial reason for the deep infusion of Japanese arts and art crafts into American consciousness. Much like the fairs themselves, the Craze embodied the internationalist spirit that the progressing Industrial Revolution encouraged, thanks to the way advances in communications spread information, facilitated opportunity, and enhanced relationships. The expression was coined in a British architectural publication in 1872, the year that Iwakura Tomomi's mission arrived in England.

By the 1860s, details of Japanese society—weddings and funerals, bathing customs, women's lives, the judicial system, foods, architecture, topography, entertainments, clothing, "the gentle art of tattooing,"[2] and the particulars of manufacturing and craft production—filled American

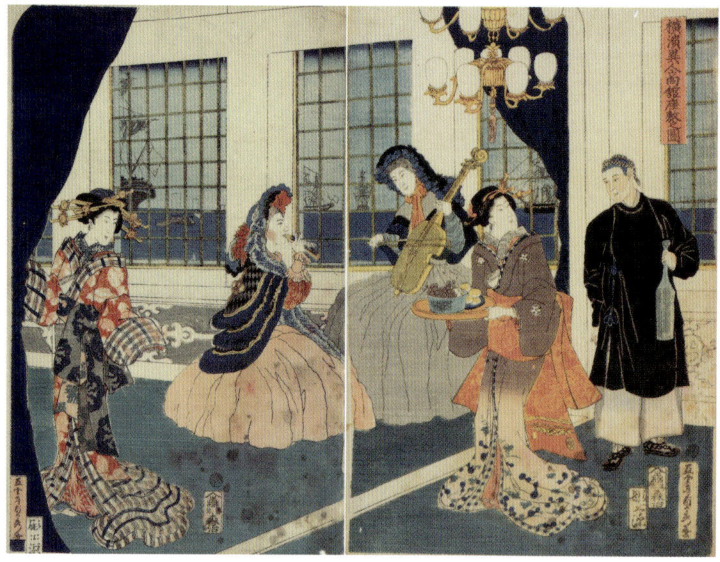

Utagawa Sadahide. *Yokohama ijin shōkan zashiki no zu (Parlour of a foreign mercantile house in Yokohama)*; Yokohama woodblock print; 1861; each 14.57 x 9.25 inches. Center and left panels of what was once a triptych depicting foreign residents dining and listening to music in their elegant home in Yokohama, Japan.

books, periodicals, and newspapers, most provided by growing numbers of missionaries, diplomats, and business people who had taken up residence in the country. Readers considered these recounts—whether intelligent and informative, skewed by idealizations and prejudices, or hypocritically ruing the vanishing of traditions as irrelevant to Japan as any modern society—brought to vivid life right before their easy chairs by their stereoscopes. Deemed essential to the up-to-date home, library, and school from the largest cities to the remotest rural hamlets, these contraptions were centerpieces of an educational philosophy that regarded an encounter with a three-dimensionally projected photograph equivalent to actually "being there." Japanese subjects comprised a large body among the millions of pictures taken by photographers sent abroad by American companies, hawked by door-to-door salesmen, or sold by catalogue and subscription.[3] Such resources certainly expanded an awareness of Japan; but, in reality, they only reinforced entrenched attitudes regarding Japan and Japanese, much like the international expositions did.

Meanwhile, Japan itself beckoned visitors for its exoticism and as a harbinger of the future as travel grew increasingly pleasurable, prompting reviewers to muse, "In view of the really palatial steamers now to be found on the Pacific Ocean, a flying trip to Japan will soon be considered the natural sequel to a trans-continental tour."[4] Visits revolved around traditional cultural meccas like Kyoto and, above all,

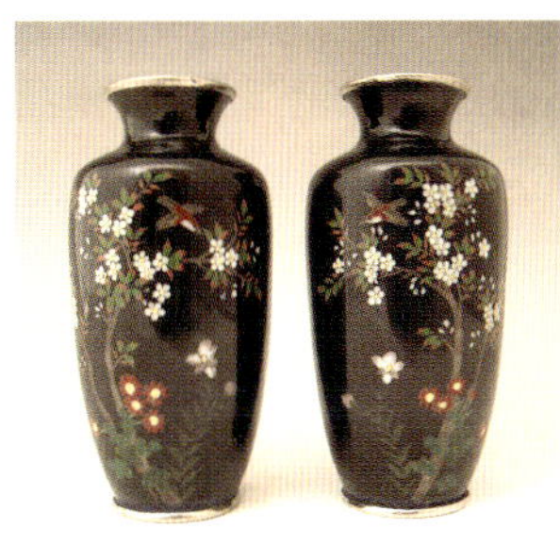

Above: Miniature vases; ca. 1900–1910; cloisonné; 5 inches high. These are excellent examples of the internationalism of the export style; an unknown yet highly skilled Japanese craftsman created these matched vases, whose mirror-image cloisonné bird-and-flower motifs rely upon intense high-gloss colors that were among Gottfried Wagener's most important technological innovations for Japan's enamel industry.

Right: Vase; ca. 1893; cloisonné; 67.72 inches high. Created for exhibition at the 1893 Columbian exhibition in Chicago, this colossal vase required the collaboration of six of Japan's top designers, enamellists, metalsmiths, and a painter of international repute. Its ornate faux-textile handles, classic shape, and breathtakingly executed, painterly depiction of hawks look to the combination of French and Asian taste that had consistently earned Japan such high critical acclaim. Courtesy of the Nasser D. Khalili Collection of Japanese Art, London, England.

Kobe and Yokohama—cosmopolitan ports defined by their Western orientation—with many resident foreigners located there. In Yokohama, "you might live in its foreign settlement a year without seeing a Japanese house, eating a Japanese meal, or knowing as much of native life and sights as you might learn of Chinese life by an hour's visit to Chinatown in San Francisco."[5] Tourists invariably dedicated serious time to broad "Curio Street," where, enticed by shops lining each side and extending for half a mile, the novel need to bargain freed one from any ". . . conscientious scruples about 'Jewing.'"[6] Cheap items made for foreign tastes that Japanese derisively referred to as *Yokohama muki* figured prominently among the offerings, much as they dominated the Japanese stalls at the international expositions. For the less sophisticated, simply obtaining an object in Japan sufficed as proof of its authenticity. But, if most was gimcrack, some was exceptional.

As much or more than the bronzes, embroideries, ceramics, furniture, and ivories designed to Western fantasies and tastes, the craft of enameling epitomized Japanese export philosophy. Originating with the technique of cloisonné, which the Japanese called *shippō,* it was a hybrid in every sense of the word. Shippō had appeared in Japan mainly in the waning years of the Tokugawa period, as a trial-and-error replicate of admired Chinese examples. The Meiji government, whose missions such as Iwakura no doubt encountered superb Western examples, identified it as an admired craft and

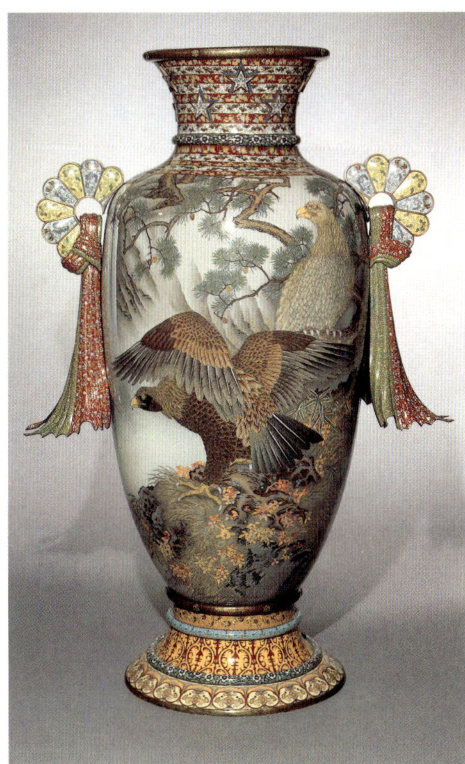

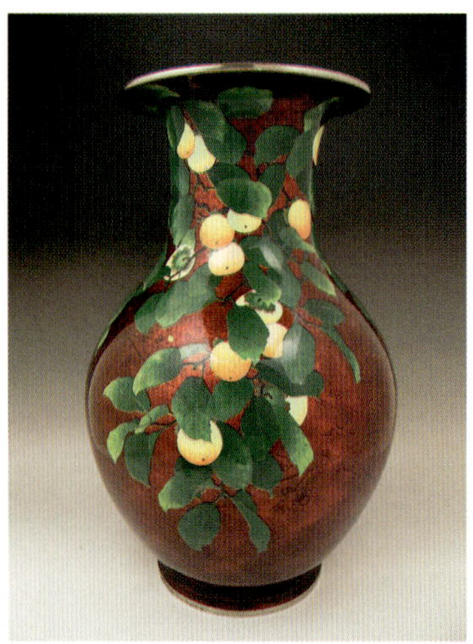

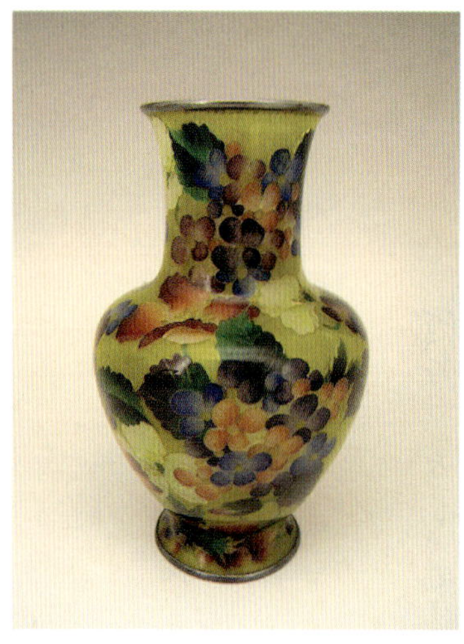

Above, Left: Andō Jūbei. Enamel vase; ca. 1895–1900; 18 inches high. This large vase combines two techniques—fruiting persimmons executed in cloisonné over plum, and chrysanthemum blossoms engraved into the metal surface beneath the transparent enamel—in a method known as *basse-taille* in Europe and *akasuke* in Japan. A founding figure in the art-enamel industry centered in the city of Nagoya, Andō was not only one of its finest art craftsmen but also a gifted businessman. His Andō Company was one of Japan's most successful export firms.

Above, Right: Bud vase; ca. 1900; enamel with silver wire; 4.75 inches high. This vase illustrates one of the tour de force techniques in which Japanese enamellists excelled. *Plique-a-jour* enamel is a technique producing a transparent object netted throughout with a lacework of silver wire.

targeted it for development. An astute decision at the top levels of the industry to employ the technical talents of the German Gottfried Wagener improved enamel color and quality that facilitated exceptionally gifted and dedicated craftsmen. Within forty years—a blink of an eye in Japanese art traditions—shippō had attained global preeminence for innovative technique, meticulous execution, and astounding feats of size, detail, and delicacy. Craftsmen, who sometimes collaborated over several years to produce a single work, began winning exposition competitions as early as Vienna in 1873. Names such as Namikawa Sōsuke, Namikawa Yasuyuki, Hayashi Kodenji, Andō Jūbei, and others became familiar to discerning collectors, who critiqued their works and made them the focus of interviews by major American publications. But, as harsh assessments at the Columbian exhibition in Chicago made clear, the drive to meet market demands inevitably resulted in a flood of run-of-the-mill work. While it diminished the craft in the eyes of many in Japan and the United States, these lesser works could also be quite pretty and found a ready market for a time. The distinction between the two levels of quality, however, became an issue for dealers and collectors.

Meanwhile, with the floodgates now open, no American desiring Japanese objects had to rely upon travel or even a visit to an exposition to obtain them. Just as seeing Japan through a stereoscope was as good as being there, all you had to do was go to your local downtown or open your Sears or Montgomery Ward catalogue for something "Japanese." What amounted to one-tenth of Japanese exports[7] from the late 1870s to the 1890s had grown to approximately $33 million dollars worth by 1900,[8] an amount in excess of $6 billion today: antiques from the old regime to new furniture and accessories that looked delightfully strange to American eyes in terms of decoration, color, or detail but in every other way suited American uses with respect to form, function, material, and size. It sent a mixed message to American buyers.

Following Yamanaka & Company's successful lead, by the 1890s, high-end Japanese concerns such as First Japan Manufacturing and Trading Company, and M. Marunaka & Company all had retail locations in major cities such as New York, Boston, Chicago, and Philadelphia, or were affiliated with high-end specialty shops, art dealers, and department stores like B. Altman and John Wanamaker. For a wider price range, shops of all sizes could be found in large cities to small towns across the continent, some owned by Americans such as John Scott Bradstreet in Minneapolis; George Turner Marsh and Frederick H. Deakin in San Francisco; J. P. Stevens in Atlanta; Herman Trost & Company, A. A. Low, and A. A. Vantine's in New York, Boston, and Philadelphia; L. D. Hyde of Newport and New York; and others owned by enterprising immigrants like Bunkio Matsuki in Salem, Massachusetts; H. Naito in Portland, Oregon; and Takayanagi Tozo, and Morimura Brothers in New York, Boston, and Chicago. At one point, New York City had more than twenty shops specializing in Japanese goods on Fifth Avenue alone. Many dealers also sold through auction houses.

It was a highly competitive world fraught with risk. Cheaper shops and dealers sold poor quality—much of it the derided Yokohama muki. They also indiscriminately mixed Japanese items with those from other exotic climes: Persia, China, India, and Turkey. While some was of

BELOW, LEFT: CABINET; CA. 1880S; LACQUER, ENAMELED AND GILDED PORCELAIN; 81.9 x 47.2 x 18.1 INCHES. With enameled and gilded porcelain panels showing detailed scenes from Japanese military legends and with fittings of *shakudo* and gilt sporting the hollyhock crest of the defunct Tokugawa shoguns, this sumptuously detailed export trade cabinet is a good example of the incongruous combinations and tour-de-force technique sought after by wealthy Japanophiles in Europe and America. Courtesy of the Nasser D. Khalili Collection of Japanese Art, London, England.

BELOW, RIGHT: Y. KONOIKE COMPANY OF YOKOHAMA. FOLDING SCREEN; CA. 1875–1900; GOLD LACQUER WITH INLAYS OF IVORY, MOTHER-OF-PEARL, AND OTHER MATERIALS; 15.8 INCHES HIGH. One of Japan's most famous creators of luxury goods produced this two-fold screen framed in silver repoussé. Courtesy of the Nasser D. Khalili Collection of Japanese Art, London, England.

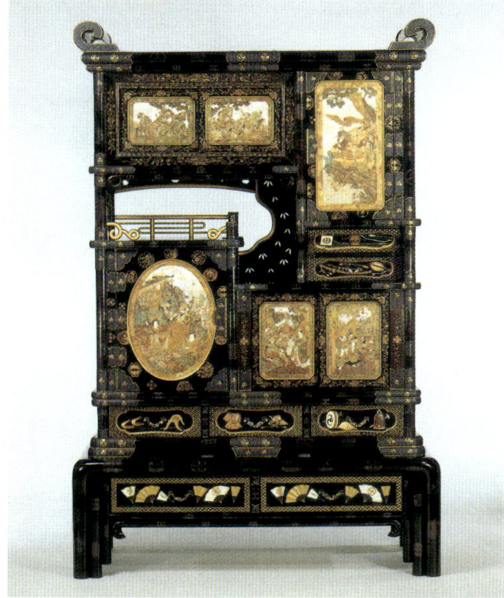

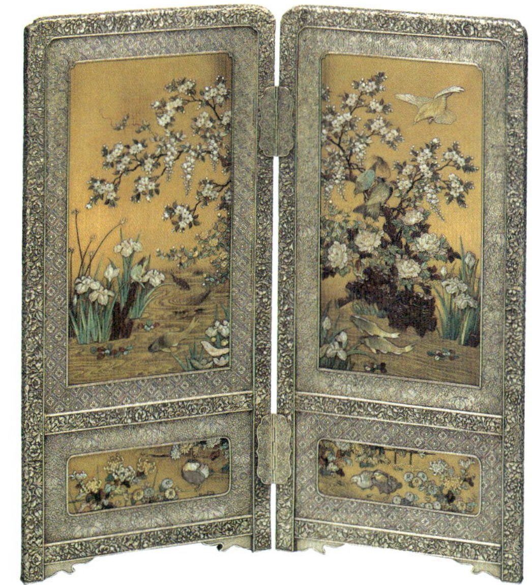

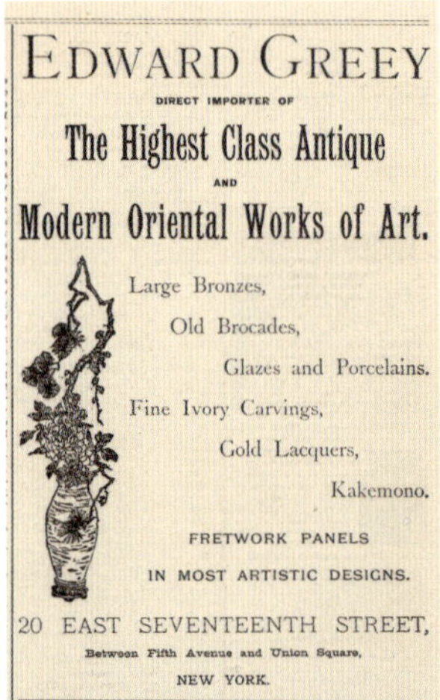

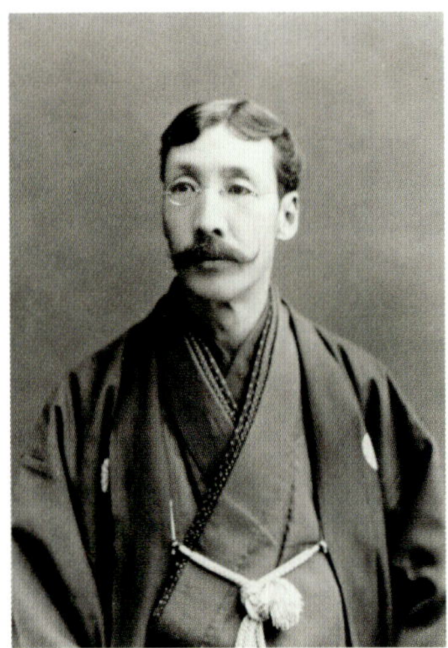

Above, Upper: Edward Greey, as he regularly advertised in *Decorator and Furnisher* beginning about April 1885. The publication ran an extensive article about his mysteriously exotic and elegant shop.

Above, Lower: Shugio Hiromichi; ca. 1887–1889.

exquisite quality, it also muddied the distinctions among them in the eyes of potential buyers. Values fluctuated with the whims of taste, and with the waning of the Japan Craze by the turn of the century, major department stores offered drastic price reductions to move merchandise. Some dealers, such as the savvy Bunkio Matsuki (1867–1940) who maintained shops in Salem and Boston, for a long period successfully insulated themselves against such insecurity through a clever combination of marketing and merchandise: With goods ranging from beautiful, high-quality antiques to export commodities made to his specifications, as well as incense, tea, and inexpensive art supplies, he encouraged sales at all levels by mixing them together with well-planned displays and judicious selection.[9] And, making an asset of his nationality, he imbued his offerings with an enticing gloss through a carefully cultivated personal mystique. In this way, he deflected the pejorative Yokohama muki identity of his lower-range wares. Matsuki became one of the most successful purveyors in the northeastern United States from 1890 to 1917. A prominent and highly regarded contemporary Edward Greey (1835–1888) did not fare as well. Returning home from his gallery one afternoon, he proceeded to his room and shot himself in the head.[10] A shocked public learned he had recently returned from Japan in a state of distress and had been hiding deep financial problems.

No hack salesmen, dealers like Greey, Matsuki, Marsh, and Takayanagi were cultivated and creative individuals who went to great lengths to foster a clientele capable of appreciating the quality objects they purveyed, even as they catered to the lower end. In newspapers, popular arts journals, and the like, they published serious articles on the connoisseurship of swords, ceramics, textiles, lacquers, cloisonné, and other topics of collecting interest. As director of the First Japan Manufacturing and Trading Company, the Oxford-educated aristocrat Shugio Hiromichi introduced the New York public to ukiyo-e prints in 1889 with the first major American exhibition, and many also to Japanese architecture, installing a model house interior on the second floor of his Broadway gallery, its "matted walls, its ceilings of Japanese wood with the bark on, and its neat, matted floor . . . worth visiting again and again."[11] He was also a member of the Imperial Art Commission for the 1904 Louisiana Purchase International Exposition and contributed regularly to periodicals and journals. In addition to selling Japanese art and antiques, John Scott Bradstreet adapted Japanese woodworking techniques to elegant designs for furniture and interiors in the homes of the Minneapolis elite. Greey, with deep ties to Japan, authored popular novels set in contemporary Tokyo and translated traditional Japanese fairy tales. Marsh, likewise fluent in Japanese and an authority on architecture and landscape design, built an innovative home that blended Japanese and Western architectural forms and aesthetics and, in conjunction with a Japanese specialist, designed the gardens for the Japanese Village at the California Midwinter International Exposition of 1894 in San Francisco. Matsuki organized well-regarded exhibitions in Boston and New York, and was asked by the Japanese government to be a judge at the World's Columbian International Exhibition in Chicago (though he did not serve); in later life he taught Buddhist studies at Columbia University.[12] In these efforts, such men created a bridge to the general public from the intellectual community and even to Japan itself.

It also made for a complicated world of varying agendas and motivations that blurred the distinctions among the artists, designers, and intellects with whom dealers mingled. Cosmopolitan and outwardly cordial, these circles percolated with rivalries beneath the surface and sometimes fissured along ethnic lines. In December 1886 the *New York Times* recorded an elegant dinner at the prestigious Author's Club hosted by Greey, whose thirteen eminent guests included his colleague and competitor Shugio and two of the country's most famous and knowledgeable collectors of Japanese art, physician William Sturgis Bigelow (1850–1926) and zoologist Edward S. Morse (1838–1925). The guest of honor was Ernest Fenollosa (1853–1908). At that time he dominated the art world of Tokyo and came to New York as one of three art commissioners of the Meiji government.[13] Fenollosa had almost single-handedly established

Below, Left: Poster from a Grolier Club exhibition; ca. 1887–1922; 27.56 × 21.26 inches.

Below, Right: Utagawa Kuniyoshi. *Chinese Warriors;* sketch; ca. 1840; ink and light color on paper; 32.48 × 65.51 inches; signed "Ichiyusai Kuniyoshi ga"; sealed. An exceedingly rare example of Kuniyoshi's work as a painter, this superb sketch was presented as a gift to the Grolier Club by Shugio Hiromichi, who remained devoted to the Club even after his return to Japan in 1889.

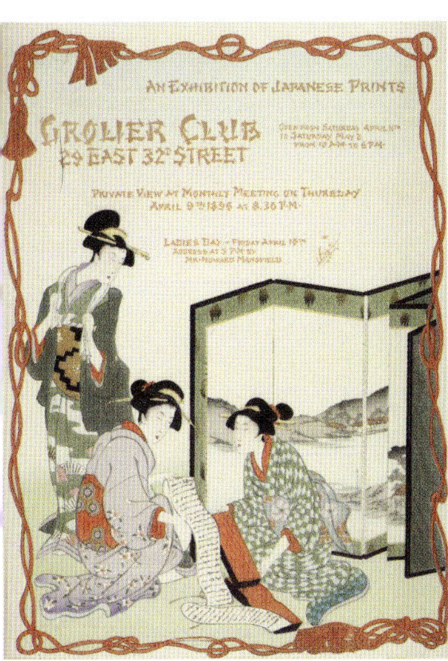

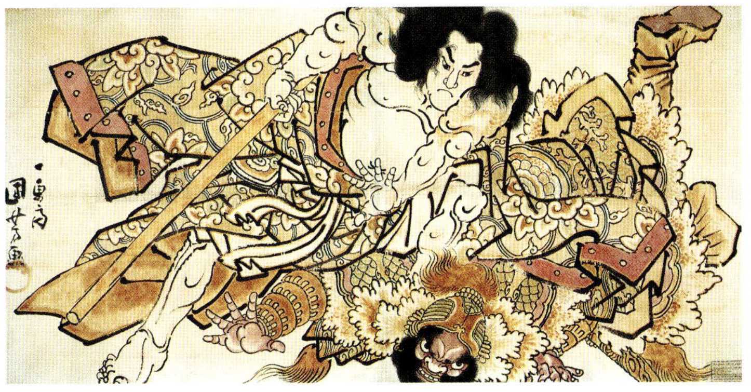

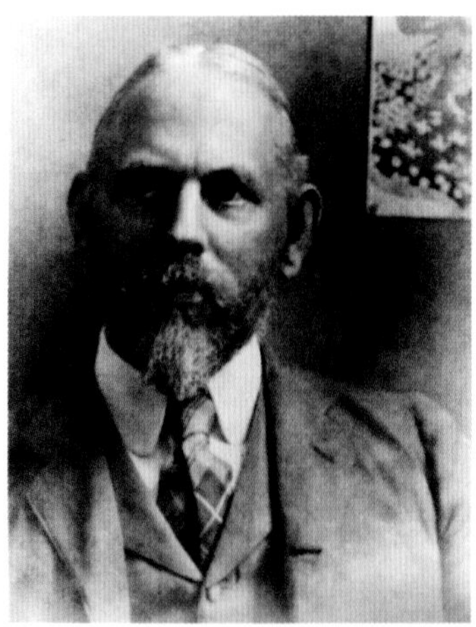

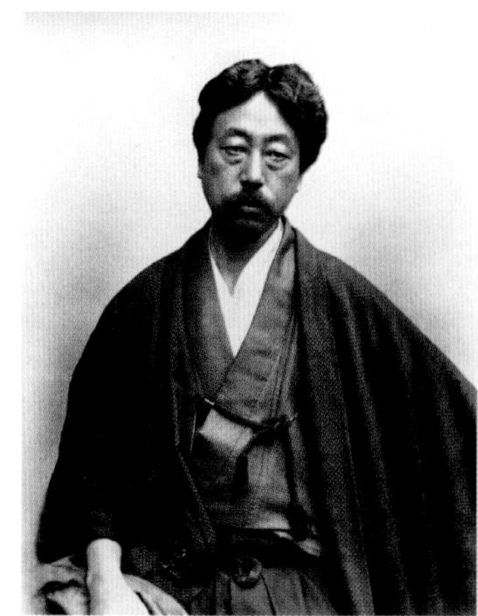

NEAR RIGHT: ERNEST FRANCISCO FENOLLOSA (1853–1908). Fenollosa was a flawed but immensely influential figure in the modern study of Japanese art on both sides of the Pacific. Courtesy of the Museum of Fine Arts, Boston.

FAR RIGHT: OKAKURA KAKUZŌ (1862–1913). He is photographed here in the elegant traditional dress that he knew Americans preferred to encounter him wearing. Courtesy of the Museum of Fine Arts, Boston.

modern scholarship of Japanese art and antiquities in both the United States and Japan, and that year, he became the first director of the Imperial Museum that, along with the Tokyo Academy of Fine Arts, he had helped to found. Emperor Meiji bestowed major awards upon him for services to the crown. He soon occupied a central position as an advocate for Japanese arts in the United States, all the while straddling the line between scholar and businessman in relationships with important dealers like Yamanaka.

Fenollosa embodied the inherent contradictions swirling around Japanese art and its appropriation by Westerners. In Tokyo, like his friends Bigelow and Morse, he associated with a number of forward-thinking Japanese for whom he served as resource and model in their nation's intellectual modernization, and upon whom he relied for substantive knowledge of Japan and, above all, Japanese art. These individuals afforded access to the collections, translations, and factual information upon which his influential theories relied. It was an awkward symbiosis with both sides in the roles of mentor and student. And, while ostensibly and conspicuously so permeated by the essence of Japan as to have become a Buddhist, Fenollosa maintained typical Western hubris by never acknowledging his apprentice role regarding the art he championed; and, worse, he harbored an astonishing agenda ". . . that, however much I may sympathize with the past civilizations of the East, I am in this incarnation a man of Western race, and bound to do my part toward the development of Western civilization."[14] In this shallow and grasping yet didactic spirit, he argued for the sustaining of Japanese art tradition and traditional

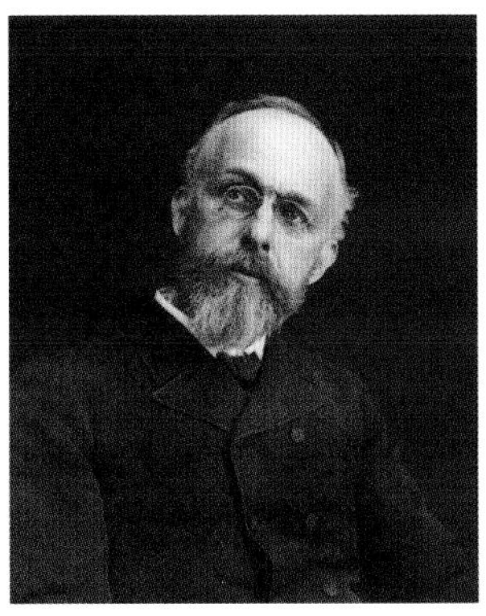

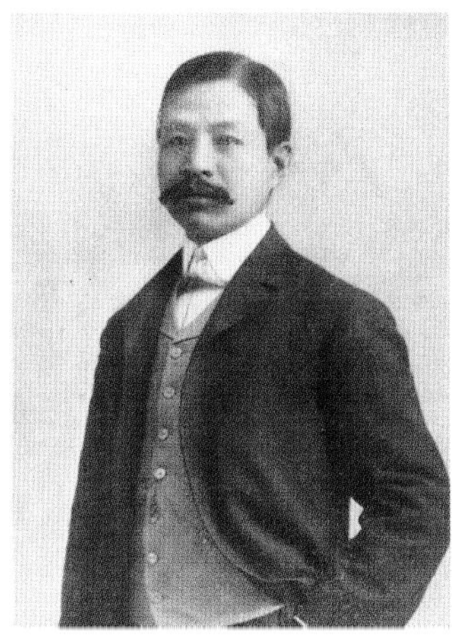

ABOVE, LEFT: EDWARD S. MORSE (1838–1925). His long and warm relationship with Bunkio Matsuki was one of the earliest and most fruitful of cross-cultural friendships. Courtesy of the Museum of Fine Arts, Boston.

ABOVE, RIGHT: BUNKIO MATSUKI (1867–1940). This photograph appeared in a little booklet entitled *Prominent Americans Interested in Japan and Prominent Japanese in America,* 1903.

Japan—as a model for the West, not for Japan itself—and, while advising the Japanese on the preservation of their heritage, simultaneously amassed a huge personal collection. It found its way to the Boston Museum of Fine Arts, where, as its first curator, he would play an immensely influential role in the introduction of Japanese aesthetic concepts to the American design world.

At home in the United States, American authorities, regardless of experience, had to rely even more upon talented Japanese to further their artistic education. The writers of the Grolier Club happily availed themselves of the expertise of their popular member, Shugio Hiromichi, as did the artists of New York's Tile Club. Bunkio Matsuki's career as a dealer began only after his arrival in Salem, Massachusetts, when a chance meeting with a repatriated Morse led to the latter's engaging him as a facilitator for his passion for Japanese ceramics. While their relationship bloomed with mutual regard, not all of them culminated with such respect or warmth. Fenollosa displaced Matsuki as a trusted last word in the eyes of collector Charles Lang Freer, whose patronage both coveted.

And absent from Greey's dinner but present as a hovering wraith was the brilliant Okakura Kakuzō (1862–1913). As bicultural as anyone of his era, his flawless English, urbane charm laced with rapier wit, exotically handsome face, and tall poised figure—often garbed elegantly in traditional *hakama,* not to mention a propensity to flaunt convention—gave him an air of erotic danger. Okakura magnetized both Japanese and American women, and, never lacking for either, scandal wafted about him like perfume; his presence was charged all the more by encyclopedic knowledge and a passion for Japanese art. These qualities, and his equally passionate sense of identity and tradition, cemented a place for Okakura among the uppermost echelons of the American elite, among whom he mingled with ease. Okakura was well known and admired, particularly in New York and Boston; he was close with Morse, Bigelow, Henry Adams, the artist John La Farge, and was intimately linked to Isabella Stewart Gardner.

All this made for a complicated relationship with Fenollosa, with whom he was inextricably intertwined and who considered these social circles his natural home. Fenollosa had advanced Okakura's knowledge of Western thought and had undeniably awakened the younger man to his heritage, first at Tokyo Imperial University and later at the Ministry of Education. But the more gifted and ultimately more knowledgeable and confident Okakura increasingly displaced the foreign Fenollosa in Japanese circles. Ultimately, government decision-makers saw them as equals, awarding both men prominent roles for the 1893 World's Columbian Exhibition: Fenollosa for selecting art submissions and Okakura for overseeing the Hōōden. The critical response made amply clear that Okakura better understood American leanings and how to capitalize upon them—something that would not have escaped notice in Japan. Meanwhile, as Fenollosa's unacknowledged dependence, condescension, and selfish agenda became increasingly obvious to Okakura, their relationship cooled. But an ironic intertwining of fate linked them one last time: extramarital indiscretion forced Fenollosa from his lofty position as curator at the Boston Museum to virtual exile in New York; a similar imprudence propelled Okakura out of Japan to Boston and into Fenollosa's vacated position. He found the Asian holdings riddled with forgeries, cataloguing errors, and historical gaps. Although Fenollosa, along with

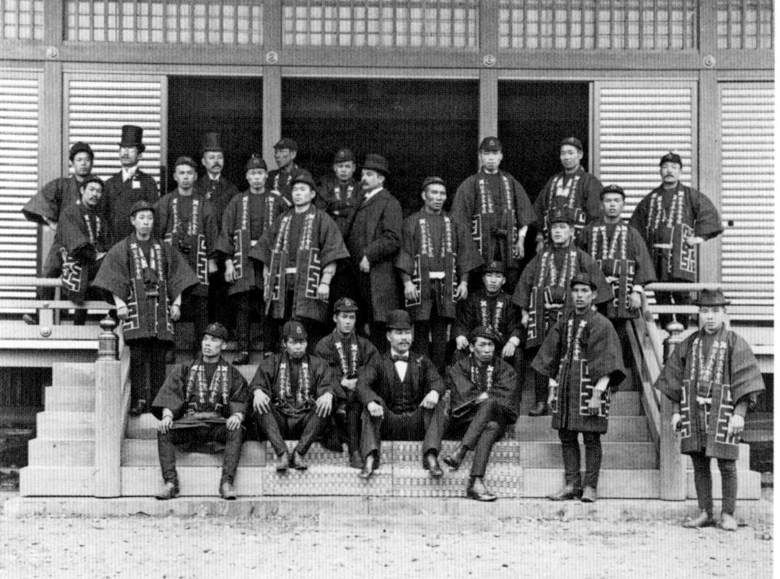

Okakura Kakuzō (1863–1913); ca. 1892–1893. Impeccably outfitted in a suit and bowler hat, he sits on the steps of the Hōōden, surrounded by the Japanese construction crew and World's Columbian Exhibition officials. Courtesy of the Chicago History Museum.

Bigelow and Morse, can be credited with starting the Japanese collection, it was Okakura who built it into one of the finest in the world. Meanwhile, he had his finger ever on the pulse of American yearnings, and his publication *The Book of Tea* (1906) initiated a generation to the idea of a unity among nature, art, and daily life in a way that, as the Japan Craze itself ebbed, struck a deep chord in the early advances toward modernism as embodied in the Arts and Crafts movement.

The Englishman Greey and the Australian Marsh are two less-well-remembered members of a cosmopolitan, transnational, Japanese art world coterie influential in boardrooms, elegant galleries, factory floors, lecture halls, and assorted publications from Tokyo, Yokohama, and Kobe, to Paris and Vienna, London, and Manchester, to the United States in Philadelphia, New York, Chicago, Cincinnati, Minneapolis, San Francisco, and St. Louis, to name only a few of the largest locales. Some merely saw opportunity for financial gain. In the ivories, prints, textiles, paintings, ceramics, bronzes, cloisonné, lacquers, and other enticements that they specialized in—authentic or made for trade—the more visionary discerned a model and language for change at a necessary time. The entire phenomenon owed everything to the easy communication and opportunities as well as to the unique challenges presented by the Industrial Revolution. In short, the Craze was created and nurtured by a web of interpersonal and commercial relations in which Japan struck the spark but Western impetus forged the result.

The Japan Craze began in France before Alcock's display at the London Exhibition of 1862, not even in connection with the exposition movement. Shortly after Commodore Perry opened Japan in the 1850s, curios and ukiyo-e prints found their way to Parisian galleries and were discovered by a number of innovative artists, among them Edgar Degas, Edouard Manet, the American James McNeill Whistler, and, notably, Whistler's friend Félix Bracquemond (1833–1914), the painter and printmaker. Although their uninitiated eyes at first confused these arts with those of China, it gradually dawned that they had encountered not only a separate and much wider body of subject matter but, even more, a distinctive approach to design and composition as well as a refreshing informality of spirit. Appetites further whetted by Alcock expanded to gluttony upon Japan's large fractious participation in the Paris exposition of 1867. After Meiji's ascension flung open the door to Japan even more widely, Europeans began to collect with fervor; in France, exhibits of metal crafts, ceramics, embroideries, and other things proved inescapably that the French could no longer take for granted their long-held preeminence in these valued applied arts. Artists and designers began to experiment in all media. By 1872, the same year a British architectural critic coined the expression the "Japan Craze," the critic and collector Philippe Burty, a leader in urging French artists to find inspiration in Japanese art, had dubbed the creative outcome of their fascination "Japonisme."

Bracquemond, hired by porcelain manufacturers Eugène Rousseau and David Haviland (the latter not coincidentally the son-in-law of Bracquemond's patron Burty) to design dishes in the 1860s, was an early bridge in the "fine" and "decorative" arts debate. He found boundless inspiration in Japanese books and albums, particularly those of Katsushika Hokusai (1760–1849). Like other European artists, Bracquemond found in them much more than exoticism. This near-contemporary, whom he could never personally know, simply overwhelmed with his towering mastery of painting, wood engraving, and block print design, coupled with interpretive brilliance and, finally, extraordinary immediacy and vitality. All went unrecognized by the Japanese, who associated his subjects and the print medium with ukiyo-e, considered merely the cheap broadsides of

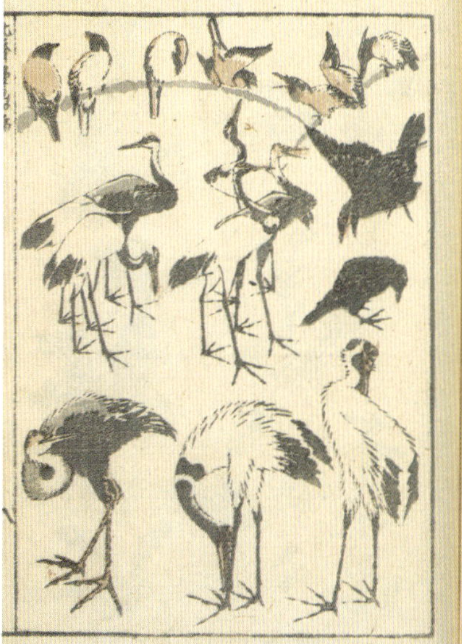
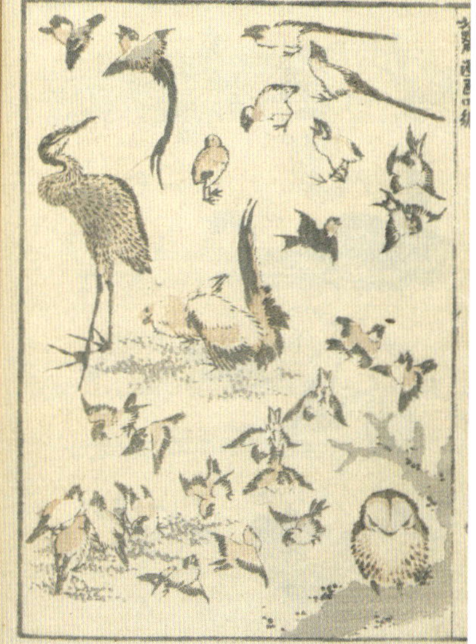

Two pages from Katsushika Hokusai's *Manga zen*; woodblock printed volumes; 1814.

prostitutes, kabuki actors, and "vulgar" everyday life. Bracquemond's story of his accidental discovery of Hokusai's work crumpled as packing in a crate of export porcelains, even if apocryphal, marks a seminal moment of nineteenth-century art history.

What foremost caught his eye was familiar to any Japanese: *manga,* meaning "caricature" or "funny picture." Hokusai had published fifteen volumes, the images not all humorous, as a no-frills resource for Japanese artists and artisans. They had been known to a few Europeans as early as the 1830s through von Siebold's Japanese museum in Leiden. But this artist's brilliance came to light, thanks mainly to Bracquemond's supposed encounter with pages torn out for wrapping. His original ink sketches of plants, animals, insects, fish, places, people in an array of situations from ordinary to odd, and virtually anything that caught the artist's endlessly inquisitive and often-amused eye, crammed as tightly as the pages would allow, lost nothing of their charm, wit, or energy in the conversion to the woodblock medium. For Westerners, their informality, droll immediacy, and encyclopedic range opened the door to a new understanding of naturalism, an exponential expansion of subject matter, and a vastly revised idea of "appropriate." Hokusai's enormous output was among the most influential ongoing inspirations from Japan for the West's most innovative designers.

Félix Bracquemond. Dish design; 1875; watercolor, pencil, and black chalk on beige wove paper; 10.43 × 11.02 inches. This design shows the influence of Japanese sources such as Hokusai's *Manga.*

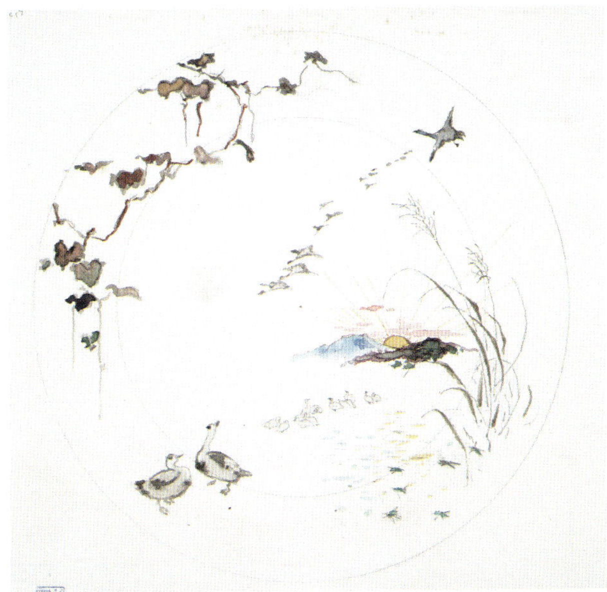

Parisians, resident Americans, and Europeans all sated their thirst for the Japanese arts flowing into France at burgeoning numbers of shops and galleries. A lucky few encountered dealers with genuine dedication, passion, knowledge, and exquisite taste. Two in particular, expatriate Japanese Hayashi Tadamasa (1851–1906) and German-born naturalized-Frenchman Siegfried Bing (1838–1905), played unmatched and complex roles in the growing Western view of Japan as a creative epicenter. At the pinnacle of European art circles, their influence extended to the United States, where they mingled with the

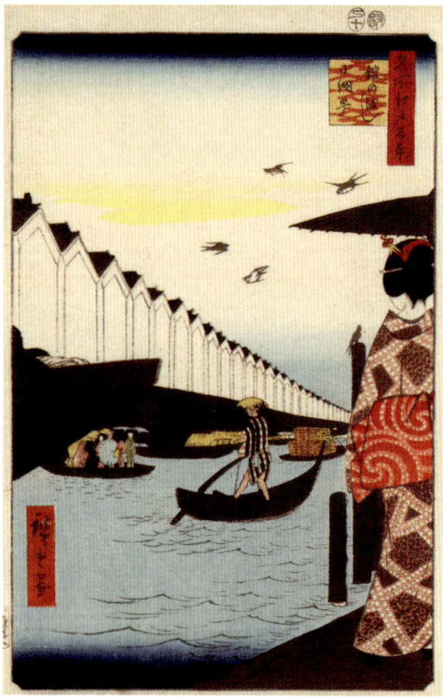

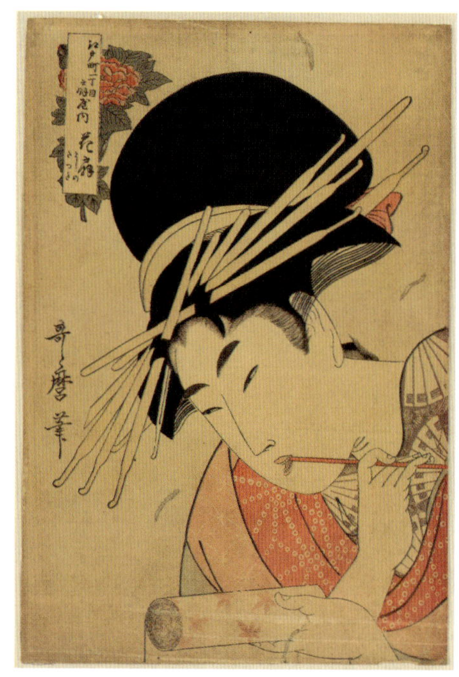

Above, Left: Utagawa Hiroshige. *Yoroi-no watashi Koami-chō (Yoroi ferry at Koami District)*; ukiyo-e woodblock print; 1857; 14.29 × 9.45 inches.

Above, Right: Kitagawa Utamaro. "Peony"; ukiyo-e woodblock print; ca. 1802; approximately 15 × 10 inches. This is a portrait of the famous beauty Hanaōgi of the Ōgiya brothel of Edo.

likes of Fenollosa and others dominating the museum, collecting, and intellectual worlds. That their respective governments officially acknowledged them in different fashions is a measure of the conspicuous role of art-related activities and achievements in the crafting of international reputations during this era.

Fluent in French from studies at elite Tokyo Imperial University, Hayashi went to Paris in 1877 as Kiritsu Kosho Kaisha's translator in its preparations for the Exposition Universelle of 1878. He stayed on, ultimately establishing an independent art house in 1899 that initially specialized in the quality ceramics, bronzes, and cloisonné he knew well from his time with the export firm. He then took advantage of the unsettled conditions in modernizing Japan to branch into traditional arts, including drawings, scrolls, screens, ivories, sword fittings, lacquer, and ceramics. He built an educated and loyal clientele by traveling all over Europe and the United States, obliging scholarly requests for translations, and charming everyone by cultivating an air of attentive mystery amid his collections in an elegant apartment on Rue de la Victoire. There he catered to each patron from private cubicles, none able to hear or see another. What they sought most were ukiyo-e prints. Over the eleven years of his

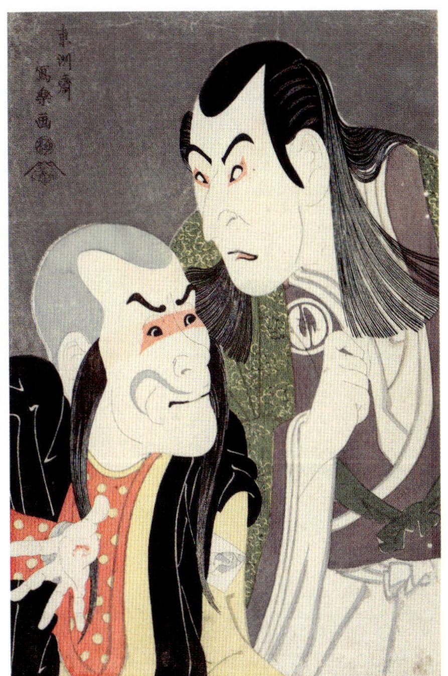

Tōshūsai Sharaku. *Actors Sawamura Hodogorō II as Kawatsura Hōgen and Bandoō Zenji as Oninosadobō*, Nishiki-e woodblock print; n.d.; ink, color, and mica on paper; 15.08 x 9.92 inches; published by Tsutaya Jūzaburō, Edo period, 1794. Courtesy of the Museum of Fine Arts, Boston: William Sturgis Bigelow Collection (11.14676).

business, he sold nearly one hundred and sixty-six thousand of them[15] by Katsushika Hokusai, Utagawa Hiroshige, Kitagawa Utamaro, Tōshūsai Sharaku, and lesser names. In the opinion of many, no other individual played a greater role in assuring the impact of this art form or in legitimizing these artists' places in the Japanese artistic canon—paradoxically due to the recognition he enabled in the West. The combination of initial Japanese indifference with Western fascination during this era led to the near-disappearance of ukiyo-e in its homeland. Later, refusing to acknowledge Hayashi's role in their belated appreciation, a remarkably ungracious and self-serving national intelligentsia excoriated him as responsible for their exodus.

But for awhile, Hayashi's transnational and cross-cultural connections, sterling reputation with Western intelligentsia, business acumen, and knowledge of foreign taste outweighed attitudes at home. The government enjoined him for the all-important international exhibitions, though Hayashi differed markedly from traditionalists on whom they also relied, notably Okakura and Fenollosa. A progressive, he believed that a vigorous "fine art" suiting a newly dynamic nation required the melding of Western concepts with the best elements of the past. His endorsement of artists working to straddle that boundary paid off brilliantly at the Columbian exhibition in Chicago: it was he who had promoted Suzuki Chokichi's *Twelve Falcons* sculptures, thereby garnering Japan's only unqualified critical success other than the Hōōden. Perhaps buoyed by this achievement, he lobbied hard for appointment as commissioner for the Exposition Universelle of 1900 in Paris, overcoming stiff aristocratic resentment that a commoner be given such standing.

Hayashi organized a combination of classic and contemporary arts designed to make the educational point of Japan's past and ongoing aesthetic sophistication. In concept, it was a reprise of the Centennial exhibition ceramic exhibit prepared by his old employer; and, likewise, it did not enjoy unqualified success—but for opposite reasons. Where Americans in 1876 had turned a cold eye to traditional ceramics, judges in 1900 deemed Hayashi's modern art selections "stale and old,"[16] inflicting on a shocked Japan the same critical embarrassment as in Chicago. But, his choice of old masterworks proved landmark. He had revealed that in addition to "merely decorative," technically cunning curios and the acknowledged brilliance of ukiyo-e, Japan boasted of glorious painting and sculpture—"high" arts worthy as models for serious artists.[17] In particular, the dramatic works of the seventeenth- and eighteenth-century Rimpa masters Hon'ami Kōetsu, Tawaraya Sōtatsu, and Ogata Kōrin dazzled the public for the first time. Wealthy Westerners now sought these for their collections, including Americans Charles Lang Freer, who later bequeathed the Smithsonian Institution, and Louisine and Henry O. Havemeyer, who did the same for the Metropolitan Museum of Art. If yet another nod only to the achievements of Japan's past, it was a victory nonetheless. But for Hayashi, the toll was extreme. Preparation of its opulent pavilion and lavish catalogue left him exhausted; the critical failures painfully humiliated him. As the price for access to imperial and aristocratic collections, his reluctant patrons in Japan had demanded that he close his Paris business, which was already suffering from a changing market. Like many of his expatriate countrymen—among them Okakura, Shugio, and Matsuki—he ultimately preferred not to make the West his home. He returned to Japan in 1905, where he died bankrupt only a year later.

Incredibly, Hayashi's enormous achievements—all accomplished in just over a decade—were arguably eclipsed by the courtly, gracious German-born Siegfried Bing (sometimes known as Samuel Bing). Though competitors, they felt mutual respect and often collaborated. So landmark were Bing's achievements as advisor, dealer, collector, intellect, passionate connoisseur, and arbiter of taste on an international scale, that France awarded this adoptive son the Legion d'Honneur. Bing's primary inspiration was, definitively, the art of Japan. Desire to sell was

Tawaraya Sōtatsu. "Ladies Among Cherry Trees"; six-panel byōbu; early Edo period, ca. 1590–1640; ink, colors, and gold on paper; each 65.12 × 148.82 inches. This pair of screens depicts a scene from the "Asagao" ("Morning Glory") chapter of the *Tale of Genji*, Japan's most famous literary work. Sōtatsu was one of Japan's seminal artists of the Rimpa movement, and this is a classic example of that dynamically asymmetrical, boldly abstracted, and opulent style. Charles Lang Freer, who probably acquired these screens around the turn of the last century when Hayashi Tadamasa introduced such works to the West, presented them as a gift to the Smithsonian Institution in 1903.

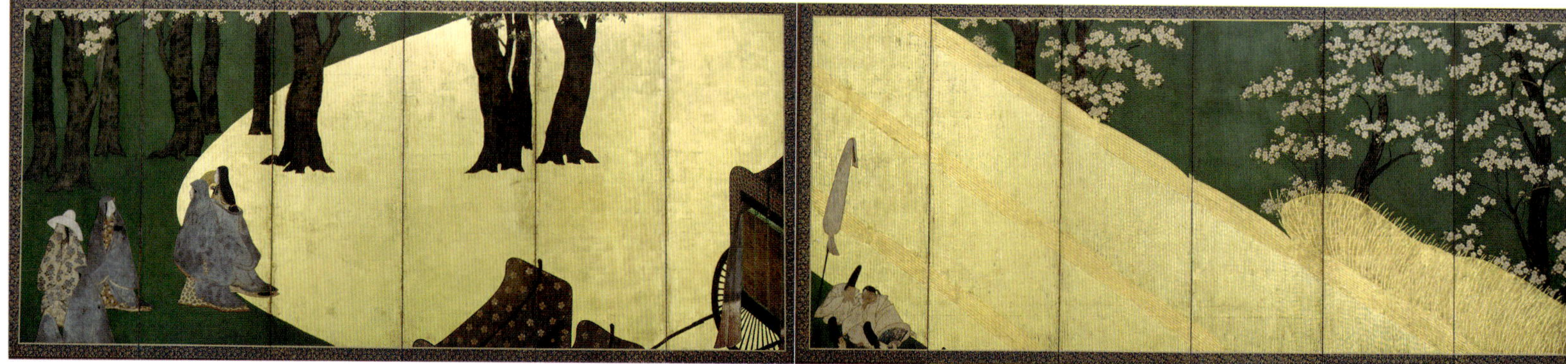

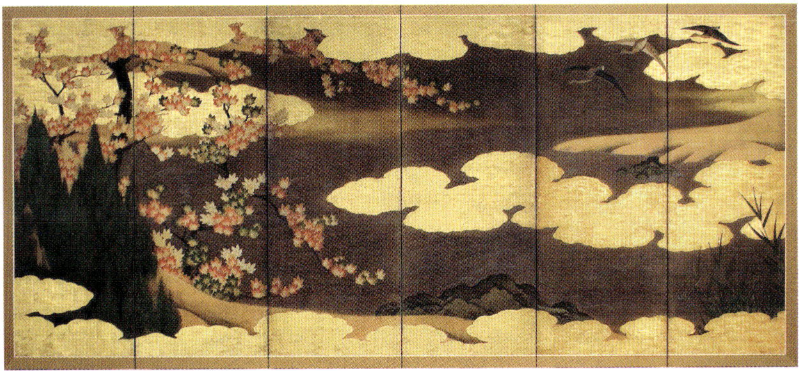

"Autumn Landscape with Geese, Maples, and Cedars"; six-panel byōbu; early seventeenth century; ink, colors gold, and silver on paper; 67.5 × 150.5 inches.

matched by a sincere proselytizing agenda that garnered him entrée and considerable support in Japan itself among aristocrats, artists, and members of intellectual circles influenced by Ernest Fenollosa.

Bing began dealing antique and contemporary Japanese arts during the flush of Europe's craze, expanding from one to several Parisian galleries from the 1870s through the 1880s. Genuine passion led him to amass a huge personal collection and to spend a year in Japan, where he immersed himself and solidified a network of sources managed through his brother-in-law, a resident consular official. Once home, the flow of porcelains, bronzes, lacquers, jades, crystals, ivories, textiles, and other objects made possible international branches of his business. He established a New York showroom and also collaborated with auctioneers and dealers there and in Philadelphia. As with Hayashi, the likes of Freer, the Havemeyers, and Edward S. Morse counted among his clients, but Bing did not content himself merely with the moneyed and the specialist. So that ordinary people could have the educational uplift of fine Japanese art, he founded collections at museums and technical schools in France, Denmark, the Netherlands, Germany, and the United States, and organized promotional shows in which the objects, not all expensive, could be purchased. Very strikingly, in light of Hayashi's preeminence, it was Bing who presented in 1890 the first comprehensive ukiyo-e show in Europe. The 725 prints and 421 books from all periods made widely known such masters as Suzuki Harunobu, Kitagawa Utamaro, Tōshūsai Sharaku, and others.[18] He followed this event with monthly private *diners Japonais* at the restaurant Le Cardinal, to which the collecting elite brought their prized prints for discussion and mutual delectation.

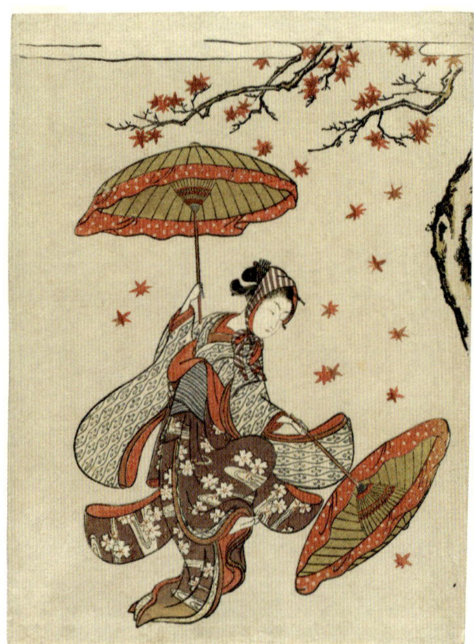

Suzuki Harunobu. "Maple-leaf Dance"; woodblock print; Edo period, ca. 1765; ink and color on paper; 11.26 × 8.54 inches. Courtesy of the Museum of Fine Arts, Boston: William S. and John T. Spaulding Collection (21.430).

By this time, the efforts of Fenollosa, Okakura, and their circle to reeducate Japan to its heritage had borne fruit with the establishment of new national and private collections and renewed veneration of ancient family and temple holdings. This drastically reduced the flow of treasures out of the country. Moreover, in the major cities of Europe and the United States, the ongoing labors of Shugio, Matsuki, Okakura, Fenollosa, Morse, Bing himself, and others had succeeded in educating serious Western collectors to "old," which they identified as "fine art," and "new" export-oriented work that largely remained denigrated as merely "decorative" or "applied art," despite Japanese initiatives to raise its profile. A critic of 1901 spoke for many in opining, "The art of Japan is dead," waxing nostalgic at the passing of a society in which "the question of adequate payment for their work never came up. The Prince supported the artist-craftsman, and all he asked in return was an occasional *inro* or *kakemono* or enamel."[19] Though the Japanese world that had inspired this romantic fantasy had ended four decades before, Western idealists did not stop from tenaciously clinging to it, abetted by the image carefully cultivated by Japan's Exhibition Bureau at the international fairs. The growing dearth of "real" art, combined with waning interest in anything else, weakened the market and brought the destruction of Greey, Hayashi, and others. Yet Bing remained undeterred, bolstered by his messianic view that saw Japanese art not as the last vestige of a dying ideal to be preserved in its antique purity but as the vital creative principle propelling an eternally youthful future. For him, Japan had given the world an *art nouveau:* as an invigorator, its heritage defined "modern."

A novel idea in itself, he introduced it innovatively as well in 1888 as the inaugural theme of a new monthly journal: *Le Japon Artistique,* the first successful Western periodical exclusively devoted to Japanese art.[20] Bing matched his expansive vision with a publication suitably grand in conception and beauty. Along with the French edition, he published in German as *Japanischer formenschatz* and in English as *Artistic Japan.* The cover of each of its thirty-six issues featured a different ukiyo-e print, sumptuously reproduced. In an era when most contents were in black and

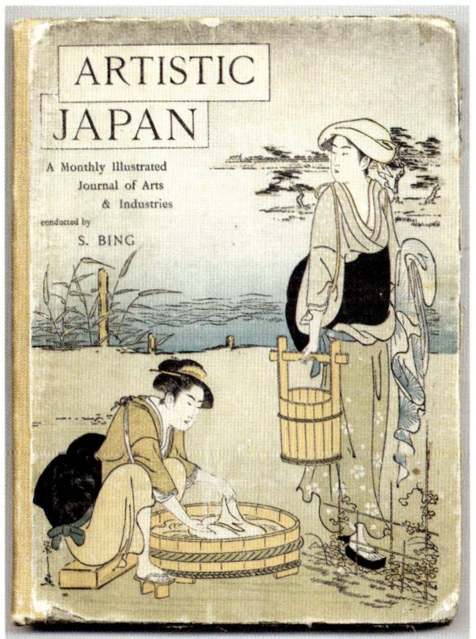

COVER; *ARTISTIC JAPAN* (1888–1891).

white, he featured exquisite color plates. And an international coterie of authorities wrote articles on prints, bronzes, textiles, swords, domestic and temple architecture, paintings, stencil techniques, mountings, color schemes, and anything else concerning Japanese arts and crafts appreciated at the time. All this came at a price aimed at the middle class. In the United States, where it was advertised in newspapers and magazines and sold in major bookstores like Brentano's in New York, a monthly perusal of *Artistic Japan* became an essential pleasure for many. Some critics, mostly Japanese, accused him of promotional aims in a time of flagging sales and of intellectual shallowness. But, if partly valid, these were flaws tempered by Bing's undeniable passion, and the success of his sincerely egalitarian educational aim "... to instruct the general public in the real and rare beauties of an Art which has hitherto attracted chiefly through its superficial qualities . . . ."[21] The sour attitude equally reflected Japan's awakening to its heritage and reluctance to admit to what its own careless indifference had allowed to slip away to Westerners like Bing, as well as its growing anxiety over losing control of its art history and aesthetics to the standards of foreigners, even the most knowledgeable.

Bing's interpretation of Japanese art as *nouveau* came from his recognition of its cohesive aesthetic of tranquility and calm, refined simplicity, and delicately sensuous, stylized nature motifs. These qualities he saw as a model for revitalizing the Western home interior.

> *Whilst our industrial arts have in consequence assumed a stiff and conventional character destructive to the boldness of originality, Japan appears to have indulged in freedom from and laxity of rules and method. Not that the Japanese artist emancipates himself from all rule, or ever lets his fancy wander at haphazard. Far from this; the constant guide whose indications he follows is called "nature"; she is his sole, his revered teacher, and her precepts form the inexhaustible source of his inspiration. . . . Under such influences the lifeless stiffness to which our technical designers have hitherto so rigidly adhered will be relaxed by degrees, and our productions will become animated by the breath of real life that constitutes the secret charm of every achievement of Japanese Art.*[22]

His admonition to "always start a work of art by remembering its function and intended place"[23] would shortly be distilled to "Form ever follows function" by the American architect Louis Sullivan, known to have been influenced by him.

Expanding on his proselytizing mission, Bing traveled widely to find artists and craftsmen in whose work he saw the creative absorption of these concepts. In 1895 he opened an elegant Parisian shop to showcase them, opulent with stained glass, wall paintings, wrought-iron railings and grilles of stylized plants and flowers, and model rooms of integrated décor and color schemes. He called it *Maison de l'art Nouveau,* giving a name to a style. There he sold Japanese prints and other items as well as an eclectic array of new designs by an international roster of talent, among them American Louis Comfort Tiffany, with whom he had developed a close relationship. He expanded his reach at the Exposition Universelle of 1900 in Paris with *Art Nouveau Bing,* a pavilion of six meticulously and elegantly executed model rooms. It ignited a fad in Scandinavia, Germany, and the Austrian Empire—places already noted for forward-thinking design[24]—and inspired manufacturers in the United States to introduce mass-produced furniture in the art nouveau style for middle-class pocketbooks. But the fad was brief. As befitted one truly avant-garde, the conservative tastes dominating France, England, and the United States found Bing too radical. Their public gawked and critics berated. Within a few years of his death, an influential American writer on household décor excoriated, ". . . and to complete the tale of iniquities, the shocking 'art nouveau' demonstrations of what an utterly unbalanced and depraved, and we might add starved, imagination could descend to."[25]

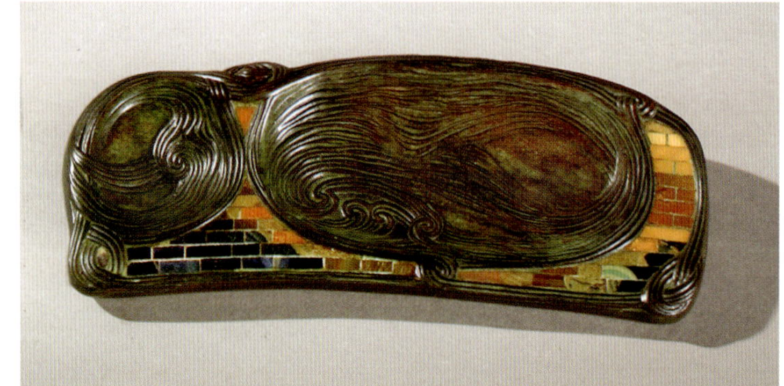

Tiffany Studios. Pen tray; ca. 1900; bronze and mosaic; 8 inches wide x 2.75 inches deep; signed and marked "8C685." This tray displays the cohesive design and sinuous line that Bing identified as inspired by Japanese aesthetics and essential to his concept of Art Nouveau.

Deep historical, cultural, linguistic, and economic ties allied American tastes closely to those of England. There, the Japan Craze burned brightly for nearly two decades, due in no small part to a single London enterprise and individuals in its sphere. In 1862 the shop ultimately called Liberty & Company opened to dispose of Alcock's unsold property from the London exhibition. The first and most influential purveyor of Asian objets d'art, in particular those from Japan, it carried the Craze to its English peak by 1875. Liberty & Company operated on the same idealistic premise as the international expositions—that of directing a rising middle class to the edifying value of high aesthetic standards. It was the prospering of Liberty, whose shipments from Japan were greeted by crowds,[26] and similar companies that so fanned demand that it led to over-expansion of export production. Combined with rising costs from improved living standards, this adversely affected Japanese quality to positive effect on the future of European design: Liberty ventured into its own household items, tastefully blending Celtic and Renaissance motifs with those Japanese elements appealing to English sensibilities: asymmetry, simplicity, sensitivity to medium, and sometimes unconventionally modest materials. The distinctive result attained international popularity and came to epitomize British art nouveau.

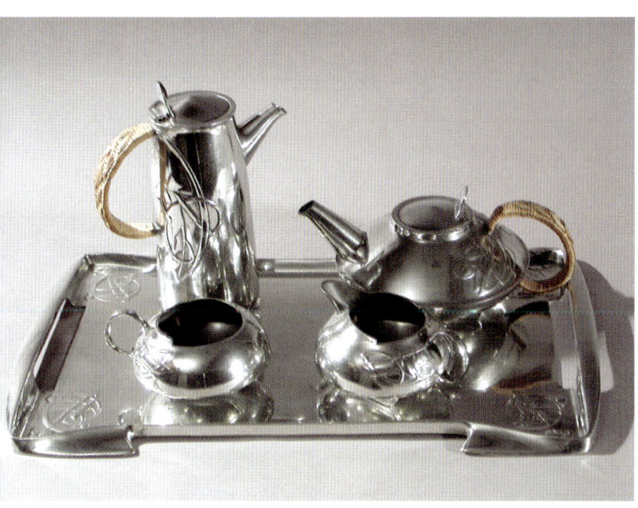

Archibald Knox. Tea service; ca. 1901; pewter; tray, 19.75 inches long x 12.5 inches wide; signed "Liberty + Co 0231." A five-piece English Art Nouveau tea service melds Japanese elements to the designer's signature Celtic motifs through the asymmetry of its interlace design, when viewed from the side, and in its contrasting handles of simple woven rattan.

Liberty's version shared with its French cousin a Japan-inspired ideal of craftsmanship and good design principles. But Bing and his followers enthusiastically took a cue from the Japanese agenda at the expositions, diving into the "fine art–applied art" debate by offering very expensive objects of opulent materials and by elevating individual craftsmen and designers as artists, such as Tiffany. Liberty and its circle took a democratizing direction by emphasizing inexpensive materials and adapting traditional methods to mass production. In this way Liberty's tea services, furniture, textiles, ceramics, and other products opened a bridge of taste between social classes in England and became suitable as models for American manufacturing; thus its spirit and intent advanced the movement toward modern design.

Among the artfully inclined, Japan-inspired avant-garde who took profit, pleasure, and sometimes both from Liberty & Company were bohemian society architect E. W. Godwin, nonconformist designer Christopher Dresser, and that doyen of aesthetes, Oscar Wilde. In addition to knowing each other, these individuals also consorted with similar circles abroad—those dominated by Bing, Hayashi, and Bracquemond in France, and in America by such figures as Okakura, Fenellosa, and artists and designers like Louis Comfort Tiffany and John La Farge. They were active with manufacturers producing goods for the well-appointed home on both sides of the Atlantic. In this way their ideas and design initiatives mingled and exerted considerable influence in the United States, even though not all of them actually spent time there.

E. W. Godwin (1833–1886) never set foot in Japan, but by the time Liberty & Company assumed its name, he had been collecting Japanese art for fifteen years. In addition to pleasure, Godwin found it a resource in a quest to improve a domestic design he considered deplorable. He was one of the first to recognize that the distinctiveness of Japanese society meant that Japanese design likewise did not find a natural habitat beyond native shores; and so he advocated not replication but creative adaptation, which did not preclude requiring his family to wear kimonos while at home. Other sources drew him, in particular Chinese furniture, but for most of the 1870s he considered Japan his primary inspiration and dubbed his style "Anglo-Japanese." Textiles, lacquers, ceramics, furniture, ukiyo-e, manga, family crests known as *mon,* and edifying books from France such as Aimé Humbert's *Le Japon illustré* offered a cornucopia of ideas: curved lintels and built-in storage, geometric grille patterns, peacock and chrysanthemum motifs, color schemes of sage and peach and gold and soft blue, textured surfaces such as matting, and accents of ebonized surfaces and brass-capped terminals. His vision emerged as plainly painted walls, bare floors graced with a few "Turkey" carpets, ukiyo-e prints and blue-and-white Chinese ceramics artfully arranged, and his own stained glass, textiles, ceramics, tiles, and plainly elegant furniture that he placed upon casters and kept to a minimum for easy movement and cleaning. This he considered an essential antidote to the French-inspired amplitude of swags, stuffing, and exotic pastiches then prevailing—in his view, not just tasteless but even unsanitary in an era where not even royals escaped the perils of infectious disease. He carried out his ideas for wealthy clients, his friend James McNeill

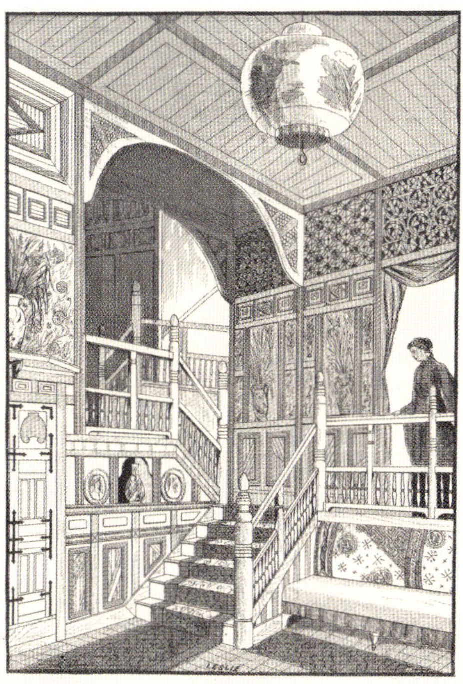

E. W. Godwin. Hall and staircase design; 1877. Originally the frontispiece illustration in William Watt's *Art Furniture*, the enduring influence of the Anglo-Japanese design style was evident in this unattributed reappearance in the January 1884 edition of *Decorator and Furnisher*.

Whistler, Wilde, and himself in homes he occupied with a series of desirable women, including an open liaison with the actress Ellen Terry. His Japan-inspired, radically austere aesthetic prompted Whistler to quip approvingly, "If you want to be comfortable, go to bed."[27]

In contrast to both John Ruskin and Siegfried Bing, Godwin embraced mass production. Relationships with Liberty & Company and other firms brought his ideas from the moneyed bohemian world to a middle-class clientele. And the era's new easy communications and international mind-set extended Godwin's influence to the United States, even though he never traveled there. At the Centennial exhibition an English furniture firm featured a Godwin-designed cabinet with incorporated Japanese lacquer panels. More enduring in impact were his Anglo-Japanese furniture designs and prolific, witty, and opinionated articles on décor and architecture in print on both sides of the Atlantic, in particular a catalogue entitled *Art Furniture*. Published in 1877 by the high-end manufacturer William Watt to advertise his firm's offerings, it featured individual pieces and suites and detailed drawings of the ideal settings incorporating Godwin's favorite Japonesque details. Its text informed readers of the essence of his philosophy: "The furniture and decoration throughout have been the result of a study of Japanese form adapted to modern English wants."[28] Extensively reprinted in whole and in part, *Art Furniture* influenced American designers into the late 1880s. Even more direct were innovative wallpaper designs of intricate two-dimensional patterns based upon Japanese geometric and nature motifs. Produced for the American market by American firms, they found their way into well-to-do homes.

Many tangents were united in Christopher Dresser (1834–1904), who wore an assortment of professional hats over a groundbreaking career as one of the first and most visionary in the new field of industrial design. He produced astonishingly forward-looking textiles, furniture, ceramics, carpets, wallpaper, glass, and silver plate. Astute and prescient in business, he worked with a huge array of manufacturing concerns for which he developed cutting-edge methods. Intellectually brilliant and, like Bing, a natural educator, he lectured and published widely. In the process he breached entrenched barriers of class and race, and left an indelibly positive imprint upon international political and business relations—all thanks to the fact that his exceptional capabilities came packaged in an engaging personality and generous spirit. Japanese arts were often the impetus behind these achievements.

Early studies in botany perhaps predisposed the working-class Dresser to the arts of Japan whose nature motifs, along with unusual materials, striking visual organization, and technical virtuosity captured his eye. Although familiar with a collection at the South Kensington Museum as early as the 1850s, he credited Alcock as his epiphany, thanks to the intimacy gained from drawings the obliging elderly diplomat allowed him to make of objects at his exhibit, some of which he purchased. These inspired ceramic, wallpaper, and textile designs much in the spirit of those by his upper-class contemporary Godwin, who freely expressed his approval. With a shared interest in mass production of middle-class-oriented products, the two became friends despite a climate of social snobbery, opening the door to the socially influential Oscar Wilde and others.

Dresser's comparatively extensive knowledge, successful Japan-inspired designs for firms like Minton, Wedgwood, and Watcomb, and his intellectual and business connections attracted the Iwakura Mission when it arrived in London in 1872. The mission enlisted his assistance for upcoming expositions; this linked him to Kiritsu Kosho Kaisha (and Hayashi Tadamasa), which soon turned to him in the selection of ceramics for display at the Centennial exhibition in Philadelphia. His growing aesthetic sophistication cemented a cross-cultural professional profile rare for the time, so that 1876 became a watershed in his career and in Western applied arts: the British government appointed him emissary to present a gift of decorative arts to Japan's newly established Imperial Museum. Dresser's dream of visiting the country became a reality. His stay of nearly a year placed him with Edward Greey among the earliest, very small number of Westerners whose claim to expertise in Japanese arts rested on actual knowledge of Japan. It preceded by a decade or more the stays of Americans Fenollosa and Morse, as well as Bing, all of whom found a model in his energetic activities. The trip, before and after, directly impacted design in the United States.

In Japan, Dresser took full advantage of a red carpet welcome that included the unheard privileges of an audience with Emperor Meiji, an open door to imperial art collections, and unfettered access all over the country. An entourage of translators, guides, sketch artists, and photographers in tow, he crisscrossed seventeen hundred miles to acquaint himself with over one hundred Buddhist temples, Shinto shrines, and famous sights; he met priests, artists, connoisseurs, and people high and low; he observed artists and craftsmen at more than seventy potteries as well as workshops for metalwork, basketry, textiles, embroideries, toys, lacquer, and bamboo, and documented it all with over a thousand photos. Japan's nascent mass manufacturers welcomed his advice. Dresser's connection became deeply personal when his sons moved to Japan, one permanently with a Japanese wife, to run operations for his import firm, Londos & Company. Meanwhile, a new understanding of Japanese aesthetic principles transformed his work; he disavowed his earlier designs as cluelessly "ornamentalist." More important for American designers, architects, and artists were his concerted activities to educate the public to his new ideas through exhibits, lectures, and, above all, publication. The *New York Times* was not alone in hailing the arrival of his seminal book of 1883, *Japan, Its Architecture, Art and Art Manufactures*. The earliest serious exploration of Japanese art traditions in English, it was for many years the only publication that gave Japanese architecture its critical due.

Christopher Dresser, for Linthorpe Art Pottery. Vase; 1879–1890; 17.5 inches high; stamped "886" with maker's mark "Ch Dresser." The austerely economical lines, wide lip band of oxidized copper, and slightly iridescent streaked glaze in intermingling shades of brown, cream, and moss green reveal this classically shaped large vase as a post-Japan design.

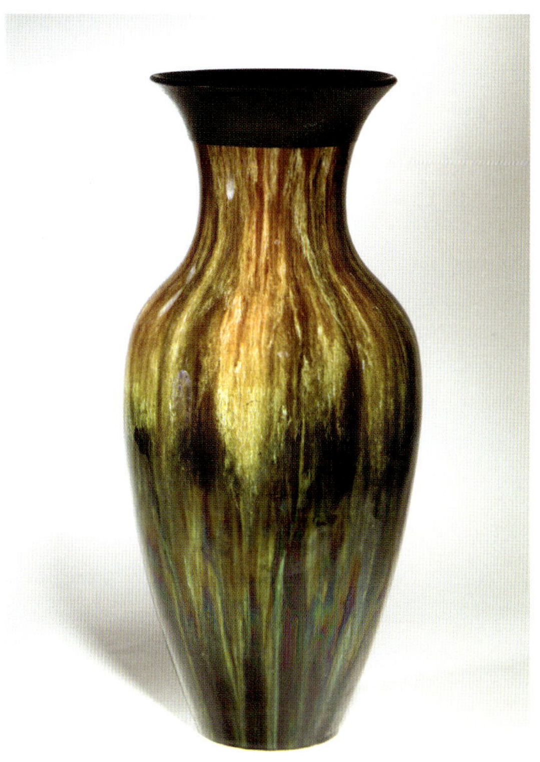

But before all of this, the long sea and overland journey to Japan took Dresser to the United States. His packed nine-week calendar left no time to record his impressions, but it afforded a reporter a vivid one of him: "The Doctor, as he is generally termed, is a full-grown Cockney—black of beard, bright of eye, and who would talk a man into a state which American ingenuity illustrated some time ago by a skeleton in a deal box; but his chat is charming."[29] In Philadelphia he toured the Centennial exhibition, including British exhibits featuring his own designs, and lectured at the Pennsylvania Museum and School of Industrial Art. Newspaper commentary hints of his warmth and accessibility in contrast to virtually everyone else, describing him as ". . . one of the most intelligible and sympathetic of the many experts who swung over to our shores entangled in the fringes

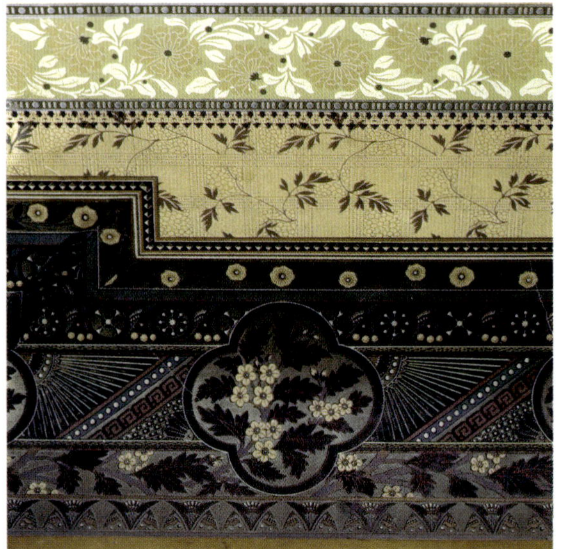

of the International Exhibition. Where the French experts were insulting and contemptuous, where Italian experts were boastful and vague, where Japanese experts were out of the question, Dr. Dresser was definite, communicative, and understood by all."[30] He followed with a major stop in Chicago, and brief ones in Council Bluffs and Salt Lake City, and finally San Francisco. There he stayed a few nights in the Palace Hotel, one of the newest and most luxurious in the country, and met up with fellow guests, the Japanese Centennial commissioners. They all quickly became a very convivial company and then proceeded to Japan by the steamship *City of Tokio.*

While in the United States, Dresser entered into business agreements with several wallpaper manufacturers and retailers. This meant that designs he soon would lament as "ornamentalist" would become a benchmark between emerging American tastes and its perception of Japanese aesthetics. But if this contributed to conventional direction, far more important to the future was a budding friendship with Charles Tiffany and his son Louis Comfort. The Tiffanys, who for several years had been experimenting with Japanese motifs such as in Hokusai's *Manga,* had a natural desire to get to know Dresser, whose knowledge extended beyond that of connoisseur intellectuals like Fenollosa (whom they also knew) to the artist's intimate sensitivity to technique and material. They enjoined Dresser to acquire "Japanese rarities" while on his trip. Incredibly, on top of the huge quantity bought for his concerns, he acquired an additional eight thousand pieces of lacquer, metalwork, enamel, ceramics, and textiles for them. Later for sale in Charles Tiffany's elegant shop, they excited "a far greater interest than those exhibited in a museum."[31] At prices ranging from $10 to $1,000, one could have plates with chrysanthemum motifs, cloisonné enamel teapots, mixed-metal bibelots and vases, ceramic sake bottles (Tiffany fanned the mood by providing free sake, which Americans compared to Madeira), or a Satsuma incense burner decorated with deities with faces like "the monkeys in Central Park" and "before which the disciples of Buddha have worn out their knees for generations." The bronzes put the store in "a Japanese uproar"; others, as the "Dresser Collection of Japanese Curios: Articles Selected for Tiffany & Co.," were auctioned in 1877; and the Tiffanys kept a large group of the very best

Above: Wallpaper frieze; installed in 1882. This frieze is a Japan-inspired, diagonally banded, geometric and floral border interspersed with floral cartouches. In situ and untouched since its installation, the original coloring seems to have been a brown, dark red, ochre, and white in the subtle hues associated with such things as Japanese ukiyo-e; the ornate conventionality reflects the "ornamentalist" taste that Dresser came to bemoan as a result of his direct experience of Japan but which retained considerable popularity.

Facing, Upper: Komai family of Kyoto. Vase; Meiji period; iron with gold and silver inlay; 4 inches high. Even more than the exotic look of the famous Kyoto landmark of Kinkakuji—formed in a cartouche and surrounded by cherry blossoms and leaves exquisitely and minutely inlaid in precious metals—the miniature size and precise balance on a delicately tiny foot made this vase the epitome of what Westerners admired in Japanese smithing skills. The signature of Komai shows it to have been created by a member of one of the most famous metalsmith families of that period.

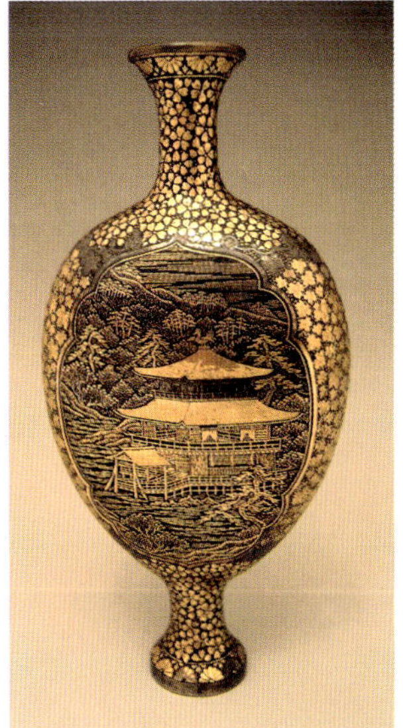

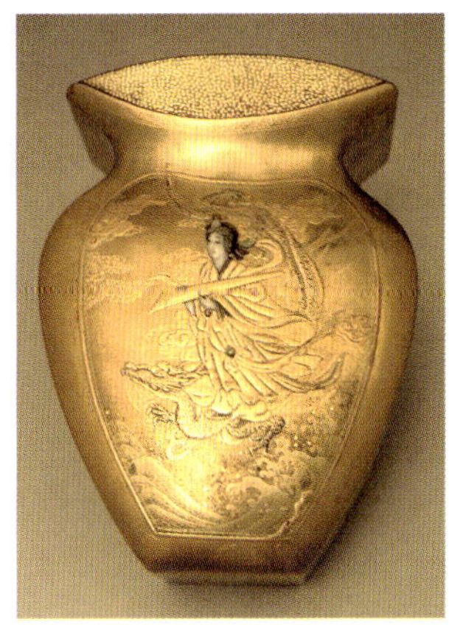

Above, Lower: Jar-shaped box; Meiji period; gold lacquer in high- and low-relief, inlaid gold flecks, ivory, and mother-of-pearl; 3.75 × 2.75 × 1.78 inches. This small Shibayama-style box has a motif of the goddess Benzaiten and typifies the opulent materials, tour-de-force technique, exotic themes, and unusual shapes with which the finest Japanese export wares enthralled well-heeled buyers at America's finest shops.

for themselves for pleasure and inspiration. They also enjoyed Dresser's exceptional expertise over the course of a close relationship. Dresser claimed to have influenced Louis Comfort in particular. If that is possibly an overstatement, it is not too much to say that Tiffany's most innovative designs benefited from Dresser's insights, making Japan the axis of two transformative figures in the history of modern design.

It was only natural that the individuals who most defined "Japanese art" in the Western public eye were Westerners themselves. Not only did their foreignness create a barrier, but also, in entangling their art with their political and economic agendas, the Japanese had set themselves an impossible task requiring that they create a public image that was simultaneously traditionally native and progressively cosmopolitan. At home, Japanese society could neither fully accept nor credit those few countrymen nimble enough to balance national identity and the outward-looking internationalism the new world demanded. Meanwhile, the motivations, agendas, and comprehensions of Westerners like Fenollosa, Bing, and Dresser naturally suited the society onto which such men grafted this borrowed aesthetic. But altogether, if naïve and clueless at worst, respectful and presciently aware at best, this mix of Americans, Germans, Englishmen, Frenchmen, and Japanese created a petri dish for a culture of change in which Japanese art emerged as the lingua franca of modernism.

1. *Hours at Home,* October 1867, 557.
2. *New York Times,* July 21, 1901.
3. Babbitts 1987.
4. *Godey's Magazine* 1898, 136, 816.
5. Finck 1895, 10.
6. *Putnam's Magazine,* June 1868.
7. Earl 1999, 31.
8. *Winterthur Portfolio* 1991, 23.
9. Sharf 1993, 20.
10. *New York Times,* October 2, 1888.
11. *Art Amateur,* February 1886.
12. Sharf 1993, 42.
13. *New York Times,* December 5, 1886, 10.
14. As quoted in Benfey 2003, 84.
15. Segi 1980, 169.
16. Jackson 2000, 101.
17. Put 2000, 24.
18. Weisberg 1990, 29.
19. Crippen 1901.
20. Put 2000, 77.
21. Bing 1888, 2.
22. Ibid., 5, 6.
23. Ibid., 13.
24. Weisberg 1990, 232.
25. Eberlein et al 1919, 167.
26. Wilkinson 1999, 71.
27. Soros 1999, 207.
28. As quoted in ibid., 185.
29. *New York Times,* May 6, 1877.
30. South 1877, 120.
31. *New York Times,* May 6, 1877.

4

HITHER AND THITHER

The Japan Craze Crosses America

In far Japan, that panoply has made tremble, Dead warriors, when it sheathed some form of might / While near it those belligerent spears assemble / That flashed, I am sure, in some hot Buddhist fight. / But strangely are set beside their savage grimness / A screen that birds and flowers make rich to see: / And slippers that perchance, in odorous dimness, Have graced an emperor's daughter sipping tea! —EDGAR FAWCETT[1]

In January 1882 a twenty-seven-year-old Oscar Wilde, of flowing locks and resplendent cape, velvet knee breeches and lace-embellished shirts, disembarked from the S.S. *Arizona* in New York. Dubbed "The Apostle of Aestheticism" by a quizzical press, he had come to enlighten the American masses with a menu of lectures, including "The House Beautiful," "The Decorative Arts," "Art Decoration," "The Interior and Exterior Decoration of Houses," "Decorative Art in America," and "The Relation of Art to Other Studies." Over the six years since the Centennial exhibition, the public now anxiously awaiting him had been flooded, rained, and infused with "Japan"—at subsequent expositions, in the media, in shops and mail-order catalogues—cajoled and guided by the likes of Matsuki, Greey, Shugio, Marsh, and a host of others including Wilde himself, standing as he did at the center of the British Japan Craze. Their enthusiasm for his words of wisdom stretched his tour to two hundred

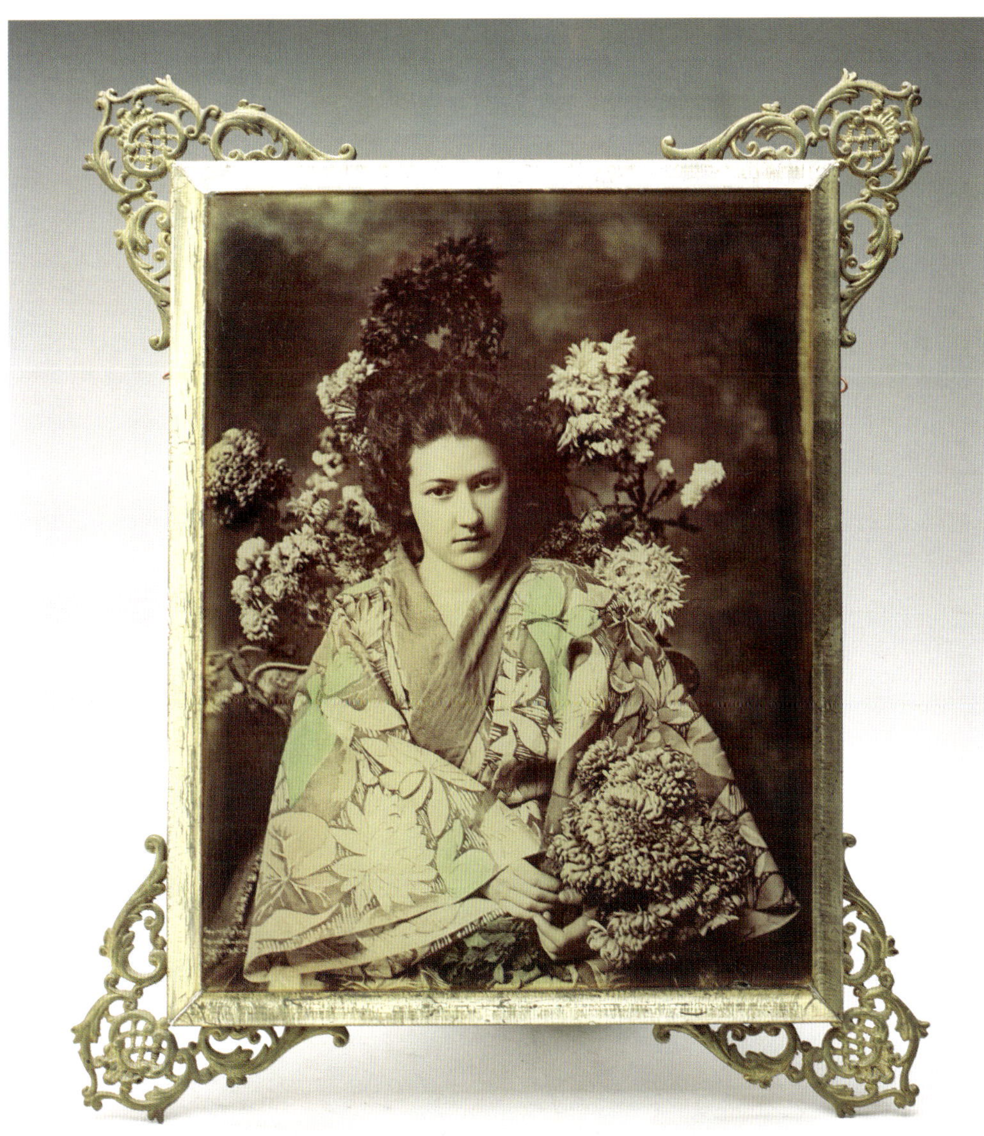

"Japanese" maiden; photograph; 1890; 14.75 x 12 inches.

and sixty days and one hundred and forty engagements from one end of the continent to the other, not only in big cities but also in places like Fort Wayne, Macon, Vicksburg, Richmond, Utica, Williamsburg, San Jose, and Leadville as well as locales large and small in Canada. He fanned their besottedness all the more, opining before audiences and to the press on how Japanese art as the ideal of aesthetic perfection exacted its impact:

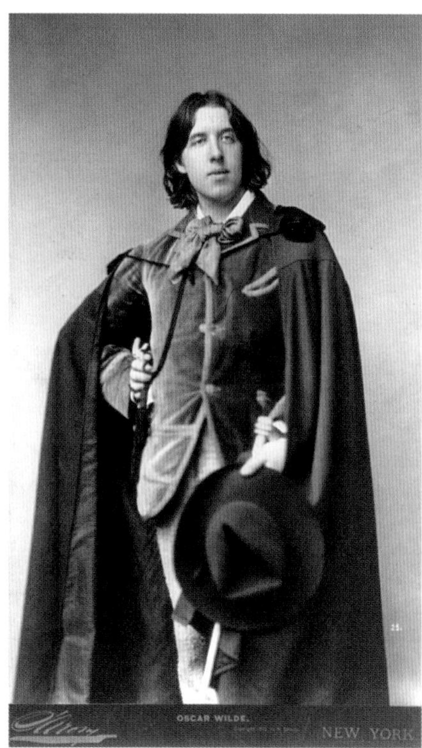

Oscar Wilde; ca. 1882.

The secret of the influence of Japanese art here in the West is that it has kept true to its primary and poetical conditions, and has not had laid on it the burden of its own intellectual doubts, the spiritual tragedy of its own sorrows. In its primary aspect, a painting has no more spiritual message than an exquisite fragment of Venetian glass. It is a certain inventive and creative handling of line and color which touches the soul—something entirely independent of anything poetical in the subject—something satisfying in itself.[2]

Finger ever on the pulse of his time and of human nature in general, Wilde intuited more fully than the more seriously regarded intellects of the day that in the world they lived in, the point was not Japanese art itself but what it had accomplished once unmoored from the land of its birth and cast into the giant foreign pond where it had no natural home. With the likes of Fenollosa, Morse, Matsuki, and Okakura, he shared the recognition that Western inspiration to date was sparked mainly by attraction to surface exoticism. But while they and others bemoaned and disdained this state of ignorance, Wilde's sense of detachment allowed him to perceive a liberating force in the disconnected, spontaneous, impressionistic engagement with the art of Japan, valuable for itself alone and as a path of discovery to more compelling qualities behind it. That engagement perfectly distilled the ideal of creative enlightenment at the heart of the Aesthetic credo that he championed—brought to gorgeous fruition by his friends Godwin, Dresser, and Whistler—while Japanese art itself presented the embryonic form of what was to come in the West: what later would be called modernism. Art Nouveau would soon be the earliest step in that direction. And perhaps uniquely in his wry fashion, he recognized and, even more, respected the active Japanese role in this process, as he articulated very precisely a few years later:

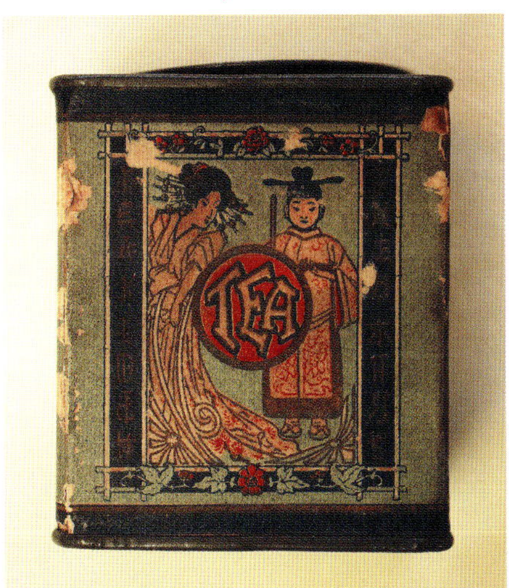

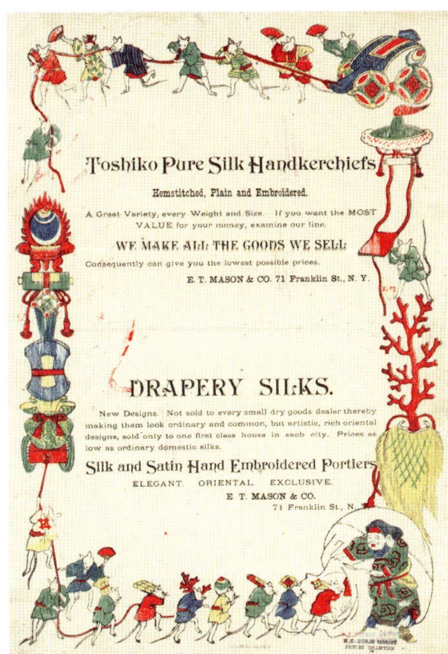

ABOVE, UPPER: TEA CANISTER; CA. 1900–1915; TIN WITH PAPER COVER.

ABOVE, LOWER: ADVERTISEMENT FOR TEXTILES, FROM A NEW YORK PURVEYOR OF JAPANESE GOODS; CHROMOLITHOGRAPH; N.D.; 12.6 × 9.06 INCHES.

No great artist ever sees things as they really are. If he did, he would cease to be an artist. . . . Now, do you really imagine that the Japanese people, as they are presented to us in art, have any existence? If you do, you have never understood Japanese art at all. The Japanese people are the deliberate self conscious creation of certain individual artists. If you set a picture by Hokusai, or Hokkei, or any of the great native painters, beside a real Japanese gentleman or lady, you will see that there is not the slightest resemblance between them. The actual people who live in Japan are not unlike the general run of English people; that is to say, they are extremely commonplace, and have nothing curious or extraordinary about them. In fact the whole of Japan is a pure invention. There is no such country, there are no such people . . . the Japanese people are . . . simply a mode of style, an exquisite fancy of art. And so, if you desire to see a Japanese effect, you will not behave like a tourist and go to Tokio. On the contrary, you will stay at home, and steep yourself in the work of certain Japanese artists, and then, when you have absorbed the spirit of their style, and caught their imaginative manner of vision, you will go some afternoon and sit in the Park or stroll down Piccadilly, and if you cannot see an absolutely Japanese effect there, you will not see it anywhere.[3]

The America he encountered as locomotives carried him to points north, south, and west must have intensified Wilde's astute eye for the droll aspects of this fascination: traveling troupes of Japanese acrobats offering diversion from his arduous schedule; the tea he imbibed daily, likely from "the Flowery Kingdom" as well—Japan being America's primary source to the tune of over sixty-one million pounds. A passing glance at any newspaper or magazine would have greeted him with an abundance of store ads for parasols, "odd little calendars of fancy red crepe" inside "ridiculously small Japanese shoes,"[4] "Net Suki" purses and "queer tobacco pouches,"[5] doll furniture, handkerchiefs with printed borders, embroidered tea cloths, jardinières, inexpensive what-not shelves of "mottled bamboo,"[6] and Satsuma bowls "for as little as $3.50." The rare quiet moment to read would have revealed articles proclaiming Japanese toilet objects "all the rage,"[7] along with draperies and

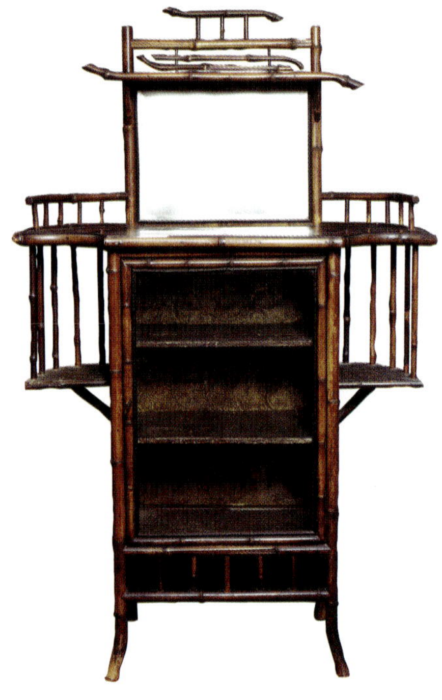

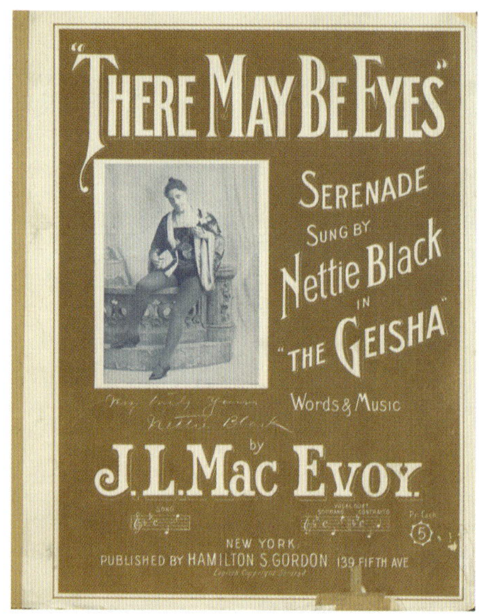

bedspreads of imported gauzes, crepes, velvets and batistes named "Ki Ki," "Banzai," "Sikok," and "Kiou-Siou," patterned with poppies or stripes in novel colors, not to mention teapots with handles shaped like mice. Others advised "Japan" as the way to impress: cunningly designed *carte de visite* cases covered with figured silk,[8] church fairs themed after Boys' and Girls' Day celebrations,[9] and springtime "sociables" decorated with wisteria sprays, paper lanterns, and fans, the kimono-wrapped hostess gracefully serving tea to guests enjoying themselves lolling upon floor cushions. That easily could have brought to mind women from bohemian to the ordinary who materialized their exotic daydreams in pictures of themselves dressed to match those of real Japanese ladies that flooded the stereoscope market. He might have cast a jaded glance on other fantasies by artists like Charles Dater Weldon (1855–1935), who tugged at peoples' lurking ambivalence and fear of the unfamiliar with eerie images of toddler-sized Japanese dolls mysteriously coming to life and stealthily approaching American children—asleep, vulnerable, and unaware. People sampled kumquats and loquats, and steamed their rice Japanese style[10]; soy sauce found its way into bottled meat dressings[11] and chrysanthemums into gardens. Up-to-date brides celebrated with luncheon and breakfast tables decorated "Japanese style" with vases of cherry blossoms and dishes, placemats, party favors, lanterns, and dolls. Entertainers sang "The Japanese Sandman," "In Old Japan," "In a Tea Garden (A Japanese Romance)," "Tokio Rag," "Lotus Land," and "When Bhudda Smiles." In the increasingly free association of such dilettantish diversions, Wilde must have recognized not only the disconnect from actual Japan but also the natural vigor of positive change in American life.

While the Japanese worked as hard as ever to stoke Western interest, by the year of Wilde's visit to America, the Japan Craze in Europe had crested, succumbing to fad fatigue, to the Victorian urge for clutter, and to the English thrall of India, thanks to the Raj. The fade would accelerate with the deaths of the main proponents of Japanese taste; all were gone

FACING, UPPER: CURIO CABINET; CA. 1880–1890; "MOTTLED BAMBOO" LINED WITH LEATHER PAPER; 36.5 × 33 INCHES.

FACING, LOWER: SHEET MUSIC FOR *THE GEISHA*; 1897. This was only one of many flamboyantly interpreted Japanese themes that abounded in popular theater and music throughout the Gilded Age.

RIGHT: C. D. WELDON. *DREAM-LAND*; ORIGINAL PAINTING RE-CREATED CA. 1883, AS AN ETCHING BY S. J. FERRIS.

BELOW: JOHN ROGERS. *PHRENOLOGY AT THE FANCY BALL*, CAST PLASTER; 1886. Feeling the bumps on the cranium of a wary Pooh Bah, a phrenologist reveals the nature of the mysterious character and alarming intelligence of the inscrutable Japanese. Though the sculpture playfully depicts the popular parlor game version of a then-seriously-regarded pseudo-science, it hints at the underlying anxieties Americans and Japanese alike felt about each other. One of the most popular sculptors of the Gilded Age, Rogers rendered it in cast plaster in order to make it an affordable accent to any middle-class home.

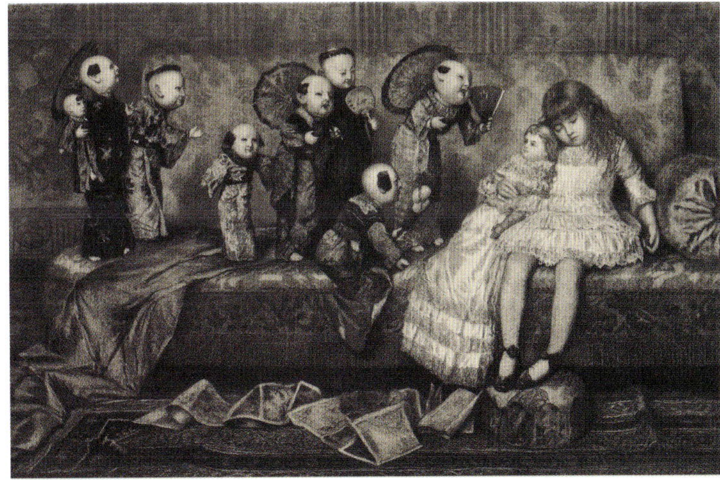

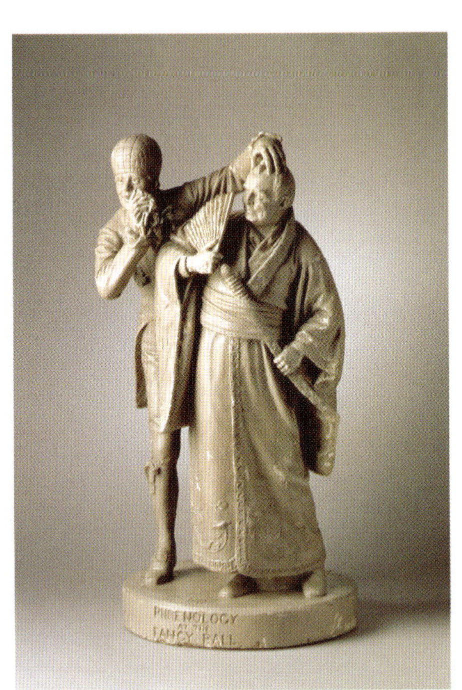

by the first years of the new century, including Wilde himself. But in the United States, the Japan Craze burned brightly for two more decades, for beneath its surface silliness, a process of true assimilation was unfolding in response to economic upheaval, changing social patterns, and greater sophistication. In the world of mass production that now typified the American market, the Japanese artistic ideal of economy, simplicity, and functionality provided creative ideas for products to meet middle-class needs and quality demands. Aesthetically, it offered a welcome alternative model to the condescending Europeans as an inspiration in the quest for the creation of an "American" taste.

The beginning made itself evident in the vibrant world of merchandise promotion that blossomed along with American manufacturing. Here, "Japan" and Japanese art played distinct roles. Exoticism—made all the more fetching, thanks to chromolithography—offered innovative ways to attract the public to new products it didn't know it needed. A splash at the 1876 Centennial exhibition, this inexpensive print technology transformed advertising from black and white into a rainbow and prompted companies to distribute small trade cards by the thousands. Their novelty and charm unleashed a collecting craze "absolute in its intensity."[12] In just the manner Wilde described, "Japan" proved irresistible to companies taking their cues from P. T.

Right: Candy box; ca. 1920; enameled tin with photo transfer; approximately 6 x 4 inches. For an appealing image, a candy company makes good use of one of the most popular Japanese photographic themes of the day, and adds a border of scribble intended to pass as Chinese characters to underscore the desirable exoticism of their product.

Below: The Strobridge Litho. Co. (Cincinnati & New York). Poster for Barnum and Bailey Circus; ca. 1898. Japanese acrobatic troupes regularly toured the United States on their own and in larger circuses.

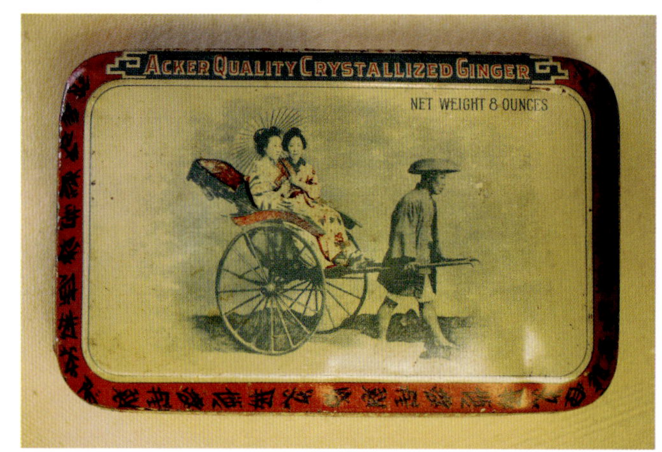

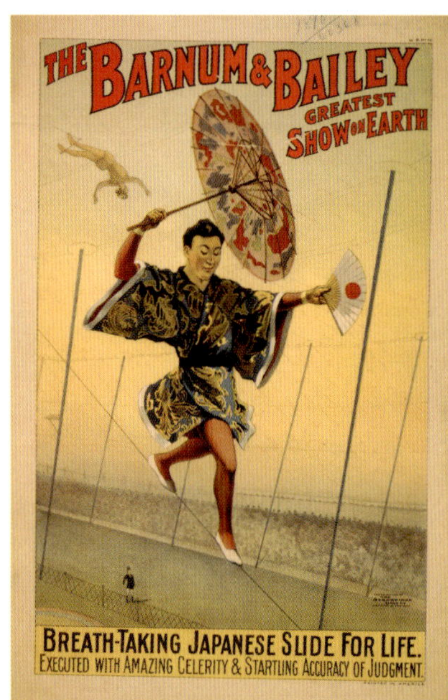

Barnum, who credited his smashing promotional success for his circus to the "humbug philosophy" of flamboyant display inspiring his posters. Early designers' quests to delight and attract by such means resulted in amusing incongruities, bizarre juxtapositions of image, and, in an era as unselfconscious as it was unsubtle, in product names that may have perplexed or even grated on many a Japanese: a kimono-clad blonde with Japanese parasol, advertising for American Eagle Tobacco; a scantily clad "geisha" promoting gelatin for pies; another daintily tripping through puddles aided by an umbrella and *geta,* re-envisioned from wooden thonged sandals into waterproof men's collars; Japanese acrobats selling patent medicine; "Amer-jap" fish food, "Jap Rose" cosmetics, "Jap-a-lac" lacquer paint, and "Japanese Corn Files"; and packaging featuring ersatz "Japanese" writing. By 1906 there was even toilet paper called "Japanese Crepe."[13] So compelling did people find these fantasies that many designs from Wilde's day lasted into the 1920s and beyond, riding the crest of another technological leap to enamels that adhered to the surfaces of tin cans.

But more important to the future was a new recognition of the lessons Japanese aesthetic principles offered to improve advertising effectiveness. Chromolithography enabled the Victorian love for detail to express itself exuberantly. A general fascination with the abundance of the new mass-produced world prompted many merchandisers to emphasize sheer variety and quantity. Combined with lack of pictorial

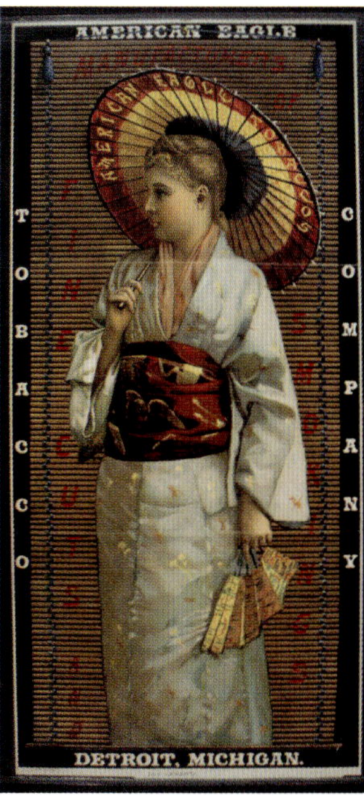

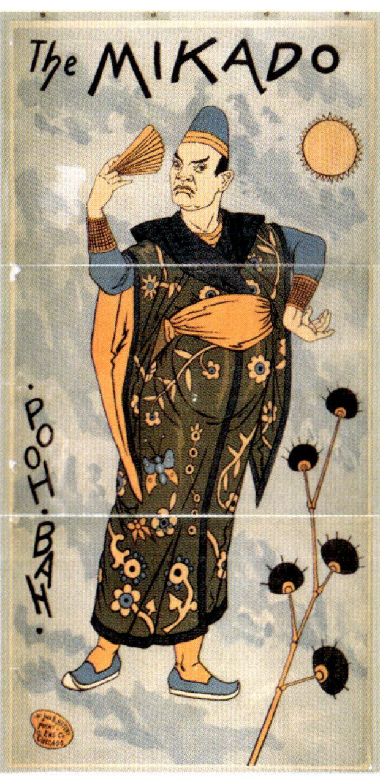

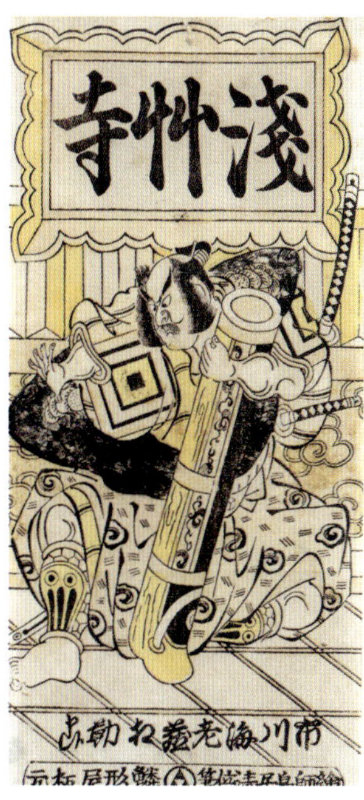

ABOVE, LEFT: ADVERTISEMENT FEATURING LILLIE LANGTRY; CHROMOLITHOGRAPH; CA. 1884. Incongruously garbed in a kimono and daintily grasping a fan and parasol, the famous actress and beauty advertises American Eagle Tobacco.

ABOVE, CENTER: "POO-BAH"; COLOR WOODBLOCK PRINT; 1885; 80.71 × 40.94 INCHES. A poster from the Gilbert and Sullivan comic opera *The Mikado* takes inspiration in composition and dramatic poses from Japanese playbills.

ABOVE, RIGHT: TORII KIYOMASU. *ICHIKAWA EBIZŌ*; UKIYO-E WOODBLOCK PRINT; CA. 1736–1741; 12.13 × 5.67 INCHES. This playbill for a swashbuckling kabuki drama, depicting a famous actor on stage with the signature prop of his role beneath the framed name of the play in bold graphics, displays all of the qualities that inspired the most talented of designers in America's nascent advertising industry.

sophistication, the quest to impress had resulted in congested, aesthetically unpleasing and visually confusing ads. Astute companies sought a more effective strategy to make their products stand out irresistibly. The most talented practitioners of the new profession of commercial art, noting their own attraction to Japanese media, brought their trained eyes to an analysis of how the formal power of its design attracted and influenced. In ukiyo-e, they recognized the components of the ideal ad: an unambiguous simple message accomplished by making a primary visual element both symbolize and extol the subject. "The Japanese . . . are poster makers by instinct. . . . [W]hat better ground work could a student of composition have than a knowledge of a few of the principles that underlie Japanese composition. These people are great in composition, great in color, marvelous in observation and drawing, and indescribably prolific in symbols."[14]

Wilde's visit could be described as a kind of exclamation point in a running Japan-inflected dialogue between Britain and North America, the incongruities and twists of which only accelerated with Gilbert and Sullivan's landmark operetta *The Mikado*—coincidentally under the hand of Wilde's own impresario, Richard D'Oyly Carte. Presenting a daffy and delightful fantastical "Old Japan" as a satirical Doppelganger of contemporary Britain, the success of *The Mikado*'s London premier in 1885 immediately spawned one hundred and fifty "unauthorized" versions worldwide, including one in New York where D'Oyly Carte obtained the first of many injunctions to stop it. The official premier that July at the Fifth Avenue Theater, with a cast of the most prominent show names of the day, ran for two hundred and fifty performances before moving to Chicago and points west,[15] starting a continuous run of almost one hundred years.

Some in Japan took offense, misreading it as a mockery of their contemporary society rather than a vision of a fantasy past, but growing urbanity outweighed such perceptions. Japanese attendees of the original New York production noted ridiculous errors, such as Pooh Bah's costume not being that of a retired nobleman "but rather that of an old

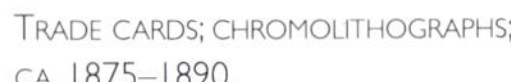

Trade cards; chromolithographs; ca. 1875–1890.

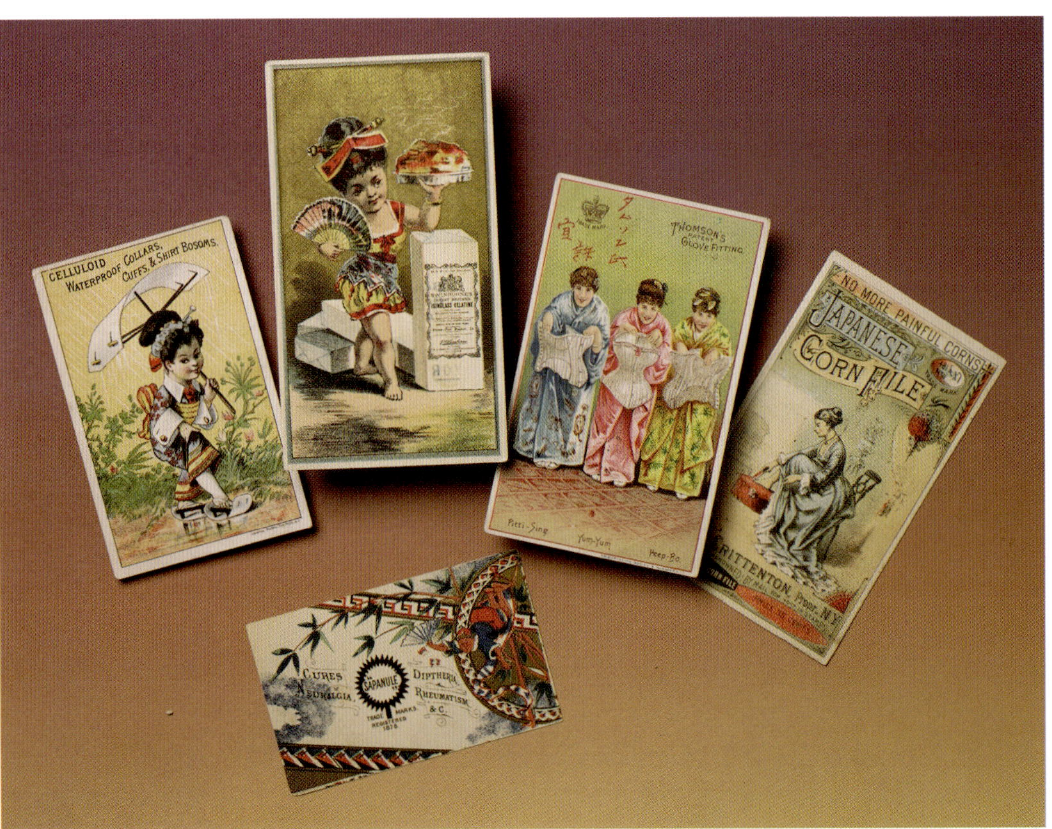

retired wrestler."[16] When a nervous British government banned London performances in 1907 to avoid upsetting a visiting Fushimi Sadanaru, that same royal who had represented Japan at the St. Louis exposition in 1904, the prince expressed disappointment at the lost opportunity, while an accompanying journalist who was fortunate enough to find an unauthorized production professed himself "deeply and pleasingly disappointed." Expecting "real insults" to his country, he had found only "bright music and much fun."[17] Meanwhile, *The Mikado*'s tongue-in-cheek vision of "Japan" instantly embedded itself in Western popular culture, inspiring a genre of "Japanese" melodramas, musicals, and the like, and surfacing in culturally scrambled advertising and marketing, such as Thomson's Glove-Fitting Corsets featuring the Three Pretty Maids—YumYum, Peep Bo, and Pitti Sing—who, had they ever existed, would not have worn corsets at all.

1. *Art Amateur,* September 1, 1879, 67.
2. *New York Times,* January 10, 1882.
3. Wilde 1905.
4. *Art Amateur,* May 1903.
5. *Art Amateur,* July 1903.
6. *Art Amateur*, June 1903.
7. *New York Times,* April 18, 1880.
8. *Art Amateur,* March 1903.
9. *Ladies' Home Journal,* November 1906.
10. *Arthur's Illustrated Home Magazine,* March 1881.
11. *Ladies' Home Journal,* November 1906.
12. Laird 1998, 90.
13. Hosley 1990, 119.
14. *New York Times,* February 16, 1896.
15. http://xroads.virginia.edu/~MA02/volpe/theater/theater/plays.html
16. *Art Amateur,* December 1885.
17. http://xroads.virginia.edu/~MA02/volpe/theater/theater/plays.html

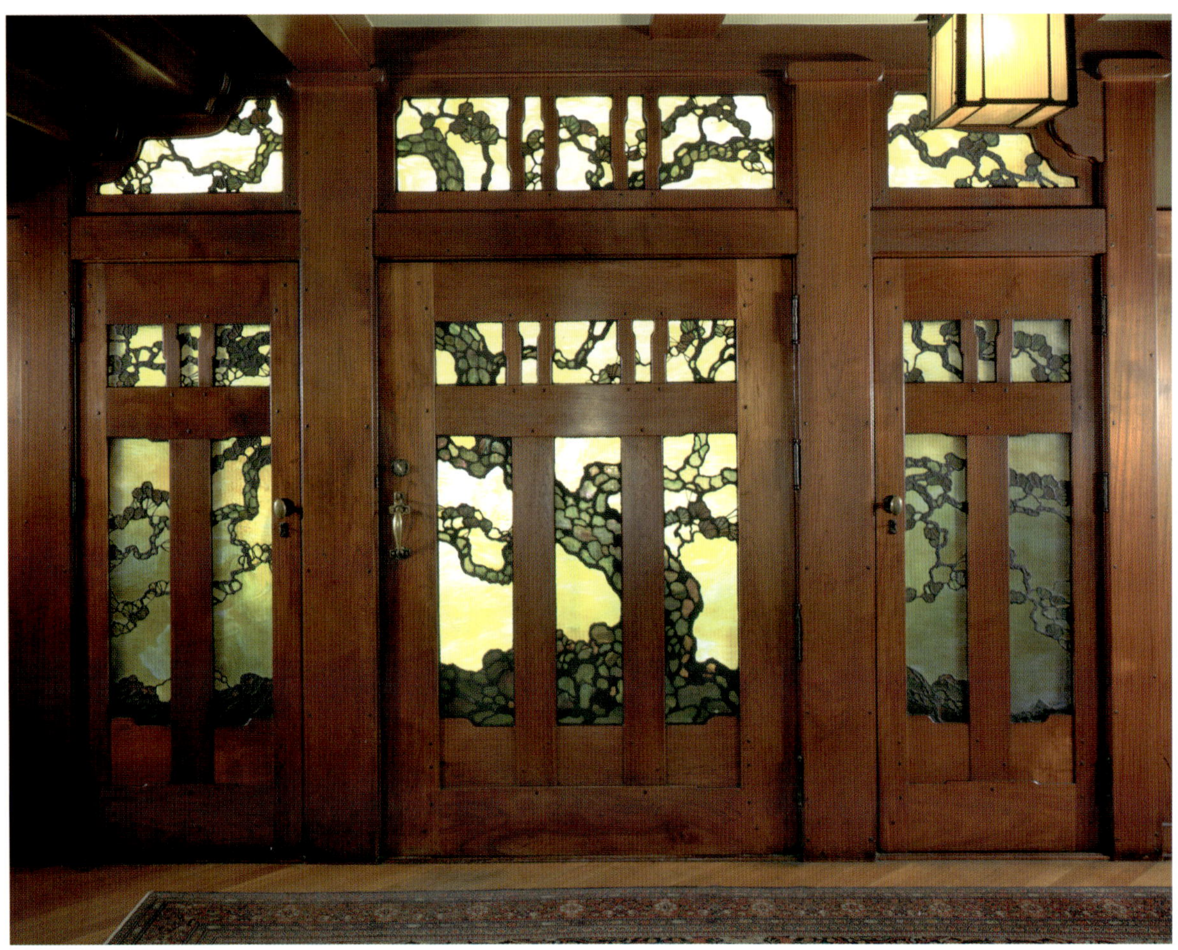

Greene & Greene. Front entry, Gamble House; 1907–1909; stained glass. A live oak design (also called "The Tree of Life")—its gnarled trunk and gracefully fanning branches luminous in green, brown, and yellow glass—spans the entire front entry of the Gamble House and bears a strong resemblance to the gold-backed tree motifs that typically graced the *tokonoma*, the alcove of Japanese palace interiors of the Edo Period. In Meiji times, such designs were a vestige of Japan's feudal past replicated for Westerners in the Hōōden and similar edifices erected at international expositions.

5

Ins and Outs of a Room

The Tasteful Speak "Japanese"

A degraded taste and a vicious way of living will as surely show itself in bad style as nobility and purity will find expression in noble and pure works . . . ."[1]

Though unleashed by the international expositions and continuously fed by Japanese export and traditional manufactures, and arts and crafts, the Japan Craze was framed largely by enthusiastic Westerners—despite the best efforts by the Japanese to control the public's image of themselves and their heritage. But if the pronouncements with which the Western media peppered itself on taste, quality, design concepts, and aesthetics as relating to their life and values frustrated the Japanese, the impact on the West of it all—whether accurate or skewed by misunderstanding and condescension—was wide-reaching and profoundly positive, most lastingly in the United States. Even the superficial fascination with a romanticized "Japan" that, much like "Turkey," "China," and "Egypt," often revealed itself as charged, eroticized exoticism could be said to have fanned interest beyond the narrow familiarities that defined the lives of many. More significant and enduringly, principles of asymmetry, abstraction, stylization, surface effect, humble as well as costly materials, utility, and unusual techniques—all of which the perceptive gleaned from serious study—infused Western design with new vigor of arrangement, color, methods, medium, and subject matter, especially a wide-ranging appreciation of the ordinary. This changed the very atmosphere in which people lived their lives and, to the thinking of the time, uplifted the characters of those within it. The very totality of the assimilation would be proof of success.

Significant in this creative process were two persistent misconceptions, both of which liberated Western artists: first, the cherished notion that in not distinguishing between "fine" and "applied" art, the Japanese regarded *everything* as "art" (rather than the very different implications of having no such umbrella concept as "art" at all); and second, that contemporary Japan retained the last vestiges of a medieval society dominated by high-minded artisans as equated with the nostalgic ideal of a long-lost Europe. As the gothicism-inspired architect William Burges observed upon viewing Alcock's display of 1862, "truly the Japanese Court is the real Mediaeval Court."[2]

Both notions elevated the Japanese as exemplars of creative genius and interpreted their entire visual culture as the natural result of "fine art" standards universally applied, with all of the high moral implications of the term. This added weight to those who overthrew the era's tendency to rigid categories in favor of a blurring of distinctions among artist, designer, and decorator, and provided a unifying rationale for the constellation of arts and crafts comprising interior design. Now, a bridge linked those who created the "fine art" regarded as the highest form of human expression to an equally idealized and all-important realm: the home and those who presided over it—women. In Britain and America, many authorities on decorating were artists or closely connected to the art world. Both groups included women, who had emerged in America as innovative advocates of home-related art crafts as appropriate employment for middle-class women struggling in the aftermath of the Civil War. But for all the discussion of what was "Japanese" in design, it rarely accorded in any way to the practices of Japan, about which most knew or cared little. All felt free to apply the principles they gleaned according to how they understood them, anywhere and any way they liked, for the world they knew. This evolved as Americans moved from the eclectic internationalist opulence of Aestheticism to a national identity of taste in the quietly simple, rustic elegance of Arts and Crafts—in part inspired by growing understanding by Americans of the suitability of Japanese aesthetic principles to their own changing world.

With ties of culture and language to Great Britain, then at its imperial apogee, Americans naturally looked first to English taste as a model despite discomfiture at being condescended to as uncultured upstart materialists. But in a twist befitting the era's exuberant internationalism in its bespoken Aesthetic style, a landmark interpretation of "Japanese" taste in England came at the hands of an expatriate American—James McNeill Whistler. Flamboyant, infuriating, and extravagantly gifted—a close friend of E. W. Godwin, with whom he collaborated, and Oscar Wilde, whose drawing room ceiling he later embellished with dragons—Whistler's ambitions in the world of two dimensions extended from pictures and their frames to the walls themselves. In 1876 he took it upon himself to redecorate those of industrialist Frederick Leyland's dining room. Popularly known as the Peacock Room, it is the finest example of the eclectic exoticism characterizing the early years of the Japan Craze.

The project all but obliterated the expensive work of another gifted and influential architect and decorator influenced by Japan, Thomas Jeckyll (1827–1881). The shock deeply unsettled the delicate emotional constitution of Jeckyll, who already had shown signs of instability and would later suffer a career-destroying mental breakdown. The

THE PEACOCK ROOM, LOOKING SOUTHEAST. Featured here is the wall with the famous "dueling peacocks," Whistler's pictorial excoriation of Leyland.

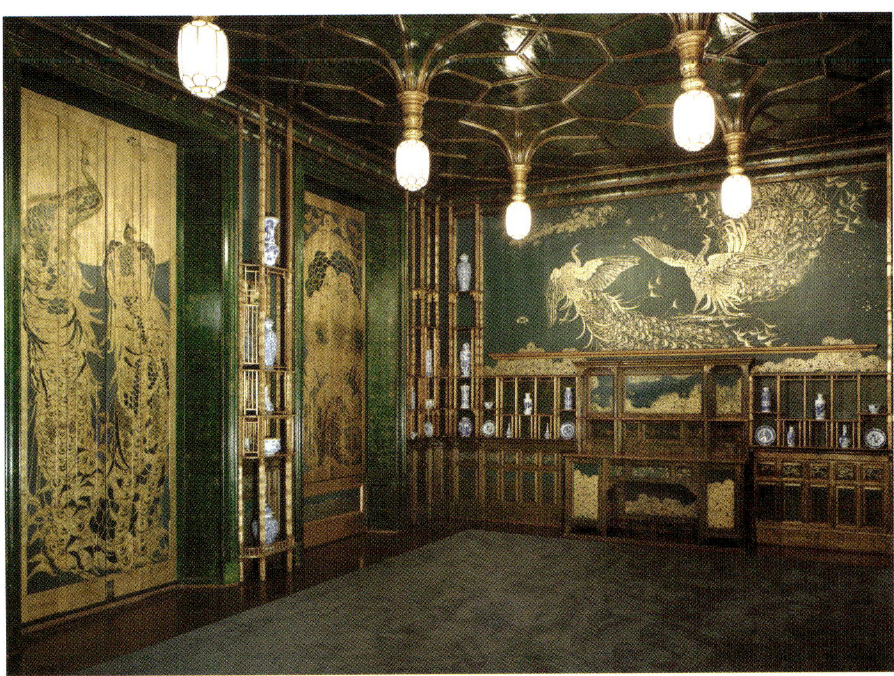

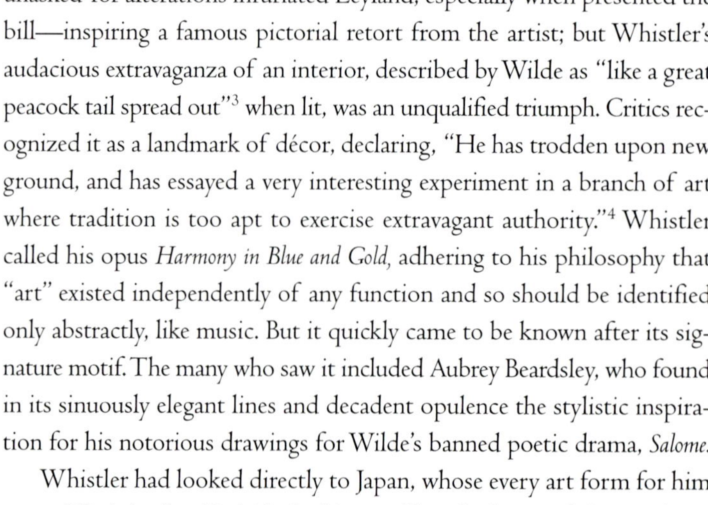

unasked-for alterations infuriated Leyland, especially when presented the bill—inspiring a famous pictorial retort from the artist; but Whistler's audacious extravaganza of an interior, described by Wilde as "like a great peacock tail spread out"[3] when lit, was an unqualified triumph. Critics recognized it as a landmark of décor, declaring, "He has trodden upon new ground, and has essayed a very interesting experiment in a branch of art where tradition is too apt to exercise extravagant authority."[4] Whistler called his opus *Harmony in Blue and Gold,* adhering to his philosophy that "art" existed independently of any function and so should be identified only abstractly, like music. But it quickly came to be known after its signature motif. The many who saw it included Aubrey Beardsley, who found in its sinuously elegant lines and decadent opulence the stylistic inspiration for his notorious drawings for Wilde's banned poetic drama, *Salome.*

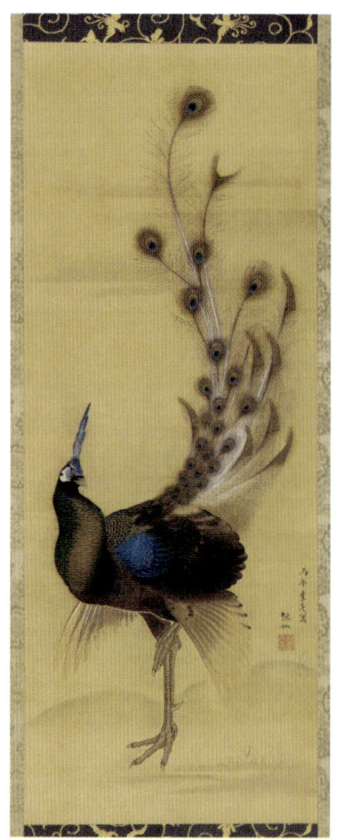

Whistler had looked directly to Japan, whose every art form for him exemplified the "rarified ideal of beauty"[5] at the heart of the Aesthetic philosophy to which he adhered. His interests leaned toward ukiyo-e and lacquer, which he began collecting years before in Paris. With eclectic inspiration, Whistler declared he wanted the effect of a lacquer box—objects of great appeal to Victorians for the rich variety of pattern and technique to be found on a single object.[6] Whistler's design emphasized two patterns in countless variations, replicating the textural and metallic effects of Japanese lacquer techniques by building up surfaces beneath the gold and silver, and even including metallic dust. Looking to Japanese screens as inspiration for the doors and windows, he borrowed the square patterns characteristic of their large expanses of gold and their dimensional effects in the way he used the hinged shutters as folding formats. The inspiration for peacocks came from paintings and ukiyo-e prints, for while no Japanese artist decorating a wealthy patron's home would have looked to ukiyo-e, Whistler, who likely neither knew nor cared about its low-class aura, adored them.

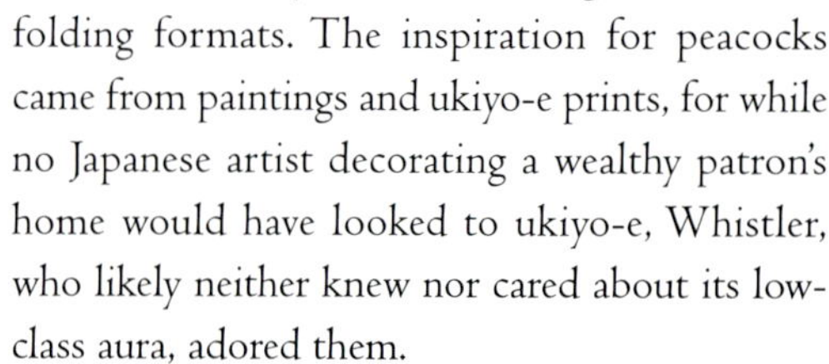

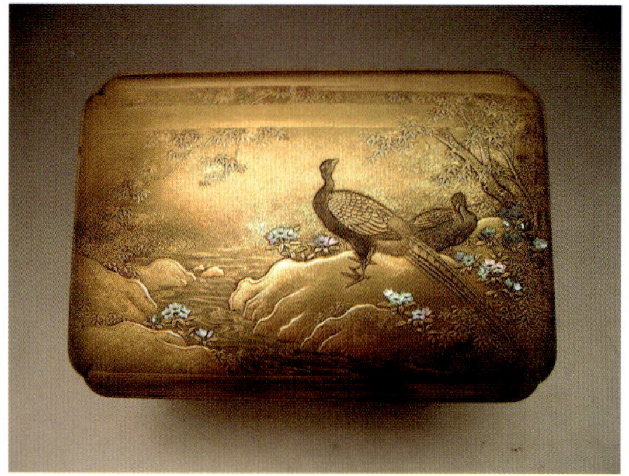

Along with sunflowers and lilies that were the signature motifs of Aesthetic taste, peacocks owed their popularity to the enthusiastic promotion of Wilde, who linked them to both medievalism and Japan. For the latter, they were considered the requisite decorative complement to jars, vases, and bowls of blue-and-white porcelain, especially those ornamented with a design of plum blossoms against a net-like pattern of cracked ice. These were first available in the Asian antiques shops of Paris and Amsterdam, and a dealer named Murray Marks had established himself as the indisputable king of the market for such pieces in London. His shop became a favorite haunt for many, including Whistler and his friend Dante Gabriel Rossetti, who coined the popular misnomer "hawthorne jars." The raging fad for hawthorn jars sent prices to fantastic highs, assuring that they would become indispensable statements for the wealthy. Frederick Leyland owned a huge collection that he displayed in the obligatory way: in the dining room on an elaborate "Japonesque" shelving constructed of spindles, centered over the fireplace mantel. If necessary, the shelf could extend on either side. Leyland's shelves took up all four walls and surmounted the doors.

Facing, Upper: Mori Sosen. "Peacock"; hanging scroll; Edo period, late eighteenth century; color and ink on silk; 68.23 x 22.95 inches.

Facing, Lower: Tiered box and matching tray; Meiji period; gold, mother-of-pearl, silver inlay, and silver-lined interior; 6.25 x 4.15 x 3.75 inches. Naturalistically observed pheasants by a stream in autumn—executed in four different lacquer techniques—make this box and tray epitomize the opulent look that Whistler sought to replicate on a grand scale in the Peacock Room.

Above: James McNeill Whistler "Hawthorne" jar; n.d.; pencil, pen, ink, and wash on paper; 8 x 5.28 inches; in *A Catalogue of Blue and White Nankin Porcelain Forming the Collection of Sir Henry Thompson* (1878).

While Japanese blue-and-white porcelain had long been exported to the West, "hawthorn" wares were largely Chinese. Yet, most considered their presence inextricable from "Japanese" taste. This was despite the fact that Europe enjoyed greater familiarity with Chinese ceramic arts due to Japan's historic isolation and the Dutch trade monopoly that had jealously controlled imports until only a few decades before. Similarly, certain lines of Aesthetic furniture possessed more of a Chinese appearance overall, unsurprising given that Chinese society did not carry out most activities while sitting on the floor and thus offered more readily adaptable furniture. Yet Godwin and his imitators dubbed it all "Anglo-Japanese," much as had already occurred in the eighteenth-century Chinese Chippendale style of "Japanned" lacquer. Some of the confusion could be attributed to antiques traders selling both Japanese and Chinese items in shops with misleading names. Quality dealers like Boston's Bunkio Matsuki, San Francisco's George T. Marsh, New York's Yamanaka, and lesser establishments like Vantine's were typical in their heavy emphasis of Japanese arts while also featuring objects from China.

But, lack of sophistication and confusion sown by dealers notwithstanding, Japan itself was the real source of Japanese dominance in the somewhat-fuzzy distinction between Japan and China in Western eyes.

Below, Upper: "Japanese" bed; as published in *Decorator and Furniture* 4, no. 1 (1884): 16. Ornate spindled lattices and a boxy shape emphasizing straight lines typified this bed as "Japanese" in the eyes of the period, but it borrowed much more from the tastes and sleeping furniture of Qing Dynasty China.

Below, Lower: Incense box; late Ming Dynasty, ca. early seventeenth century; lacquer; 2.76 inches diameter. This *kogo*, carved with a fruiting spray of lichees, was discovered with a label indicating that it had once been among the fine Chinese objects sold by George Turner Marsh, the preeminent West Coast dealer of the era, who was especially noted for Japanese art and antiquities.

Contemporary Japan's outsized presence at the international fairs contrasted with a much less ambitious Chinese one that was not even an official government initiative until 1904 in St. Louis. Like Japan, other Asian nations struggled with impoverishment and Western encroachment, but their leaders lacked Japan's foresight in sacrificing to invest the necessary resources for an ambitious economic, political, and public relations initiative. This assured that Japan's vastly smaller and historically less influential culture would loom disproportionately large in the public eye. Success in capturing the Western imagination, accurately or not, established "Japanese" as a dominant element in a generalized Orientalism extending to Moorish, Persian, Egyptian, Indian, and, of course, Chinese fascinations. While this would change with evolving fads, and the emergence of Arts and Crafts ultimately would cause the shedding of these superficial veneers, it opened the door to many principles inherent in Japanese art, and these would remain.

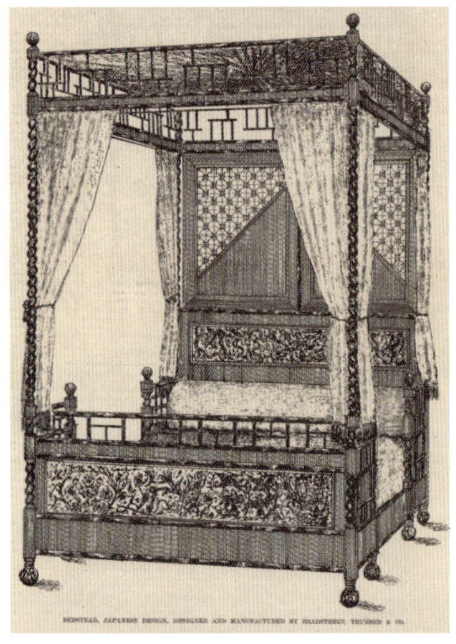

For the uninitiated Western public it could be very difficult to separate one from the other. Because Japanese art crafts targeted to the West stood wholly outside the Japanese frame of reference with respect to desirability, unlike traditional art forms, there existed no established canon of decoration or appearance from a Japanese perspective. This left artisans and designers completely free to tailor modern work to foreign expectations that, in light of the murky Western knowledge of Asia, inevitably led to mix and match. Looking to the successful precedent of older export initiatives in ceramics under Dutch direction that adopted Chinese motifs, brilliant color, and abundant decoration, a similar approach for contemporary export items came logically. After all, foreigners clearly liked them. In the new Westward-looking era, the Japanese found such aesthetics, materials, and shapes, even when based upon traditional forms, in every way inappropriate for any conceivable purpose except, perhaps, when necessary to look or be "Western."

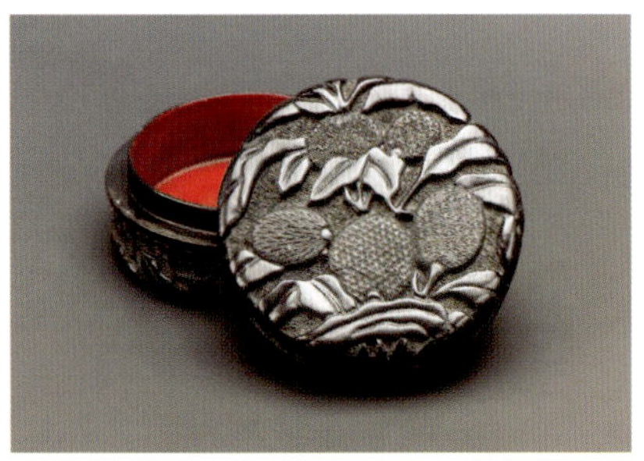

A far more complex factor lay in Japan's two millennia under the cultural umbrella of China. This had left Japanese traditional arts with a clearly Chinese streak of themes, motifs, pictorial styles, techniques, media, and forms, all fully acknowledged by the Japanese as integral yet distinct from the purely Japanese in their visual heritage. These elements, which

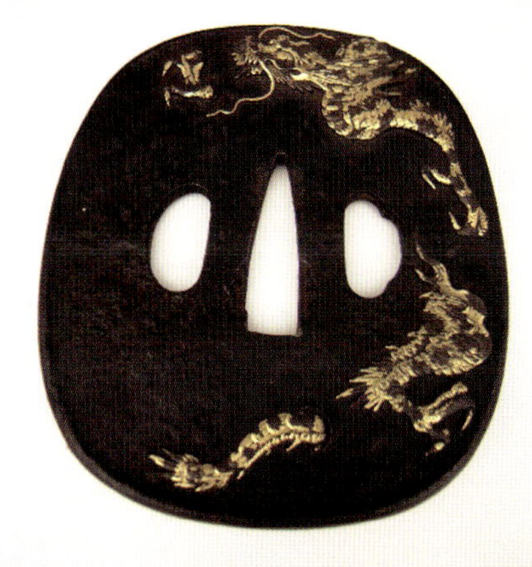

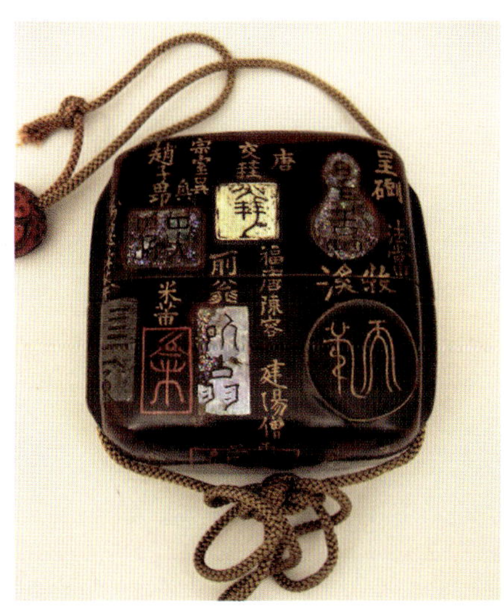

Above, Upper: Sword guard; Edo period; gold inlay bas-relief; 3.15 inches high. A Chinese dragon writhes across a *tsuba* of iron and precious metals, the quintessential samurai martial accessory.

Above, Lower: Inro; Edo period; lacquer with abalone inlay; 3.35 inches high. Seal motifs featuring Chinese characters in archaic style make a handsome decorative motif on this small traditional container for medicines, an indispensable accessory for the Edo-period Japanese gentleman.

historically had served certain functions in public and private life, commonly appeared on traditional objects of enormous attraction to Westerners: folding screens, sliding wall panels, scrolls, certain ceramics, and many, many works in bronze, ivory, and lacquer, such as sword guards, medicine boxes called *inro,* and their cunningly carved toggle-like attachments known as *netsuke.* Objects of these types just as often displayed purely Japanese themes. In antiques shops and the primitively organized exhibitions available to the vast majority of Western devotees, all appeared indiscriminately mingled, leaving people unaware of the distinctions among them. Most were indifferent anyway. Whistler, typical of his day, responded only to aesthetic inspiration, seeking to create for Leyland's dining room "something quite wonderful"[7] that would complement his ceramic collection and, not coincidently, harmonize with Whistler's own portrait of Mrs. Leyland, destined to have pride of place on one wall.

Among English society artists and designers and their moneyed clients of avant-garde inclination, Whistler's statement for Frederick Leyland sparked a host of other dining rooms in the "Japanese taste," as well as libraries, morning rooms, boudoirs, and parlors. And, perhaps encouraged by the era's hallmark activity of mingling between financially straitened British nobility and title-and-status-seeking robber barons, similar rooms began to appear in the urban palaces and country retreats of America's uppermost crust after the 1876 Centennial exhibition brought the Japan Craze across the Atlantic.

In the United States a few people like Bunkio Matsuki in Massachusetts and George Turner Marsh in California experimented with interiors that sought to adapt Japanese design conventions to Western domestic patterns, but as a Japanese and a deeply knowledgeable Westerner, they were exceptional. America's millionaires had different expectations; to create their sumptuous spaces like the English upper crust with whom they competed, they turned to society's most prominent architects and designers. Although Christopher Dresser's *Traditional Arts and Crafts of Japan* appeared in 1882, Edward S. Morse's *Japanese Homes and Their Surroundings* in 1885, and Siegfried Bing's *Artistic Japan* in 1888,

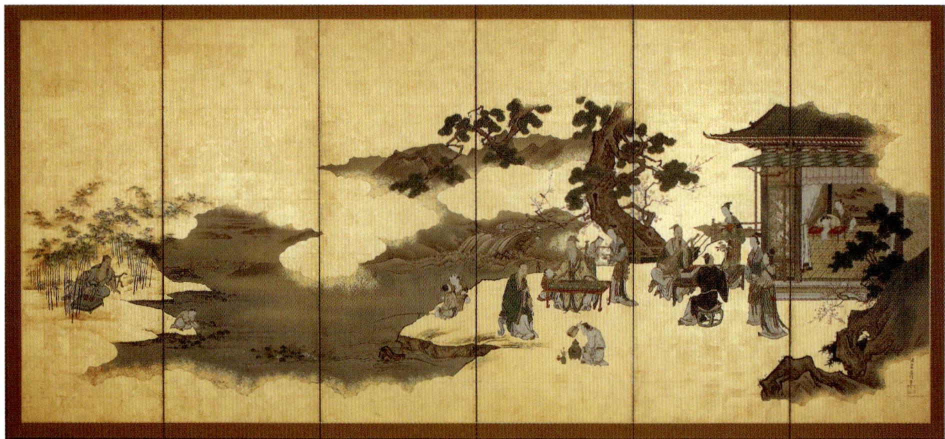

Above: Tōun Masunobu. "Music & Calligraphy"; six-panel byōbu; Edo period, late seventeenth century; ink and color accented with gold leaf and gold dust on paper; 67.75 x 149.5 inches; signed "Tōun Masunobu"; sealed "Soshin." This folding screen was once one of a pair depicting the four traditional accomplishments of the Chinese scholar: Music, Calligraphy, Chess, and Painting. The artist, also known as Kanō Masunobu, was a prominent member of Japan's most important school of artists until the fall of the Tokugawa shoguns. For several hundred years, Kanō artists specialized in creating paintings of classic Chinese themes in a Chinese-derived style for the palaces of Japan's most powerful aristocrats, who understood them as such.

Facing, Upper: Wallpaper designs. Cutting-edge designers considered the effect of three dimensions the worst possible taste for wallpaper and openly emulated the Japanese talent for formalized two-dimensional pattern. Among their favorites from Japanese design were random and asymmetrical motifs as in this frieze miscellany of daisies against a lattice-like ground, extant and in situ in the 1882 Cohen-Bray House (facing, upper left), whose more immediate inspiration may have been a pattern by Owen Jones, published in *Decorator and Furnisher* (October 1882) as part of an extensive article that noted Jones' own debt to "Oriental masters" (facing, upper right).

which were all informative resources, for many years any nod to authenticity took a backseat to the Victorian penchants for upholstered comfort and decorative abundance according to the morally infused rationale for "domesticity."

With the spirit of Whistler's free adaptations gone wild, they found inspiration from all of Japanese arts, applied with equal abandon to otherwise conventional western décor. Designs from Japanese textiles or ceramic decoration found their way into fireplace surrounds, decorative friezes, and the like. Nearly all such spaces featured built-in and free-standing irregular display shelves and faux bamboo. Dragons turned up everywhere. Alcoves, asymmetrical built-in cabinetry, and other essential functional components of Japanese interiors transmogrified into stylish decorative embellishments; exterior architectural forms such as temple roofs and brackets found new homes on library and dining room walls. Americans easily equated the opulent paintings on the *fusuma* (sliding wall panels) of the most formal Japanese spaces with wallpaper, no doubt encouraged by Japanese manufactures who obligingly created export designs resembling them. Designers also diverged from innovative Western models such as the thematically united elegance of Whistler's Peacock Room and, even more, the austere ideal urged by Godwin, whose bare-bones interior for Whistler's home actually excited public ridicule. Combined with deep red and dull gold finishes and, of course, an amplitude of similarly styled furniture, cushions, and draperies, as well as the obligatory "Turkey" carpet, and then mixed with pottery, bronzes and ivories, fans and parasols shading fireplaces and light fixtures, tasseled

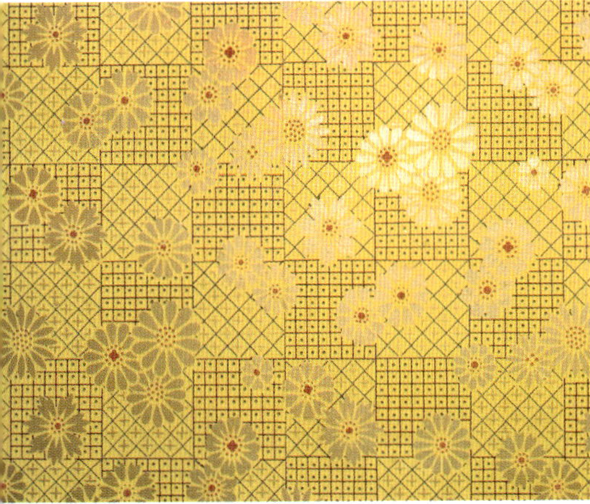

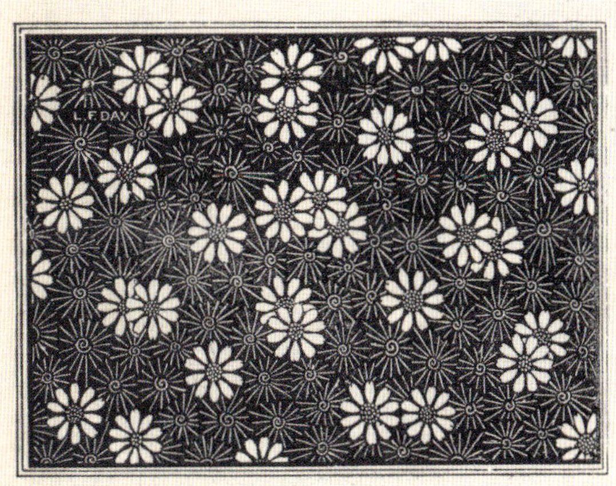

Below: Library, Louis Comfort Tiffany's Bella apartment, New York City; as published in *Artistic Houses*, 1883. By mounting a *ranma* in the doorway between the library and dining room of his New York apartment, Tiffany replicated the position of these elegantly carved grilles, which in Japanese interiors served to ventilate and support the sliding wall panels that divided interior spaces. The library also featured opulent wallpapers in a miscellany of Japanese floral, fan, and botanical patterns, and a writing table whose asymmetrical shelving and carved and reticulated floral ornamentation alluded to Japanese taste.

lanterns, and a smattering of objects from China, India, and elsewhere, it all added up to a crowded "oriental" pastiche.

New York emerged as a center of this fashion. Among the more restrained were the dining room and library of Louis Comfort Tiffany's apartment. There, walls and ceilings were an olio of Japanese wallpapers and included carved antique architectural grilles called *ranma,* the ventilating transoms for *fusuma* whose placement Tiffany replicated decoratively by installing them at the top of the doorways. More opulent rooms had walls faced with imported Japanese embroideries and inset with lacquered panels encrusted with ivory and mother-of-pearl. Reviewers regarded these congested spaces as genuine, their appeal derived from their daring and therefore slightly unsettling look. A *New York Times* writer managed to sound simultaneously timorous and rapturous in describing the small, overstuffed "Japanese" parlor of William H. Vanderbilt's Fifth Avenue mansion—which featured split-bamboo paneling, beams and doorways ornamented with red lacquer and gilt, and architecture-inspired built-in shelving—as an "odd-looking room" with a ceiling "shaped like that of a real Japanese house."[8]

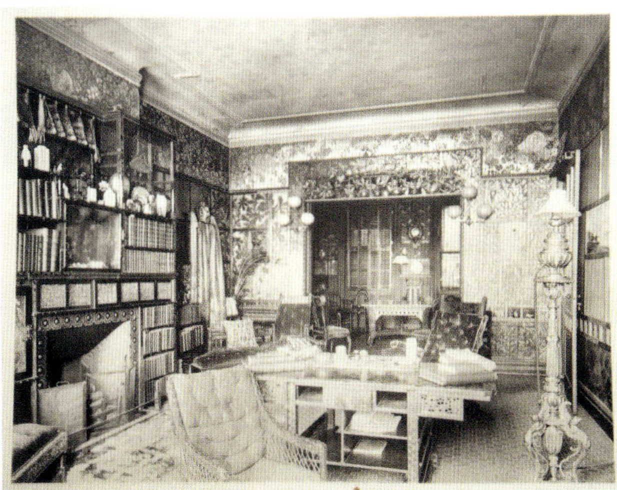

The more conventionally minded satisfied the obligatory exotic touch with carefully selected Japanese accents placed deliberatively in spots considered appropriate, such as on a dining room mantelpiece, on a parlor or library whatnot shelf, or in an entry hall. Choices typically included ceramics from Satsuma, Kutani, or Imari, calling card trays of Japanese-export cloisonné enamel, bronze vases and figurines, ivory carvings, hanging scrolls, and the occasional lacquered table or cabinet, a design of twining branches traversing a fireplace surround, or an asymmetrical detail of woodwork, while the overall atmosphere maintained a European sensibility. Typical of these more conservative spaces, the dining room of Ulysses S. Grant contained a delicate Japanese folding screen with a bird and flower motif, while his parlor displayed another mounted with fans on the top of the piano and a pair of ebonized cabinets in the ornately hybrid Victorian-Japonesque style typical of high-end art furniture export companies like Yamanaka. The dining room of another society scion displayed an elegant ceiling of roundels set with asymmetrical textile and figural motifs. The intent was not just to create a stylish effect but also to convey to visitors the sophistication and depth of character that only knowledge of such objects could imbue and to inspire the owners to live accordingly.

Below: Library fireplace, William Vanderbilt's home; as published in *Artistic Houses*, ca. 1883.

Facing, Upper Left: Calling card receiver; ca. 1890–1900; cloisonné enamel; 5.25 x 12.7 inches; unmarked. This Japanese export has a classic motif of flying cranes and water grasses.

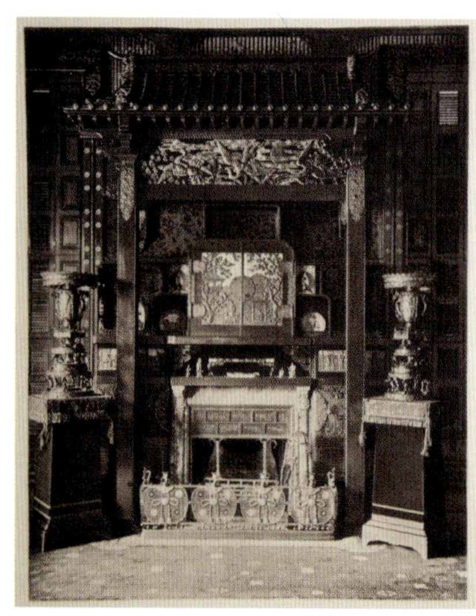

Photos of these society Japonesque interiors became highlights of the exploding art book and periodicals industry of the 1870s and '80s. The premier example, *Artistic Houses, Being a Series of Interior Views of a Number of the Most Beautiful and Celebrated Homes in the United States with a Description of the Art Treasures Contained Therein,* appeared in 1883–1884, so expensive and limited in quantity as to be primarily a self-congratulatory badge for the grandees whose homes it featured. But middle-class aspirants could avail themselves readily of less pricey but still high-end, often beautifully produced, American and English publications, among them *The Decorator and Furnisher, The Art Amateur, Art Journal, The Art Interchange, American Architect and Building News, American Art Review, The House Beautiful, House and Garden, Country Life in America,* and—somewhat later and intended for a broader demographic—*The Craftsman.* These and newspapers featured the work and commentary of top creative minds, who expounded on American design and analyzed Japanese aesthetics, craftsmanship, architecture, and other areas of interest. The illustrations of Japanese patterns, furniture, and the like that accompanied these densely written articles often lacked much if any explanation linking them to the text, virtually inviting open

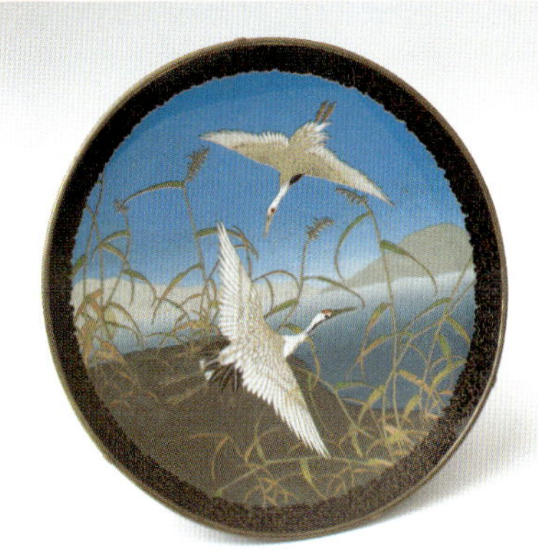

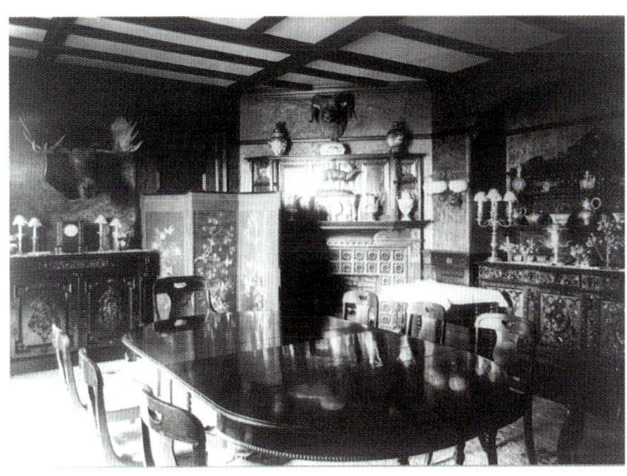

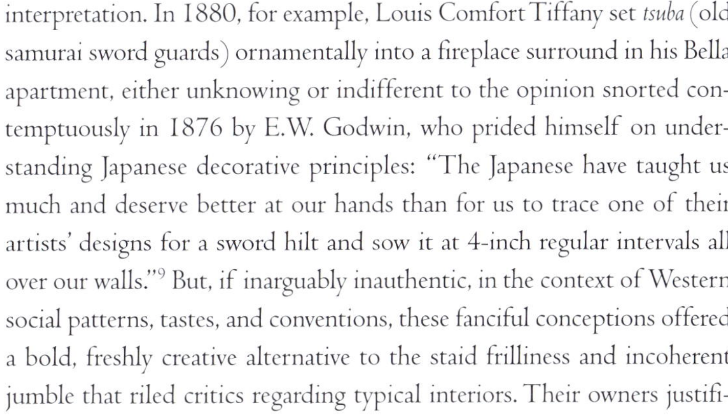

Above, Right: Japanese embroidered folding screen; dining room, President Theodore Roosevelt's home, Washington, D.C.; ca. 1904.

Below: Japanese library, William H. Vanderbilt's home; as published in *Mr. Vanderbilt's House and Collection*. This view shows the split bamboo paneling, the exposed rafters and built-in asymmetrical shelving, a plethora of decorative ceramics and bronzes, and the exotically bright color scheme of this fanciful room.

interpretation. In 1880, for example, Louis Comfort Tiffany set *tsuba* (old samurai sword guards) ornamentally into a fireplace surround in his Bella apartment, either unknowing or indifferent to the opinion snorted contemptuously in 1876 by E.W. Godwin, who prided himself on understanding Japanese decorative principles: "The Japanese have taught us much and deserve better at our hands than for us to trace one of their artists' designs for a sword hilt and sow it at 4-inch regular intervals all over our walls."[9] But, if inarguably inauthentic, in the context of Western social patterns, tastes, and conventions, these fanciful conceptions offered a bold, freshly creative alternative to the staid frilliness and incoherent jumble that riled critics regarding typical interiors. Their owners justifiably pointed to them with special pride as having met the lofty criteria of pundits with brilliance and, before taking up residence in their mansions, often opened the doors to the masses for a discreet yet public viewing.

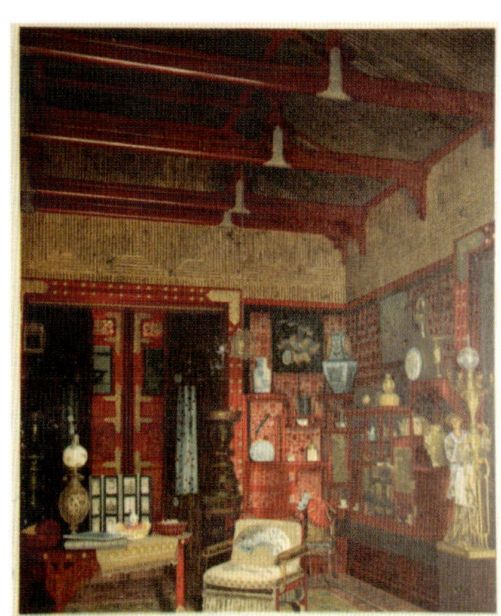

Housewives had to learn how to incorporate such heady inspiration into their more ordinary domestic domains. For this, they turned to a wide selection of publications that, with authoritative and often condescending tone, guided them through the complex shoals of "meaningless," "commonplace," "false," "pretentious," "cold," and "uniform" towards an island of physical and spiritual comfort achieved by visual virtues of harmony, softness, grace, delicacy, warmth, quiet, timelessness, and, above all, "individualism." Periodicals such as *Ladies' Home Journal* offered advice monthly. Manuals, among them Charles Eastlake's *Hints on Household Taste*, an English publication, went

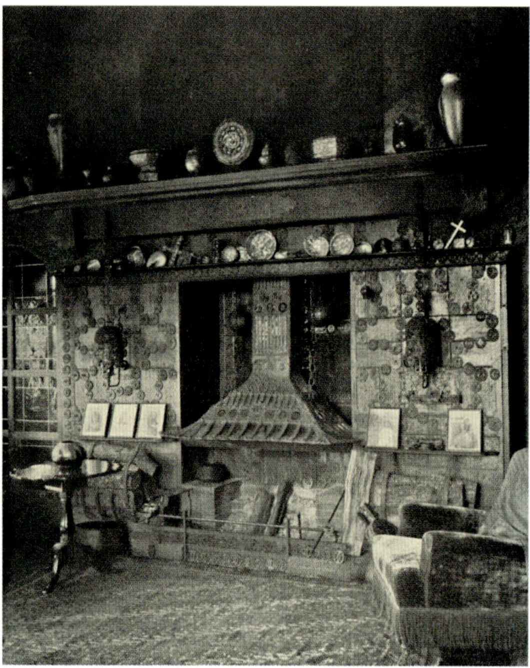

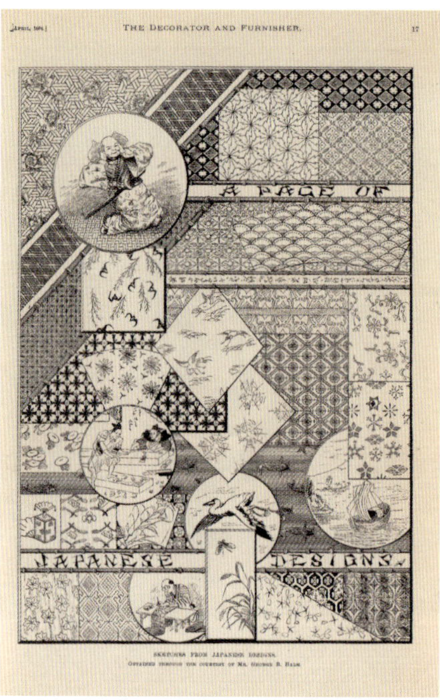

Above, Left: Fireplace surround, Louis Comfort Tiffany's Bella apartment, New York City; ca. 1880. *Tsuba* (sword guards) were embedded in the fireplace surround, a fashion that E.W. Godwin excoriated but many found exotically charming.

Above, Right: Traditional Japanese motifs; 1880s; as published by *Decorator and Furnisher* (April 1884): 17. Regularly published samplers displayed such motifs as water currents, lattice-blossoms-butterflies, cranes, bamboo, plum tree branches, stylized blossoms, banana leaves, basket weaves, overlapping circle or floral patterns, *noshi* bundles, hemp leaves, tortoiseshell, joined broken crosses, rhombuses, maple leaves on streams, *Tale of Genji* symbols, auspicious Chinese characters, and horsetail plants as models of good taste. In featuring them, the designer of this particular sampler also adopted an appropriately "Japanese" composition and font style.

into nine American editions between 1872 and 1886, and *The House Beautiful, Essays on Beds and Tables, Stools and Candlesticks* by American art critic Clarence Cook appeared in 1877 and went into multiple editions. Gustav Stickley took their ideals in new directions in 1901 with his progressive magazine *The Craftsman.*

To educate on the cultivation of artfulness and thus the capacity to recognize, appreciate, and, finally, create beauty, the manuals and home magazines alike urged homemakers to train their eyes by studying superior fine and applied arts and décor. The mandate of individualism emphasized general principles over rigid formulas. Eastlake referred neither to Japan nor Japan-inspired taste in his *Hints.* But, set on a path of guided yet free discovery, readers saw in the formalism of Japanese patterns and practical yet beautiful traditional arts and art crafts a close accord with Eastlake's idealized medievalism and his hygiene theories through which he called for sparse interiors, simple furnishings, and unified schemes. Japan-inspired asymmetrical arrangements and motifs met the criterion of "individualism." Cook looked to Japan for some of his inspiration. In addition to furniture in the "Anglo-Japanese" style originated by Godwin, he referred directly to Japanese products in the text and in illustrations of

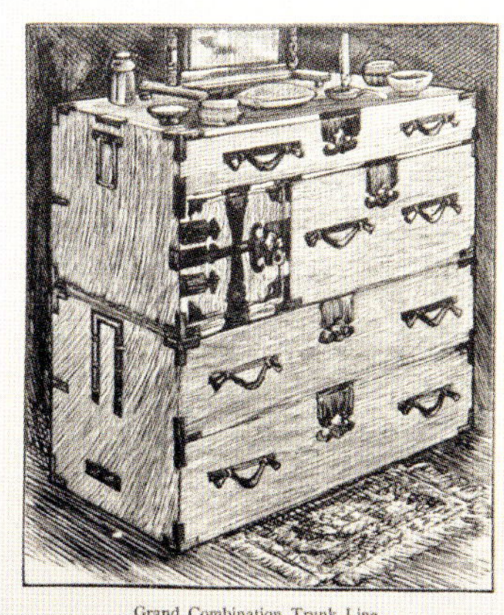

décor, including export fans, tables, and vases. Japanese traditional objects also found favor in Cook's promotion of antiques as desirable in the artistic home, making an example of a storage chest and a large folding screen depicting a landscape with figures.

Cook did not use the chest's proper name, *tansu,* or that of the screen, *byōbu,* which he notably misidentified as "Indian." In fact, as Tiffany's fanciful sword guard fireplace surround made clear, for all its importance as a look, "Japanese," much less Japan itself, was really not the point in the end. As the *Ladies' Home Journal* advised, having a Japanese room entailed not simply accumulating a lot of Japanese objects together in one space but creating "a perfect fusion of Oriental with Occidental ideas."[10] This meant the appropriation of certain visual concepts: creamy-colored carpeting to suggest *tatami* floor mats, a curtain on only one side of a window or an odd number of objects on a mantel, a minimum of furniture, or an ogee-shaped hole in the middle of a window shade. In this way, both Japan and "Japanese" acted as signatures of a look referred to as "artistic," an aspect of "taste," the defining quality of Aestheticism's domestic realm. The nod to Japanese aesthetics was one of several that met the criteria for the "artistic" interior, neo-Egyptian and "Moorish" being among other exotic styles to be combined with neo-Gothic, neo-Classic and neo-Renaissance. The Vanderbilt mansion, for example, included rooms with other schemes. But while these other "oriental" tastes peaked and quickly passed, the concerted efforts by Japanese themselves and influential enthusiasts to keep Japanese export manufactures and traditional arts at the forefront of public attention provided both time and impetus for their inherent principles to be absorbed.

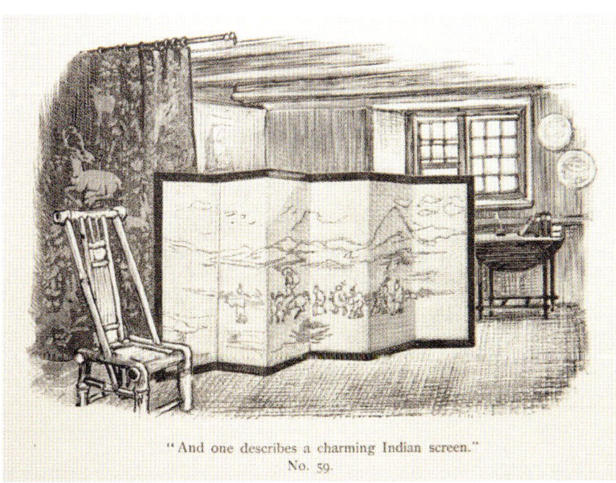

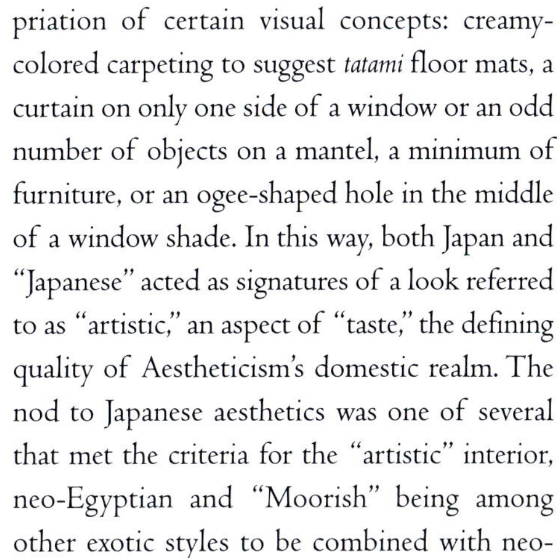

ABOVE, UPPER: TANSU; AS PUBLISHED IN *THE HOUSE BEAUTIFUL* (1881), 290. Clarence Cook went on at length about the practical virtues of this Japanese chest and even suggested that readers could have something made that would incorporate its best features, but he never identified it as Japanese or by its proper name.

ABOVE, LOWER: BYŌBU (FOLDING SCREEN), AS PUBLISHED IN *THE HOUSE BEAUTIFUL* (1881), 181. Deploring the long narrow parlors of New York abodes as "an affliction," Cook looked to the ancient Japanese custom of curtain dividers and standing folding screens as "elegant" solutions, although his book illustration misidentified the latter as "Indian."

Because the Japanese manufactures so carefully conformed to market desire, their success was a direct influence on decorating. At the St. Louis exposition in 1904, observers singled out Japan and Germany as the two countries toward which Americans should turn for lessons in household decoration. "No housewife should omit seeing . . . the beautiful Japanese living rooms. . . . Simplicity and perfect taste mark them in every detail. No stuffing of rooms with crudely designed and unnecessary furniture!"

one declared, going on to describe the "spring salon" featuring walls hung with pictures in cut velvet, shelves with cloisonné vases, and "typical Japanese furniture" as a "typical Japanese room."[11] Emphasizing wall treatments as the backbone of a room's entire scheme, critics prized Japan's textiles, papers, and imitation leathers first for their motifs: their lattices and medallions, stylized blossoms, vines, butterflies and birds, and asymmetrical liveliness did not commit the cardinal sin of denying the flatness of the wall. Secondly, they found a model for color, an essential believed to affect physical and mental well-being. The secondary and tertiary hues and dull metallic accents and backgrounds that designers first discerned in Japanese ukiyo-e prints were replicated by manufacturers in wall treatments of subtle harmonious combinations. Innumerable advertisements in all manner of publications testify to the popularity of tough matting for floors and walls, and decorative leather paper prized for neutral color, durability, and ease of cleaning, a virtue at a time when dust and dirt were believed a major source of illness.

In this decidedly mixed fashion, "Japanese" taste and Japan itself passed from the world of the stereoscope and the preciously artificial anachronistic vision offered by Japan at the international expositions into the homes of the urban middle class—that "strange mixture of romance and finance," as Oscar Wilde acerbically observed. Most of

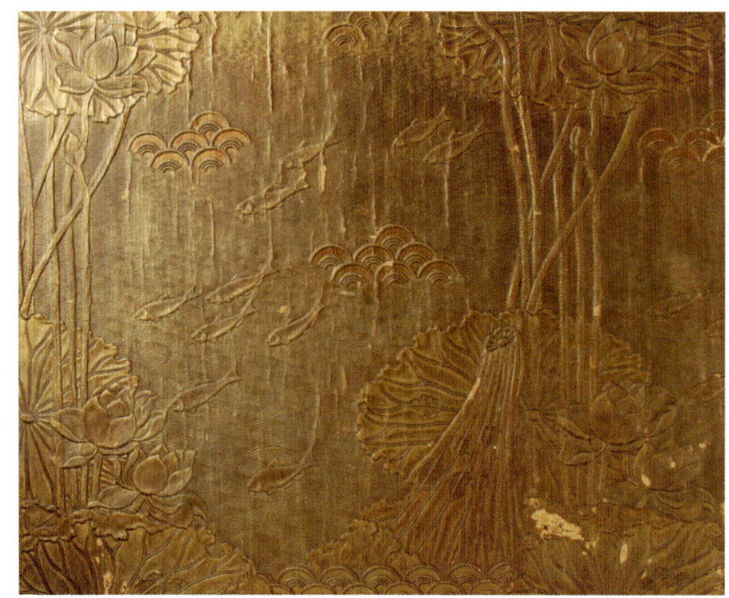

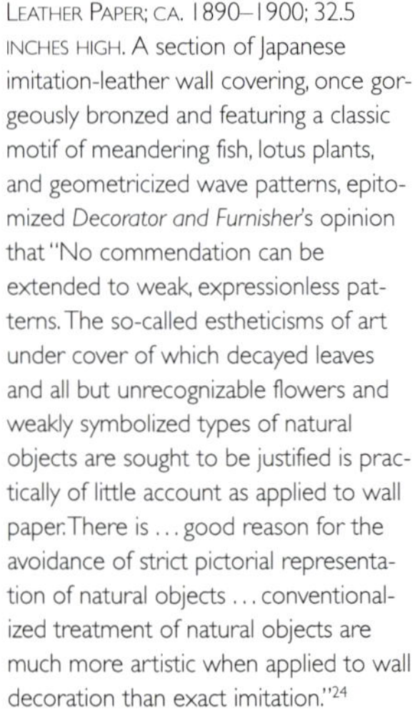

Leather Paper; ca. 1890–1900; 32.5 inches high. A section of Japanese imitation-leather wall covering, once gorgeously bronzed and featuring a classic motif of meandering fish, lotus plants, and geometricized wave patterns, epitomized *Decorator and Furnisher*'s opinion that "No commendation can be extended to weak, expressionless patterns. The so-called estheticisms of art under cover of which decayed leaves and all but unrecognizable flowers and weakly symbolized types of natural objects are sought to be justified is practically of little account as applied to wall paper. There is . . . good reason for the avoidance of strict pictorial representation of natural objects . . . conventionalized treatment of natural objects are much more artistic when applied to wall decoration than exact imitation."[24]

what tastemakers extrapolated accorded with their own requirements for an artful environment; in short, they found in Japanese taste what they needed to see.

The elite commissioned the furniture that graced their mansions. But, as insecure parvenus in the upper class and its tastes, they largely acquiesced to the makers to assure a unifying vision for furniture, carpets, upholstery, paints and wall treatments, draperies and chandeliers, mantels, mirrors, mosaics, objets d'art, and clocks. In this way, masterminds of cabinetmaking joined the ranks of those who defined style. William Vanderbilt's Japanese room, like the rest of his mansion's interior, was the crowning achievement of the top furniture designer of the Centennial Exhibition era—Christian Herter of Herter Brothers. His vision defined the homes of the Gilded Age preeminent from coast to coast, extending all the way to the White House of Ulysses S. Grant. There, Herter turned to Japanese export velvets, satins, and brocades for the upholstery and curtains, and selected a folding screen to accompany his furniture. The inclusion of such an object came naturally; Herter's showroom offered a wide selection of Japanese decorative arts obtained through none other than Hayashi Tadamasa. Herter also collaborated with Kiritsu Kosho Kaisha, whose craftsmen reportedly spent four years bringing to fruition a pair of enormous mixed-metal vases bearing an elegant Japonesque motif of chrysanthemums designed by Herter himself, a telling example of the internationalist language that Japanese aesthetic conventions had become.

Christian Herter; created in Japan by Sugiura Seitaro of Kiritsu Kosho Kaisha. Vase; 1877; 36 inches high; bronze and mixed metals. A hybrid of European and Japanese decorative motifs, this vase (one of a pair) is typical of Herter's work, a telling example of the internationalist language that Japanese aesthetic conventions had become.

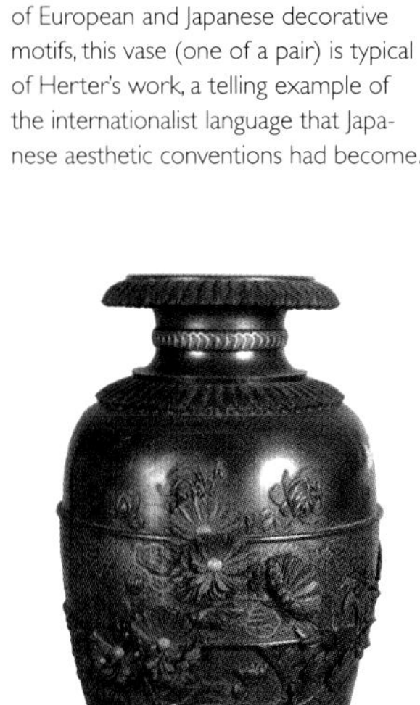

An emigrant German in New York by way of Paris, Herter embodied the cosmopolitan mind-set and tastes to which his upper-crust clientele aspired. Like the Japanese themselves, he found inspiration in the cultural mélange of the expositions—in his case Japan-tinged: Anglo-Japanese designs by Godwin, Dutch pieces hearkening back to the elegant lacquers from their days of monopoly with Japan's old regime, and, of course, Japanese furniture in export and traditional styles. Herter's appropriations accorded completely with the free-ranging outlook encouraged by the fairs, mingling Japan-derived motifs and stylistic conventions with classical, Italianate, and other elements. For him, "Japan" consisted of ebonized surfaces, carved lattices and spindles, and, above all, exquisite marquetry of birds, flowers, scrolling vines, bamboo, and, in particular, a signature

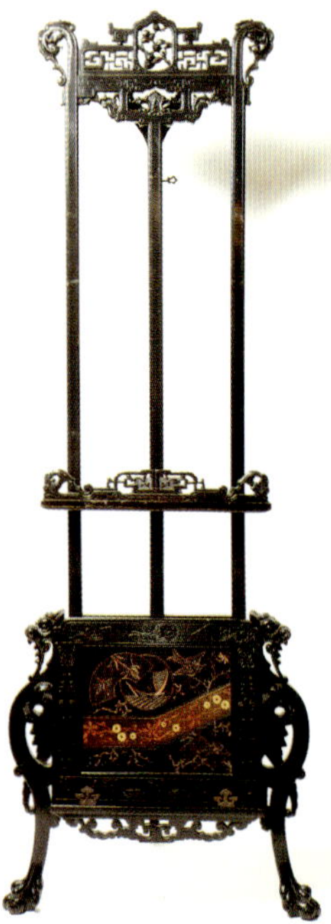

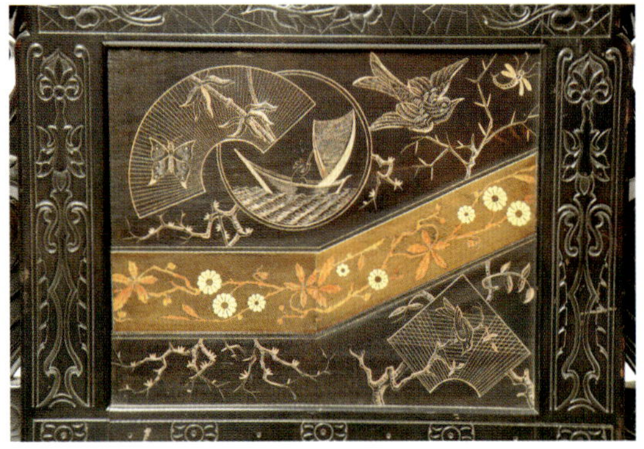

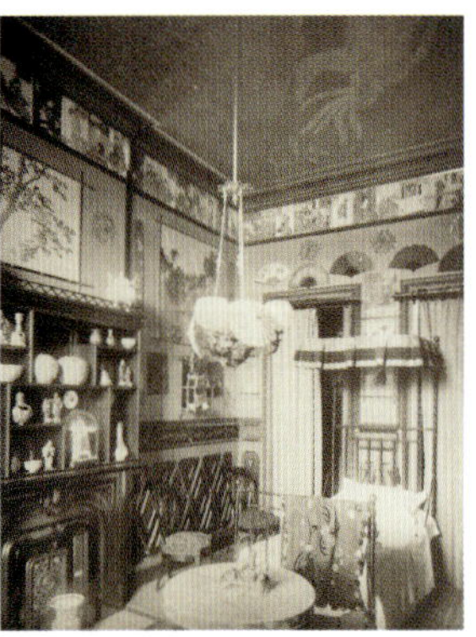

Above, Left and Center: Herter Brothers (attributed). Easel and detail; ca. 1880s; wood and marquetry; 80 inches high; unsigned. A miscellany of favorite "Japanese" features includes an ebonized finish, geometric and botanical reticulations, chimera legs, and a panel featuring random floating fans, cartouches, birds, and branches around an inlaid asymmetrically disposed *obi* (sash), whose daisy-form roundels (one of Gustave Herter's signature motifs) link this easel to Herter Brothers' designs of the 1880s.

Above, Right: Bedroom, William A. Hammond's home; 1879; as published in *Artistic Houses* (1883). One of the earliest examples of "Japanese" taste in the United States, this bedroom dazzled with an asymmetrical ceiling design in black and gold, a frieze made from mounted ukiyo-e prints, walls covered with fans, and exotically themed pictures framed in bamboo. One decorative feature much imitated, thanks to magazines that picked up the idea and affordability within reach of the most modest homes, was miniature parasols used as shades for gas lamps.

daisy form based upon a Japanese crest, or *mon*. The flat formalism of these inlays reflected "Japanese" via the influence of Dresser and Godwin. In some cases, panels dismantled from actual Japanese cabinetry or enameled or porcelain roundels found their way into his designs. In keeping with Aestheticism's pervading view, Herter's well-heeled clients considered his superbly crafted, stylistically sophisticated, and visually rich furniture as works of art in their own right.

By the early 1880s other companies aimed progressively at a middle class increasingly desirous and able to replicate on a modest scale the sophisticated décor in which the wealthy nurtured their spirits. At the top stood Kimbell & Cabus (which was, like Herter, owned by cosmopolitan Germans), followed by Cincinnati-based Mitchell & Rammelsberg, one of the era's most successful mass-manufacturers whose market stretched across the South and West of the United States. All sold furniture featuring spindles, faux bamboo, flat surfaces, dragon motifs, geometrical hardware, and other features adopted from Anglo-Japanese styles and marketed as such. Godwin himself disdained the ornate carving and applied figural motifs typical of these pieces as lacking the principles of lightness, simplicity, practicality, and cleanliness that he prized. Yet they, not Godwin's taste, set the tone of American Japonisme, not just by themselves but also through the model interiors featured at international exhibitions and in retail showrooms that educated their clientele as to arrangements and accoutrements for a tasteful décor. For their part, Japanese manufacturers saw opportunity: it was this ingrained American taste for *horror vacui* that inspired Yamanaka & Company's bizarrely oxymoronic Horiuji sofa.

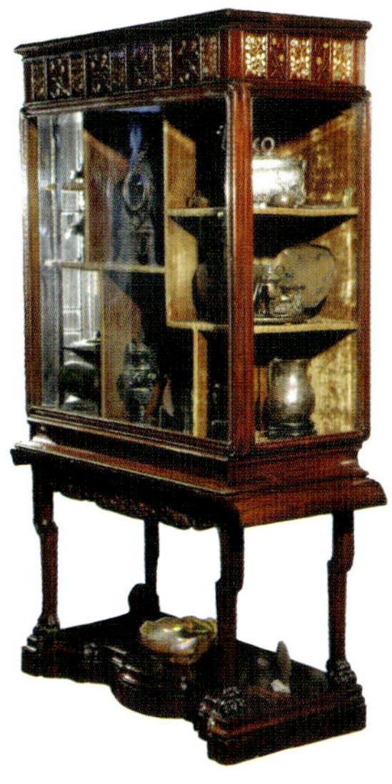

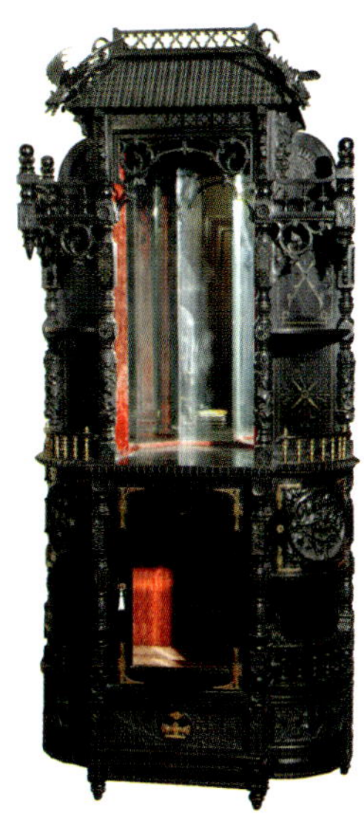

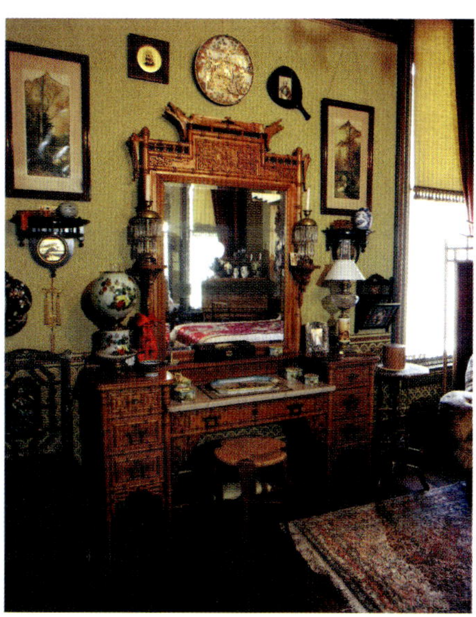

ABOVE, LEFT: HERTER BROTHERS (ATTRIBUTED). CABINET WITH FRIEZE; CA. 1880–1890; 73 INCHES HIGH; UNSIGNED. An eclectic combination typical of Herter work, this vitrine of cherry wood features an upper cabinet of "Japanese"-style asymmetrical shelving and an inlaid ivory and mother-of-pearl frieze of flowering stems alternating with ordinary garden pea vines; it sits upon a base of conventional Western taste.

ABOVE, CENTER: KIMBELL AND CABUS. MIRRORED CABINET; CA. 1880–1890; EBONIZED WOOD; 84 INCHES HIGH. Accented with brass spindles and fittings, this cabinet is an orgy of carved and engraved exotic references seen as "Japanese"—most notably, its "pagoda" roof surmounted by fantastical birds and the two beautifully carved roundels displaying a bird hunting through flowering shrubbery, stalking his butterfly prey on one side and capturing it on the other.

ABOVE, RIGHT: MITCHELL AND RAMMELSBERG. LADIES' DRESSING TABLE; CA. 1880–1890; CHERRY; 86 × 63.5 INCHES. This table displays faux bamboo legs and detailing that includes writhing serpents, birds, and a flowering branch in bas-relief at the top of the mirror frame.

For the vast majority of Americans, the Japan Craze, despite its intensity, never amounted to more than dilettantish fascination in the quest for the artful interior and the identity it imbued. Most ignored taste arbiters' directives to be sparing. Preferring the example of high society and of furniture companies, people availed themselves of tourist trade screens, fans, and parasols in brash colors, garish embroideries, photographs, and tacky porcelains found at department stores and specialty shops. Those who could afford it delighted in bronzes, lacquers, and ceramics of extraordinary technical virtuosity. They mingled imported Japanese Western-oriented objects with Western-made Japonesque works, exotically patterned wallpaper, and draperies. The exuberance largely spent itself with the economic collapse of 1893. Japanese export manufacturers faltered at this moment, failing to recognize the transformation in mood and lifestyle. From this point onward, the vogue waned, along with its companion exoticisms and Aesthetic taste. But Okakura Kakuzō and his circle had correctly read the direction that two decades of exposure and education had taken American talents and taste, unveiling the ideal model at the symbolic divide between past and future at the Chicago Columbian exhibition. This was the Hōōden. The masterstroke of this building and its contents ensured that Japanese art would remain at the crossroads of American architecture, applied arts, and design at a time of innovation. It was integral to the emergence of major overlapping initiatives in the

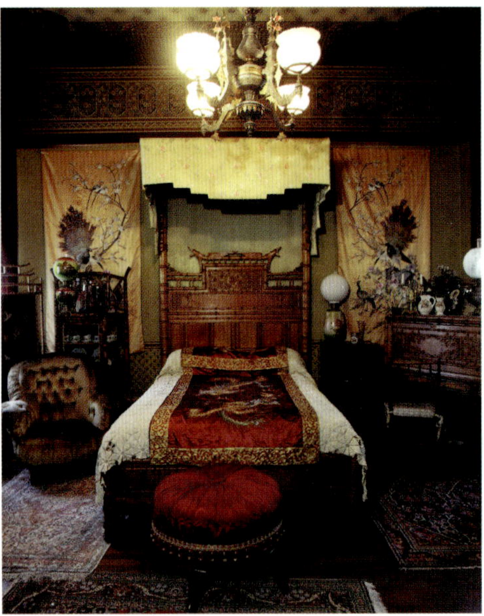

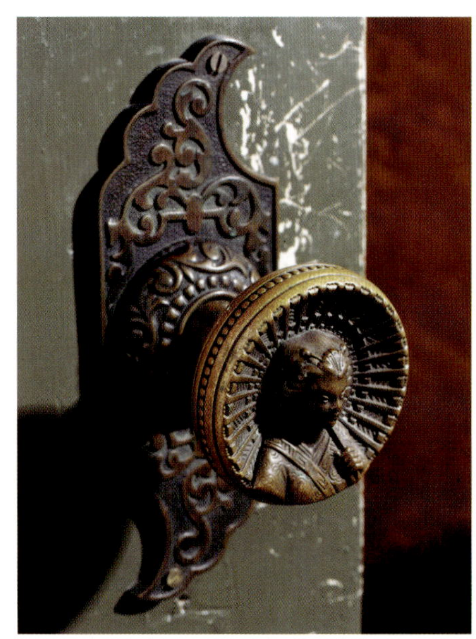

Mitchell and Rammelsberg. Bedroom suite; ca. 1880–1890. / Doorknob ca. 1885; 2.15 inches diameter. In the "Japanese taste," this room is accented by period Japanese-export embroidered peacock hangings and mottled bamboo cabinets; a doorknob featuring YumYum from *The Mikado* is one of a large array of Japan-inspired door fittings made by companies such as Russel & Erwin Manufacturing Co. that enabled rooms to be thematically correct to the last detail.

establishment of an American style—the Arts and Crafts movement, early Art Nouveau, and the first stirrings of modernism.

Economic upheaval following the Panic of 1893 accelerated several trends with far-reaching consequences to the American home: A sharp lowering of magazine prices to keep the publishing industry alive actually caused it to expand. New magazines spread ideas about taste as never before. In a change of even greater impact, middle-class matrons before the Panic reigned over their homes, directing several employees to the tedious maintenance of their cluttered interiors; their daughters often had only one servant or even none. The altered domestic environment required a new taste, efficient to maintain but still possessed of aesthetic loftiness to infuse the family and bestow dignity upon the housewife who created and maintained it. The return of prosperity and optimism renewed desire for a quintessentially American-style representative of an increasingly assertive middle class's sense of itself as the true face of American society. The quest found a natural resolution in melding the simple ideals of Ruskin's medieval revivalism with the practicality and restrained elegance of traditional Japanese interiors and their contents. Attraction for the hybrid furniture and bibelots of Japan's export industry began to wane. The contrast had been made vividly real for the thousands who visited the Hōōden in Chicago. The more curious, especially architects and designers, learned details through Edward S. Morse's authoritative *Japanese Homes and Their Surroundings,* which became one of the most influential resources of the era.

These trends unified in the emergence of the American Arts and Crafts movement, guided by the voice of Gustav Stickley in his visionary magazine *The Craftsman* beginning in 1901. Through his own essays and those of his contributors, an exceptionally diverse group that included John La Farge and Bunkio Matsuki, Stickley articulated an internationalist philosophy grounded on the theories of his predecessors Ruskin, Eastlake, and others: the home as a moral nucleus, a flawed design harmed while a harmoniously beautiful domestic environment uplifted accordingly, and the importance of individualism of expression. But unlike Ruskin, Eastlake, and even Cook, Stickley placed Japan high among his many inspirations. Over its sixteen years of publication, *The Craftsman* offered its readers more articles specifically about Japan than almost any other nation, on everything from the arts of ceramics, damascene, and gardening to the customs of funerals and sake drinking, as well as references to Japanese aesthetics scattered throughout writings on virtually every other subject. *The Craftsman* pointed to the arts of Japanese medievalism as models of utility, balance, and logic. It presented Japanese prints as guides to ideal color schemes, the "utmost subtlety" and "intimacy of tone" of their muted greens, blues, grays, yellows, pinks, and browns—"the despair of the Occidental decorator."[12] These became hallmarks of Arts and Crafts color, while the prints themselves, along with folding screens and paintings, were suggested as the perfect accoutrements of the

HŌŌDEN INTERIORS; 1893; AS PUBLISHED IN *THE HŌŌDEN (PHOENIX HALL), AN ILLUSTRATED DESCRIPTION OF THE BUILDINGS ERECTED BY THE JAPANESE GOVERNMENT AT THE WORLD'S COLUMBIAN EXPOSITION, JACKSON PARK, CHICAGO.* Two rooms, both described as "libraries" by Okakura Kakuzō in the booklet he made available to the interested, revealed the extremes of Japanese taste in the most authentic way most Americans would ever see. The flamboyant fans and floral motifs on the *fusuma* (sliding walls) of the interior known as the *shosai* (right), an opulence that had long inspired designers of the waning Aesthetic era, contrasted starkly with the restraint of its twin (left), whose calm style based upon Zen Buddhist aesthetics inspired the growing Arts and Crafts movement to emphasize plain and unfinished materials and the geometric beauty of structural elements.

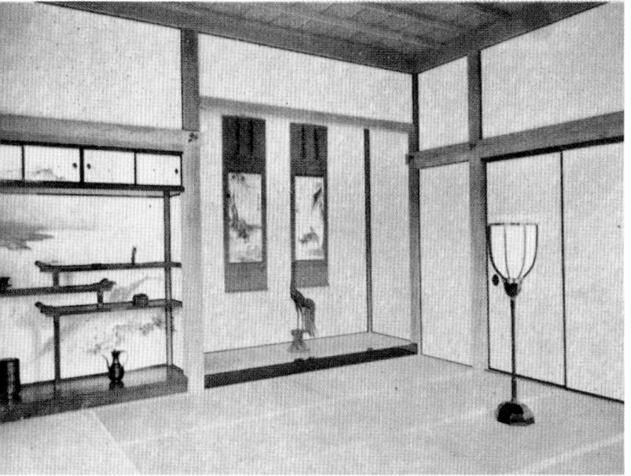

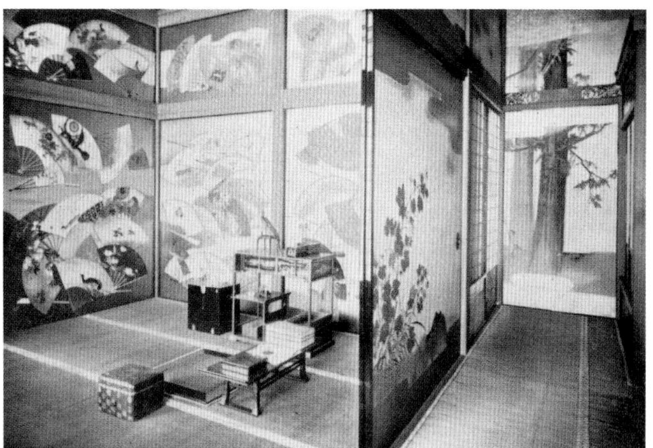

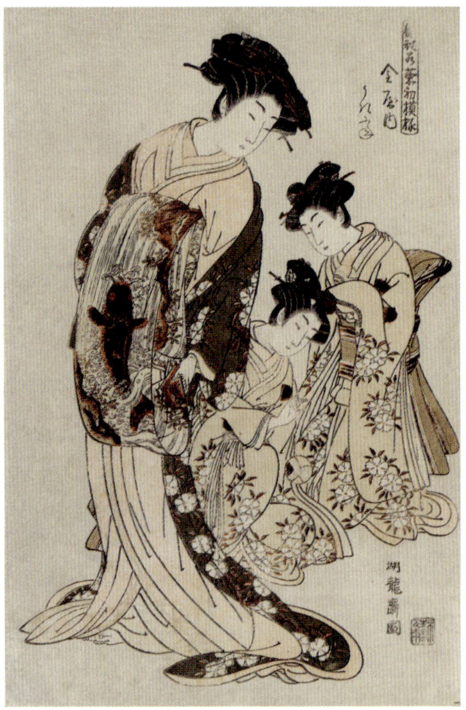

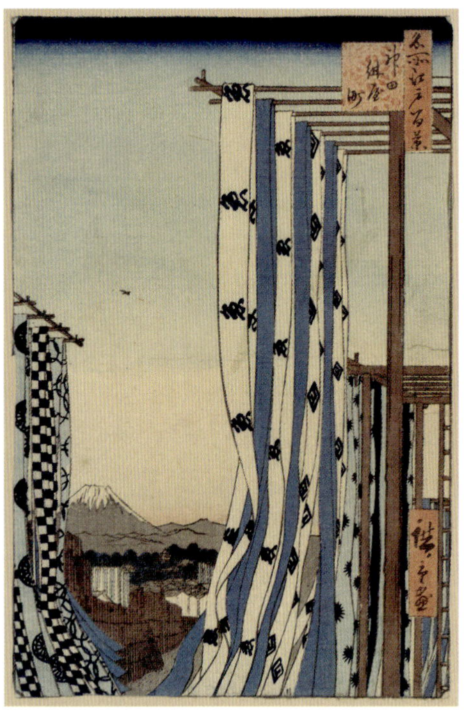

Above, Left: Isoda Koryūsai. *Kanaya uchi ukifune (Ukifune of the house of Kanaya)*; ukiyo-e woodblock print; ca. 1772–1780; 14.96 × 10.04 inches; from the series *Hinagata wakano no hatsumoyō (New Designs of Young Models)*.

Above, Right: Utagawa Hiroshige. *Kanda Konyachō (Dyers' Street in Kanda)*; ukiyo-e woodblock print; 1857; 13.94 × 9.72 inches; from the series *Meisho Edo hyakkei (One Hundred Famous Views of Edo)*, published by Uoya Eikichi.

tasteful décor. They excoriated contemporary Japan as "evilly influenced" by Western commercialism while extolling traditional, ordinary—even poor—Japanese as the embodiments of the Arts and Crafts ideal: "Where a nation of people express their highest spiritual attainment through an art or craft, the workman will inevitably achieve fitting surroundings for his toil, and all unconsciously the laborer himself and his workroom will illustrate the beauty he finds in his own soul . . . labor and beauty thus became completely interwoven. . . ."[13] Stickley had ample precedent in looking to the Japanese past as a beacon for the Western future. But the cost of *The Craftsman* placed these ideas within reach of people of modest means for the first time, enticingly combined with his view that tasteful and therefore morally uplifting design grew naturally out of honest labor, deserved by those who labored for the common good; and that the ideal they fostered in their home lives projected outward, giving impetus to the life of the nation. In this way, idealism about Japanese tradition became linked to a wider idealism about American national character.

Perhaps most important, *The Craftsman* went head-to-head with a persistent shibboleth that Japan possessed "no architecture." Conventional critics saw its stylistic links to the Asian mainland as derivative, its reliance upon wood and paper as trivial while dismissing its magnificent stone castles as "big curios," some going so far as to say, ". . . all art is based on architecture—Japan has no architecture—therefore Japan has no art."[14] *The Craftsman* singled out Japanese architecture as sharing pride of place with that of ancient Greece and medieval Europe, considered the world's greatest, and standing alone as "the most perfect mode in wood the world has known."[15] Turning "derivative" on its head, Stickley proposed it as the model for America, due to Japan's uniqueness as the "vortex of the East,"[16] the pure distillate of a society that had drawn to itself the entirety of Asian culture, therefore embodying everything essential to the modern. To his mind this translated into "honesty," simplicity in construction, rejection of false ornamentation, the "meeting of all actual requirements in the simplest and most direct way,"[17] and visual incorporation into the surrounding landscape. *The Craftsman* considered Japanese appreciation for the physical qualities of materials an aesthetic to be prized, pointing especially to the focus on the subtle beauties of wood grain, texture, and color, but also noted with approval that even mundane components like plaster benefited from sensitive attention. He considered the absence of furnishings, subtle color schemes, and wide-open spaces a laudable austerity conducive to fostering a "perfect artistic feeling" and a sense of repose. Unsurprisingly, the inhabitants of such interiors represented ordinary Japanese of old-fashioned values—frugal, warm, sincere, and devoid of artifice. In this way, Japanese traditional architecture became the metaphor for its occupants and a symbol of what its essential qualities could accomplish for the spirit of ordinary Americans. Looking stubbornly backward to an idealized Japanese past, *The Craftsman*, like many other commentaries, dismissed out-of-hand contemporary Japanese architecture that was responding increasingly to the needs and aspirations of a modernizing society and, by implication, dismissed those who lived in it as well.

TABLE; CA. 1900; 20 INCHES HIGH. Combining the simple sturdy construction and restrained line of traditional American cottage furniture with delicate artistry in a skilled replication of floral motifs inspired by Japanese textile patterns, the union of practicality and aesthetic sensibility in this occasional table is the epitome of Arts and Crafts philosophy.

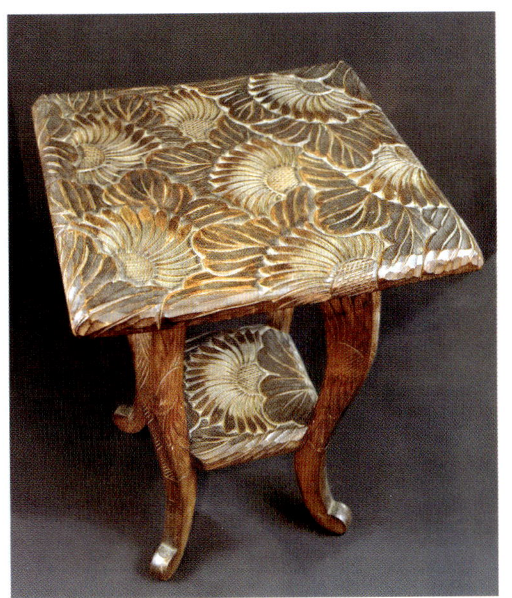

Stickley made his concept of simple artful living coherent and real for readers with building plans and interiors—as often as not, small, tidy, and simple reflections of his ideological emphasis on the working class. Its apotheosis, the bungalow, became the defining image of the Arts and Crafts movement. Modeled on the bare-bones rest houses of the British Raj, the bungalow was infused with Japanese architectural concepts not only due to theories like Stickley's but also thanks to emigrant Japanese laborers who left their mark on details of construction and sometimes in its restrained ornamentation. By the end of the nineteenth century, "simplicity" came to be a byword for "Japanese."[18] The bungalow suited the mind-set and everyday life of American society overall in the aftermath of the Panic of 1893. Beneath their millions, many of the wealthy wanted to see themselves as simple and unaffected working individuals. In this way Stickley's influence extended upward, with the bungalow reaching an elegant and expensive epitome at the hands of the talented brother architect-engineers Charles and Henry Greene of Pasadena. Wealthy patrons allowed them to indulge in the highest standards and to develop a cohesive vision that became a model of superior craftsmanship and forward-thinking design. To paraphrase an old adage, "modesty is in the eye of the beholder."

The Greenes are thought to have found revelation in the Hōōden at the 1893 Chicago exhibition. It sparked a fascination for Japan otherwise satisfied only from photos, journals, collections, and other later fairs such as the California Midwinter Exposition of 1894 in San Francisco and, above all, the Louisiana Purchase International Exposition of 1904.[19] Charles Greene in particular immersed himself, collecting sword guards and delving into the esoterica of Buddhism, of which he declared himself an adherent. Japan's tradition-based buildings at the fairs allowed him to bring his engineer's eye to a close study of Japanese architecture that he likely combined with concepts from Morse's book on Japanese homes. And, given his inclinations, he well may have found direction from one other source: the deceptively modest *The Book of Tea* by Okakura Kakuzō, the urbane intellectual mastermind of the Hōōden itself. In it, Okakura presented the first explanation in English of the philosophical underpinnings of Asian aesthetics; his elucidation of the tea ceremony revealed for the first time that asymmetry, proportion, simplicity, muted color, austerity, and sense of repose were not mere conventions but products of a deep moral, ethical, and spiritual foundation having all the profundity of anything in the West. Okakura wrote *The Book of Tea* to educate his friends among the Boston elite, but the moment was timely: thanks to its brevity, clarity, and highly readable style, its influence rapidly spread. In continuous new editions and translations, *The Book of Tea* became

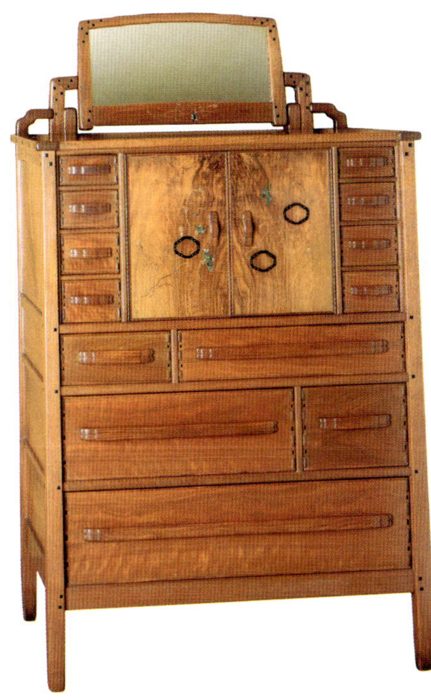

Above: Charles Greene. Chiffonier; 1908; black walnut, oak, ebony, glass, various minerals, and metal; 62 × 37.25 × 21 inches; repository: University of Southern California, The Gamble House. Greene avidly collected sword guards and turned to them as inspiration for a number of designs in the Gamble House. He replicated not only their shapes in furniture and cabinet glass but also their decorative motifs, which adapted Japanese-style geometric formalism and random objects to Western designs.

Right: Box; late Meiji to early Taisho periods, ca. 1900–1920; lacquer; 9 × 8 × 4.5 inches. A *nuri bako* features a design of scattered *tsuba* (sword guards) and other samurai weaponry accessories.

the essential guide for the adaptation of Japanese principles to Western as well as American design. In the process, it also introduced the concepts of Zen and Taoism to Western minds, sure to have been immensely attractive to Charles Greene.

In all of this, the Greene brothers found features ideal to dwellings and life in the Southern California climate. Their 1908 masterpiece, the vacation home of industrialist David B. Gamble, features the characteristic deep eaves, low-slung layered roofs, deeply recessed porches, simple balustrades, and naturally aged wood typical of Japanese religious structures and farmhouses. These made astute choices for ventilation and for protection from the sun. They also imbued rustic elegance and ease. Inside, true to Stickley's vision, the natural finish of abundant woodwork, unadorned neutral-colored walls, and a lack of clutter produced an atmosphere of restfulness and coolness. Built-in storage made for efficient use of space and clean interior lines, holding furniture to a minimum. And compared to the era's typical homes, the Greenes' asymmetrical arrangement of rooms to one another offered flexibility in furnishing and function, adaptability to relaxed social patterns, and better ventilation. Asymmetry also allowed the building's shape to conform to the contours of the site, a Japanese-derived convention so important to the two architects that they engineered the driveway invisible from the street.[20]

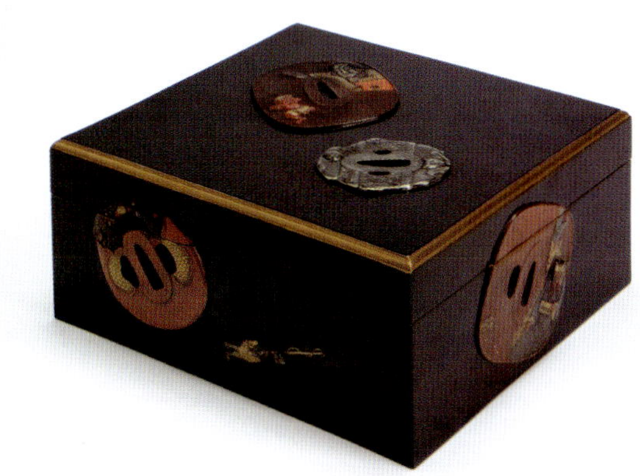

In addition to these practical innovations, the Greenes also indulged in exquisite embellishment. In the front hall, a California live oak in luminous stained glass spreading across the entry suggests as its inspiration the pines backed by gold leaf, traversing the walls of Japanese samurai palace interiors, and, indeed, such motifs were among those ornamenting the central hall of the Hōōden and other buildings that modeled such aristocratic spaces. Exposed ceiling beams, stairway structural components strapped with steel, and decoratively exposed peg heads drew inspiration from castle interiors. More unconventional adaptations occur throughout, in the sword guard shape of the table and cabinet glass in the dining room, in the switch plates and door pulls, and in the inlay of the bedroom furniture designed specifically for the house.

It was this successful union of ideas from Japan with the "nonnegotiables" of Western lifestyle that made the Gamble House so comfortable for all its "Japanese" qualities. Amazingly forward thinking, it marked the beginning of modernism. But not straying far from the admonitions of the *Ladies' Home Journal,* the Gamble House design retained the Western conception of a home in every key way: rooms dedicated to specific functions like dining and sleeping, solid walls and closing doors to ensure privacy, generous spaces, curtained windows, and the standard component of tables, beds, bureaus, and chairs. A book of the time described the Greenes' work in general as "the utmost limits to which Japanese architecture could be stretched and still meet American requirements."[21]

It took Frank Lloyd Wright to create a genuine revolution in the American interior, an achievement of which he was quite aware. Wright prized the romantic myth of the lone genius but admitted to a sole muse: ukiyo-e prints. He explained to one client, "I have never confided to you the extent to which the Japanese print per se has inspired me. I never got over my first experience with it, and I shall never, probably, recover. I hope I shan't."[22] Wright adored ukiyo-e. He collected them, decorated his homes and studios with them, and made a lot of money dealing in them. His draftsmen styled presentation drawings after them. It is no coincidence that he counted Shugio Hiromichi, who had introduced Japanese prints to the American public, among his closest friends. In writings Wright distilled exactly what ukiyo-e taught him: first, geometric structure that organizes parts into a larger unity, creating an organic whole; second, a supreme principle of simplification, eliminating the insignificant to produce a sense of drama.[23] He said that "to dramatize a thing is to do precisely what a

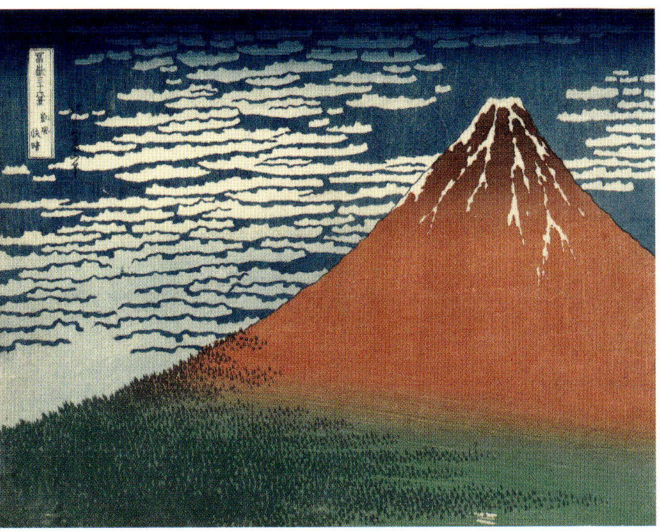

Katsushika Hokusai. *Gaifū kaisei (Fine Wind, Clear Weather,* also known as *Red Fuji)*; nishiki-e woodblock print; Edo period, about 1830–1831; 9.61 × 15 inches; from the series *Fugaku sanjūrokkei (Thirty-Six Views of Mount Fuji)*, published by Nishimura Yohachi (Eijudō). Courtesy of the Museum of Fine Art, Boston: William S. and John T. Spaulding Collection (21.675b).

Japanese does with these prints. . . . Well, now, buildings can be like that, too . . ."[24] Organic organization and elimination of the insignificant had been the central tenets of Japan-inspired innovators as early as E. W. Godwin, but Wright's appreciation for the natural drama of Japanese aesthetics allowed him to bring these previously recognized qualities to a new level. As a trio, they are hallmarks of modernism.

Ego kept Wright from admitting anything other than ukiyo-e as an influence. But his early experience, visual evidence, and even technological impetus suggest otherwise. Japanese architecture was a model too. Wright had apprenticed with the gifted and influential Louis Sullivan, a man well-acquainted with Japanese art who had worked with firms that designed homes with Japonesque details. Wright also knew Ernest Fenollosa, with whom it would have been impossible that the subject of Japan would not have come up. And he encountered Japanese architecture exactly as the Greene brothers likely had, at the Hōōden in 1893. There, like the Greenes, he saw in material fact the concepts that he previously could only have read of in recently published books. Wright is known to have visited the Hōōden countless times over the fifty-three years it stood.

When comparing the exterior of the Hōōden to Wright's early Prairie-style homes, parallels are obvious: steeply pitched roofs, wings arranged at sharp angles to one another, deep eaves, large covered entry, and the contrast of stucco and exposed wood beams. But the Hōōden offered other ideas. In addition to décor details in the arrangement of hanging scrolls, furniture, tea implements, and ceramics displayed in its three interiors, he saw the structural concepts of modular design, partition walls, sliding door panels, exposed support beams, asymmetrical room configurations, open flowing space, an overall horizontality, as well as simplicity and plainness of materials, and opulent ones expressively employed. All had been noted by others and would be adapted with skill by the Greenes. But as Wright himself noted, he found an added asset in the dramatic air of these spaces that united all of these elements. This must have inspired him in completely rethinking interior spaces.

Interiors had become a new and interesting design challenge. It was not only due to the increasing informality of domestic life and democratic social ideals that so inspired Stickley, it was also thanks to technology. Plate glass had appeared in the mid-1880s, with new possibilities for window size, interior light, and even interior walls. Even more important, central heating had come into common use by the late nineteenth century, ending the need to enclose every room and to warm it with a fireplace. With these and other innovations, architects literally could think out of the box for the first time. But few besides Wright had the imagination to do it, and his frequent visits to the Hōōden suggest that its open flowing interiors had a great deal to do with his conceptual leap.

One such interior, the Tokugawa room, replicated the reception room of the samurai aristocrat and, not coincidentally, occupied the central space in the Hōōden complex. Wright's early revolutionary design for the living room of the Darwin D. Martin House of Buffalo, New York, draws strikingly and creatively on the primary feature of such spaces: dramatic flowing openness around a single, stationary visual anchor. Expansive and with almost no walls, Wright's focal point is a freestanding fireplace dividing the living room from the front entry. Enveloped by a rambling wisteria vine executed in gold and colored-glass mosaic, the fireplace bears an uncanny resemblance to the sole unmovable wall of Japanese interiors—an ornamental alcove called a *tokonoma*. In the most formal of these spaces, the tokonoma is completely decorated, often with tree or flowering plant imagery against a backdrop of gold. The wisteria itself, a classic Japanese

Below, Left: Central Hall (the grand *Jodan-no-ma*) of the Hōōden; 1893; as published in *The Hōōden (Phoenix Hall), An Illustrated Description of the Buildings Erected by the Japanese Government at the World's Columbian Exposition, Jackson Park, Chicago.* This view shows Japanese décor at its most opulent and palatial, resplendent with wall paintings, ornately carved, gilded, and lacquered *ranma*, coffered ceilings, and the *tokonoma* (alcove) with its stylized tree in brilliant color against a golden ground of the type that may have inspired architects such as Wright and the Greene brothers.

Below, Right: Living room, Darwin D. Martin House; 1905. The view of this gracefully proportioned, sparsely furnished room shows its anchor and focal point: the freestanding fireplace ornamented with wisteria in gold and multicolored mosaic.

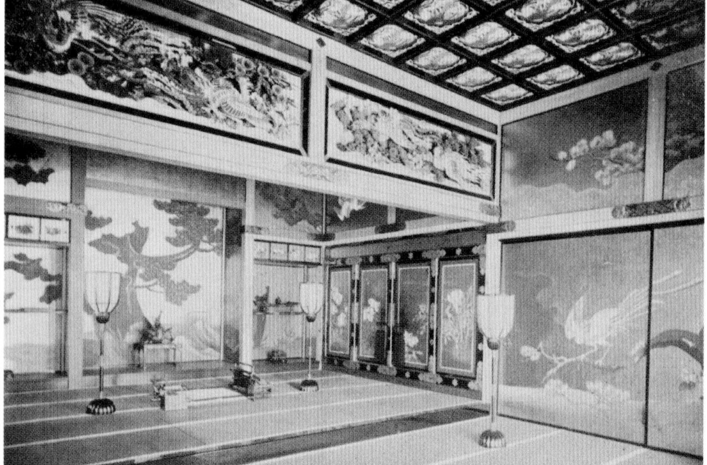

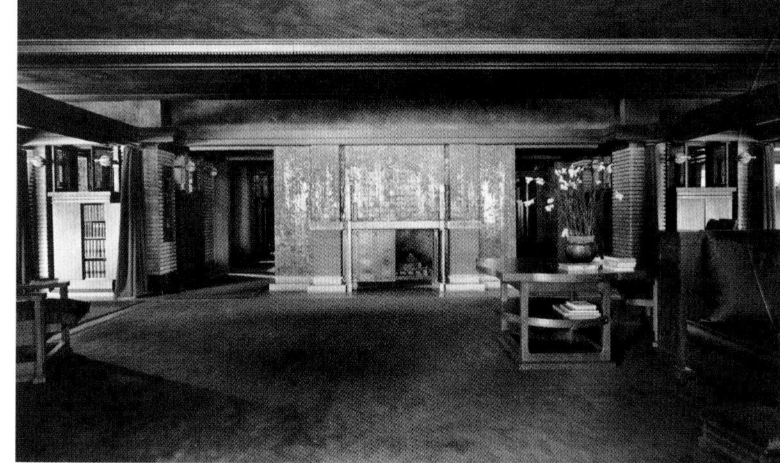

motif, was among those recorded as appearing on the walls of the Hōōden's Tokugawa room. In Wright's hands it became a unifying theme for the Martin House; besides the fireplace, he adapted it in abstract form to the stained glass windows and planted it in the gardens. Also similar to such Japanese interiors is the horizontality of the space, including the beam of wood that divides the ceiling, whose placement strongly resembles that of the *ranma,* or transom. Wright designated scant furnishings—a very few, very simple chairs and tables. Finally, with the open spacial flow into the adjacent library, Wright adapted the Japanese manner of erasing the distinction between one space and another, the inflow of light from the other room arguably taking a cue from the absence of exterior walls to the outdoors. Completed in 1905 just before Wright's first trip to Japan and preceding even Okakura's *Book of Tea,* the most likely source of inspiration other than architecture books would have been the Hōōden.

The Martin House was built three years before the Greenes built the Gamble House, but it looked way beyond. More telling is to compare it to Whistler's Peacock Room. The mere twenty-nine years from one to the other witness a true transformation. With delighted abandon, Whistler borrowed from everything that caught his eye, yet the Peacock Room did not essentially differ from others of its time: it had an elegant surface that set it apart from and above its peers. Wright conceived the Martin House with the eye of a deeply thoughtful purist, paring both Western and Japanese concepts to bare bones and combining them to create something fundamentally new. The difference reflects the genius of Wright. It is also due to the power of Japanese art when allowed to speak for itself rather than being made to answer to Western ideas of the exotic.

1. Smith 1875, 161, 162.
2. As quoted in Gere 2000, 43.
3. Ibid., 62.
4. Merrill 1998, 222.
5. Ibid., 65.
6. Ibid., 238.
7. Ibid., 212.
8. *New York Times,* August 25, 1881.
9. As quoted in Banham 1999, 294.
10. *Ladies' Home Journal,* October 1895.
11. Francis 1913, 398.
12. *The Craftsman,* November 1903, 136.
13. *The Craftsman,* February 1910, 517.
14. *International Studio* 1, no. 3 (1896): 140.
15. *The Craftsman,* May 1906, 198.
16. Ibid., 198.
17. Ibid., 192.
18. Lancaster 1983, 75.
19. Based upon recent research by Bruce Smith.
20. Mackinson 1998, 118.
21. Lancaster 1983; reprint 1963, 109.
22. Meech 2001, 231–32.
23. Ibid., 70.
24. Ibid., 72.

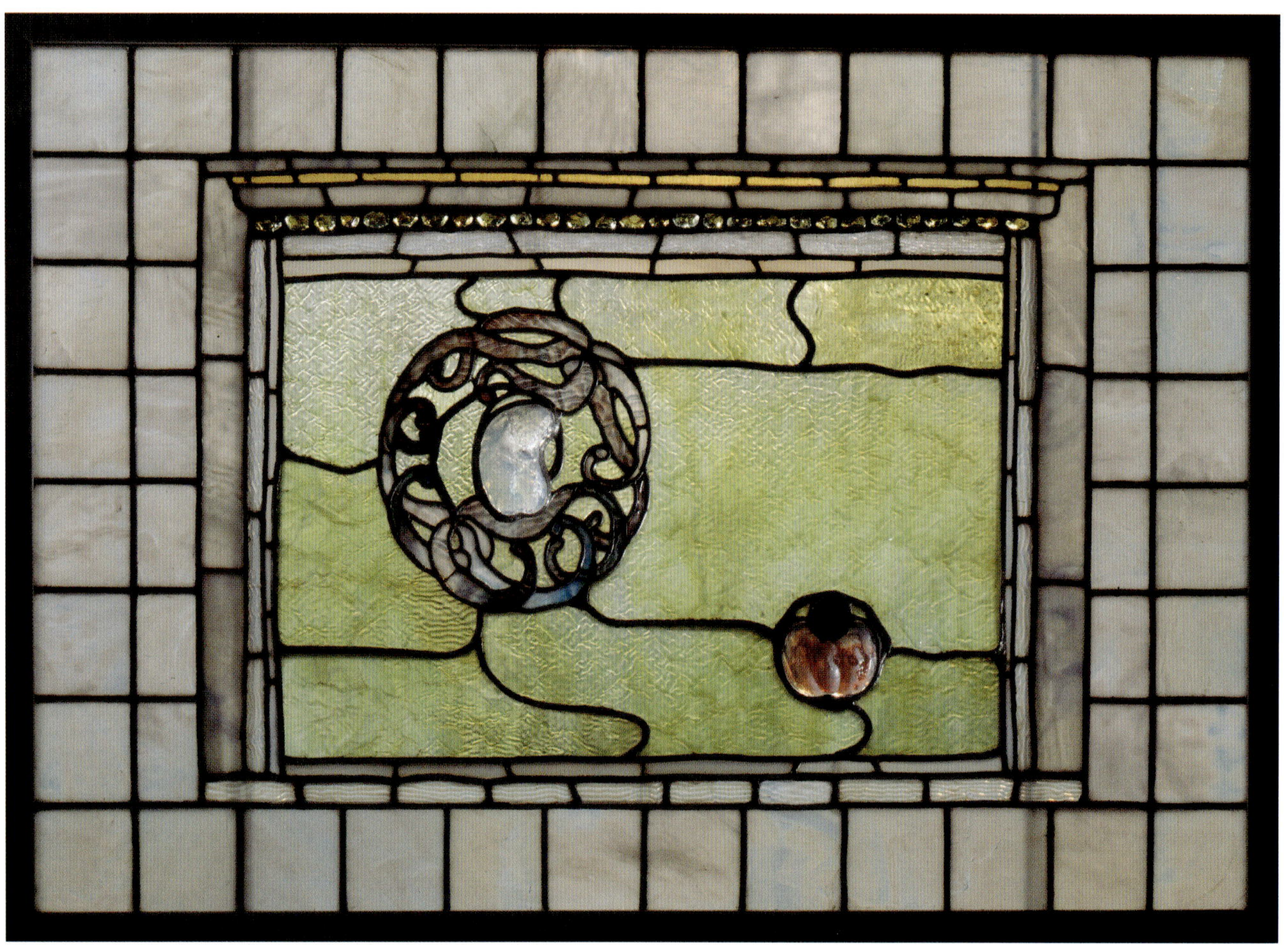

Louis Comfort Tiffany, Tiffany Glass and Decorating Company. "Tsuba"; glass window; 1882–1900; leaded opaline glass; 31.5 x 43.5 inches. Tiffany carried through his interest in *tsuba* (sword guards) into his designs. One particular favorite not only inspired this seemingly abstract window design but also was used directly to create decorative impressions in ornamental glass tiles.

6

Glass and Textiles

The Creative Assimilation

The Japanese have very appropriately been called the "French of the East."[1]

From the onset of Aesthetic taste around 1876 through the Arts and Crafts movement and into the emergent modernism of the twentieth century's opening decades, American architects and interior designers prized stained glass. And while Japanese motifs and concepts initially had no place in such a quintessentially European art form, they became indispensable to its transformation from staid antiquarianism into a vigorous, secular decorative art and, even more, an identifiably American one—perhaps the first to earn a legitimate claim to exerting international influence of its own. The relationship between stained glass and ideas from Japan was truly representative of the era's internationalist mentality that uprooted foreign things to mingle with others in a swirl of creative abandon.

No other material matched stained glass in attaining the era's cherished twin goals of utility and beauty: It provided privacy and masked unpleasant views in towns and cities increasingly clogged with vehicles and blighted by factories and miles of electrical and communication lines. Inside it substituted for draperies and united interior schemes with jeweled veils of color, its images casting an appropriate theme about a room. With all concerned deeming stained glass the quintessence of good design, no new home was complete without at least a nod to it. But, before technology reduced costs, only the wealthy could indulge. Prices that began at $10 a square foot for a workshop window ran to $100 for the design of an established artist.[2] The aspiring middle class contented itself with sandblasted and pressed glass panels that began at around $2 or better, designs etched through a contrasting layer of a single transparent, brightly colored glaze costing about double that[3]—all either purchased ready-made by mail order or perhaps custom-copied based on designs published in decorating magazines. In this way, a taste that originated with religious themes in Gothic Revival churches found its way into parlors, libraries, foyers, and stairwells.

Japanese-influenced motifs comprised a popular category of themes that began in the mid-1870s with influences from abroad. European window designs were published in American journals. Emigrant artisans, particularly from England, likely brought with them Christopher Dresser's observations on the compatibility between Japanese design and stained glass. In a short time America's most exceptional talents began experiments that coalesced into a style everywhere identified as "American,"

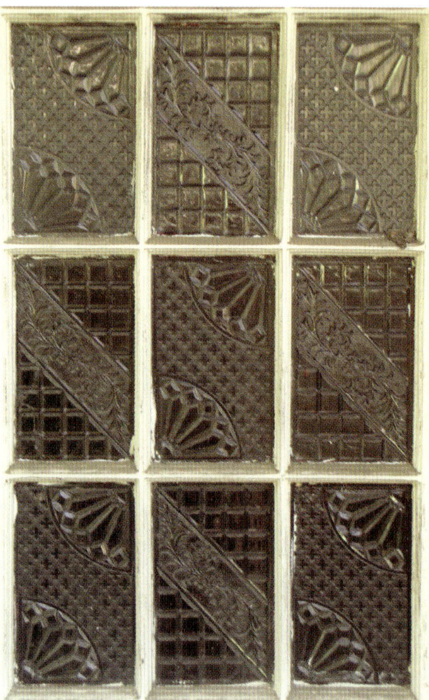

Below, Left: Door; undated; pressed glass panes. Diagonally disposed fans and ribbons make a Japanese statement in the front door of an 1880s home in Richmond, Virginia.

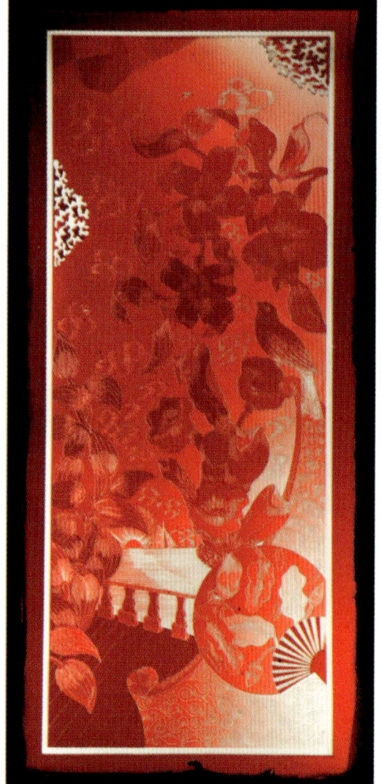

Below, Right: Door panel; ca. 1880–1890; layered etched glass; 26.25 inches. The etched ruby glass displays a romantic balcony harbor scene, viewed through the Japanese pictorial conventions of extreme close-up, sharply cropped floating fans, foliage, birds, and flowers.

even when practiced in Europe: painterly conceptions incorporating translucent glass with opalescent striations of color plated in layers for nuances of tone, the various parts united by their dark leading lines, and the near elimination of painted accents—all elements that, in addition to various formal and thematic references to Japan, suggest a Japanese attitude often noted and emulated by Western artists in their sensitivity to the inherent qualities of the materials.

The transformation had begun by 1881, the year William H. Vanderbilt completed his Fifth Avenue palace, when the very newness and cost of the fashion made artist-designed windows indispensable vehicles for a conspicuous parading of wealth. A large bay with a top frieze and sides of peacock designs in "the Japanese style" destined for this mansion so impressed a *New York Times* journalist when he saw it in the maker's studio that he made it the focus of his opening remarks on the décor of that now-vanished home. Its designer John La Farge, the mastermind for all of the mansion's stained glass, would later be described poetically by Gustav Stickley as the creator of "virile work, graceful in composition, palpitating in light and harmonious in color."[4] Stickley also credited La Farge as the originator of a stained glass style not only recognizably "American" all over the civilized world but, even more, presenting "a new kind of beauty for a new civilization."[5] Stickley's opinion, a thinly veiled allusion to a heated dispute between La Farge and Louis Comfort Tiffany, reprised the atmosphere of vicious competitiveness propelling much of the era's creativity, notwithstanding the lofty spiritualism and ideals that Japanese aesthetics supposedly imbued.

STAINED GLASS WINDOW; AS PUBLISHED IN *DECORATOR AND FURNISHER* 4, NO. 5 (AUGUST 1884): 167. The internationalist spirit of the late nineteenth century reveals itself in the American publication of a British design for a stained glass window incorporating the West's favorite Japanese features: birds, fish, and bugs in random fans, and a backdrop of blossoming plum.

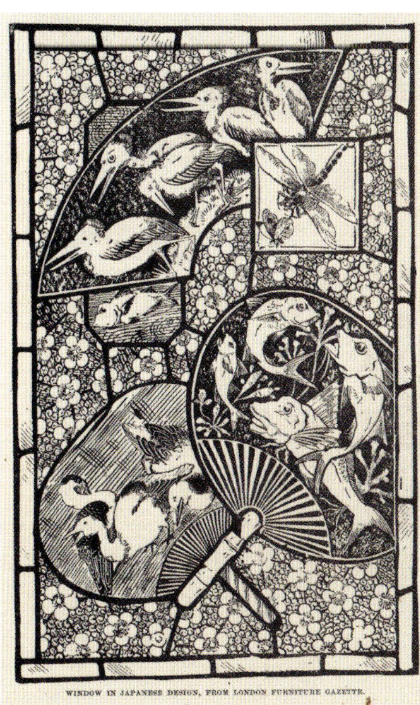
WINDOW IN JAPANESE DESIGN, FROM LONDON FURNITURE GAZETTE.

Artist-intellectual par excellence and one of the most influential creative minds in nineteenth-century America, La Farge made no secret of his use of Japanese aesthetic concepts, formal devices, and pictorial themes because he believed borrowing to be an avenue to good design. They led him to innovations in painting and book illustration even before his landmark experiments in stained glass. Sharing his knowledge in speaking and in prolific writing, his stature as one of the earliest and most influential authorities on the subject gave his opinions considerable weight in shaping American perception. It grew from a deep abiding intimacy indivisible from his cosmopolitan character. La Farge was among the first Westerners,

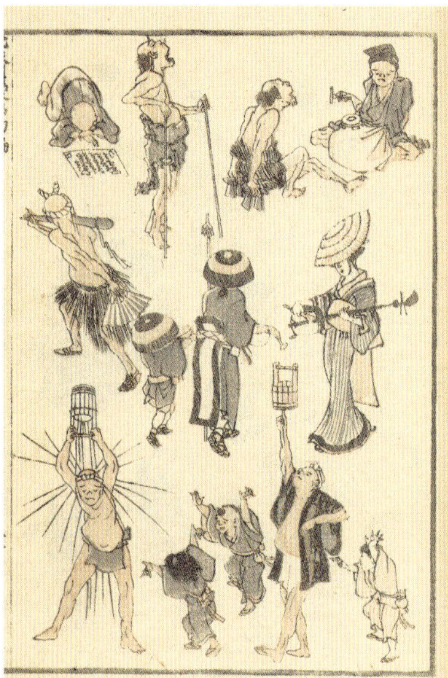
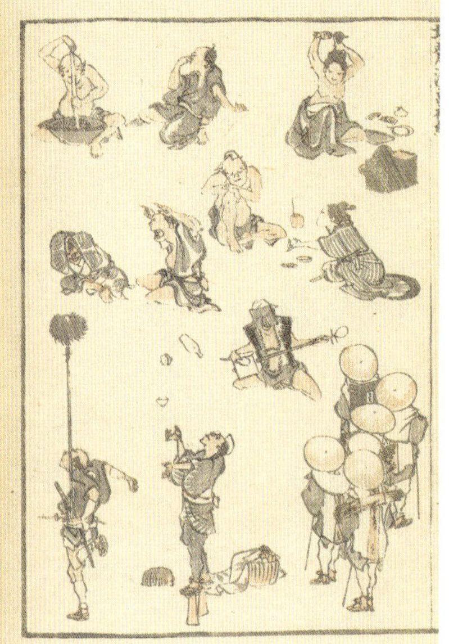

Two pages from Katsushika Hokusai's *Manga*; 1814. John La Farge adapted Hokusai's humorous character studies from the *Manga* for his earliest-known stained glass window.

and possibly the first American, to collect: In 1856, he was still in his twenties when family ties brought him to the Paris circles of Bracquemond. The experience led him to abandon law for art and also to acquire a book of illustrations by Hokusai—possibly the *Manga*—making engagement with Japanese art part and parcel with his identity as an artist. Beginning in 1863, La Farge went on to import prints directly from Japan by Utagawa Hiroshige, Utagawa Kunisada, Utagawa Kuniyoshi, Utagawa Toyokuni, Yanagawa Shigenobu, and others, as well as sword guards, ceramics, lacquer, paintings, and textiles. Marriage to Commodore Perry's grand niece brought him into a family that strongly identified with its illustrious ancestor's achievement. More direct and fruitful were personal relationships with Ernest Fenollosa and, above all, Okakura Kakuzō. Both began in 1886, when La Farge journeyed to Japan with Henry Adams. Okakura facilitated La Farge's travels in the country. Two years later, Okakura stayed with La Farge in New York. La Farge's dedication of a major lecture series on Japanese art to Okakura, who dedicated the *Book of Tea* to La Farge, speaks of a genuine and rare ability to transcend the baggage of cultural superiority and typecast exoticism typical of the era. By this time, La Farge had established himself as one of the top creators and authorities in the decorative arts of the day. On the subject of Japan he was a confident and independent thinker: the academic theorist Fenollosa dismissed ukiyo-e prints at this point in his career; the artist-intellectual La Farge prized them.

Japanese art seems to have been intertwined with La Farge's move to stained glass from the outset. He shared the general philosophy of adherents of Aestheticism who viewed art as a single entity rather than as individual ranked categories. To La Farge, the value of glass as a medium equaled that of the painting and prints with which he had already established a major reputation. But La Farge went farther with glass, aiming to reach the "successful blending of the two opposites of realism and decoration" that he saw as Japan's unique contribution to design. This brought his work progressively to a transformational sophistication. La Farge's earliest-known windows, a set of three referred to in a letter of 1875 and likely extant in a private collection, were composed of leaded roundels on which he replicated a miscellany of images from Hokusai's *Manga* using a transfer process enhanced with simple color. In other words, these were conventional windows. Six years later, the now-lost Vanderbilt peacocks—described by the dazzled *New York Times* reporter as "hundreds of bits of colored glass"—suggests that by 1881 La Farge had moved well away from the simple replications of exotica of typical stained glass designs to a refined assimilation of Japanese motifs and aesthetic principles in much the way he already had in his paintings and illustrations.

John La Farge. "The Fish" (or "The Fish and Flowering Branch"); ca. 1890; leaded stained glass; 26.5 x 26.5 x 2.5 inches. Courtesy of the Museum of Fine Arts, Boston; Edwin E. Jack Fund and Anonymous Gift (69.1224).

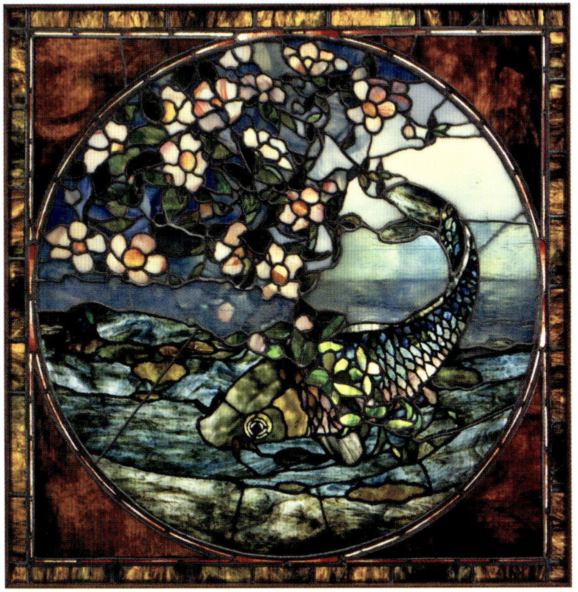

La Farge, like Dresser, learned to separate Japanese design concepts from the exotic motifs in which they appeared. Both recognized the placement of realistically observed nature motifs within a flat, formalized abstract structure, so typical of Japanese design, as an intellectual approach intrinsically suiting the material qualities of stained glass windows. But, while Dresser commented on glass, he never actually delved into its design. La Farge went beyond theorizing to active experiment and, in looking directly at Japanese arts for guidance, discovered a spectrum of possibilities. He sought inspiration in particular from textile stencils and ukiyo-e prints, in part due to their suggestiveness regarding the configuration of leading line that he considered the backbone of design. In an influential article of 1870 he pointed to the linear beauty of the Japanese print as an essential inspiration. In this way, what had always been a mesh of meaningless lines became an organized and logical structure dictated by the subject it portrayed and therefore an active element of the composition itself. La Farge also praised Japanese compositional approaches, such as carefully balanced, rigorously edited asymmetrical arrangements and the practice of extreme close-ups that gave even modest subjects a powerful presence. These devices maximized the pictorial surface, adapting the motif to its surroundings and creating the contemplative yet commanding effect that he prized.

Motifs typical in all Japanese media led La Farge to experiment. Fish, butterflies and grasshoppers, sparrows and peacocks, and modest cottage garden lattices and their flowers as well as irises, chrysanthemums, and apple blossoms, with morning glories and peonies his particular favorites—all highly informal subjects that were not considered sufficiently lofty for serious painting and unheard of for stained glass until that moment. La Farge's vision elevated the most mundane things to the level of art. Above all, Japanese prints mesmerized him with intricate combinations of pattern and complex harmonies of color. In these he perceived a jewel-like quality of change according to time of day and, with it, the sensation of passing time. In an inspired moment, he recognized that the irregularities of color and texture found in reject batches of pot-metal glass could replicate those qualities, resulting in designs with completely new effects of luminosity and pictorial subtlety. Windows with motifs drawn from ordinary gardens, executed with elegant linearity, and made exquisite with opalescent striations of color completely changed the art of stained glass to a definably American look.

"Carp"; textile stencil; Meiji period, ca. 1880–1900. Perhaps in part due to the popularity of goldfish and koi introduced as pets to the American public during the late nineteenth century, swimming carp were among the most common motifs in many media and among the most inspirational to American designers.

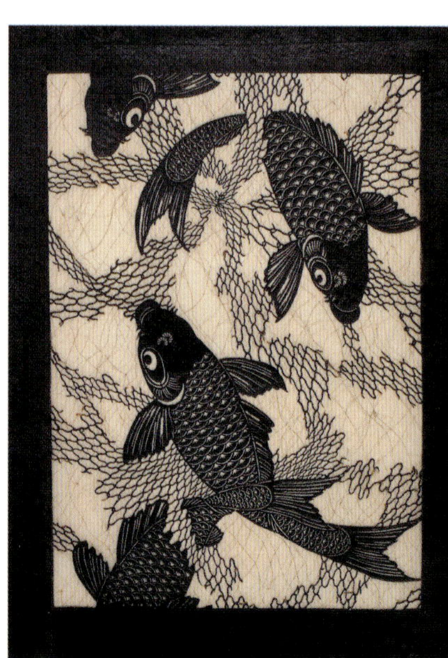

At his death in 1910, La Farge was lauded by a prominent critic as "the most salient artistic personality in America. In culture, no artist since the Renaissance has surpassed him."[6] Such an accolade made clear that La Farge stood as master and towering influence across an intellectual and artistic spectrum. Yet consensus did not extend to the realm of stained glass windows despite his undeniable prominence in that preeminent decorative expression of the Gilded Age.

Below, Upper: Louis Comfort Tiffany, ca. 1908.

Below, Lower: Two pages from Katsushika Hokusai's *Manga*; 1814. La Farge and Tiffany's beloved cottage flowers as they appear in Hokusai's *Manga*.

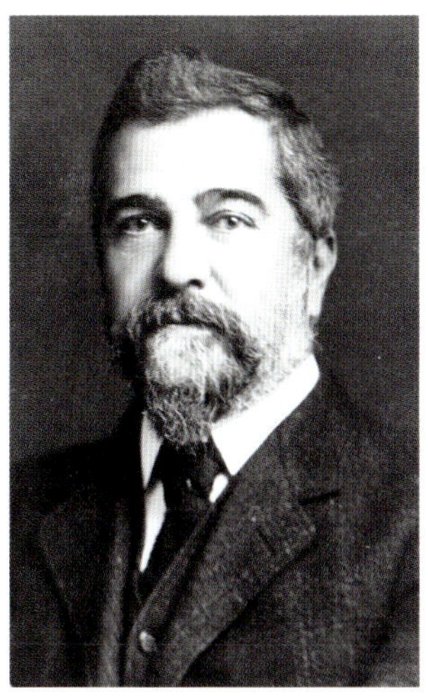

Stained glass also had drawn the attention of the formidably talented and enterprising Louis Comfort Tiffany. What began in the 1870s as a cordial accord and shared interest between an elder established and young emerging talent collapsed into open animosity by 1881, the year of La Farge's Vanderbilt commission. Both La Farge and Tiffany might have unhesitatingly pointed to the Japanese ideas in the prisms of beauty they each cast across the rooms of the wealthy. But the bitterness and litigiousness of their dispute gave the lie to the era's stubbornly cherished notion that art of any sort inherently brought people's finer characters to the fore: here, the qualities inspired by Japanese tradition, having transformed the art itself, served only to witness the naked pursuit of lucre, artistic dominance, and prestige.

Tiffany had conveniently decamped for Europe around the time discussions on a joint business venture for stained glass windows fell apart. An incensed La Farge, possibly perceiving a duplicitous ploy to steal expertise, sought to thwart his young rival from competing for prestigious clients. He obtained a patent for window-grade opalescent glass and followed up by suing Tiffany for infringement. Tiffany countered with a patent for structural techniques, unsuccessfully seeking to stop La Farge. By 1883 the two desisted, likely having come to their senses that the very success of their respective innovations had led to a much greater

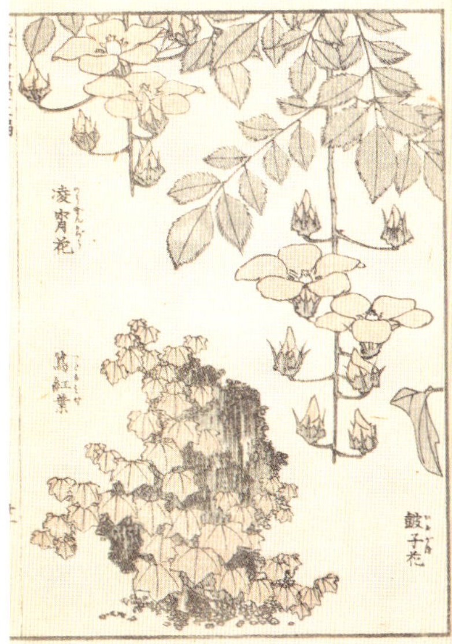

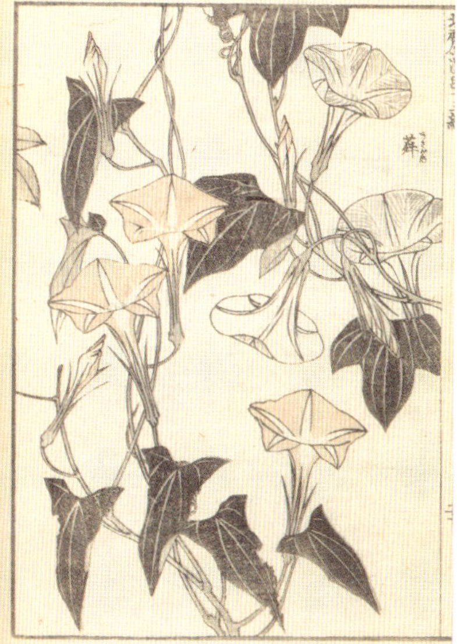

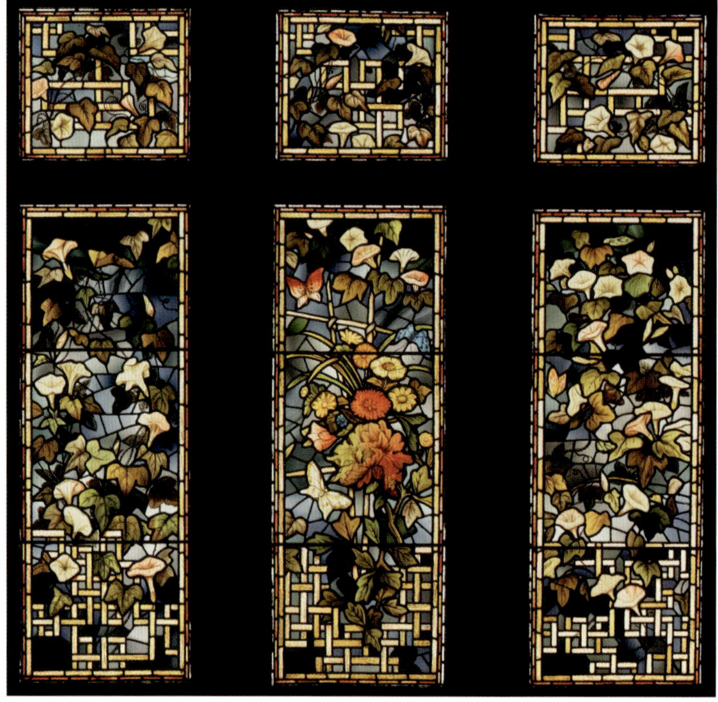

Probably Daniel Cottier, formerly attributed to John La Farge. "Morning Glories"; six-panel window; ca. 1877–1878; stained glass; 110.5 x 72 inches; from William Watts Sherman House, Newport, Rhode Island. Butterflies flitting through a brocade of cottage flowers entwining a lattice fence, this window displays some of La Farge's most imitated design elements, nearly all of which adapt from a variety of Japanese sources, including screens, textile stencils, manga, and ukiyo-e prints. Courtesy of the Museum of Fine Arts, Boston; Gift of James F. and Jean Baer O'Gorman (1974.498 a–f).

threat from imitators than from each other, and both had other legal and financial distractions. But mutual ire went unabated for decades, each lining up supporters. In 1889 La Farge received the French medal of the Legion d'Honneur as the inventor of opaline glass. That same year an influential American publication credited Tiffany with that achievement. Each attempted to one-up the other with commissions, display, and in the media, their relentless ungentlemanly duel as typical of the era as the high-toned language of spiritual uplift accorded to art overall. In the end, Tiffany prevailed, the natural outcome of being younger, longer-lived, artistically more diverse, and more commercially enterprising. Indeed, had it not been for their status in the decorating philosophy he did so much to shape, Tiffany would not have been so wedded to stained glass windows as the measure of his image and success. The very wealthy who could afford commissions allowing the kind of creative exploration he sought were too few to sustain a business. In 1893 at the Columbian exhibition in Chicago, as La Farge's star faded in the background, the top prizes awarded for his windows were only several among fifty-four medals for a series of other entries.

"Wisteria and Poem Cards"; two-panel screen; Edo period, late seventeenth–early eighteenth century; ink, color, gesso, and gold on paper; 66.25 × 74.5 inches. A *byōbu* displays the lattice patterns and country blossoms so novel to La Farge and other creative minds of the period.

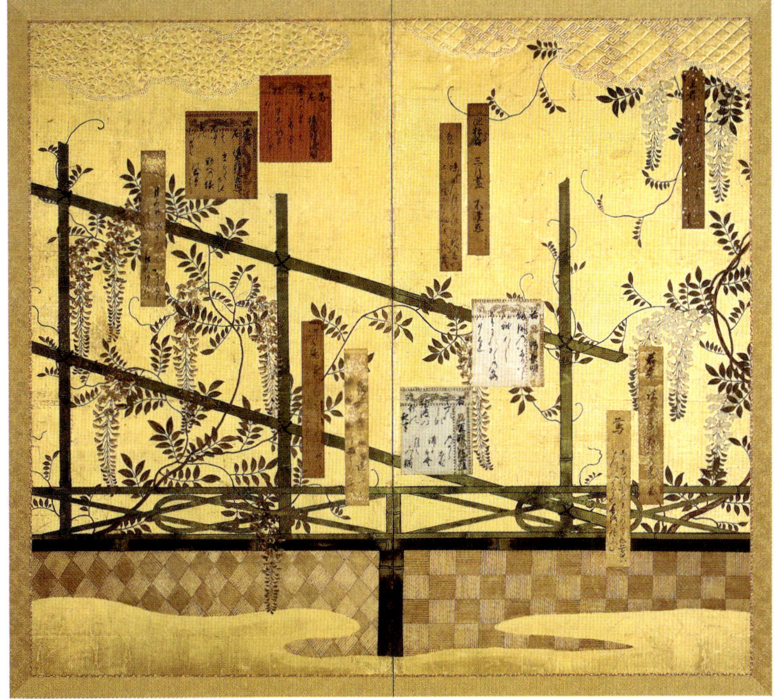

In his ventures, Tiffany built upon a background much like that of La Farge: trained painter and socially connected cosmopolitan with links to the Japan-infused Parisian avant-garde. In America he worked with some of the same artisans and mingled in the same artistic and intellectual circles, many with an abiding interest in Japan. But if their attraction to Japanese art began similarly, the two men ultimately stood far apart in ways that are suggestive, particularly for Tiffany. Japan never figured among his exotic travels; affinity with individuals like Okakura, Shugio, Hayashi, or even Matsuki, all of whom he undoubtedly knew, does not seem to have factored. Tiffany typified the indirect perspective of most Americans and Westerners by remaining within the "comfort zone" of people like himself in his exposure to Japan and its arts, in his case supercharged by his talent and by the environment of money and momentum afforded by his father Charles' landmark luxury goods and jewelry business, Tiffany & Company. It is likely that Edward C. Moore, his father's chief silver designer until his death in 1891, played a significant role as a creative mentor to Louis Comfort. One of the earliest American collectors of Japanese art, the gifted Moore brought his own

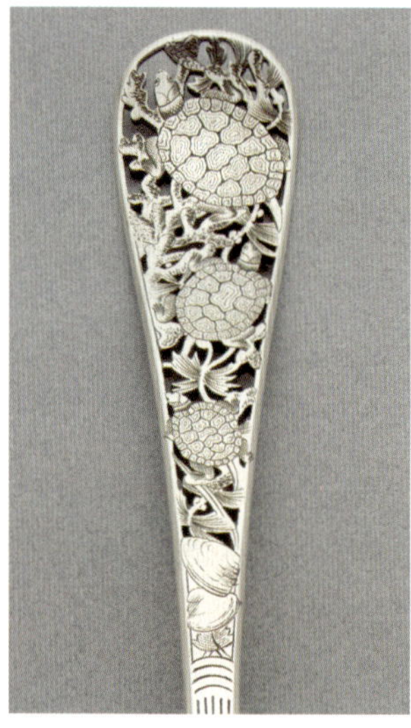

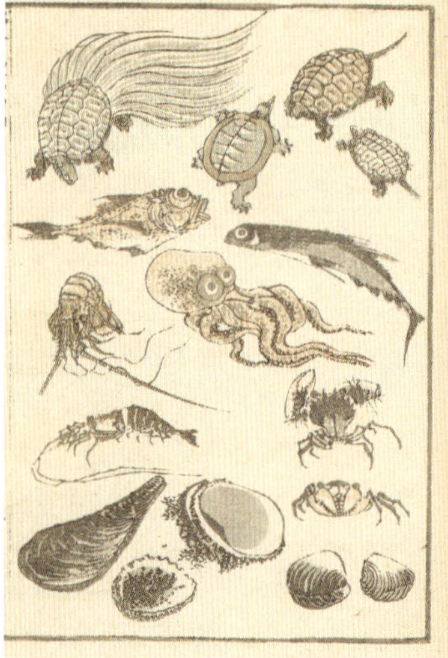

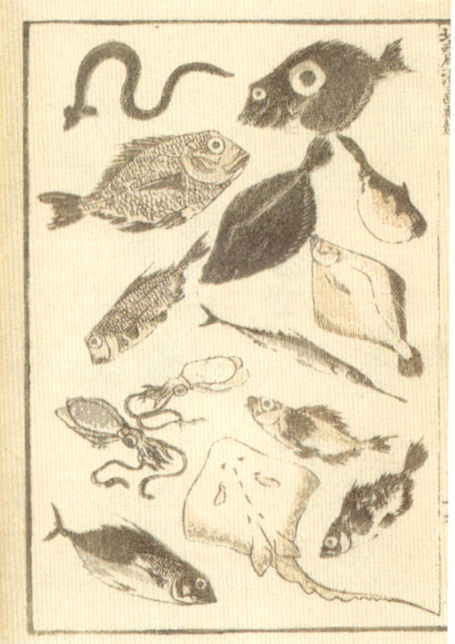

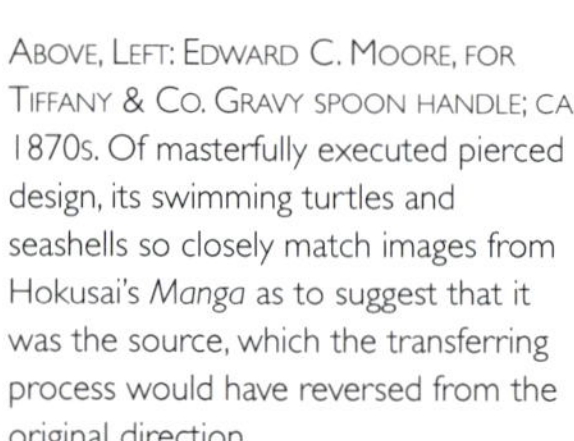

Above, Left: Edward C. Moore, for Tiffany & Co. Gravy spoon handle; ca. 1870s. Of masterfully executed pierced design, its swimming turtles and seashells so closely match images from Hokusai's *Manga* as to suggest that it was the source, which the transferring process would have reversed from the original direction.

Above, right: Two pages from Katsushika Hokusai's *Manga*; 1814. Motifs from this artwork were adapted by Edward C. Moore in some of his designs for Tiffany & Co.

Right: Poster highlighting art glass by Louis Comfort Tiffany; undated, before 1905. Advertisement used for an exhibition sponsored by Siegfried Bing.

Facing, Upper Left: Louis Comfort Tiffany, Tiffany Studios. "Daffodil"; window; ca. 1916; leaded opaline glass; 31.5 × 19.5 inches. The extreme close-up view of the daffodils and the high horizon line of this delightful window are conventions Tiffany adapted from ukiyo-e prints by masters such as Hiroshige.

aesthetic discernment to a taste initiated in Paris beginning in the 1850s that he was still refining into Tiffany's adulthood and first sojourn in Paris in 1868. Also, while still in his twenties, Tiffany developed a relationship with Christopher Dresser. When this seminal figure met the Tiffanys in 1876 during his American stop en route to Japan, they enjoined him to acquire art for them. The pottery, textiles, wood, basketry, metalwork, lacquer, and prints Dresser purchased joined what became a huge collection for study, reference, and pleasure. Not only did Dresser thus markedly shape Tiffany's taste, but he also claimed to

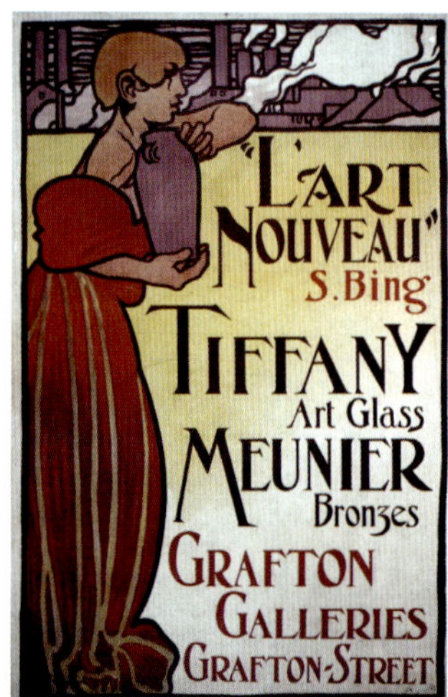

have swayed Louis Comfort's developing approach to design—sharing the benefits of his own transformative experience from the trip. Dresser may also have served as a model through the all-encompassing breadth of his design interests, every one infused with ideas from Japan. Lastly, Tiffany counted Siegfried Bing, a deeply knowledgeable collector, among his closest friends. Bing considered Tiffany's work the epitome of his idea that Japanese art principles lay at the heart of art nouveau, and he worked

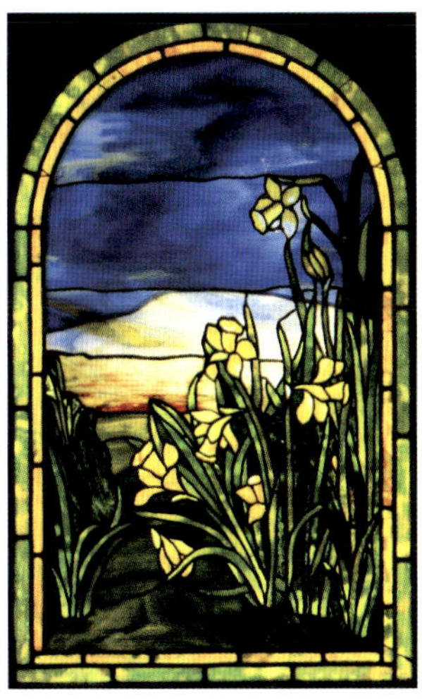

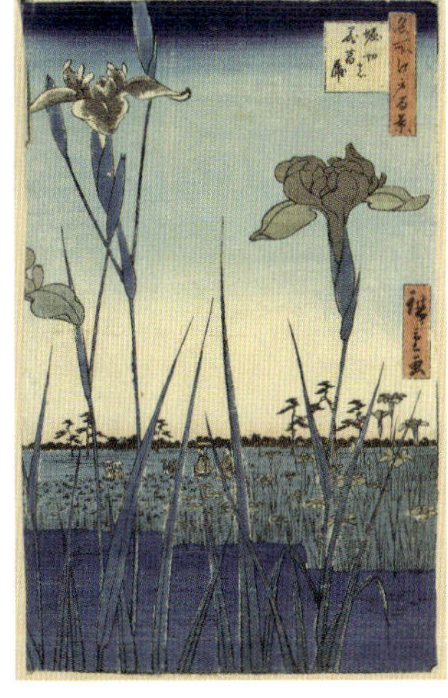

tirelessly and with great success to establish Tiffany's reputation in Europe. In America, Tiffany's Japan-infused, richly assimilative vision transformed American mass taste.

Tiffany brought to Japanese art the mind and eye of a true child of the Aesthetic movement: absent starry romanticism or moralizing overlay, the pursuit of beauty his sole aim. Such clarity of purpose led to liberating interpretations of the horticultural themes that figured among his deepest passions and to a celebration of the inherent qualities of medium. Both found endless expression in all of his work: opaline glass, dramatic lead line, nature motifs, and compositional devices such as asymmetry, sharply upturned picture planes, and extreme close-ups, much like La Farge's work—all looked to Japanese woodblock print compositions and color schemes. In many of his figural and landscape "paintings" in glass, he subsumed these Japan-derived devices to near invisibility. But other more experimental efforts adapted sword guards in strange still life arrangements or mounted magnolia, wisteria, and other large plant motifs in clear glass so that their forms created a frame or lattice through which a distant view appeared, bringing to actual experience a visual device of the masters Hiroshige and Hokusai

ABOVE, RIGHT: UTAGAWA HIROSHIGE. *HORIKIRI NO HANASHŌBU (HORIKIRI IRIS GARDEN)*; UKIYO-E WOODBLOCK PRINT; EDO PERIOD, 1857; 14.2 × 8.75 INCHES; AS FEATURED IN *MEISHO EDO HYAKKEI (ONE HUNDRED FAMOUS VIEWS OF EDO)*, PUBLISHED BY UOYA EIKICHI.

BELOW, LEFT: LOUIS COMFORT TIFFANY, TIFFANY GLASS AND DECORATING COMPANY. "MAGNOLIA"; WINDOW; CA. 1885; LEADED GLASS; 52.87 × 18.50 INCHES / 52.87 × 19.13 INCHES / 52.87 × 19.02 INCHES. Three panels of what was probably once a five-panel composition reveal distant views through a web of blossom-laden branches, a visual technique typical of Japanese prints that fascinated and inspired not only Tiffany but also avant-garde artists of the Impressionist and related movements.

FAR RIGHT: UTAGAWA HIROSHIGE. *MAMA NO MOMIJI TEKONA NO YASHIRO TSUGIHASHI (MAPLES AT MAMA, TEKONA SHRINE AND TSUGI)*; UKIYO-E WOODBLOCK PRINT; EDO PERIOD, 1857; 14.2 × 9.25 INCHES; AS FEATURED IN THE SERIES *MEISHO EDO HYAKKEI (ONE HUNDRED FAMOUS VIEWS OF EDO)*, PUBLISHED BY UOYA EIKICHI. Courtesy of the Museum of Fine Arts, Boston; William S. and John T. Spaulding Collection.

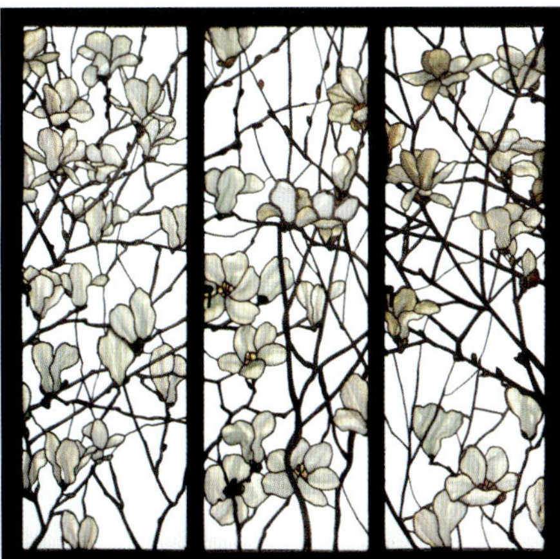

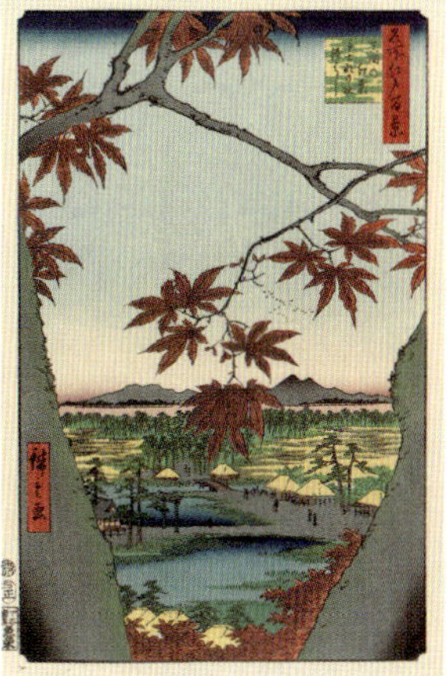

in the miniature world of the print. Tiffany showed similar inventiveness in other signature explorations such as lampshades whose lead lines replicated those of spider webs, bunched bamboo canes, or lotus pads.

In pairing stained glass and bronze, Tiffany's lamps combined two of the era's most highly regarded decorative arts on a small, relatively accessible scale; with their freshly envisioned nature-based designs, this assured they would be sought after from the moment he offered them in 1899. Yet, Tiffany did not regard his lamps very highly and avoided calling attention to them. They contradicted his vision of himself as an artist, for though hardly mass produced, they were conceived by talented designers under his direction rather than by his own hand, and all but the most exceptional were created in multiples. But his money-losing business required them as a cost-effective use for the vast quantities of scrap glass left over from windows, and he may have thought to tap a huge market for something that everyone needed. But Tiffany's prices ranged from what today would be $550 to almost $14,000, and the electrified versions added to his line the second year were a measure of their place as luxury items, for only a fraction of even the most well-to-do had wired homes at the time. Like virtually everything else he offered, Tiffany's lamps were for the few, but his vision so appealed that it spread like pond ripples.

That appeal came not just from the desirable materials but also from an astute reading of popular taste that by now had firmly assimilated

Below, Left: Tiffany Studios. "Spider" lamp; ca. 1902; Favrile glass; 18 inches diameter x 14.5 inches high; shade signed "Tiffany Studios New York 337"; base signed "Tiffany Studios New York 337." Six panels resembling a spider's legs divide a web-like shade of mottled translucent amber glass above an inverted mushroom base in brown/green patinated bronze.

Below, Center: Louis Comfort Tiffany, Tiffany Studios. Reading lamp; ca. 1902; 30 inches high. Leaded Favrile glass in a cobweb design shades a base of blooming field narcissus in mosaic. Originally an oil lamp, it was converted to electricity.

Below, right: Louis Comfort Tiffany, Tiffany Studios. "Pond Lily" globe on newel post; after 1900; leaded opaline glass.

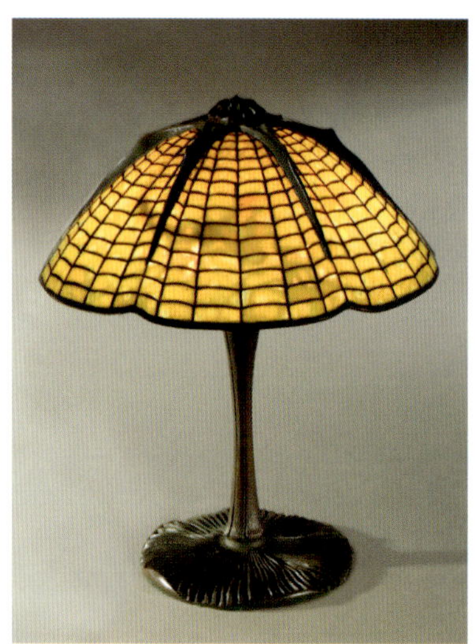

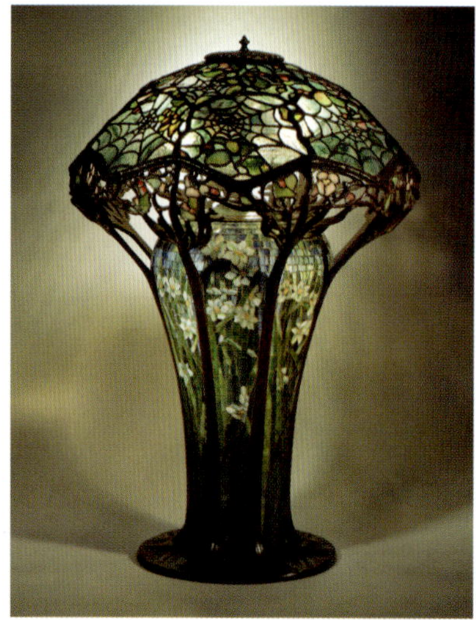

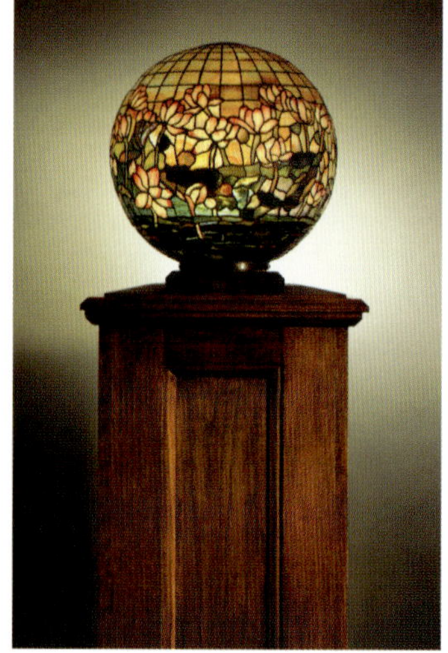

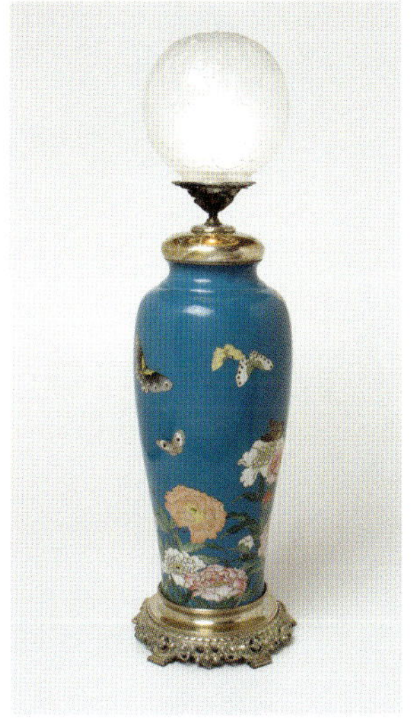

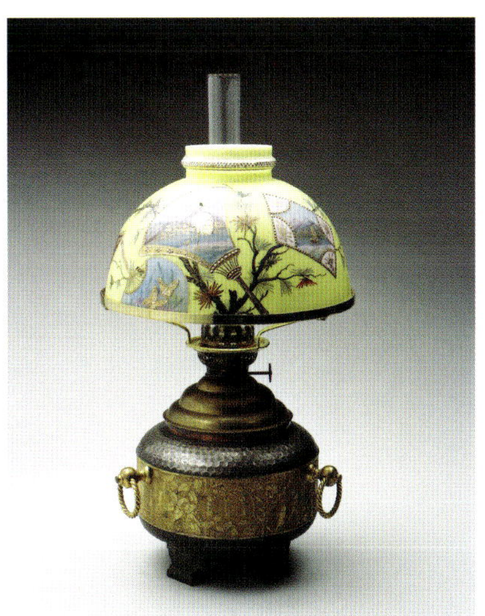

NEAR RIGHT: LAMP WITH GLOBE SHADE; CA. 1880–1890; CLOISONNÉ; 33.46 INCHES HIGH. The body of this converted Japanese vase has a motif of poppies and butterflies in finely executed cloisonné.

FAR RIGHT: DERBY SILVER COMPANY. OIL LAMP; CA. 1880–1890; PEWTER AND GILT BRASS; 28 INCHES HIGH. This lamp is ornamented with a band of miscellaneous motifs, including cobwebs, vines, flowers, ribbons, and Japanese figures; the shade, period but not original to the lamp, is decorated with random fans and flowering branches, among the most visible of adaptions from Japanese design.

BELOW: DUFFNER & KIMBERLY. "POND LILY" LAMP; CA. 1905; LEADED OPALINE GLASS; CA. 1905; 26 INCHES HIGH. This company was a short-lived art-glass manufacturer that attempted to compete directly with Tiffany. Its lamps equaled Tiffany Studio's high quality and expense, but its blatantly imitative designs lacked the vigor and charm of Tiffany's original vision and obscured a distinct brand identity, contributing to the company's demise in 1913.

things Japanese. Tiffany's designers took no risks with their motifs of carefully observed, asymmetrically arranged garden bugs and flowers, or even the quietly witty sensibility. They tapped into a liking well-established in Aesthetic ceramics and brass; in glass, Mount Washington Glass and other companies offered lamp shades whose motifs of randomly scattered fans and twining vines in soft pastels recalled Satsuma ceramics. Beautifully made exports from Japan in novel and expensive materials such as cloisonné featured butterflies, birds, grasshoppers, spiderwebs, frogs, and floral sprays. Tiffany's reenvisioning combined the most desirable of materials, superb color, fine execution, and, above all, bold pared-down elegance that owed to an ability to discern the essential qualities of the most successful Japanese design and adapt it to a Western form—this set him apart and moved American design forward toward the Arts and Crafts and the Art Nouveau movements.

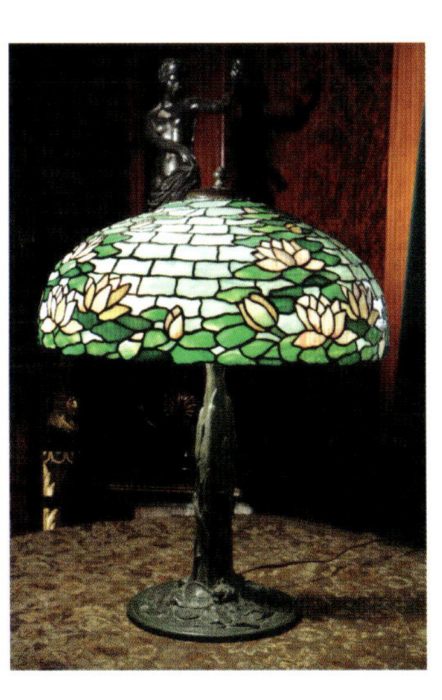

Tiffany's success with innovative lamp design was preceded by an even greater one with his Favrile glass. Favrile was also an enterprising and shrewd business decision that built on an established fashion; though expensive, it was a more attainable luxury with prices that ranged between the modern equivalents of $180 and $1,000. Moreover, it gained an immediate boost from Siegfried Bing, whose enthusiasm resulted in enormous sales in Europe, acquisitions by major museums, prizes at the most prestigious art fairs and at the Paris exposition of 1900—all culminating in Tiffany being awarded the Legion d'Honneur.

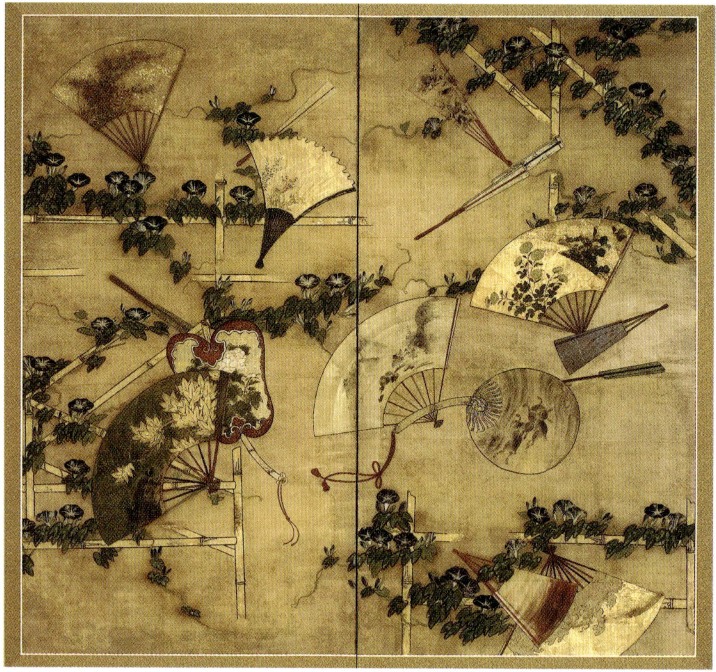

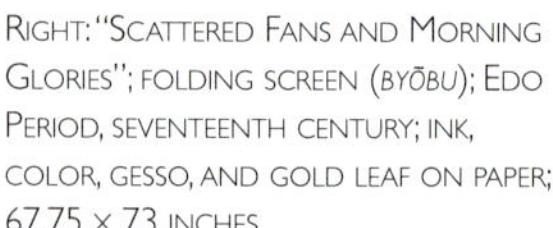

Right: "Scattered Fans and Morning Glories"; folding screen (*byōbu*); Edo Period, seventeenth century; ink, color, gesso, and gold leaf on paper; 67.75 x 73 inches.

Below: Favrile vase; as published in *The Art Work of Louis C Tiffany*. In 1914 Louis Comfort Tiffany and Charles De Kay, prominent arts critic for the *New York Times* and a founder of the National Arts Club, published an expensively produced book entitled *The Art Work of Louis C Tiffany*, which featured this vase as a supreme example of Favrile glass. Its unmistakable nod to the Asian double-gourd shape, known to American artists mainly through Japan, was possibly inspired by works in his vast collection and also by Christopher Dresser, who had replicated Japanese bronzes of this shape in ceramic form.

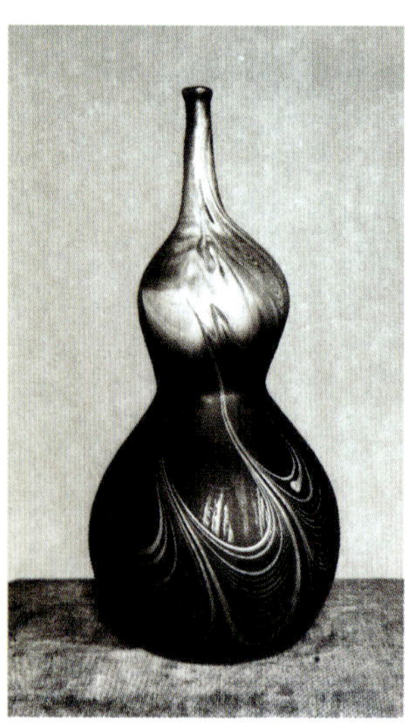

Bing, who had commissioned from Tiffany ten windows based upon designs by some of the era's most prominent avant-garde artists, of course featured Favrile in his shop. Its Japan-infused aesthetic, so sophisticated and forward-looking as to be transformational, perfectly articulated his art nouveau philosophy. Tiffany himself never used the term *art nouveau* and possibly did not want to be limited by one definition of "modern."

With Favrile, Tiffany took advantage of a vogue ongoing nearly twenty years. At the Centennial exhibition in 1876, Venetian and English glass of dazzling color, fantastic shapes, and opulent enameled and gilded ornament revived the legendary arts of the island of Murano in contemporary forms. The modern pieces embodied Aesthetic ideals as promoted by Eastlake, then at the peak of his influence. Desire for Murano-style glass quickly spread and spawned a thriving American competition that enthusiastically experimented with a repertoire of color, shape, and ornament. Perhaps it was the tales of techniques jealously guarded to the point of maiming betrayers that led American exhibitors to detect an appealing whiff of exotic taboo in Murano, for they typically displayed "Venetian glass" next to ceramics from Japan

NEAR RIGHT: TRUMPET VASE; CA. 1876–1885; PINK AND CLEAR MURANO GLASS WITH ENAMELS; 22.5 INCHES HIGH. The Japonesque taste for fans and cartouches of flowering branches and birds appear with typical Murano touches, including pendants of clear glass drips and enameled decorations, making this vase by an unidentified maker the epitome of Aesthetic style; the stand is made of blackened iron.

FAR RIGHT: EMILE GALLÉ. "SPIDER WEB" VASE; CA. 1900; 8 INCHES HIGH; SIGNED "GALLÉ." This classic example of Art Nouveau style presents a realistically observed spiderweb and red maple leaves in blood red and blue over clear glass.

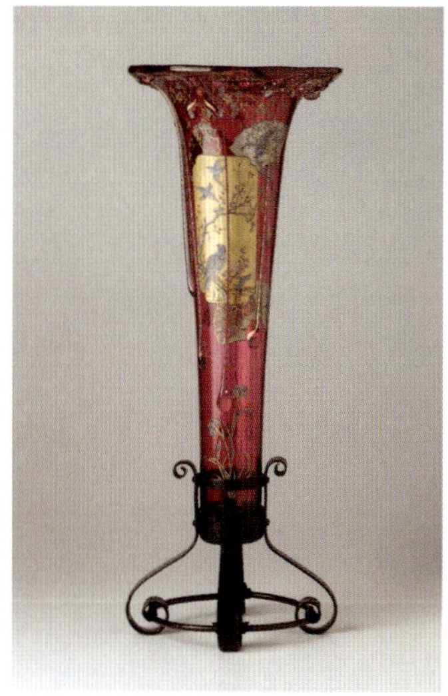

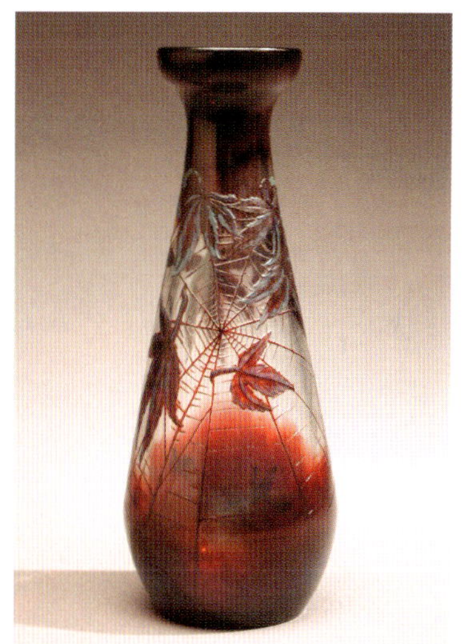

and China. In this way, the merging of the two tastes may have been inevitable: American companies producing silver plate collaborated with glass companies to feature in their catalogues trumpet vases with elaborate metal bases—a classic Italianate combination—some of which displayed intricate patterns of cartouches asymmetrically disposed and laced with meandering floral vines in the style of Satsuma vases but executed in delicate, transparent colored glass.

Impossible to mass produce, Aesthetic-style Murano renewed appreciation for the skilled, experimentally adventurous artisan and, with it, a recognition of "art glass." By the late 1880s an avant-garde trend emerged in France led by Émile Gallé (1846–1904), who considered Japan his chief aesthetic influence to the point of adding "a la japonica" on some of his signed pieces. Gallé's family had a long-standing relationship with Charles Tiffany, who sold their factory's ceramics and glass, including his critically acclaimed work, at Tiffany & Company. In Gallé's work, Tiffany encountered not surface exoticism, but true assimilation of essential principles and themes, among them abstracted nature-based forms, dramatic line and silhouette, asymmetry, closely observed botanical and zoological motifs, novel color schemes, utilization of the inherent qualities of the material, and efficient design—the same inspirations Tiffany brought to his windows but envisioned for vases, bowls, and other items. On meeting Gallé himself in 1889, Louis Comfort found a kindred spirit and knowledgeable willing resource.

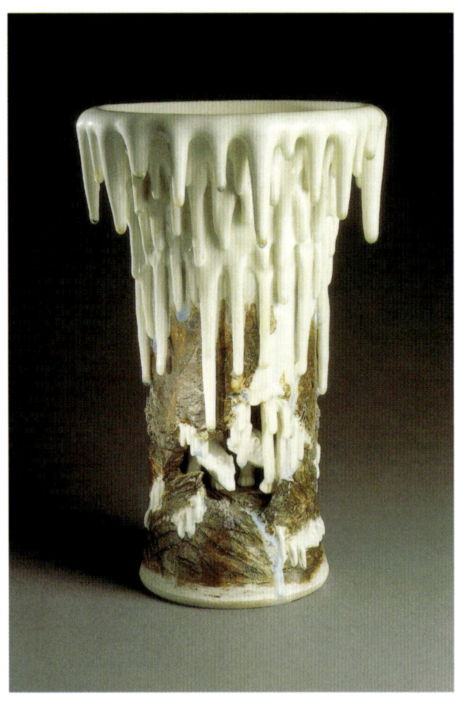

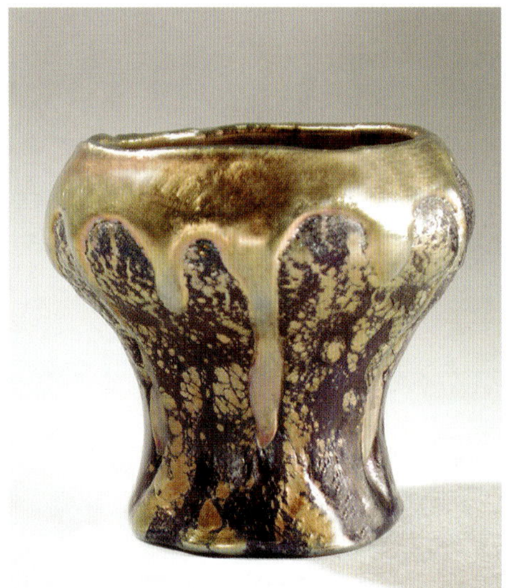

Returning to the United States, Tiffany established workshops staffed with an international roster of talent whose names, unlike Gallé's practice, he endeavored to keep from the public eye. Not a glass artist himself, he needed their expertise and interpretive skills to make his vision a reality but desired that the product be identified as entirely his own. Literally and conceptually Japan figured strongly in his eclectic concept. The term *Favrile* revived an archaic French word meaning "handmade" but Tiffany embraced in spirit some of the prime identifications with Japanese art crafts: appreciation for the craftsman's hand through fine technique and his spirit through sensual delight in the physical properties of material. The method of fusing variously colored strands of molten glass looked to Murano. Its hallmark opalescent and metallic sheens had been inspired by the iridescent surfaces of ancient glass excavated from ruins in the Mediterranean. Unstated but equal to these were aspects perceived as Japanese or inspired by them: forms such as classic nature-based double gourds and jack-in-the-pulpit blooms, with undulating leaf and floral motifs embedded in many of these pieces. Certain other innovations, such as his distinctive "lava ware," although suggestive in name of the eruptions of famous European volcanoes, actually took their stylistic cues from the Japanese practice of mending damaged ceramic rims with an undulating "glue" of gold lacquer. Japanese craftsmen, noting Western fascination with this look, had begun to exploit it in exaggerated fashion in their export lacquer and ceramic wares. And above all, there is the delight in the interaction between the furnace and glass medium itself, allowing the shapes to deform and the glazes to follow their natural inclinations in the spirit of Japanese tea ceramics, of which he owned many.

Tiffany debuted Favrile to international acclaim at the Chicago exhibition of 1893. Perfectly in step with—even propelling—the

FACING, UPPER: MIYAGAWA KOZAN WORKSHOP. VASE; CA. 1910; MOLDED AND ENAMELED PORCELAIN; 12.24 INCHES HIGH; MARKED "MAKUZU." Vases with ornamental versions of the traditional Japanese taste for the unfettered random look of running glazes and lacquer mends made an early appearance among Japanese export wares in many media, becoming increasingly exaggerated over time. Courtesy of the Nasser D. Khalili Collection of Japanese Art, London, England.

FACING, LOWER: TIFFANY STUDIOS. VASE; CA. 1908; FAVRILE GLASS; 4.25 INCHES HIGH; SIGNED "L. C. TIFFANY FAVRILE 5611C." This iridescent "lava" vase has organic design simulating lava flow over blue basaltic rock.

American trends toward Arts and Crafts and Art Nouveau, it was only the latest example of his uncanny sensibility for the pulse of the times that had revealed itself from the outset of his career, when avant-garde meant the Japan-infused Aesthetic taste. This, too, he had done much to define collaboratively beginning in 1879 as establishing partner in Louis C. Tiffany & Co., Associated Artists, America's first interior design firm. So swiftly did its vision strike a chord that *Artistic Houses* featured seven interiors whole or in part its work. These included Tiffany's own apartment and several rooms of the refurbished White House, an astonishing feat for an enterprise lasting only four years, and for Tiffany personally, who had not previously attempted interior décor. Associated Artists found inspiration in all of "the Orient," but Japanese concepts provided much of the structural unity behind the look they achieved.

Associated Artists principals—Tiffany, Lockwood de Forest, Samuel Colman, and Candace Wheeler—conceived a cohesive interior whose beauty emphasized relative sparseness in which attention to every element's individual flawlessness added up to a totality of perfection, one that expressed the disposition, sophistication, and individuality of the owner. The basic concept did not differ radically from ideas already afoot; Tiffany actually echoed Whistler's approving quip regarding E. W. Godwin in his comment, "We must be artistic first and comfortable afterward—if possible."[7] But Associated Artists cemented these ideas in the minds of the American public, and attaining design coherence through collaboration was a novel idea. Each specialized in a different aspect of décor: Tiffany in glass and tiles, de Forest in furniture and wood, Colman in color schemes, and Wheeler in textiles. Japan figured throughout their thinking in several ways, most superficially in ornamental components such as imported leather papers, furniture, and objets d'art that they combined with furniture of their own design and from other places. More definitively, inspirations such as Japanese prints guided them to a radical departure from garish color schemes of red, blue, and gold, a custom so entrenched that some critics found their emphasis on delicate pastels, gradations of hue, and metallic accents "barbarous." "Japanese" color schemes as much as anything made their work a risk for society's conventionally minded and infinitely interesting to iconoclasts like Samuel Clemens, who delighted in the interiors created for his Hartford home.

Japan also provided a more direct reference in motifs incorporated into fittings and furnishings. These were adapted from the growing number of

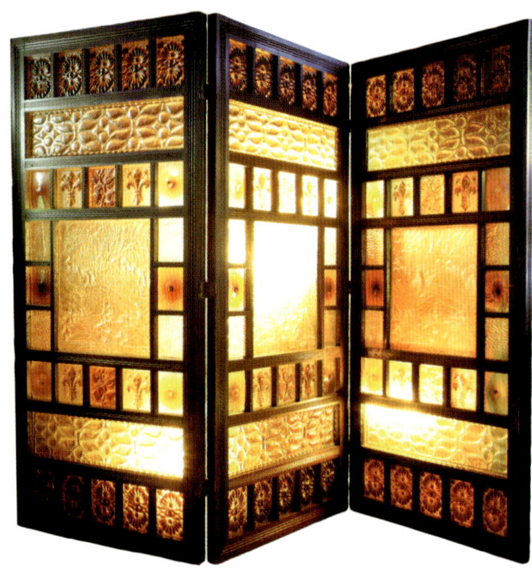

Above: Screen; ca. 1879–1881; pressed amber glass and wood; 64 inches high; signed "Associated Artists." Almost certainly designed by Louis Comfort Tiffany, this standing screen incorporates large square panels that, in extreme close-up, display fruiting olive branches in a delicate intermingling, taking its cue from Japanese textile patterns based upon naturalistic plant forms.

Facing, Upper: Portieres, Japanese; ca. 1880–1890; burgundy velvet; 117 inches high. Embroidered in metallic threads, these doorway curtains are typical of the finely executed textiles created by Japanese craftsmen for the export market.

Western publications on Japanese design, such as Thomas W. Cutler's *A Grammar of Japanese Ornament and Design* and Théodore Lambert's *Motifs décoratifs tire des pochoirs japonais,* and, above all, from direct sources of the enormous study collections of Colman and Tiffany, whose personal possessions alone included scores of antiques and contemporary items of all sorts, among them lacquers, cloisonné, leather pouches, tea caddies and tea bowls, sword fittings (including sword guards in the thousands), armor, ivories, architectural elements, paintings, folding screens, and books of paper samples.

Borrowing Japanese motifs directly or treating Western botanical themes according to the formalized yet realistically observed tenets of Japanese design became a hallmark of Associated Artists' work. Tiffany expanded his glass beyond windows to such furnishings as folding screens with impressed botanical motifs and in the stenciled patterns and wallpapers designed by Tiffany, Colman, and Wheeler, whose very first effort inspired by Japanese color schemes and fondness for ordinary garden insects and plants won the $1,000 first prize in a manufacturer's competition.

Candace Wheeler (1827–1923) had joined Associated Artists already well primed with Japan-influenced ideas. Her skill with the needle had been honed by a gifted eye and an informal and semiformal education in which Japanese art was intertwined from the outset. Her social circles brought her into regular contact with La Farge and Colman; she possessed an urbanity acquired from years of living in European cities. But, like Tiffany and many others, her transformative experience was through Japan's charming and landmark presence at the Centennial exhibition in 1876. Following the reaction to their debut effort at the Vienna exposition of 1873, which critics called a "revelation," Japanese organizers featured embroidery prominently, including fabrics and folding screens whose depictions of figures, animals, anthropomorphized insects, flowers, and other motifs combined painting with ornamentally stitched relief and detail. American home

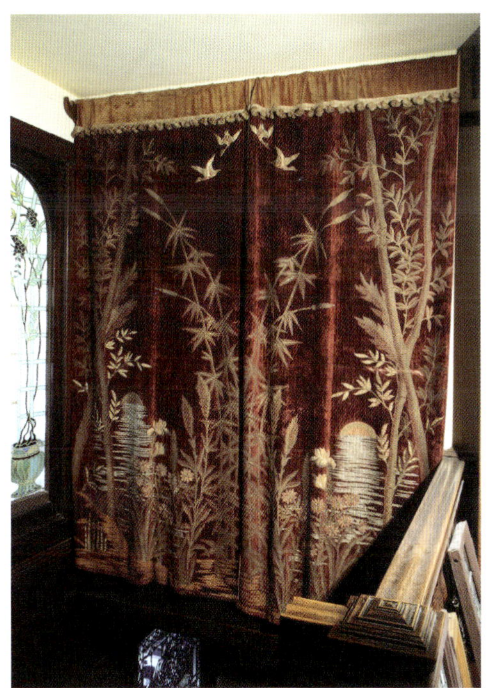

magazines soon recommended them as ideal curtains for windows and doorways, the latter called *portieres,* and found them "particularly well-suited for draping over the back of a piano."[8] In addition to this direct, if artificial, inauthentic introduction to Japanese textile arts, Wheeler also encountered some of the earliest examples of assimilated Japanese design in the exhibit of Queen Victoria's Royal School of Needlework at the Centennial exhibition.

For Associated Artists' projects, Wheeler supervised the needlewomen executing heavy gold- and silk-embroidered designs whose novelty and quality often attracted enthusiastic response. She was noted in particular for portieres, then deemed essential to the well-dressed room. For these, she frequently began with the mass-produced, high-quality brocades for which Japan was becoming well known and enhanced them with appliquéd designs in a variety of themes. But she also developed sophisticated patterns based upon Japanese precedents. One of her first mass-produced designs, of carp lazily swimming through the spiraling eddies of water, adapted a classic Japanese design commonly found on stencils for textile printing. Perhaps heeding a popular misconception of the carp motif specifically as "Japanese" and popularized as a perfect example of the Japanese craftsman's estimable talents of observation, or because goldfish had captured the public fancy as novelty pets, Wheeler continued to experiment with the theme as well as with other naturalistic Japanese motifs such as shrimp in nets, ocean waves, and maple leaves. She also delved into Japanese-style formalizations, sometimes in direct borrowings of chrysanthemums, irises, lilies, and others such as nasturtiums and daffodils that followed pundits' admonitions to adapt Japanese design concepts without slavishly imitating them.

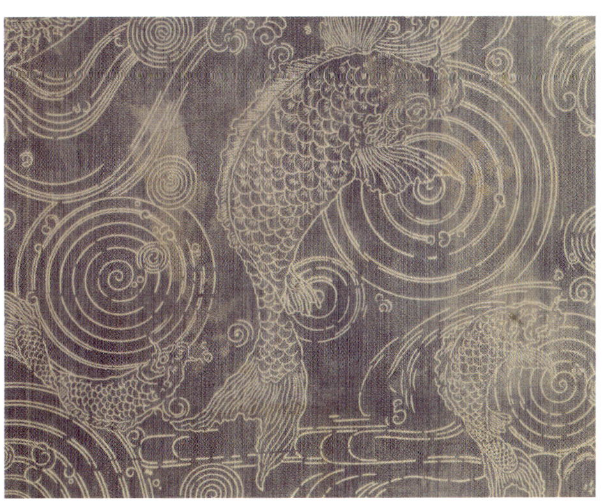

Above, Lower: Candace Wheeler; manufacturer unknown. "Swimming Carp"; textile; ca. 1883–1900; discharge-printed cotton denim; 53 x 18.5 inches.

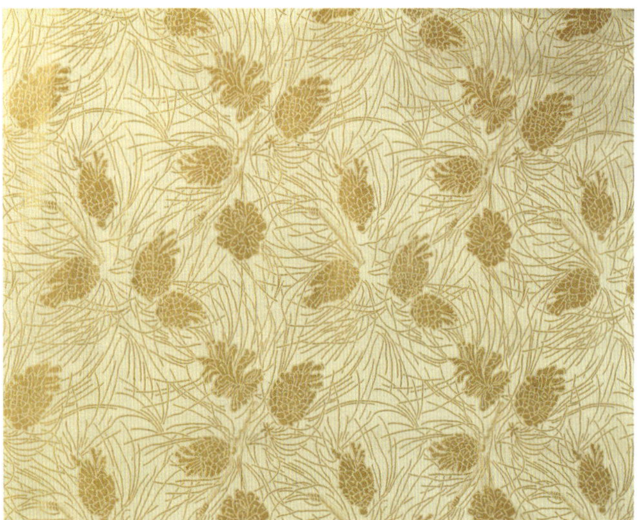

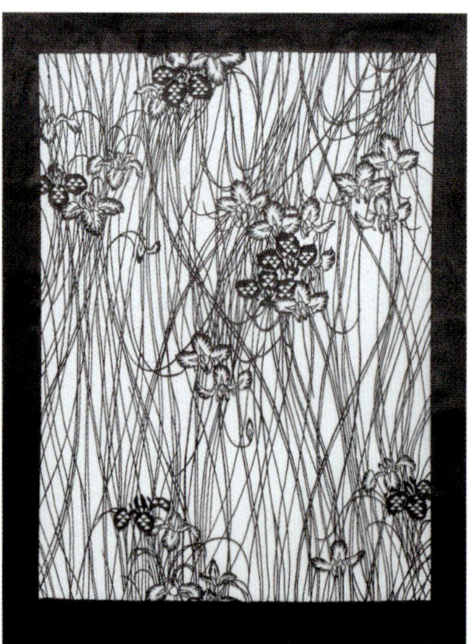

ABOVE, LEFT: CANDACE WHEELER; MANUFACTURED BY CHENEY BROTHERS. "PINE CONES-AND-NEEDLES"; TEXTILE; CA. 1883–1900; SILK; 10.5 × 50 INCHES.

ABOVE, RIGHT: "IRISES"; TEXTILE STENCIL; MEIJI PERIOD, CA. LATE NINETEENTH CENTURY. Based upon the formalized realism of an extreme close-up of iris blossoms amid tangled foliage, this design typifies the types of Japanese patterns that so inspired Wheeler, Tiffany, and other forward-thinking designers.

When the four partners amicably went separate ways in 1883, Wheeler retained the name Associated Artists for her own business, going on to become America's preeminent textile and wallpaper designer of the 1880s and 1890s, and one of the most influential opinions on taste. This she brought to an eager mass audience. Her prolific writings on textiles and interior design in publications geared toward a general readership, among them *The Atlantic, Art Amateur, Harper's Bazaar, House Beautiful,* and *Home Needlework,* as well as authorship of books on a range of subjects deemed essential to the well-run home—including embroidery, household arts, rug making, and, most importantly, her manual on decorating, *Principles of Home Decoration*—culminated in her directing the design for the Women's Building at the 1893 Columbian exhibition in Chicago. In this role, she would have been intimately involved with the Japanese installation: an entire interior of the "typical" Japanese home whose simple interiors offered a low-key domestic model to the developing Arts and Crafts style to contrast the opulence of the Hōōden.

Wheeler's work originated with the Aesthetic movement taste that she, as Tiffany's partner, helped to shape in the United States, and, like him, she would always cater to an elite clientele. But her writing for mass publications brought to middle-class women her philosophy of elegant simplicity, high standards, and elevated view of handwork as an important aspect of décor at the very moment that the Arts and Crafts movement was gaining momentum, and matched the ideals of Stickley and his circle. *The Craftsman* featured many articles on needlework and many extolling aspects of Japanese art and life but, oddly, nothing on Japanese needlework despite its popularity and strong critical approval describing it as "the limit of human attainment."[9] But needlework societies and other self-improvement groups eagerly embraced not just Wheeler's point of view but also the Japan-infused sensibility of many of her designs, if not her sense of style. Department stores held popular embroidery clinics under the guidance of Japanese artisans advertised as "world famous." Home publications featured patterns for doilies, centerpieces, bed quilts, and pillows featuring graceful meanderings of irises, cranes, leaves, dragons, and other motifs, as often as not contributed by Japanese artisans of repute or respected art world figures such as Bunkio Matsuki. These often related the history of the motif along with detailed how-to descriptions and recommendations for color schemes, a combined edification that assured Japanese ideas would retain relevance and propel tastes forward towards the simplicity and subtlety characteristic of the Arts and Crafts movement.

1. *Saturday Evening Post,* July 13, 1878.
2. *New York Times,* December 4, 1881, 14.
3. Based on quotes for the glass for door frames in the Sears Roebuck & Co. Catalogue, 1897.
4. *The Craftsman,* January 1911, 336.
5. Ibid., 330.
6. *Bulletin of the Metropolitan Museum of Art,* December 1910, 284–85.
7. *New York Times,* June 10, 1877.
8. *Art Amateur,* March 1880.
9. *New York Times,* April 23, 1893.

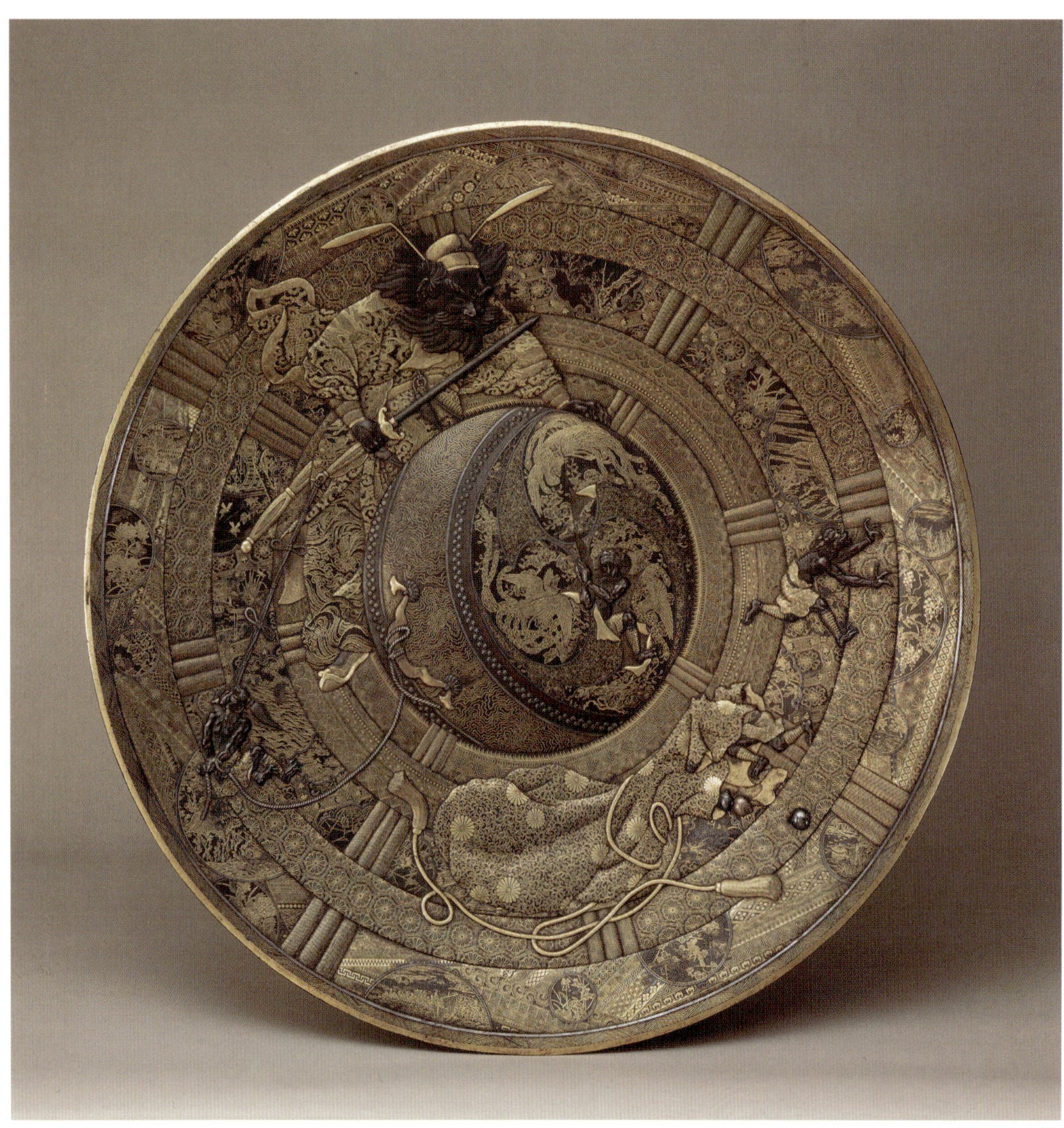

KOMAI, OF KYOTO, JAPAN. CHARGER; CA. 1903–1913; IRON WITH GOLD AND SILVER INLAY AND RELIEF; 22 INCHES DIAMETER; SIGNED ON THE UNDERSIDE "NIHON KUNI SAIKYO KOMAI SEI" ("MADE BY KOMAI, OF KYOTO, JAPAN"). The mesmerizing vortex of swirling, minutely brocaded pattern into which the mythical figures of Shoki the Demon Queller and his supernatural adversaries all but disappear shows this charger to be a hallmark example of the Komai family output. Founded about 1841, its workshops produced some of the finest damascene work in the world for the export trade between about 1873 and 1915.

7

Silver and Bronze

The Gladiators of the Tabletop

". . . in all the articles of Japanese manufacture, we see a minuteness of workmanship and finish such as no Christian people can afford the time to emulate."[1]

The international expositions were only the most conspicuous and prestigious arenas in an overall atmosphere of competitiveness that defined every aspect of the Gilded Age. Japan had shown itself to be a master player in realms of immense significance to people of the time—domestic goods that created the "house beautiful." Their accomplishments had so revised the rules of style that desire to compete and beat the Japanese at their own game as much as pure artistic fervor propelled many creative minds: Japan-inflected taste resulted in sales. A positive development, what began with pastiche and shallow exoticism over time became genuine appropriation and, with it, a radical upgrade in American design. The Tiffanys, arguably the most gifted in this process, never forgot that there was money to be made in gorgeousness.

From the outset, critics extended paeans to Japanese metalwork for originality, quality of design, color harmony, and precision of execution. A decorative art highly esteemed in Europe and long dominated by the French, the Japanese examples dazzled Westerners from their first encounter with the strange, daringly unconventional designs and tour de

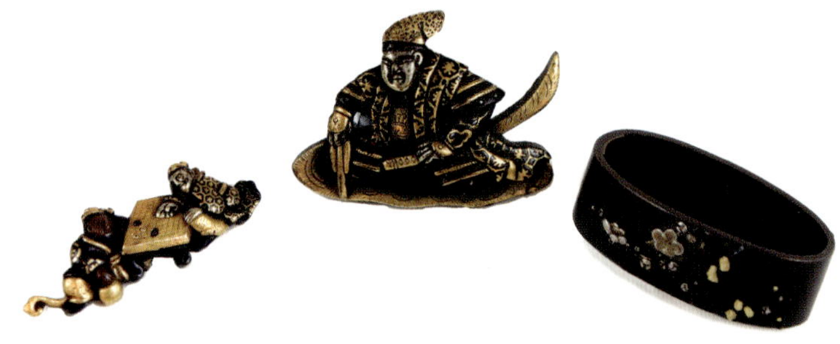

RIGHT: MENUKI AND FUCHI; EDO PERIOD, PROBABLY THE EARLY HALF OF THE NINETEENTH CENTURY. Finely executed ornaments for the sword hilt, these are typical of the samurai accessories that found their way out of Japan in large numbers with the end of the feudal era. The pieces on the left and in the middle are *menuki* (hilt decorations)—one depicting tiny figures playing chess and the other a warrior—and the piece on the right is a *fuchi* (a ring that fits around the base of the sword hilt), which displays a design of cherry blossoms.

FACING, UPPER LEFT: USUBATA-STYLE VASE; MEIJI PERIOD, CA. 1870–1880; BRONZE, EXECUTED IN BAS-RELIEF WITH INLAID GOLD, SILVER, AND MIXED METAL; 27 INCHES HIGH; SIGNED "TŌKYŌ-JU, SHŌJUSAI SHIGEYUKI." Depicted are courtiers under a cherry tree, with birds, flowers, and hanging gold poem cards on the reverse.

FACING, UPPER RIGHT: VASES; CA. 1880–1890; METAL MIXED AND BRONZE; 8.6 INCHES HIGH.

FACING, LOWER LEFT: VASES; CA. 1880; 12 INCHES HIGH.

FACING, LOWER RIGHT: HAVILAND & CO., LIMOGES, FRANCE. VASES; 1876; PORCELAIN; 8.27 × 10.24 INCHES; SILVER ALBUMEN PRINT BY CENTENNIAL PHOTOGRAPHIC CO. Two ornate vases, decorated with angels and the American Eagle, commemorating the United States' establishment and Centennial, were exhibited in Philadelphia, their trumpeting angels and encrusted detail epitomizing the French taste that the Japanese replicated exotically in their export bronzes and ceramics.

force expertise in casting, forging, inlay, and artificial patination, and their highly novel coloristic mingling of iron, steel, lead, bronze, copper, gold, silver, and a host of unusual alloys. From huge sculptures to tiny sword fittings, master of extreme simplicity or breathtaking detail as need required, the Japanese smith transcended the astonishingly primitive tools and workshops in which he plied his craft. With centuries of aristocratic patronage behind him, he epitomized Ruskin's romantic image of the perfect artisan. Esteeming their own smithing tradition as they did, Westerners unsurprisingly concluded that metalwork was the epitome of Japanese art and sought it avidly. Matsuki, Greey, Marsh, Shugio, and their competitors scoured Japan for the discards of the old regime, bringing back everything, from religious images to weapons, to an enthusiastic American public. Louis Comfort Tiffany and architect Charles Greene were among the many lured by old sword guards of the defunct feudal military, Tiffany's collection swelling to four thousand pieces.

Such fascination revealed to the Japanese government not only a moneymaking opportunity but, just as important, an answer to their dilemma regarding an ancient venerated craft, whose practitioners still sustained something of their old prestige but whose livelihoods now suffered acutely from the demise of the samurai and the economic straits of Buddhist temples. Both their skills and their traditional status could be turned to advantage in light of the West's idealized vision. Attention quickly turned to developing metal craft for the export market. Bronze held particular appeal for the high value Europeans accorded their own, especially that of the French, whose decorative bronze industry benefited from considerable state support and consequently defined the world standard. At the top of the Japanese line stood versions of the huge one-of-a-kind, extravagant European pieces that had become de rigueur entries at the international expositions, where their splendor served as

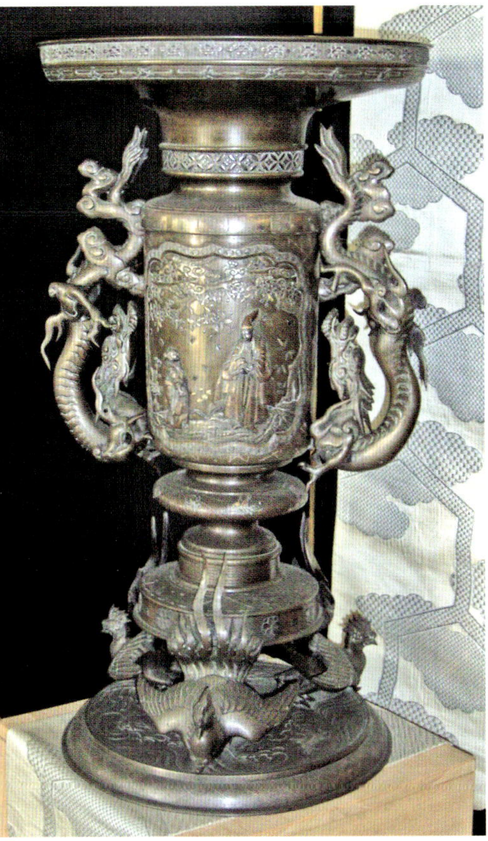

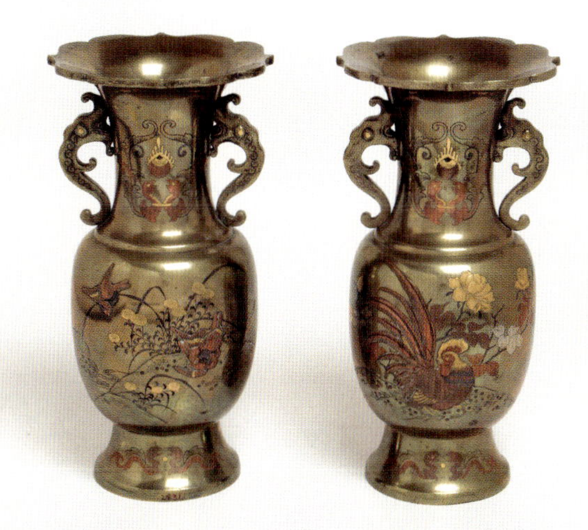

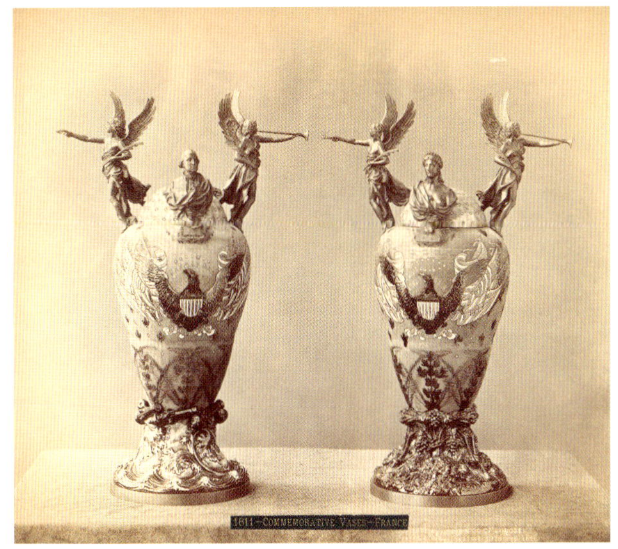

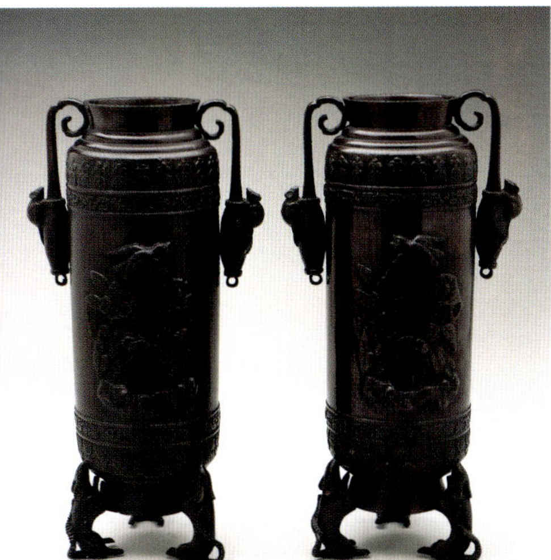

statements with which to astound fairgoers with the genius of a nation's artisan community. In devising a characteristic style, the Japanese took aim at the prevailing French by marrying Japanese motifs, techniques, and forms to the ornate Gallic aesthetic. For each piece, Japan's top artisans, often collaboratively, dedicated hundreds of days to casting, chasing, and construction, the awestruck accolades with each world's

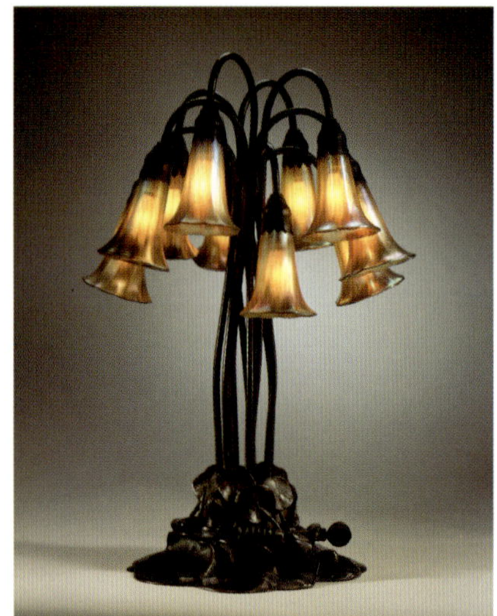

Louis Comfort Tiffany. "Pond Lily" lamp; ca. 1902; bronze and opaline glass; 21 inches high. Tiffany was awarded a grand prize at the 1902 World Exposition in Turin, Italy, for this piece, which judges deemed had transformed the standard lamp form into sculptures from nature. This was Tiffany's highly innovative response to the new freedom afforded by electrical wiring that removed the need for a bulky oil receptacle, in which he brilliantly melded naturalism to utility, a concept that originated with Japanese metal craftsmen.

fair spurring them to ever-greater feats of size and intricacy with which to flabbergast the public. In the minds of many a judge, the Japanese succeeded in besting their French rivals, earning them a parade of gold medals. Pieces in a descending range of size, quality, and cost found their way into homes across the country, making Japanese bronzes ubiquitous in stylish American interiors. Mingled with the Edo-era antiques in Western shops and displaying undeniable technical expertise in their crisply articulated intricate details, the best of these works only added to the confusion in Western minds between "authentic" and "inauthentic" Japanese art. They also made Japanese metal crafts the standard to be met. Louis Comfort Tiffany's cast-bronze lamp bases shaped like inverted mushrooms, lily pads, and the like looked to Japanese bronzes in their precisely observed nature-based themes and gently witty sensibility.

For quality and charm, an example already had been set by Louis Comfort's father, Charles, and his aggressive rival John Gorham, at the forefront of a large group of American silver manufacturing firms striving to take on Japan even as they sought to outdo each other in what became a premier American art. Japanese references were part and parcel of this development, appearing at Tiffany and Gorham in the late 1860s almost simultaneously with technological advances in the industry. Charles Tiffany even boasted in company literature that in his offerings he would be "even more Japanese than the Japanese themselves."[2] The Japanese were not happy with the outcome of his challenge. Tiffany bested them with a surprise triumph at the Paris exposition of 1878, where he won the grand prix. His designers under Edward Moore had gone farther than simply replicating "Japanese taste"; in its aesthetics and principles, they had found the means to push design in a new direction. Dresser concurred, as did Siegfried Bing, who recognized that "the borrowed elements were so ingeniously transposed to serve their new function as to become the equivalents of new discoveries."[3] These accolades acknowledged only part of a process by now well underway in which Japanese ideas propelled American metal crafts from Aesthetic taste into the divergent contemporary trends of early modernism: Arts and Crafts and Art Nouveau.

This leap was a large one. Japanese fine metalwork rested on a very different foundation from that of the West. Limited natural resources

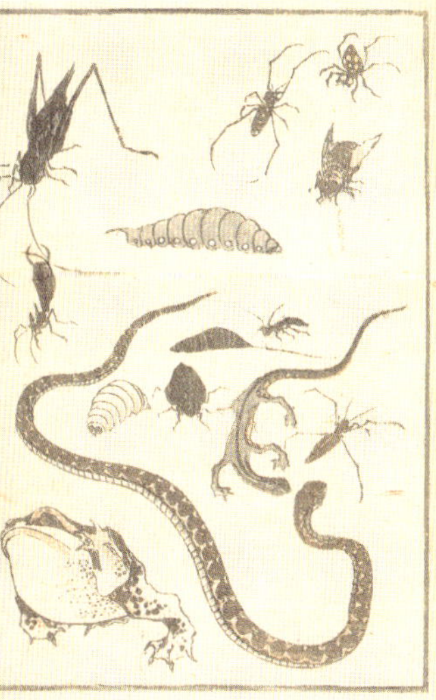
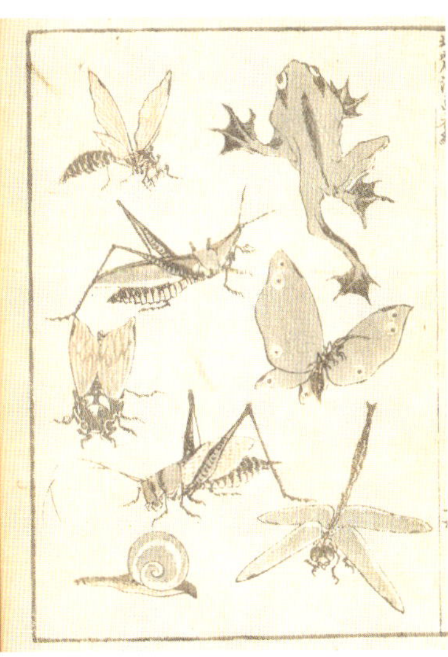
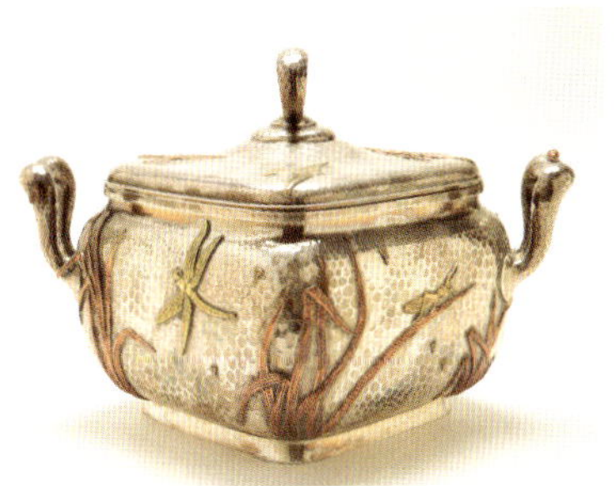

had led artisans traditionally to use gold and silver very sparingly with great effect and, until spurred by competition with the West, to delve little into silversmithing—the craft in which Tiffany & Company and Gorham Manufacturing had established international reputations. But, with the Japanese example having radically raised the public sense of the possible, American designers began to completely rethink their aesthetic approach, resulting in innovative adaptations of motifs, techniques, and materials to Western utensils and containers. The Japanese meanwhile presented a new challenge by turning their inventive design sense to

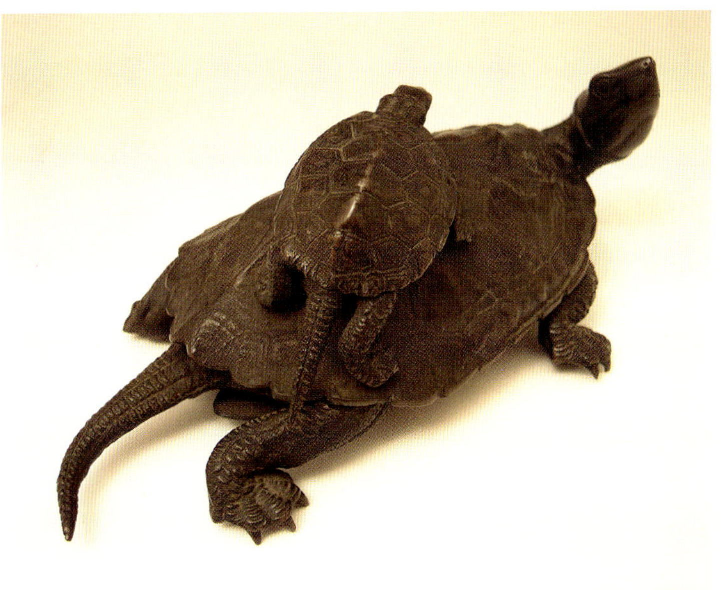

Above, Left: Page from Katsushika Hokusai's *Manga*; 1814. Some of the motifs from the page were adapted in silver by Edward C. Moore for Tiffany & Co.

Above, Right: Tiffany & Co. Covered bowl; ca. 1880; silver and mixed metals; 7.75 inches high. Marked "Tiffany & Co. 214.5034.192." Probably designed by Edward C. Moore, this lidded serving bowl features a hammered surface, mixed-metal appliqués of bugs and grasses, and a squared shape, which take their cues from Japanese precedents and closely resemble other designs of Moore's from this period that have been linked to the influence of Christopher Dresser.

Right: Ashtray; early–mid Meiji period, ca. 1890–1900, bronze; 6.5 × 2.5 × 4 inches; signed "Kanryū." In the hands of skilled Japanese metal craftsmen, practicality often acquired charm through the melding of closely observed animal behavior with functional requirements, as in these clambering turtles that form a hinged ashtray.

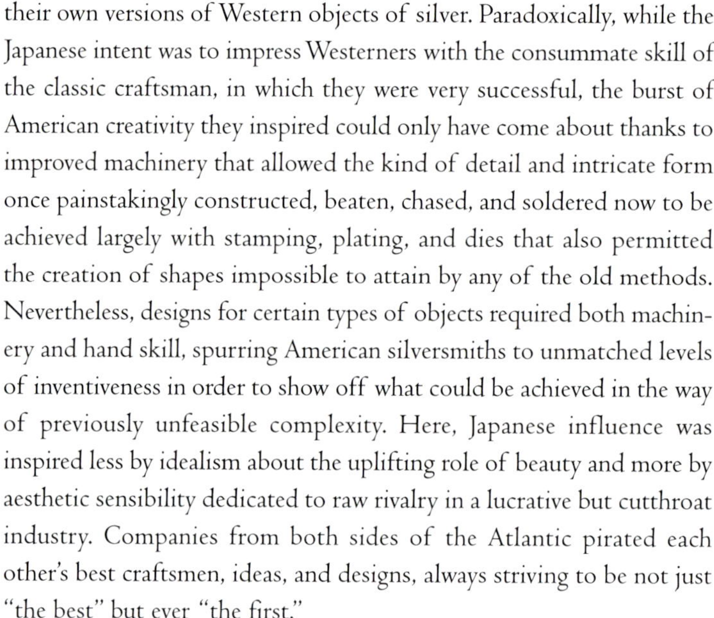

their own versions of Western objects of silver. Paradoxically, while the Japanese intent was to impress Westerners with the consummate skill of the classic craftsman, in which they were very successful, the burst of American creativity they inspired could only have come about thanks to improved machinery that allowed the kind of detail and intricate form once painstakingly constructed, beaten, chased, and soldered now to be achieved largely with stamping, plating, and dies that also permitted the creation of shapes impossible to attain by any of the old methods. Nevertheless, designs for certain types of objects required both machinery and hand skill, spurring American silversmiths to unmatched levels of inventiveness in order to show off what could be achieved in the way of previously unfeasible complexity. Here, Japanese influence was inspired less by idealism about the uplifting role of beauty and more by aesthetic sensibility dedicated to raw rivalry in a lucrative but cutthroat industry. Companies from both sides of the Atlantic pirated each other's best craftsmen, ideas, and designs, always striving to be not just "the best" but ever "the first."

COVERED VASE; MEIJI PERIOD, CA. 1885; PRECIOUS METALS AND ALLOYS, ENAMEL; 17.32 INCHES HIGH; MARKED "OZEKI SEI" ("MADE BY OZEKI"). With its finial of Shoki the Demon Queller surmounting an egg-shaped container densely webbed with wisteria and butterflies, three vanquished demons its feet, the Chinese fairy-tale theme and silver filigree with *shakudo*, gold, and cloisonné accents make this lidded vase a tour de force example of Japanese work in precious metals and exoticism for the very top of the export market. It was crafted by one of the most successful art craft concerns of the Meiji period. Courtesy of the Nasser D. Khalili Collection of Japanese Art, London, England.

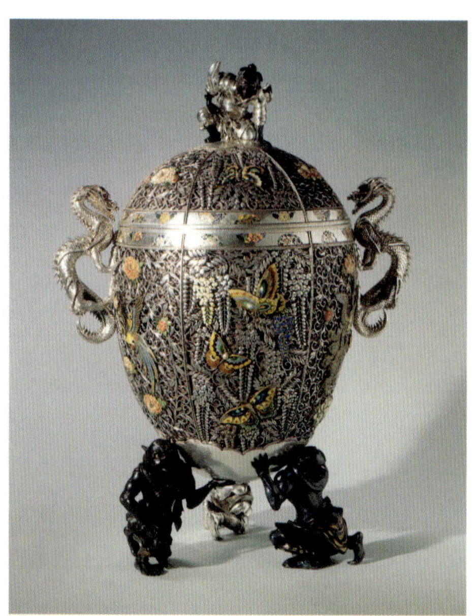

While the newspaper society pages delighted in describing the enormous services of gold utensils and serving pieces on which the Vanderbilts, Astors, and Delanos prided themselves for their most elegant occasions, the era regarded those in silver as premier American luxury items, indivisible from social class and lofty moral and artistic associations.[4] Discoveries of huge ore deposits and advances in mass production and silver plating had made impressive flatware and hollowware services an affordable and necessary extravagance, as social aspirants followed the upper-class dining trend to the style *à la russe.* An opportunity for opulent and decorous display in which meals unfolded as a sequence of courses in a set order at the hands of attentive servers, dining *à la russe* reached its extreme in the United States and, according to the *Ladies' Home Journal* in 1890, especially in New York, "where the art of dinner-giving . . . now flourishes as nowhere else in the world."[5] Commodore Perry willed his son a set of dining accoutrements that took up six "immense cedar chests"; among

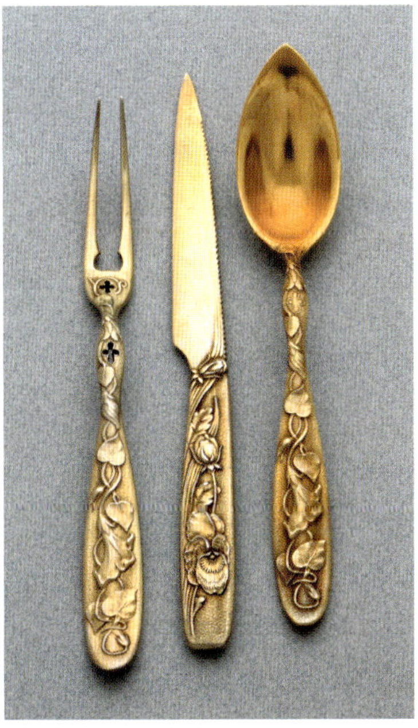

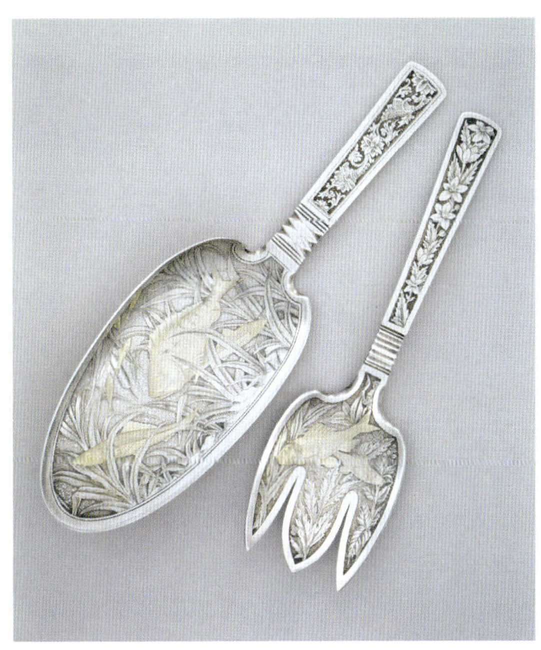

ABOVE, LEFT: TIFFANY & CO. FRUIT SET; INTRODUCED IN 1872; SILVER GILT; LENGTH: FORK, 5.8 INCHES; KNIFE, 6.1 INCHES; SPOON, 6.5 INCHES. Attributed to Edward C. Moore, these utensils for preparing oranges at the dining table include a spoon and fork embellished with a morning glory and a knife detailed with a pansy. The flatware design is entitled *Vine*, which featured informally rambling garden-flower motifs and stippled ground that are characteristic of Japanese-inspired patterns.

ABOVE, RIGHT: GORHAM MANUFACTURING CO. FISH SERVERS; CA. 1885; STERLING SILVER WITH GILT WASH. These beautifully engraved and etched servers depicting fish in a watery habitat take their cue from the intimately observed Japanese designs that, combined with the formalized patterns of the handles, make a classic and elegant example of Aesthetic eclecticism.

its necessities were tea and coffee services, serving pieces, fish and venison dishes, and a large covered dish inscribed "In acknowledgement of the signal service which he has rendered to the nation and to the world by his able and successful negotiation of the treaty with Japan."[6]

Coupled with the era's aversion to touching food with the fingers, dining *à la russe* led to utensils specific to each course and comestible. As improved technologies for canning, farming, and transportation brought evermore variety to American tables, manufacturers seized on the opportunity to create even more "need": mangos, berries, chicken legs, celery, ice cream, oysters, lobster, bread, grapefruit, and sardines all now received individual, specially designed forks, spoons, knives, scrapers, or tongs. By the 1890s the trend had reached absurd proportions, with some companies offering as many as one hundred forty-six different pieces in a given pattern.[7] Fanned by skillful advertising and catalogue sales, the American market for holloware and flatware in solid silver and silver plate exploded. Company designers found themselves under enormous pressure to create lines that stood out from the competition or capitalized on the success of others.

Japanese motifs and techniques proved inspirational. As early as the 1860s, well before the Centennial exhibition brought the Japan Craze to

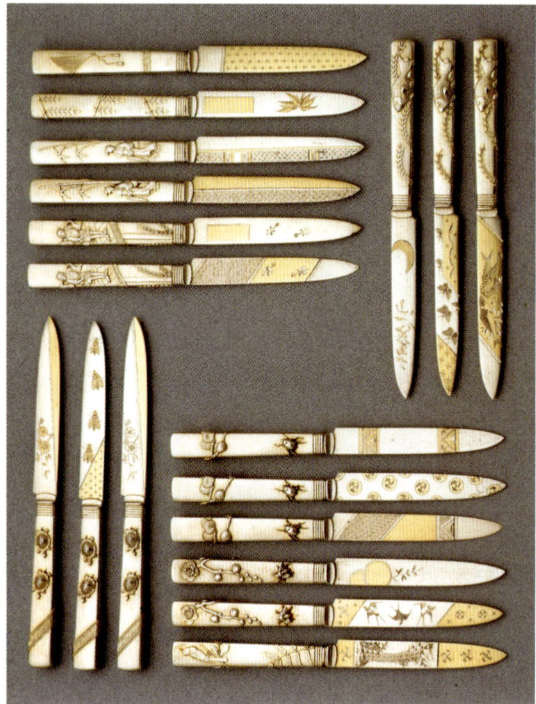

Tiffany & Co. Kozuka; n.d.; sterling silver and gilt; 8.25 inches long; marked "Tiffany & Co., Sterling." Elegant little knives, erroneously mythologized in Western minds as the tool of samurai ritual suicide, *hara kiri*, were found by Western smiths to be very adaptable in size and shape, lending the American dining ritual of dessert all the more enticing for a romantically dark frisson. Tiffany and Gorham made some of the best kozuka-inspired sets. These by Tiffany re-create the spirit in the fanciful miscellany of gilt-washed, asymmetrically engraved, and applied patterns and insect motifs, but they bow to American sensibilities in the emphasis on polished silver.

the United States, Tiffany and Gorham devoted serious attention to developing Japonesque designs, especially for their prestigious art lines targeted to the wealthy. Versions from France, then at the peak of its Japan frenzy, probably sparked the initial interest. Novel patterns designed for the premier firm of Christofle were exhibited at expositions and written about in periodicals, not to mention seen by the likes of Edward C. Moore on his periodic visits to Paris. American designers arrived at true appreciation for Japanese craftsmanship and design by further availing themselves of the addition of collections such as that obtained for Tiffany by Dresser or Moore's own extensive private libraries of Japanese sources. These by now extended beyond Hokusai's *Manga* to include others, among them *Kacho Gaden,* pattern books of designs such as *Musa Koeki Mocha,* and Western sources on Japan such as Louis Gonse's *L'Art Japonais,* Siegfried Bing's *Artistic Japan,* and Christopher Dresser's *Japan, Its Architecture, Art and Art Manufactures.* It met with low labor costs that permitted exceptional attention to detail and high standards of craftsmanship, with landmark results in solid silver and sometimes top-of-the-line silver plate.

The "Japanese" flavor that emerged first took the form of suitable motifs such as dragonflies, turtles, fans, flowers, textile patterns, and figures often copied directly from Japanese sources. By the mid-to-late 1870s it expanded to include the coloristic effects of mixed metals and, into the 1880s, increasingly rounded forms of arresting minimalism, given the typical tastes of the time. Critics particularly praised Tiffany designs for simplicity and boldness of form, and the "subtle appreciation of the Japanese of contrast and effect."[8] Designers responded to their clientele's attraction to anything suggesting the direct presence of the craftsman's hand by turning to techniques of texturing that Japanese smiths employed to offset motifs and add play of light. Though never reaching the high degree of refinement of *nanako* ("fish roe," or raised dots), *ishime* (punch or chisel marks), *tsuchime* (marks made with the side of a hammer), *amida yasurime* (long marks like rain, made with a file),

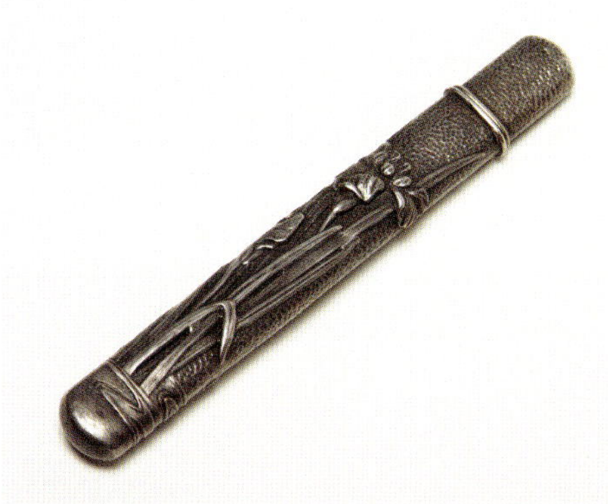

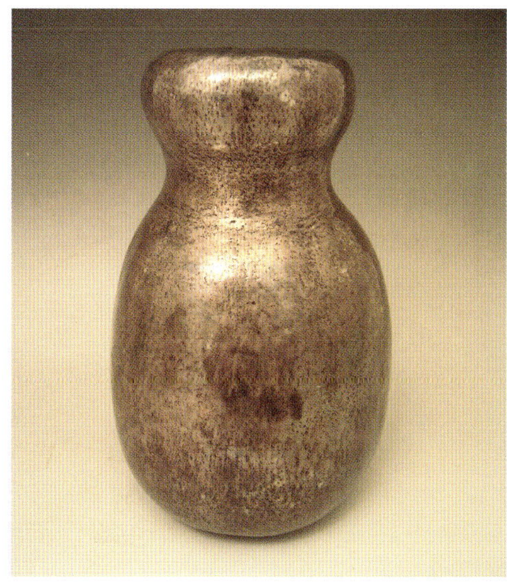

ABOVE, UPPER: AMERICAN SILVER COMPANY. POCKET PENCIL; CA. 1880–1890; SILVER; 3 INCHES LONG. The classic motif of a Japanese iris in its characteristic watery environment was skillfully replicated from Japanese sources down to its engraved and stippled effects on this elegant silver encasement and cap for a pocket pencil.

ABOVE, LOWER: VASE; LATE MEIJI PERIOD, EARLY TWENTIETH CENTURY; SILVER; 7.25 INCHES HIGH. A small gourd-shaped vase displays the textured surface effects and austere single shape that American smiths found so radical.

amida tangane (radiating lines), and *neko-yake* ("cat scratches" made with a chisel), hammered surfaces became linked with the idea of "Japanese." By the 1890s, manufacturers assured a "Japanese effect" by sending some pieces to Japan for finishing.[9] Silversmiths also replicated actual Japanese objects whose functions or shapes were amenable to Western uses. Especially appropriate were baskets, teapots, and small knives called *kozuka:* some marrying American-made blades with imported hilts, others entirely American-made replicas, they were perfect for slicing fruit; popular notions added a delightful frisson by fancifully identifying them as the blades of choice for *hara kiri.*

In combining from these and other sources, silver designers also echoed the creatively assimilative pattern of artists and craftsmen in other media, resulting in a blend that was as "un-Japanese" as the utensils to which they were applied. One of the first such flatware patterns, designed by Edward C. Moore in 1871 and named *Japanese,* paired handles displaying assorted zoologically precise, naturalistically observed "bird and flower" motifs—long used throughout Japanese arts but likely unbeknownst to Moore to be of Chinese origin—with knife blades, spoon bowls, and other surfaces engraved with textile patterns, ribbons, and a potpourri of fish, fans, people, seashells, and the like, drawn from *manga*. A classic of Aesthetic taste, the pattern inspired a trend and several imitations by the same name, compelling the ever-protective Tiffany to litigation. With time came greater sophistication in melding "Japan" to Western silver forms: *Vine* by Moore and, above all, *Lap Over Edge* by younger colleague Charles Grosjean (1841–1888). In these, assorted patterns employed "Japanese" characteristics of particular charm to Americans. Sets were organized in a method referred to as "matching," which categorized a utensil of one type with a chosen motif to distinguish it from the others in its set. There was a predilection for garden themes—Americanized to include tomatoes, wheat, grapes, and peas, as well as the specifically Japanese chrysanthemums, irises, spiders, bugs and other tiny creatures, and asymmetrical meanderings in wrapping motifs from front to back on each piece. Designers elsewhere responded with their own highly inventive, even sculptural realism: George W. Shiebler produced sardine servers and butter forks constructed of fish and grasses; Gorham offered daringly unconventional salad servers, most famously their *Narragansett* series—each piece a dense encrustation of minuscule sea creatures, all perfectly realized and lovingly rendered with the intimate naturalism observed in Japanese metal designs. Following Tiffany and Gorham's lead in hollowware, companies like Whiting Manufacturing Company and Shreve & Company turned to motifs such as netted fish, textile patterns, fruiting branches, and butterflies on pieces, from the exquisitely plain to the ornate.

Tiffany's *Lap Over Edge* versions, featuring appliqué insects and animals made of polychrome with gilt washes and articulated by etching and chasing or inlaying, were but one example of American designs featuring mixed metals. Of all Japanese techniques, painterly combinations of color, relief, and texture excited particular interest for the skill demanded and the subtlety of a spectrum of hues from gold, copper, iron, steel, silver, and, enticingly, a remarkable range of alloys and patinations. The quest for this expertise resulted in an instance of international industrial espionage in which Tiffany managed to pirate alloy formulas from the secretive Japanese, only to fall victim to a stealthy

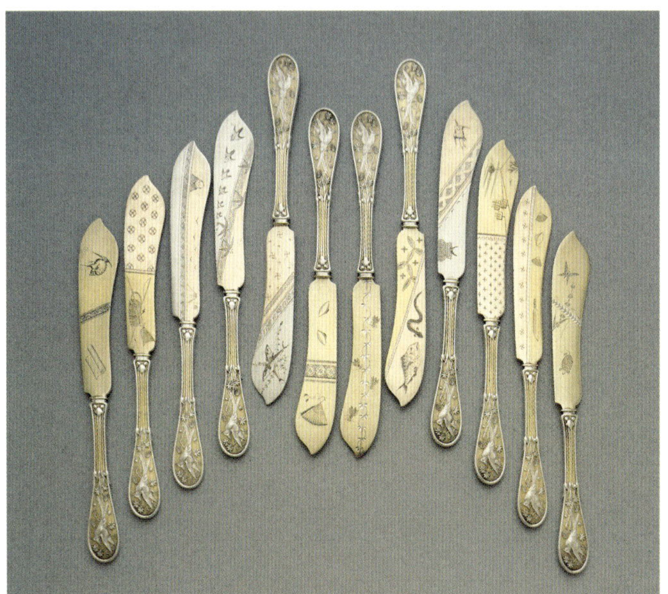

Below, Left: Tiffany & Co. Fish knives; n.d.; sterling silver and gilt; each 8.2 inches long. A set of fish knives in Tiffany's *Japanese* pattern is from a design series by Edward C. Moore, dating to 1871. It was characterized by handles decorated with bird-and-flower motifs of Chinese origin, although the source could well have been Japanese. Meanwhile, its asymmetrically disposed patterns on serving surfaces, as in the *Manga*-derived and textile motifs engraved on these blades, marked it as an early experiment in Japonesque taste, as the series name suggests.

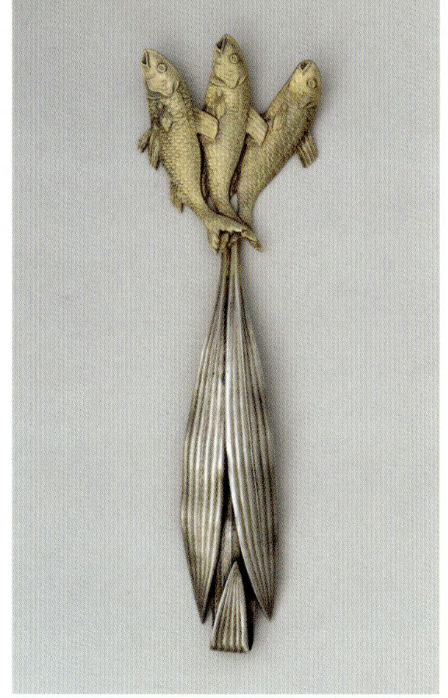

Below, Right: George W. Shiebler & Co. Sardine server, *Grass* pattern; ca. 1885; sterling silver and gilt; 6.6 inches long. A perfect adaptation of Meiji metalsmiths' melding of naturalism and function, this elegant sardine server features a cluster of minutely observed fish for the spatula and blades of grass for the handle.

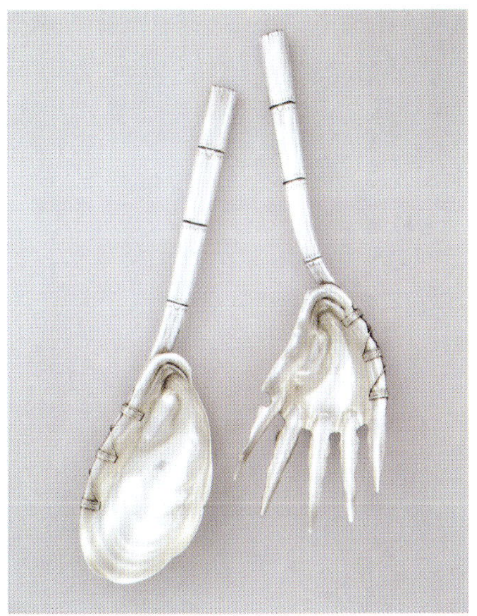

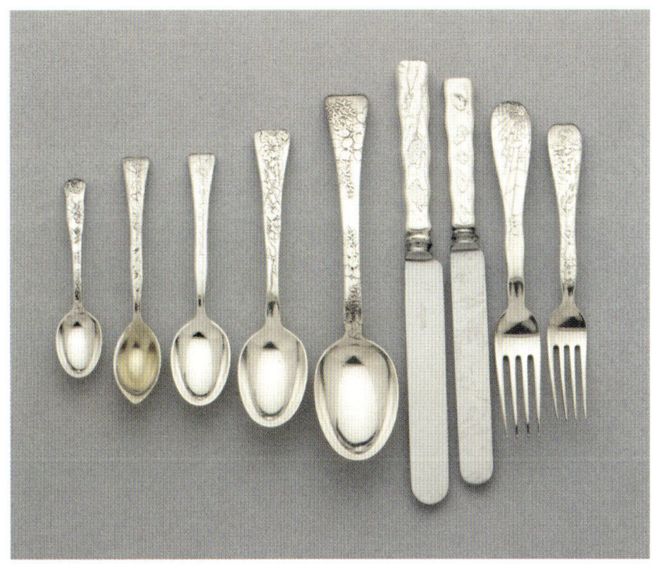

ABOVE, LEFT: GORHAM MANUFACTURING CO. SALAD SERVERS, *BAMBOO* PATTERN; CA. 1880; STERLING SILVER; 9.8 INCHES LONG. An informal yet elegant salad set, among the most radically forward-looking of Gorham designs, not only made use of favorite Japonesque motifs of bamboo and seashell but also carried Japanese smiths' clever melding of literalism to functionality to thoroughly Western utensils.

ABOVE, RIGHT: TIFFANY & CO. PLACE SETTING, *LAP OVER EDGE* PATTERN; CA. 1880; STERLING SILVER; LENGTH (L–R): LARGE COFFEE SPOON, 4.7 INCHES; ORANGE SPOON, 5.8 INCHES; TEASPOON, 5.9 INCHES; DESSERT SPOON, 7.1 INCHES; TABLESPOON, 8.65 INCHES; DINNER KNIFE, 10 INCHES; LUNCHEON KNIFE, 8.15 INCHES; DINNER FORK, 8 INCHES; LUNCHEON FORK, 7.1 INCHES. Designer Charles Grosjean's *Lap Over Edge*, a radically inventive design in its day, relied for its striking presence at the dining table upon both Japanese motifs and the "matching" method of set-making.

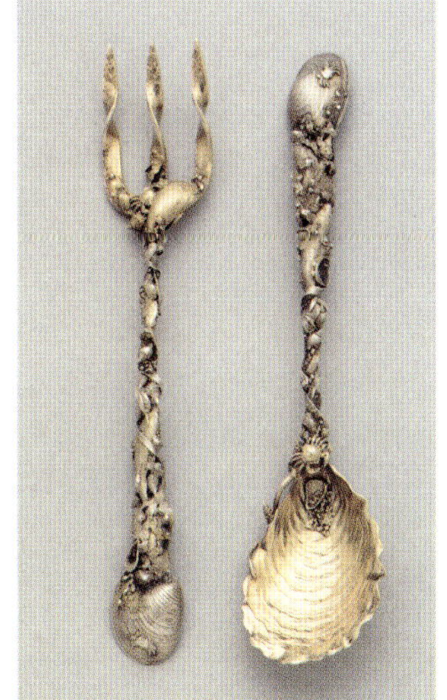

FAR RIGHT: GORHAM MANUFACTURING CO. SALAD SERVERS, *NARRAGANSETT* PATTERN; 1884; SILVER GILT; EACH 11.5 INCHES LONG. Part of an extraordinary flatware series, these salad servers are a tour-de-force of naturalism and the silversmith's art.

theft from Gorham. After much experimentation, both companies succeeded in their own versions of *shibuichi,* a gray made from silver and copper, and *shakudo,* a blue-black of copper and gold. Techniques in hand, designers excelled, and the freshness of the method freed them to create radical new conceptions that placed them at the forefront of the industry worldwide. Among the most striking adaptations to hollowware and flatware was a complex labor-intensive method called *mokume* that layered, soldered, rolled, folded, and hammered mixed metals to produce a sheet of mottled color. Color techniques, the prized mokume in particular, whetted competitive juices. French critics asserted in print that Christofle's designers, not Tiffany's, had been the first Western craftsmen to succeed with them while giving full credit to the Japanese for the origins of all such methods. But this did not prevent Tiffany's designs from triumphing at the expositions. His patterns—with their sparingly realized motifs of falling leaves, ivy sprigs, gourds,

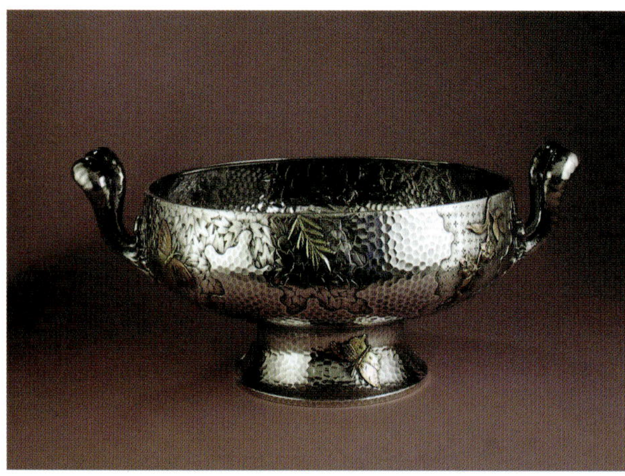

spiders, irises, leaping carp, shellfish, and cherries in silver gilt and inlaid, cast and soldered alloys, with the visual qualities of technique given full play, flatware of hammered surfaces and unconventional simplicity—anticipated tastes seventy years into the future.

Though Dresser, Bing, and many others enthused that Tiffany designs outstripped those of any other company, the wealthy could avail themselves of striking alternatives. Most innovative was Gorham's combining of silver and mixed metals on patinated, oxidized, and hammered copper, inspired by the Japanese predilection for the subtle elegance of precious accents and exquisite craftsmanship to highlight the beauty of less expensive metals. Extending the "Japonesque" from technique to theme, the appliquéd motifs from such sources as Hokusai's *Manga,* often miscellaneously combined in the "Japanese" style, found their way to tea sets, trays, smokers' accessories, vases, inkstands, mugs, candlesticks, umbrella stands, and oil lamps.

A particular favorite created in several versions was a graceful coffee ewer. Its form, with ivory insulators inserted into the handle and an ornamental band of floral scrolls ringing the base of a tall neck, hearkened to

Above: Dominick & Haff. Berry bowl; ca 1880; sterling silver and mixed metals; 5 inches high. This berry bowl amounts to a skillfully executed catalogue of Japanese references, with its mixed metal appliqués of butterflies and plant sprigs floating against a backdrop of millefleur chrysanthemums, and a stamped textile motif overlayered by a hammered surface "torn" like paper.

Right: Tiffany & Co. Dessert forks, *Lap Over Edge* pattern; ca. 1880; sterling silver and gilt wash; each 7.1 inches long; marked "Tiffany & Co./Sterling/367." Charles Grosjean produced some Japonesque designs truly spectacular in their forward-looking simplicity of shape and ornament, as in these dessert forks, highlighted by the additional element of color, using gilt-washed appliqués.

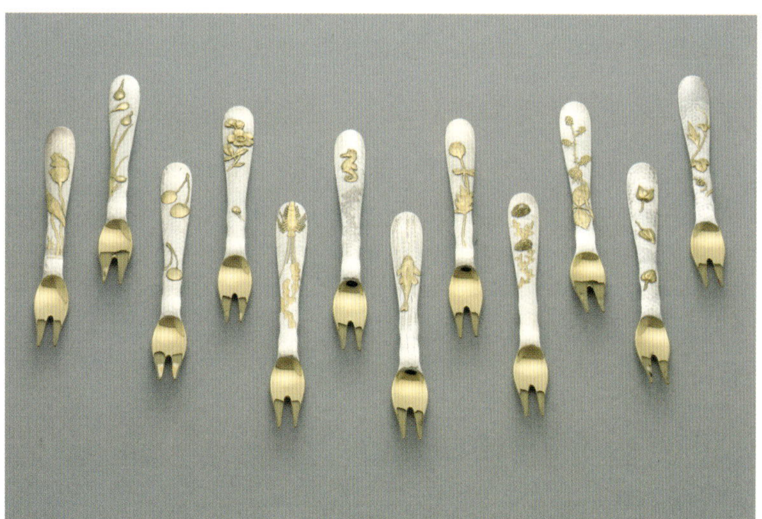

Right: Tiffany & Co. Spoons; ca. 1880; sterling silver and mixed metal alloys; each 6 to 6.2 inches long; marked "m/Tiffany & Co." To highlight the striking random patterns of the labor-intensive *mokume* technique, Tiffany designers disciplined themselves to creating designs whose flat surfaces and starkly edited shapes anticipate tastes decades into the future.

Below, Left: Gorham Manufacturing Co. Coffee ewer; 1883; copper, silver, ivory; 13 inches high; with anchor mark and "GORHAM CO, E40." This ewer is made of beaten patinated copper with appliquéd silver decoration in an eclectic combination of Turkish and Japonesque technique, motif, and shape.

Below, Right: Gorham Manufacturing Co. Platter; ca. 1882–1883; copper with mixed metal appliqué; 11.8 inches wide. American silversmiths adapted favorite motifs from Hokusai's *Manga* or similar sources to many applications and materials.

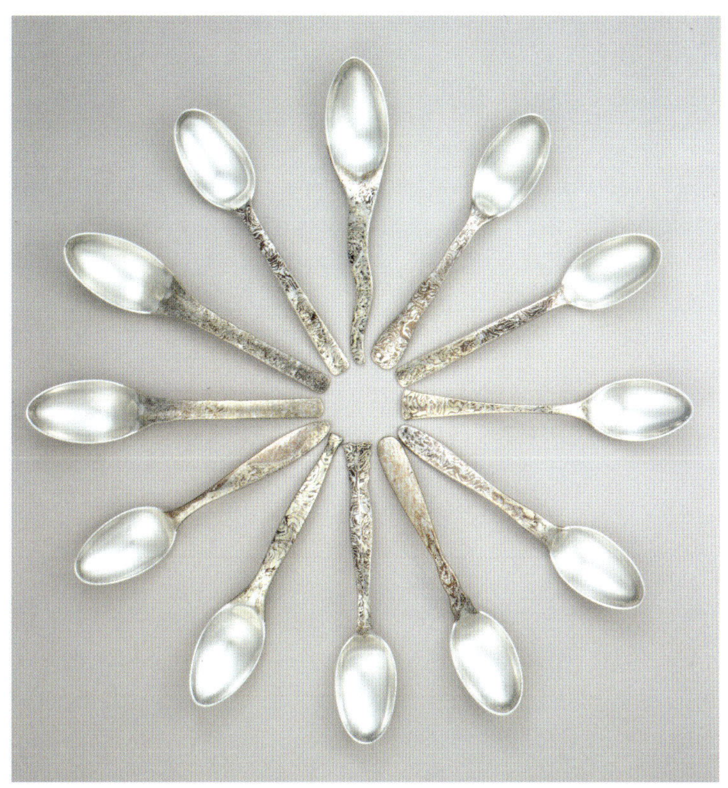

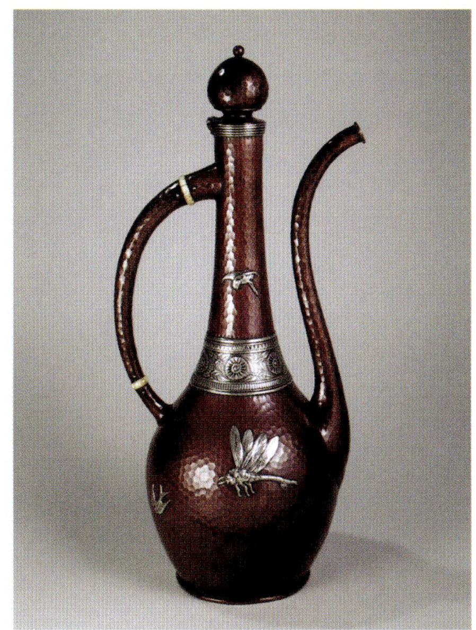

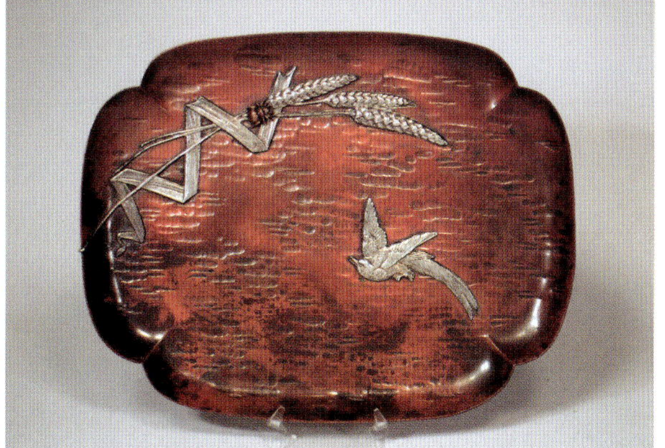

Turkey; its beaten, patinated copper body, often with realistically observed nature motifs appliquéd in asymmetrical arrangements, identified it as "Japonesque." Such hybrid classics of Aesthetic taste marked the process of assimilation of Japanese motifs and decorative principles into the broader realm of design, an evolution reflected in the yearly catalogues of mass manufacturers such as Meriden Brittania, which often featured designs under names such as *Persia* or *Venice,* whose motifs, shapes, asymmetrical ornamentation, or other features clearly marked their primary inspiration as Japanese. Many had, indeed, begun so. Using a ploy to convince the public of an endlessly varied and refreshed selection, manufacturers simply recycled old designs with new names—their motivation was not the lofty ideals associated with the Japanese craftsman but was fashion in the service of sales. With Japan, like Persia and Venice (part of Italy only since 1866)—countries all similarly exotic in the public mind—companies renamed their designs any way they liked, indifferent and probably oblivious to inaccuracy. Such incongruously inauthentic monikers gradually unmoored Japanese aesthetics and motifs from their origins, an important step in freeing them to become the neutral elements of style.

The money and sophistication of the clientele for solid silver naturally placed it at the forefront of taste. In their circles, the Japan Craze peaked in the 1880s; by 1904 Tiffany was destroying the dies for many of his best Japan-inspired patterns, even as the principles and techniques had been absorbed into the mainstream of design. But the silver plate industry was aimed toward the broader public, whose awareness and fascination for Japan began just as those they emulated had begun to shift

BELOW, LEFT: JAMES TUFTS TRIPLE SILVER PLATE. TEA CADDY; CA. 1890; SILVER PLATE; 4 INCHES HIGH. Its asymmetrical ribbon, plant, animal, and textile designs and bamboo-form frame make this tea caddy a catalogue of favorite Japonesque references.

BELOW, RIGHT: CARD RECEIVER; CA. 1885; 6.25 X 5 INCHES. Naturalistically rendered fruiting and flowering branches, often with perching birds, were among the most popular Japanese decorative devices adapted by American designers, along with their fascination for trompe l'oeil effects in unconventional media.

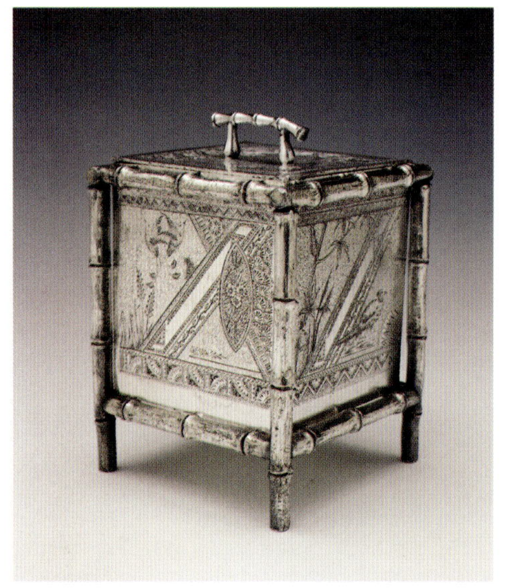

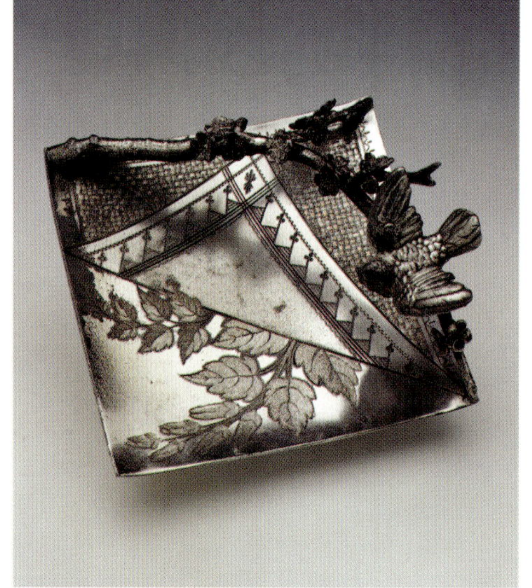

their interests elsewhere. After the Centennial exhibition introduced the Japan Craze, Anglo-Japanese styles, and the wider exoticism of Aesthetic taste simultaneously to the public, the Japanese-export ceramics and bronzes that buyers snapped up from burgeoning displays at subsequent expositions and at Yamanaka, Vantine's, Bunkio Matsuki, George Marsh, and Tiffany & Company proved irresistible inspiration to Meriden Britannia Company, Derby Silver Company, Whiting Manufacturing Co., Shreve & Company, George W. Schiebler & Company, Dominick & Haff, and dozens of others around the United States. Blending the unabated middle-class manias for Japan and silver, they offered their clientele calling card receivers, candy baskets, and other items essential to the well-appointed home, all sporting the kinds of whimsically decorative elements most noted in popular magazines of the day: fanciful fan shapes, handles and pedestals shaped like branches, naturalistic animals, cartouches laced with meandering vines, asymmetrical arrangements, and, in short, "the thousand phases of Japanese life depicted with a lively sense of their special pictorial and human value"[10]—the versatility of the medium allowing them to combine attributes previously restricted to either bronze or ceramic. Broadly commercial, these were mass-produced in a range of quantity and quality, an affordable elegance to the upwardly mobile and occasionally artful enough to appear even in the homes of the wealthy.

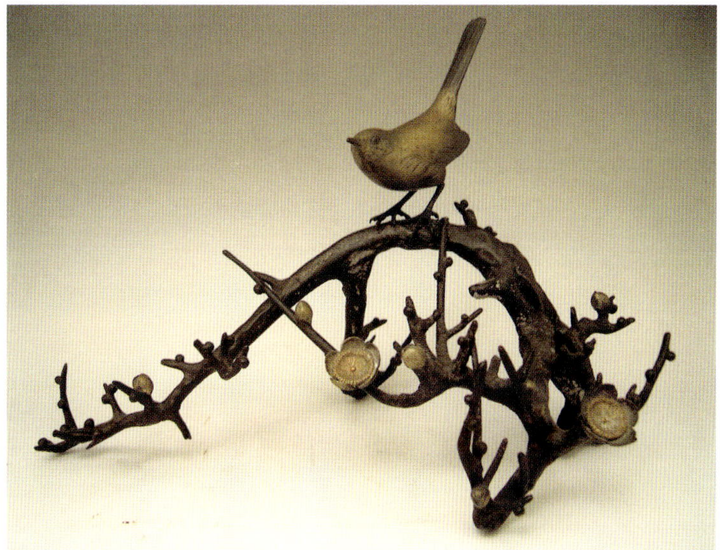

Okimono; late Meiji–early Taisho period, early twentieth century; 11 x 7.25 x 5 inches. A blooming plum branch with nightingale was fashioned in two shades of bronze in this alcove or table ornament.

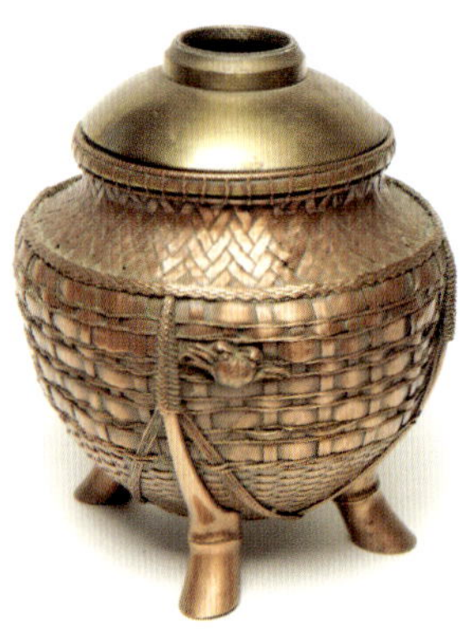

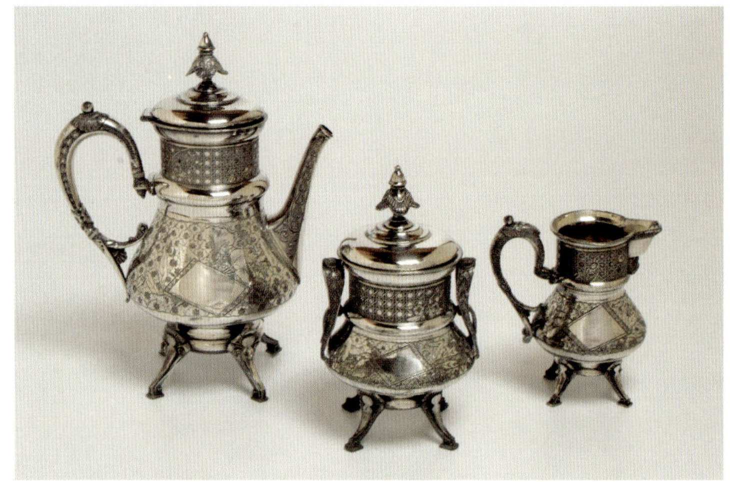

ABOVE, LEFT: OIL LAMP; MEIJI PERIOD, CA. 1890; 9 INCHES HIGH. A copper lamp shows a precise replication of several basketry weaves, bamboo, and a wandering miniature crab.

ABOVE, RIGHT: WILCOX & COMPANY. COFFEE SERVICE; CA. 1880; SILVER PLATE. Among its Japonesque references, this Aesthetic coffeepot, sugar, and creamer in silver plate includes a decorative band in imitation of basketry highlighted by stray floral sprigs.

During the 1880s and 1890s, at the peak of the taste for ornately Japonesque silver plate, the Japanese appreciation for the beauty of nonprecious metals found a welcome in another booming American industry, that of art brass furniture and accessories. Low cost and easy workability, resistance to rust, golden color, and amenability to high polish, patination, bronzing, and silvering made brass ideal for mass production. Much as with the silver plate industry, with whom manufacturers enjoyed a collegial relationship, technological advances in stamping, embossing, lathing, tubing, and the drawing of wire had freed them to explore heights of creative fancy while making a touch of glitter and opulence easily within the reach of most consumers.

The uninhibited combinations of gothic and exotic shapes and motifs sported by the products of metal manufacturers reflected Aesthetic taste at its mongrel best. But from the outset, thanks in part to the presence of English labor much as in the glass industry, Japanese concepts lay at the heart of its style, an extension of an English trend beginning in the 1870s when Christopher Dresser and others swayed the look and direction of commodities in the metals industry. One of the most talented was the unfortunate Thomas Jeckyll, whose work Whistler had so rudely obliterated in creating the Peacock Room. Jeckyll extended an elegant Japan-infused aesthetic vision beyond his upper-class patrons to the general British public. Among his most distinctive was a selection of cast-brass or cast-iron fireplace surrounds for the firm Barnard, Bishop & Barnards' coal-burning stoves. These made creative use of the

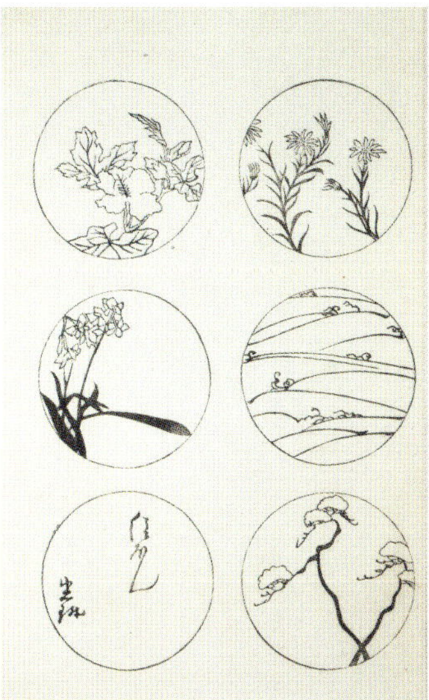

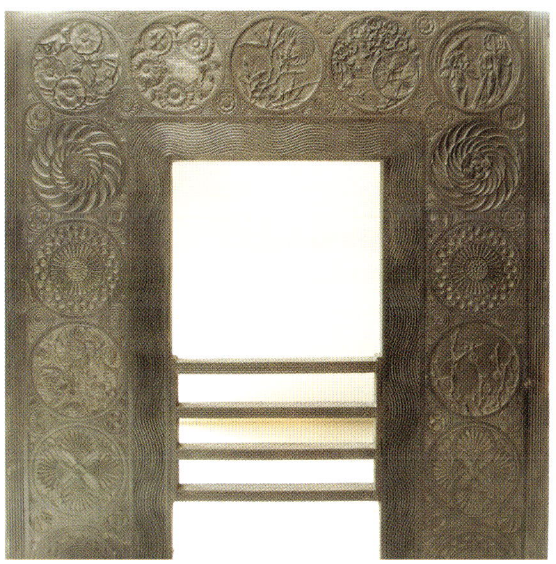

ABOVE, LEFT: SAKAI HŌITSU. WOODBLOCK PRINT; CA. 1815; PUBLISHED IN *KŌRIN HYAKUZU*. Japanese textile design conventions—such as the floral motifs asymmetrically and randomly disposed in roundels on these designs for cotton summer kimonos in the style of Ogata Kōrin immediately caught the attention of Westerners. Published in many magazines and journals, these patterns found their way into every conceivable medium.

ABOVE, RIGHT: THOMAS JECKYLL, FOR BARNARD, BISHOP AND BARNARDS. FIREPLACE SURROUND; AFTER 1873; CAST BRASS; 36 × 36.4 INCHES; MARKED "BBB/."

classic Japanese roundel-shaped family crests, stencils, and textile motifs then finding their way into many of Europe's decorative arts. Jeckyll re-created their flat geometric and floral patterns as impressions in the surfaces of the metal, disposing them in an ordered asymmetry of mingled sizes—some cropped in the Japanese fashion—against a background of fretwork or reeding. In this way, the formalized two-dimensional combination of natural and abstract form, which Christopher Dresser highlighted as one of Japan's greatest contributions to design, achieved Dresser's stated ultimate goal in Jeckyll's hands: the transformation of a mass-produced utilitarian necessity into the elegant epitome of beauty with which to elevate the life of the ordinary person.

Dresser in particular had found Japanese design principles invaluable in his extensive work with commodities of metals. But while such elegant sensibilities resonated with the likes of Tiffany, Gorham, and the artistically inclined craftsmen of their workshops, his influence on American brass companies extended only to enthusiasm for his emphasis on coloristic effects and aesthetic elevation of the inexpensive material in which they specialized. The model of simplicity in the spare gracefulness of his own post-Japan designs for teapots, kettles, ewers, boxes, and other everyday objects, and in his designs for furniture of wood, proved too plain for the American popular market. Instead, manufacturers took their cue from the less austere Anglo-Japanese ideas of

Dresser's contemporary, E. W. Godwin, using his judicious ornament and restrained constructions as a springboard for a delighted launch into ornate fancies large and small: lamps, chandeliers, mirrors, beds, shaving stands, tables, sconces, stools, easels, seating, and racks of all sorts that took full advantage of the newfound ease in producing spindles, spirals, grilles, textures and reticulations, and stamped floral and animal forms.

Among the most successful were those of the Charles Parker Company, the largest and most-diversified of art metal manufacturers. To a greater extent than the majority of its competitors, it relied upon Japanese motifs and stylistic elements enhanced with panels of glass, imported Japanese leather paper or velvet, and the color range of the many alloys produced at their huge foundry to achieve a very Anglo-Japanese look that, despite a miscellany of references, was coherent and readily recognizable: yellow brass frames made from an assortment of grilles, spiraled rods, spindles, and brackets stamped and pierced into geometric, animal, and plant shapes surrounded panels of deeply hammered or smooth patinated gray metal, often mounted with asymmetrically positioned, naturalistic, beautifully articulated floral branches in a combination of pale metals. A large yet limited group of molds and patterns meant that motifs reappeared from one piece to the next, probably a function of economy and mass production, resulted in even further stylistic unity.

Below, Left: Charles Parker Co. Hanging shelf; ca. 1885; brass and mixed metals; 33.25 × 26.25 × 7.6 inches. Within its Japonesque styling, this shelf not only uses mixed brass and other metals along with appliquéd floral bouquets and hammered surfaces but also retains its original lining of imported Japanese leather paper.

Below, Right: Charles Parker Co. Decorative panel; ca. 1885; mixed metals. This floral bouquet ornaments a small table; it is identical to the one on the hanging shelf but for its single coloration. The company controlled its costs and created a characteristic look by using the same decorative accents over and over.

Perhaps swayed by the strength of the middle-class markets for Japan-inflected Aesthetic silver

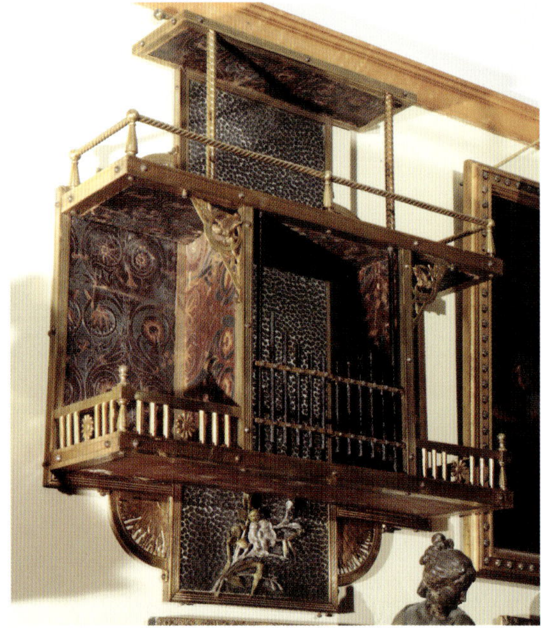

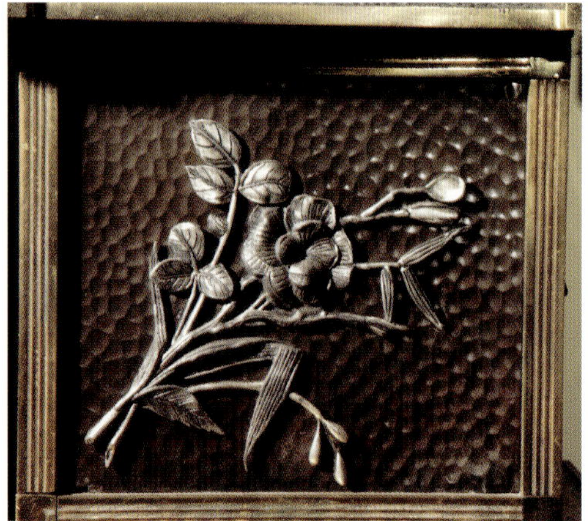

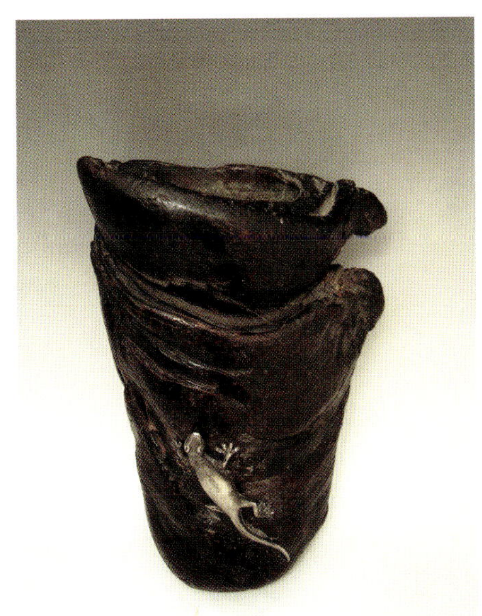

Bud vase; Meiji period; burl wood and silver; 6 inches high. An exquisitely crafted gecko in silver perches upon a rough nub of tree burl; together, they make this vase, whose striking presence belies its small size. This is an example of the unconventional vision and skill that American smiths found so inspirational in the work of Japanese artisans.

plate, brass furniture, and the like in the 1880s and early 1890s, Japanese companies and many who advised them, such as Ernest Fenollosa, misjudged the power of new trends in an American society brought to bay by the 1893 depression and its wake, as the negative reaction to many of their exhibits at the Columbian exhibition in Chicago revealed. While they would recover somewhat by the St. Louis exposition in 1904, in certain key areas the Japanese-export art manufactures industry had peaked, a victim of overextended mass production combined with dilution of quality, failure to recognize new trends, and changing priorities in the Japanese government. But the ideals that Americans associated with the Japanese artisan—that of the medieval craftsman and his aesthetic—remained both compelling and inspiring as the Arts and Crafts spirit took hold, due in no small part to the success of the public image emphasized by Japan that persisted long after their cultivation of it at the fairs had waned.

For American architecture and interior design, this idealistic vision was the reason for the impact of both the Hōōden and the Japanese interior in the Women's Building at the Chicago exhibition. It was also true with metal arts, to which articles in *The Craftsman* and other publications dedicated considerable attention as they extolled the Japanese artisan as the exemplar of his nation's living feudal spirit—the source of its industrial, social, and increasingly martial vigor. The principles they identified as guiding him in his work—functionality, quality, suitability, and economy, and the related aesthetic of simplicity, sensitivity to material, naturalism adapted to function, and the presence of the hand—epitomized what the American craftsman should strive for in his own life and work to the same broader social ends. Indeed, many very striking examples of Japanese metal crafts epitomizing all these things still were readily seen. As expensive as these one-of-a-kind imaginative creations were, their aesthetic and what that symbolized in American minds proved a natural companion to other European models in informing Arts and Crafts metalwork pegged to the new ideal of the working family and its pocketbook.

That spirit informed the taste for furnishing homes with handsome yet utilitarian American-made dishes, lamps, vases, desk sets, candlesticks, ashtrays, and the like in bronze, copper, and iron. Unlike Aesthetic

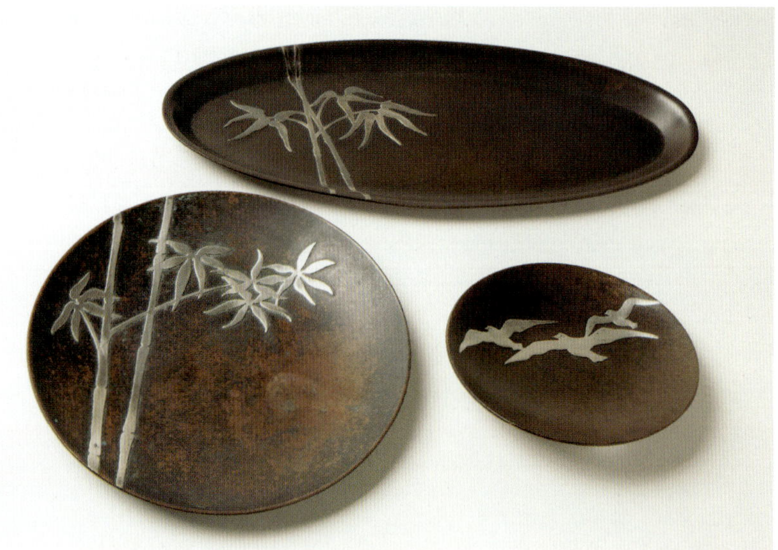

Heintz Art Metal. Dishware; 1906–1929; bronze, silver; diameter: oval tray, 9.25 x 4 inches; large dish, 5.5 inches; small dish, 4 inches; marked "AMS, bronze, sterling silver." With their closely cropped, asymmetrically placed stalks of bamboo and flying birds, three small dishes of patinated bronze with silver appliqué are typical examples of Otto Heintz' adaptations of Japanese aesthetic principles and motifs to Western forms.

movement taste, such pieces strove not for novelty, cleverness, or wit but for restraint tailored to purpose. The inexpensive materials, sturdy simplicity, and their origins in workshops of craftsmen made their relative affordability part of their aesthetic virtue. Some shops were small but high-quality personal operations, such as that of Dirk Van Erp in San Francisco, or part of arts communities with a utopian bent; the most famous was the Roycroft Copper Shop of East Aurora, Illinois. Others among them—Stickley's own United Crafts Workshops of Eastwood, New York, and Heintz Art Metal Shop in Buffalo, New York—straddled the line between mass-produced and artisan-made pieces by combining spun-metal forms with various amounts of hand finishing.

In visualizing their idealistic philosophy, the metal arts of Japan figured prominently. The elevation of inexpensive non-precious metals and the employment of hammer textures and darkly patinated matte surfaces typical of Japanese metalwork and identified as such had by now become so fully assimilated as to be neutralized of their origins, but in other instances an overt borrowing remained. Van Erp, Heintz, and others often incorporated imported Japanese ornamental papers for lamp shades or reinterpreted lantern forms by retaining the shape edited of all or most identifiably Japanese details.

Perhaps the most consistently Japonesque in spirit were the unassumingly elegant practical pieces by Otto Heintz and his staff, beginning with the founding of his shop in 1903, closely followed after World War I by the rival Smith Metal Arts Company that pirated many of his designs. Heintz looked to the quintessential Japanese aesthetic of bronze accented with precious metal ornament as his primary model. Cost-effectiveness limited him to a set number of pared-down, often compact machine-made shapes. For these he achieved variety by means of several subdued patinations—including soft bronze brown, a slightly iridescent deep red, a mottled muted green, a nickel silver, and a mottled gold tone—on which appeared a wide array of silver appliqués. Much of the quiet appeal of these pieces lay in the contrast between the sober simplicity of the dark forms and their delicate bright ornament, whose linearity strongly resembled Japanese stencil patterns. While many presented conventional Western decoration, a large proportion extended the Japanese feeling to the motifs themselves: pine branches, birds, Virginia creeper, roses, vines, and other such themes, at times of wire-like fineness, asymmetrically disposed across a dish, growing upward from the base of a vise, or dangled from the rim of an inkwell.

It was not just aesthetics and the ideal of the living artisan that Japan contributed to the Arts and Crafts philosophy and, thus, into the lives of middle-class people through the moderately priced lines of Heintz and similar companies. Japan's ongoing wrangle with international expositions over the appropriate categorization of its visual heritage and modern works in the debate of "fine" versus "applied" art had the tangential effect of legitimizing the profile of American applied arts when, at the St. Louis exposition, judges finally capitulated and removed all such barriers. Those that qualified for the most prestigious exhibit in the Palace of Fine Arts displayed a degree of novelty with a level of quality and material unaffordable to all but the wealthiest, but lesser versions were readily available. The public snapped them up, and the fair became the point of dissemination for Arts and Crafts into the general public.

1. Smith 1875.
2. As quoted in Hosley 1990, 127.
3. Bing (1895) 1970, 121.
4. Venable 1994, 123–24.
5. *Ladies' Home Journal,* December 1890.
6. Ibid.
7. Hood 1999, 40.
8. *Art Amateur,* June 1879.
9. *New York Times,* December 11, 1898.
10. *New York Times,* April 11, 1909.

8

Clay and Glaze

The Journey to Modern

. . . And on the hillside I can see / The villages of Imari, / Whose thronged and flaming workshops lift / Their twisted columns of smoke on high, / Cloud cloisters that in ruins lie, / With sunshine streaming through each rift, / And broken arches of blue sky. / . . . The snow on Fusiyama's cone, / The midnight heaven so thickly sown / . . . The leaves that rustle, the reeds that make / A whisper by each stream and lake, / The saffron dawn, the sunset red, / Are painted on these lovely jars; / . . . The stork, the heron, and the crane / Float through the azure overhead, / The counterfeit and counterpart / Of Nature reproduced in Art.

—*Henry Wadsworth Longfellow*[1]

People of the Gilded Age placed great store in ceramics, especially those they could relate to their romantic vision of the artisan-potter of old. The wealthy collected not just avidly but even competitively, devoting vast sums and developing refined connoisseurship. Critics, scholars, and dealers built notable public careers on their knowledge. Ceramics became a craze in their own right, the butt of satire in *Punch* and other publications. Asian porcelain enjoyed particular acclaim, hence Frederick Leyland's "hawthorne jar" collection that some criticized as an expression of ostentation over true appreciation. Unsurprisingly, for many immersed in the Japan Craze, ceramics more than any other art

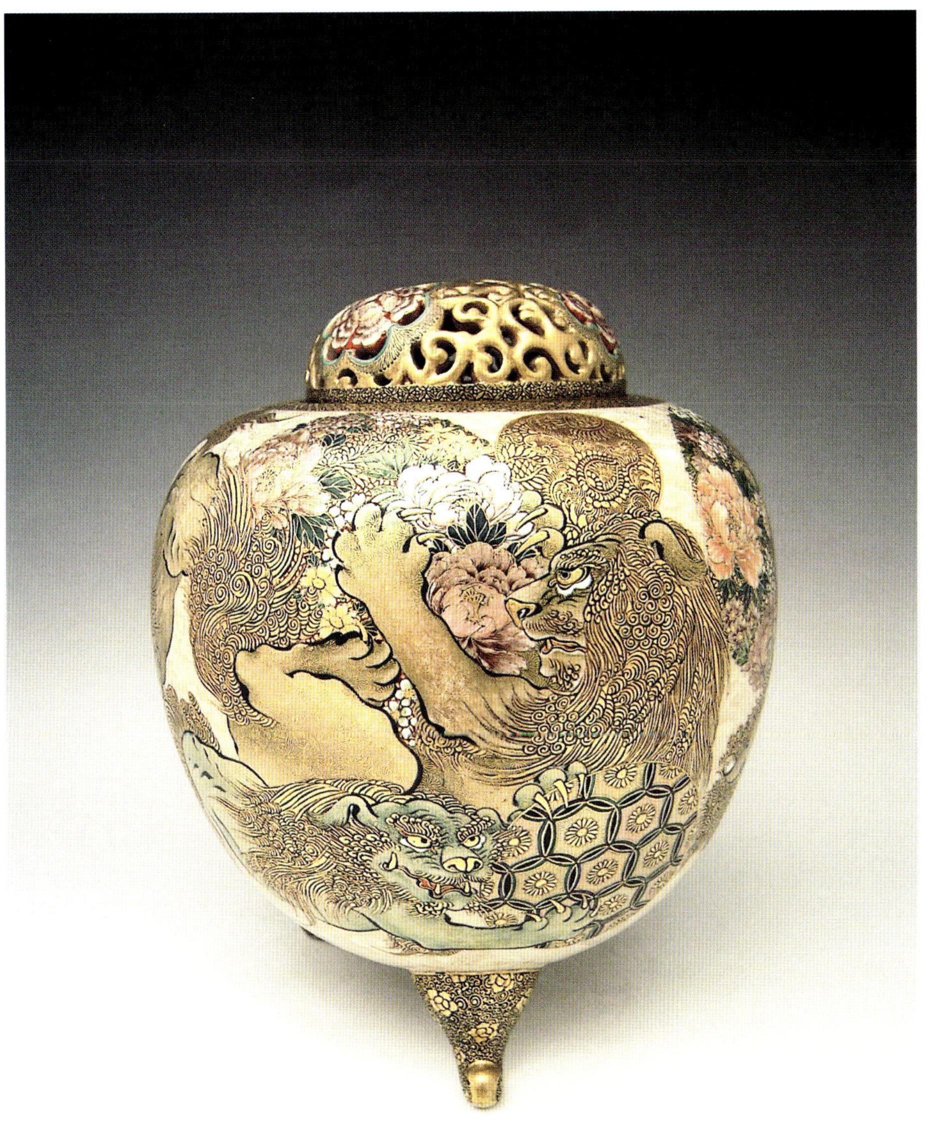

Satsuma ware incense burner; early Taisho period; pottery with gold and enamel decoration; 9 inches high; signed "DAI NIPPON YASUI SAKU" ("Made by Yasui of Japan"). This exquisitely potted and glazed Satsuma pottery *koro,* decorated with *shishi* (Chinese lion dogs) frolicking amid peonies, was among Japan's highlights featured at the 1915 Panama-Pacific International Exposition in San Francisco.

alerted to the contrast between the cherished medieval-infused ideal and "ruination" wrought by modernization. Much hand-wringing ensued over what many called a lost golden age in "the Fairy Kingdom" when, "without any thought of profit or loss, but solely with the motive artistic pride, potter and painter wrought in rivalry together to make works of art . . . ."[2] And over the first forty years after the opening of their nation to the West, there was nothing else that the Japanese more adeptly exploited than the general Western confusion regarding that ideal and the directions their taste really took them. Ultimately, as the fashion for ornate orientalized eclecticism waned, Japanese aesthetic principles found a home in the Arts and Crafts philosophy that replaced it, offering the commercial market opportunity to exploit and amateur hobbyists to experience for themselves the rectifying model of artisanal work and the inspiring aesthetic of simplicity.

In addition to what found its way to the shops of Paris from the 1850s onward, the rare photos of Alcock's display show that authentic and export Japanese wares mingled at British expositions as early as 1862, the numbers growing exponentially after 1871, for, on its groundbreaking tour that same year, the Iwakura Mission had seen treasured collections of Imari porcelain maintained by European noble families since days of the Dutch trade monopoly. Among its members, this mission included former samurai aristocrats from fiefs where these ceramics were made, who knew it to have been a profitable trade. This unexpected and flattering rediscovery of a Western fascination helped spur the new generation of export wares. In addition to its enormous potential for creating a modern market and raising the nation's international profile, a modernized ceramics industry promised a revived role for a prized art that, much like metalsmithing, found itself under stress with fading customs important to the old regime.

When the Meiji government first entered the feverishly competitive world of the expositions, its ceramics industry was still dominated by the family workshops of old. If these appealed to Western fantasies of the pure-minded medieval artisans, their products did not match the vision, for people now expected perfection obtainable only by the huge strides the Industrial Revolution had made. Exposition judges sharply criticized for inconsistent quality the same porcelains once widely admired and imitated in the days of the Dutch trade. To change that opinion, Japan enthusiastically turned to technology for its export ware. A major early

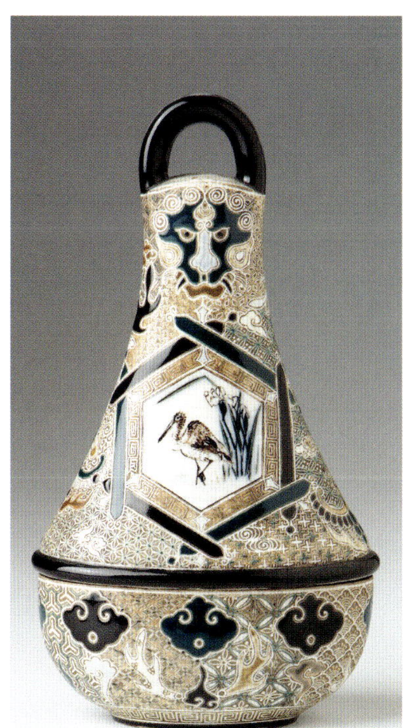

Container with lid; Meiji period; porcelain and overglaze enamels; 8 inches high. A mold-cast export porcelain, carefully designed to meet foreign demands for the exotic, eclectically mingles motifs from Chinese painting and a shape loosely adapted from ancient Chinese bronzes with a surface treatment, patterns, and colors based upon Japanese textiles. Unmarked, its mongrel qualities make its source impossible to identify, but the strong colors of teal, black, and ochre yellow suggest Kutani as a possibility.

resource was Christopher Dresser. The government regarded his 1876 visit so important that it awarded him an imperial audience followed by virtually unheard-of access to art industries, with a flock of facilitators, illustrators, and translators always in tow. As he gleaned from Japanese aesthetics for British mass manufacturing, he willingly proffered invaluable advice on modernizing their ancient venerated industry. The Japanese also imported expertise for long-term advisement. Gottfried Wagener, the German whose work with the art enamel industry helped make it the world standard, was actually first recruited for ceramic production, in which he was the single most important innovator.[3] Through him came coal-fired kilns, new organizational systems, and glazes and pigments that expanded the color range to accord with Western taste. Ceramicists went abroad to research the most commercially successful designs, visit state-of-the-art factories, and acquire technology—steam-driven wheels improved throwing; copper stencils, stamping, and spraying machines reimagined decorating. Most transformative was plaster casting. In addition to speed, it enabled the standardization and the complex constructed forms Westerners now demanded. It also meant that the same forms found their way all over Japan, styles distinguished by decoration rather than shape. By the late 1880s Japan had fully mechanized export production. This presented not only the irony that a craft admired by Americans as an epitome of Japanese artisanship and values owed a significant portion of its excellence to Western technology but also that the distinctive look of its art wares, perceived as "Japanese," in fact derived from an aggressively international mentality regarding materials, technology, manufacturing methods, market-researched design, and, increasingly, merchandising. In their awestruck attraction, many Westerners persisted in seeing old-fashioned skill in works of ever-increasing mechanical virtuosity, leading "authentic" versus "inauthentic" to become a *cause célèbre* taken on by Edward Morse, Ernest Fenollosa, and others.

As Longfellow's romantic poetic image made clear, Imari held special fascination. His "thronged and flaming workshops" did not in fact fit the description of this town on the west coast of the island of

Kyūshū, a port closely linked to the Dutch monopoly beginning in the seventeenth century. Its name had become affixed in Western minds to its chief exports, the colorful porcelains made in nearby Arita, Nabeshima, and Hirado, each a distinctive style directed expressly to the foreign market. In feudal times this region was the powerful domain of Hizen, ruled from the castle town of Saga. High-ranking Saga samurai were central in the coup that brought the emperor into the public view and Japan into the modern age. One, a member of the Iwakura Mission, had seen for himself the Europeans' prized collections of wares from his region. With such history and power for Saga in the new government, it was only natural that these porcelains would assume an important place in Japanese competition with the West, and that they would succeed.

In the eyes of many, "Imari" porcelains had always epitomized Japanese taste and Japan itself. Their hold on European imaginations inspired kilns in Worcester, England, and in Delft, Holland, to imitate them. Yet, such purely export creations had little in common with those created at these kilns that were prized by feudal lords. Their brocade-like designs—too ornate for native sensibilities—took their cue from China, for they

Below, Left: Hirado ware; Meiji period. Porcelain with cobalt blue underglaze decoration; 8.2 inches diameter. A finely molded porcelain dish is shaped as five overlapping petals, its motif of a delicately executed bamboo basket spilling over with grapes and persimmons exemplifying the "quivering realism" that commentators lauded in Japanese interpretations of natural themes.

Below, Right: Imari charger; Meiji period; porcelain with cobalt blue underglaze and enamel overglaze decoration; 18 inches diameter. Chrysanthemum and cherry motifs in ornately fluted fans against a backdrop of millefleur and Western-style brocade patterns make this large charger a particularly highly styled example of export design.

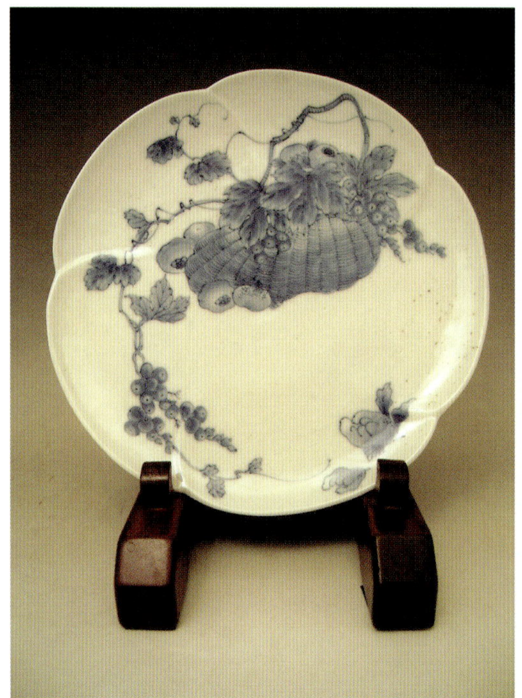

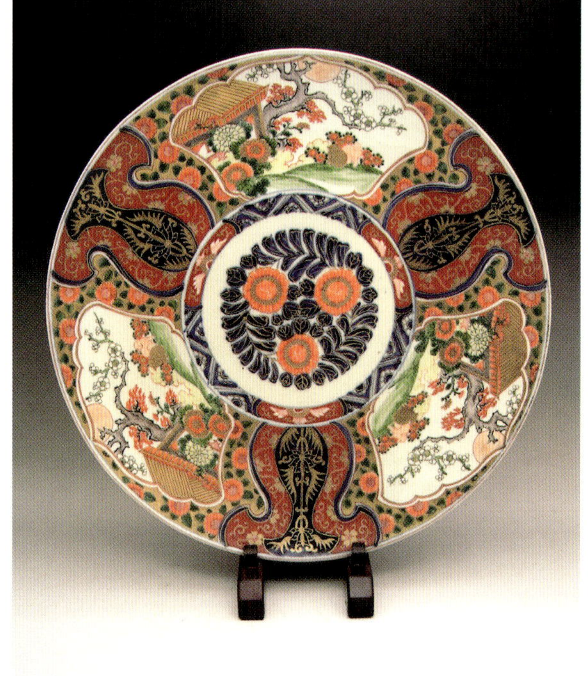

had originated in an economic opportunity provided by disruption in Chinese porcelain trade in the seventeenth century. This so-called "Old Imari" also reflected specific requests by the Dutch East India Company that strictly controlled both sides of the market. In its quest to meet the needs and tastes of its wealthy clientele, it sometimes even went so far as to present Japanese potteries with painted wooden models to copy. European collectors often had silversmiths provide elaborate mounts in a further adaptation of these expensive wares for Western tastes.

The new generation of Imari wares capitalized upon this hybrid foundation, adapting characteristic features to mass-produced precision and standardization while updating shapes, colors, and motifs to modern tastes and notions of Japan. Those from Hirado emphasized bird, flower, and animal motifs executed in brilliant cobalt blue underglaze on vases, dishes, water pots, and incense burners, and were distinguished by engraving, relief, openwork, and applied animals such as dragons. Generally "Chinese" in style and subject, Japanese qualities emerged in bold, often asymmetrical, arrangement of motifs and in their textured and sculptural exuberance that made them the artistic twins of export bronzes. In wares from Arita, cobalt blue underglaze designs typically served as the foundation for overglaze decoration in bright vermillion, green, yellow, pale blue, and metallic gold for an olio brocade consisting of floral, scroll, and geometric diaper patterns surrounding ogee, fan, or rectangular cartouches that framed figural, floral, or fauna images. Likewise originating in Chinese motifs, new versions included Japanese themes. Shapes became more ornate. Kiritsu Kosho Kaisha featured Hirado and Arita wares at the Centennial exhibition, with those from Arita enjoying pride of place.[4] Organizers considered them "fully equal to the bronzes," adding that the display "surpasses in beauty of forms and ornamentation the combined exhibit of every other nation . . . ."[5]

Imari vase; Meiji period; porcelain with cobalt blue underglaze and enamel overglaze decoration; 36 inches high. Richly decorated with the much-loved Asian motifs of peacocks, chrysanthemums, and dragons, this tall porcelain Imari vase with the flaring scalloped rim and hints of vermilion and turquoise was designed for a Western clientele.

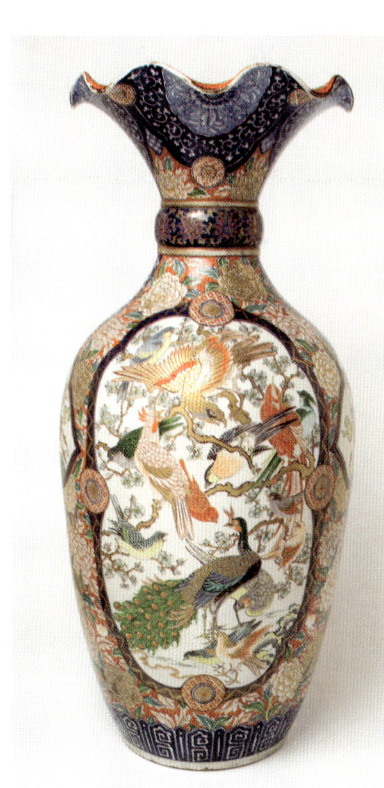

On the other side of Kyūshū from Imari, in a bay jutting into the island's southern end, the castle town of Kagoshima perched on a narrow straight, the pluming volcano Sakurajima looming a stone's throw away. The West's quintessential image of Japan, this was the home of Satsuma pottery, the Japanese ware least

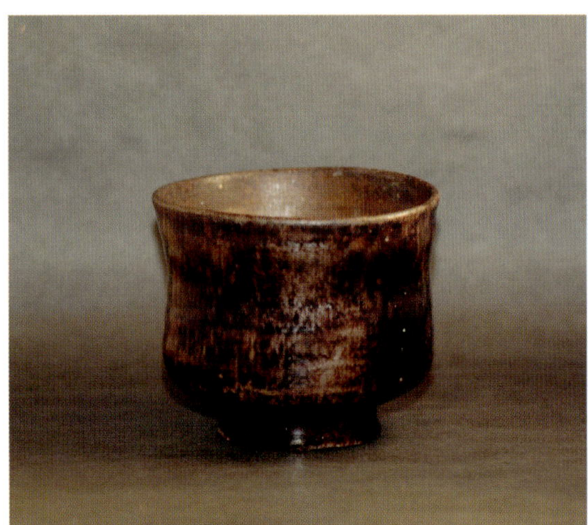

"OLD SATSUMA" TEA BOWL; LATE EDO PERIOD, MID-NINETEENTH CENTURY; POTTERY; 3.2 INCHES HIGH. Some traditional Satsuma ware was not even pale in color, but dark.

historical but most calculatingly tailored for export by its makers and, for a time, the most successful. This came as no surprise. The region's experience with European trade began with the Portuguese and Spanish in the mid-sixteenth century. Up to the end of the Tokugawa shogunate, Kagoshima was the seat of one of Japan's most powerful samurai clans, to whom trade had brought almost unrivaled wealth, an unusually forward-looking interest in imported science and technology, and direct experience of the pitfalls in dealing with the West. It was at Kagoshima that Christianity had arrived with Francis Xavier, ultimately deemed such a threat as to be brutally stamped out and instigating Japan's two-and-a-half-century ban on most of the outside world. In the shogunate's waning days, the British bombarded the city to retaliate for an Englishman's murder by retainers of the fief. Anger at Tokugawa incompetence in the face of the looming Western menace incited Kagoshima samurai to major roles in the coup that brought down the old government and abolished the feudal system. These men continued prominent in the new regime and its drive to parity with the West: the admiral whose decisive victory in the 1904–1905 Russo-Japanese War signaled Japan's arrival as a military power hailed from Kagoshima.

The debate over "authentic" raged more for Satsuma pottery than for any other Japanese ceramic. Like the porcelains of Hizen, the industry had begun relatively late and with "outsider" associations in Satsuma's case when marauding samurai abducted and forcibly resettled Korean potters in the sixteenth century. Their descendent remained "foreign" to the Japanese. These potters specialized in modest earthenware bowls, incense burners, dishes, and vases of either dark brown or eggshell color with a transparent glaze netted with fine crackles. In the late eighteenth century, they began decorating these plain pieces with floral sprays and geometric motifs in blue, green, pink, red, and gold enamel—sparing versions of designs used in Hizen. Their quiet appeal attracted a few discerning early foreigners, notably Edward Morse, who designated them "Old Satsuma" despite the decorated style not being much older than the collectors themselves.

He did so in light of what was already transpiring at the kilns, for it was only natural that Kagoshima, with its long history of Western contact and its activist role in the new government, would stand at the forefront of the aggressive quest for industrialization and national recognition. In characteristic clear-eyed fashion, Kagoshima leaders recognized the ceramics industry as an obvious opportunity. Redesigned through calculated selection to match Western ideas of gorgeousness and exoticism, the once-unprepossessing transmogrified into the opulent and densely decorated, large incense burners Westerners referred to as "clove-boilers" being among the most renowned. They revised the colorful mingled and banded *horror vacui* of their Arita cousins as "gold brocade"; the customary cartouches framed floral bouquets, scenes from Japanese and Chinese myths and legends, dainty damsels, or hosts of Buddhist and Taoist divinities. Kagoshima potters reimagined the textured surfaces and sculptural qualities of Hirado porcelains as raised clouds and waves, pearl-like encrustations, and appliquéd cicadas, birds, and dragons. Foreign delight in breathtaking detail was met with feats guaranteed to awe: critics for the 1904 St. Louis exposition could not help but extol ". . . a small Satsuma bowl in the decoration of which, with a reading glass, one could count eight thousand butterflies, and the famous 'monkey vase' upon the exterior of which two thousand monkeys were discernable."[6]

SATSUMA VASE; MEIJI PERIOD; POTTERY WITH GOLD AND ENAMEL DECORATION; 28.5 INCHES HIGH. A tall pottery vase features a scene from Japanese legend and floral motifs.

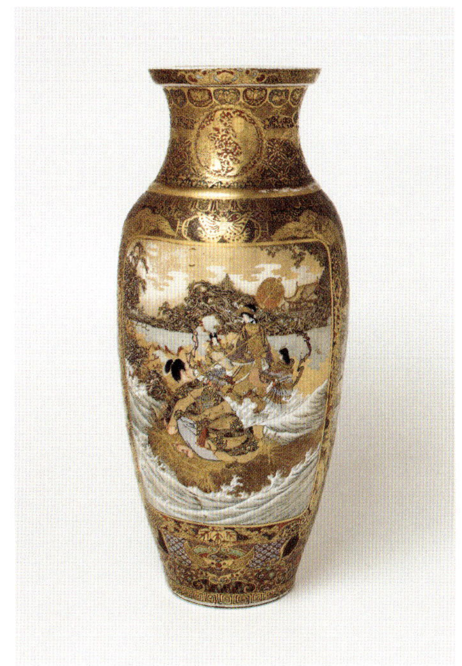

Many of the 1880s managed to link Satsuma with medieval values, attributing the best to small family workshops of pure-minded artisan holdovers, all the while ruing a feudal system that had been "utterly destroyed" and, with it, the passing of "Old Satsuma."[7] Yet, however enthralled, those priding themselves on refined connoisseurship had to be confident that the sums commanded assured authenticity—with respect not just to taste, on which Morse so persistently worked to educate, but also to provenance and quality. But Satsuma's instant popularity proved irresistible to other important ceramic centers such as Kyoto, Nagoya, and Tokyo. They followed suit almost instantly, benefiting from dissemination of techniques and styles as the travel and communications barriers of feudal times gave way to rapid unrestricted movement of craftsmen. This resulted in pieces virtually indistinguishable from one place to the next and introduced variations from the original look: bodies of mazarine blue or dark brown, the characteristic cartouches abandoned for full-body designs. As early as the Centennial exhibition in 1876, Satsuma's once-regional distinctiveness was rapidly on its way to becoming the most national of all export styles, and for all its inauthenticity, ironically the most readily identifiable as "Japanese." But, to the minds of Morse and others, there was worse: to bolster value by capitalizing on Western desire, inexperience, and gullibility, the Japanese promulgated the idea of "old" and "new" Satsuma, the unscrupulous resorting to such dissembling as soaking pieces in tea to give a patina of age or, with an eye to the foreign aversion to plainness, refiring unadorned old pieces with applied decoration. Meanwhile, manufacturers offered a range of quality and price that took full advantage of mass production and, in doing so, completely shattered the identification with the artisan that Westerners held so dear. Wailed *The Art Amateur* in 1880, "'But why is old Satsuma ware a thing of the past and inimitable?' the reader may ask. The reason is that the feudal system has been utterly destroyed.'"[8] Ultimately anyone, it seemed, could own a piece of Satsuma pottery. A victim of its own success, the fantastic prices collapsed. Newspaper commentary began to note auctions where even good pieces could be had at a fraction of what they had commanded only a year or two before. Dealers, perhaps Edward Greey

Below, Left: Kinkozan kilns of Kyoto. Satsuma-style vases; late Meiji–early Taisho period; pottery with mazarine blue and multicolored enamel decoration; 18.75 inches high. These vases employ the Satsuma practice of narrative depictions and of framing the body of a ware with contrasting neck and foot bands of ornamentation; but the use of mazarine blue as well as the all-over decoration in the main portion of the ware mark these vases as not only later versions of the style but also reflecting its dissemination to other ceramic centers.

Below, Right: Satsuma vases; late Meiji–early Taisho period; pottery with brown glaze and gold enamel; 8 inches high.

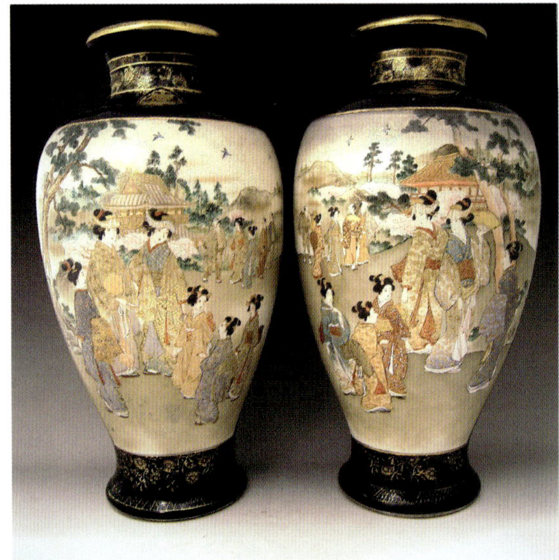

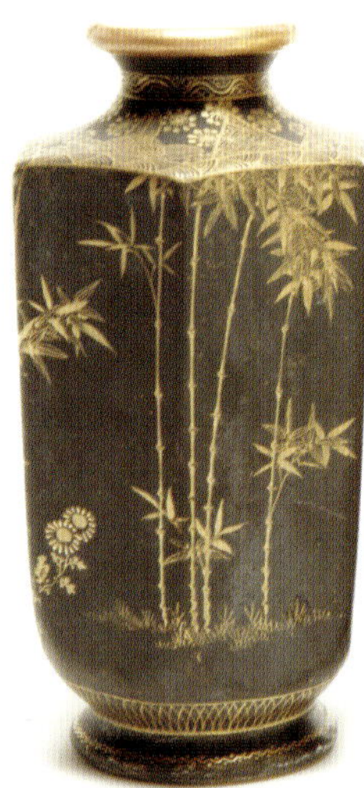

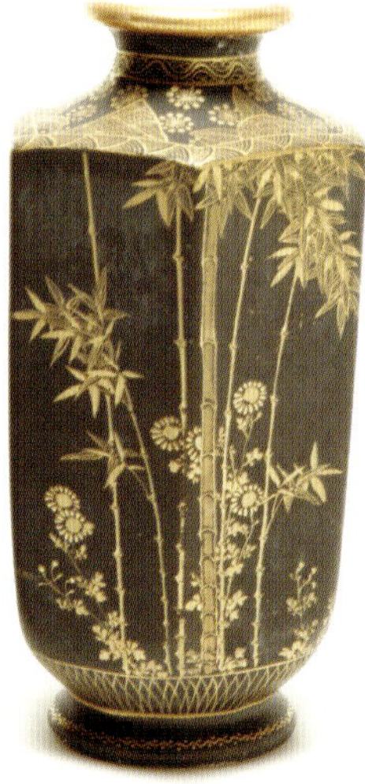

among them, lost their fortunes in the face of changing tastes and growing Western sophistication.

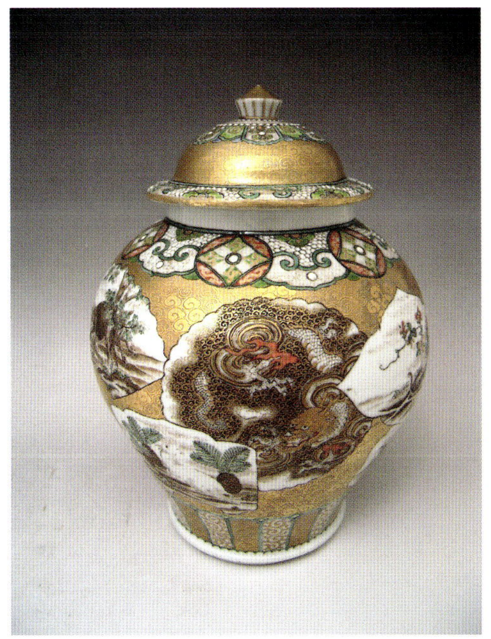

Kutani jar with lid; Meiji period; porcelain with enamel overglaze and gold decoration; 8.5 inches high. The animals of the Chinese zodiac in floating cartouches, each a different shape, show the exotic opulence combined with breathtaking precision and refined execution that Americans prized in the best export wares of these famous kilns.

Even in Tokugawa days, image sleight of hand had characterized Kutani wares. Since the seventeenth century, porcelains boldly patterned in aubergine, yellow, red, green, and blue had been prized by the Maeda clan that ruled Kaga on the west coast of Japan's island of Honshu. The name that identified these wares was that of a Kaga village, but like all porcelains, the earliest were made in Hizen. Porcelain craftsmen later operated kilns in Kutani itself for several decades but then shut down for almost a century. In the early nineteenth century, the Maeda revived production as part of a policy to bring prosperity through art crafts. They directed potters to a distinctive new look, drawing on the earlier style combined with those of Arita and Kyoto, adding motifs from Chinese painting, and using specialists brought in for that expertise. The result was an opulently embellished, finely decorated hybrid look for Japanese aristocrats. With the new regime, descendent of these samurai expanded the mercantile strategy. They proceeded with deliberation, developing extensive local educational resources, state-of-the-art production, innovative multipurpose designs, and aggressive marketing. They revived "Old Kutani" of the earliest years and introduced a new export version. Not unlike the Satsuma pottery it sometimes deliberately resembled, its look emerged from considerable research on foreign desires. Though made of porcelain, a finer and harder material than pottery, it similarly emphasized densely brocaded golden backdrops for a variety of overlapping cartouches bearing miscellanies of Chinese and Japanese themes. The aristocratic "Kutani" taste remained in the delicate drawing and dominant palate of deep red and dark green with silver accents. It was an unqualified success. By 1887 the region controlled 80 percent of the export ceramics market.[9] Its potters had won prizes at the Centennial exhibition in Philadelphia and would again in Chicago in 1893. But as with Satsuma, changing Western tastes combined with Japanese misjudgment led to overproduction, decline in quality, and, ultimately, demise.

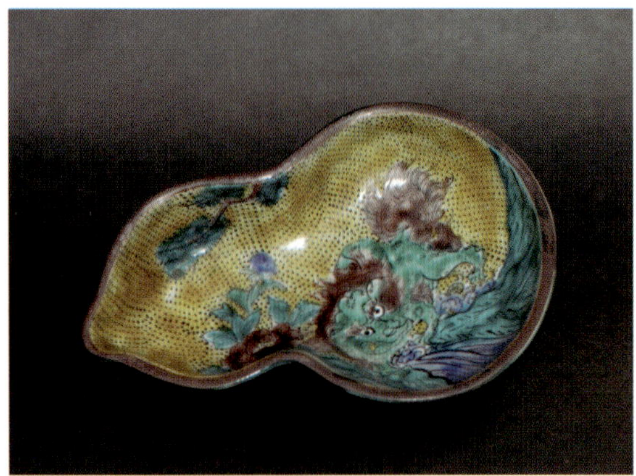

Above: "Old Kutani"–style dish; Meiji period, nineteenth century; porcelain with overglaze enamel decoration; 7.5 inches diameter. This dish, in the shape of a double gourd, depicts a *shishi* (Chinese lion dog) frolicking by a stream.

Fenollosa was particularly excoriating of the deleterious effect of the West on what he viewed as Japan's pure-mindedness with respect to ceramics:

Now the whole compound is given up to a feverish activity of work, with Tom Dick and Harry and their children slapping it out by the gross. An order is given by the foreign agent for a hundred thousand cups and saucers. "Put on all the red and gold you can" is the order . . . and the haste and roughness of the work, which is exported to America and Europe, confirms to the Japanese that they are dealing with people whose tastes are barbaric. And yet these Japanese products are regarded as attractive in our country.[10]

At the Centennial exhibition, when the art marketing firm Kiritsu Kosho Kaisha presented the first collection of Japanese ceramics ever seen in the West selected according to Japanese criteria, the most perceptive in the American decorative arts world found its 216 pieces, from ancient to modern, eye-opening and inspirational. These individuals, among them Louis Comfort Tiffany, returned to their studios and production floors to experiment with ideas that ultimately found full expression in American Art Nouveau as well as in Arts and Crafts. But the wider public—enthralled with new machine-made accuracy and tainted by tastes that critics in a few years' time would disparage as "ingrained love of display" and attraction to "tawdry and vulgar bedizenment"[11]—turned a cold eye to the drab colors, sparse and imprecise decoration, coarse textures, irregular shapes, and running glazes of traditional Bizen, Karatsu, Oribe, and the like, while delighting in the finely finished, minutely

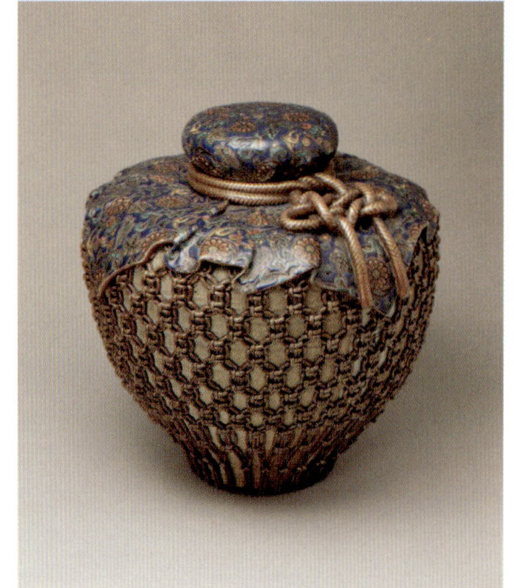

Right: Miyagawa Kozan, for the Makuzu Kiln. Lidded vase; Meiji period; stoneware with polychrome enamel decoration; 14.5 inches high; signed "Makuzu." This large covered vase combines tradition with innovation: its form an over-sized replica of a time-honored presentation container for fine teas, its extraordinary trompe l'oeil verisimilitude of a sort obtainable only by melding superior handcraftsmanship with the era's latest ceramic technology.

Kiritsu Kosho Kaisha introduced the foreign public to Japanese aesthetics as early as the Centennial International Exhibition of 1876 in Philadelphia with a collection of traditional ceramics such as these:

Below, Upper: Ko kiyomizu ware *chaire* (tea container); ca. eighteenth century; pottery with overglaze decoration; minus lid; 1.6 inches high. / right: Kuro oribe ware *chawan*, (tea bowl); ca. nineteenth century; pottery; 2.9 inches high.

Below, Lower: Karatsu ware *chawan* (tea bowl); nineteenth century; pottery with snakeskin glaze; 3.3 inches high. / right: Kiseto ware *chaire* (tea storage jar); early Edo period, ca. seventeenth century; stoneware; 3.25 inches high.

detailed and constructed pieces designed so astutely with them in mind. In the ensuing years, the message of Morse, Dresser, Fenollosa, and Okakura ran up against that of other pundits whose actual knowledge did not always match their popular influence. Dealers such as Bunkio Matsuki only complicated perceptions when, their nationality serving as a tacit seal of authenticity, they mingled genuine pieces in their shops with others custom-designed in Japanese factories to meet Western tastes. In the end, despite the "deathblow"[12] to quality and authenticity that opinion laid upon the corrupting influence of Western methods and ideas, Americans snapped up these fancies in clay, delighted with what, at its best, displayed a breathtaking technique that they attributed to Japanese artisanal genius but, in reality, was attainable only through the very technological methods they claimed to abhor. Indeed, some authorities wrote disparagingly of pieces in their own collections, the length with which they dwelt on such supposedly degenerate objects suggesting an attraction they dared not openly admit. Such popularity assured that American manufacturers would follow suit with products created in the same spirit. This resulted in some of the definitive examples of Aesthetic ceramics. However spurious their inspiration, they shared with other Japonesque objects the positive effect of shaking American tastes loose from the extreme conventionalism of the time.

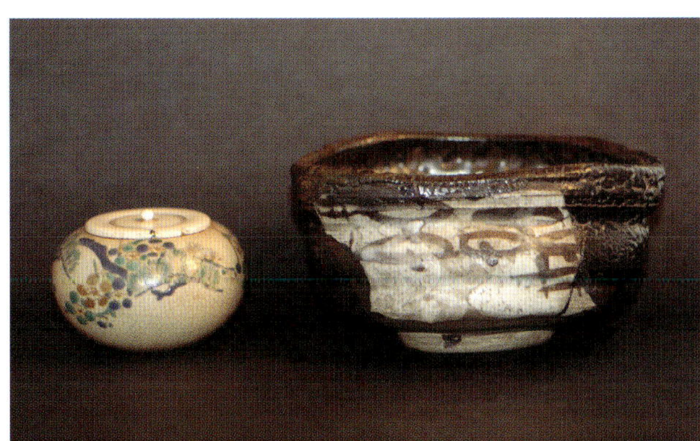

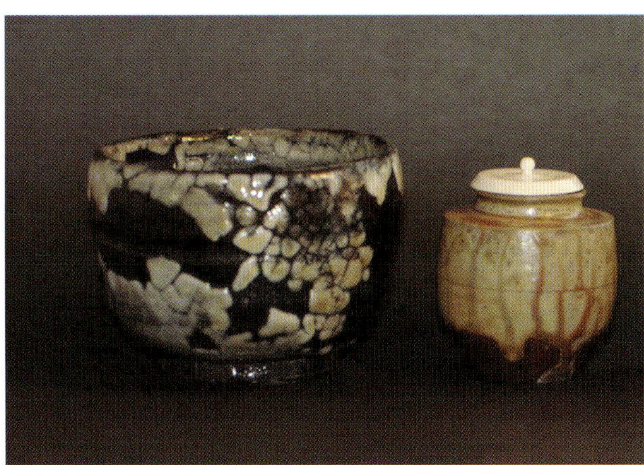

For a model on how to assimilate "Japanese taste," Americans had only to look at their own dinner tables. From the 1870s into the 1880s, as Japanese aesthetic principles inspired Dresser to radical new ideas, more literal-minded if nevertheless talented in-house decorators and designers for the huge British art and mass-market ceramics industry looked to the export style that had inspired a feeding frenzy for asymmetry, cartouches, fans, geometric patterns, flitting birds, crawling amphibians, trailing vines, and waving bamboo. All made their way to the pitchers, gravy boats, cups, and platters of ordinary dining services and tea sets. Companies used the same stencil and transfer patterns for different lines, adding colors as the price range rose. This helped to spread the fashion by assuring that it could be had by almost any pocketbook. Companies also pursued the same assimilative practices as silver plate manufacturers, assigning to overtly Japonesque designs names that simply suggested "foreign"—*Formosa, Cairo, Burma,* or even *Melbourne.* They also adapted Japonesque pictorial devices to non-Japanese themes, gracing dinner plates with vine- and leaf-laced asymmetrical cartouches bearing everything from romantic castle ruins to the British Houses of Parliament. Exported to the United States, these affordable wares established Japonesque taste in America as much as Japanese export itself, often as design ideas free of associations with Japan.

For Americans, it all came together at the Centennial exhibition in 1876. People took ceramics very seriously as prime expressions of the nation's arrival as a first-rank civilization, considering that a perfectly created vase or charger united the twin goals of industrial might and artistic profundity. Such a piece was not just functional but was something to be collected and displayed as a measure of the owner's refinement as well. A National Potters Association had been formed to encourage world-class designs expressly "American" in character, but its efforts had not paid off in the eyes of Centennial exhibition judges. Critics contrasted them unfavorably with those from China, Japan, and

Stoke-on-Trent potteries; Japonesque-patterned stoneware; late nineteenth century.

Below, Left: Pattern from Japanese sources.

Below, Right: Pattern from British sources.

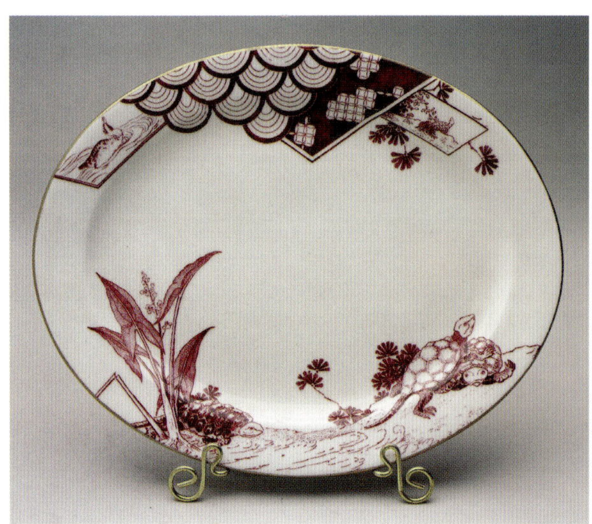

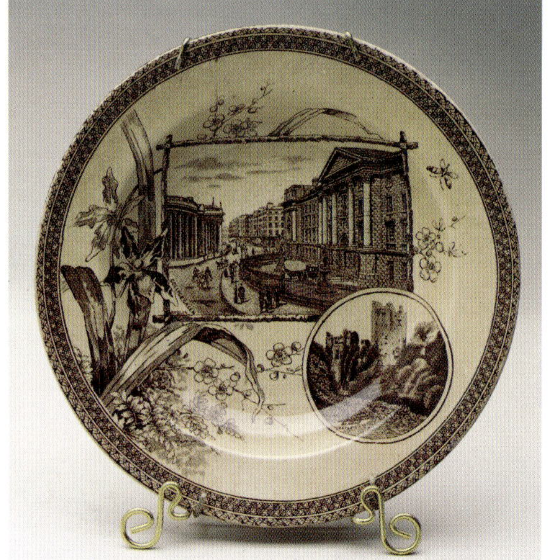

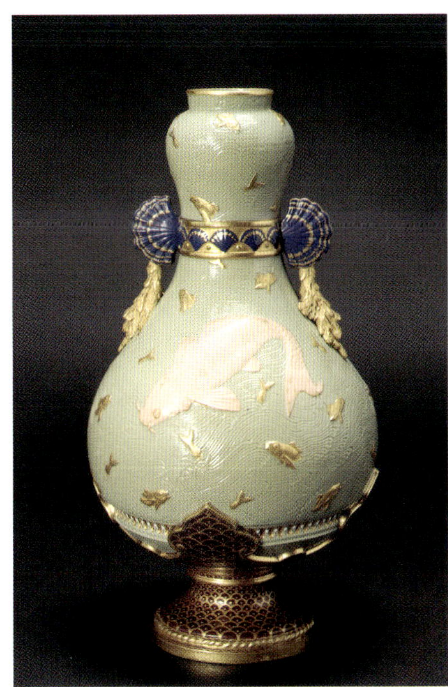

William Brownfield Company. Vase; ca. 1880; porcelain; 13 inches high; marked "Brownfield's China" and "Tiffany & Company, New York." The double-gourd shape and the motif of leaping fish amid waves were among the most popular adaptations by Western designers from Japanese sources. This vase combines these with Islamic and French motifs and colors, making it a textbook example of high international style that established a benchmark for art ceramics in the United States in the years after the Centennial exhibition. Created by world-renowned art ceramics manufacturer Brownfield, it was sold by Charles Tiffany in his elegant New York City establishment.

Europe, one going so far as to consider American wares "so poor as not to be noticeable artistically."[13] But, the chagrin must have been tempered by a touch of ironic pleasure that these judges had found European submissions likewise wanting in relation to those of the backwards Japanese, whose ceramics revealed "utmost dexterity in moulding, in evenness of line, and accuracy of contour of difficult and complicated forms."[14] And, looking from these export vases, jars, and incense burners with their awesome technique, exquisite coloration, and breathtaking size, to the novel adaptations of British dinner services and flower containers, they saw a bridge.

In the decades after the Centennial exhibition, Trenton, New Jersey, emerged as a center of an internationally competitive ceramics industry. Its fifteen factories of 1870 grew to twenty-three by the peak of the Aesthetic movement in the 1880s and continued to expand for another forty years. Trenton's ceramists bore a natural affinity for the highly successful British industrial model and its distinctive designs that their employers emulated, for many were emigrants from there. Moreover, not unlike Kutani in Japan, Trenton's kilns benefited from forceful, enlightened government support. George B. McClellan, far more effective as New Jersey's governor than he had been as general of the Union Army, directed his marshal instincts toward building a world-class ceramics industry for his state. By 1879 a school of industrial design had been founded, supported by a cutting-edge reference library and a ceramics study collection. And, also like the Japanese, McClellan believed in fact-finding missions to bolster competitiveness. He sent Trenton's star ceramist to the Exposition Universelle of 1878 in Paris.

This craftsman worked for the innovative and aggressively competitive firm of Ott & Brewer, which cemented its reputation as the nation's preeminent art ceramics manufacturer when, in an example of industrial espionage worthy of John Gorham, it enticed top craftsmen away from Belleek, Ireland. Using a closely guarded formula, the Belleek factories made exquisitely thin, lightweight, translucent ivory-colored porcelain that lent itself to shapes of exceptional refinement and took an unusually silky glaze. By 1882 Ott & Brewer was making its own

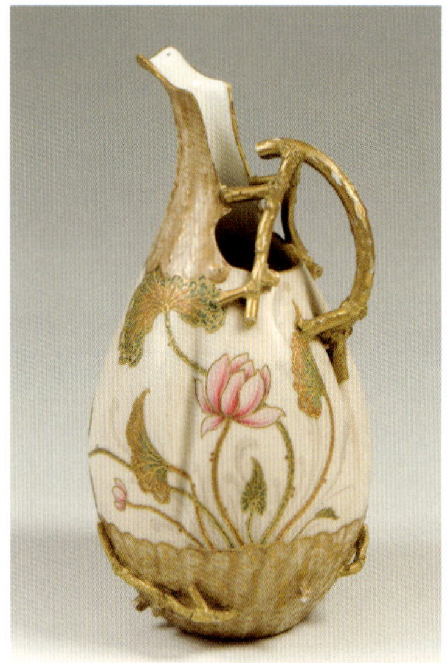

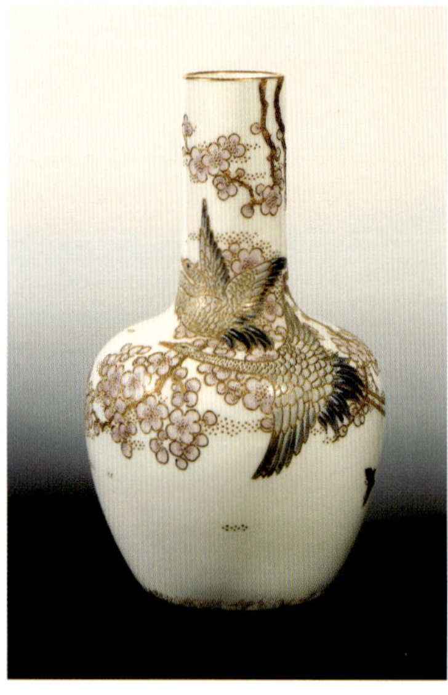

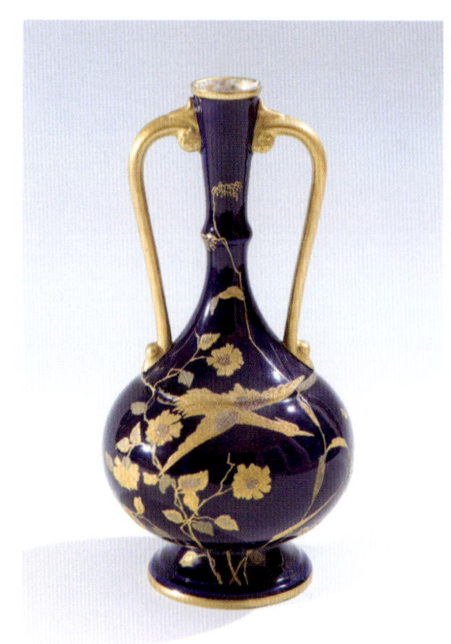

AMERICAN JAPONESQUE ART PORCELAINS; 1880–1914:

ABOVE, LEFT: JAMES CALLOWHILL (PROBABLY), FOR OTT & BREWER. BELLEEK PITCHER; 13 INCHES HIGH. Gourd-shaped with applied relief, and gold textured registers (above and below a central ornamental field) borrowing from the Satsuma style and its twig-shaped decoration and handle from sources such as bronzes.

ABOVE, CENTER: JAMES CALLOWHILL, FOR WILLETS. BELLEEK VASE; 10.5 INCHES HIGH; SIGNED "JAMES CALLOWHILL." A vase featuring cranes, butterflies, and cherry blossoms.

ABOVE, RIGHT: GREENWOOD POTTERY. VASE; PORCELAIN; 9.5 INCHES HIGH. A mazarine blue vase of Persian form, with Japanese floral and bird motifs in gold, echoing trends in British Worcester porcelain.

Belleek-style porcelain. Within a year it had made clear its competitive intent, entering this new line at a trade fair entitled America Against the World. For a decade, Ott & Brewer retained its status as the American leader, its prized ware considered the equal of anything Ireland had to offer and sold only in the finest shops, such as Tiffany & Company. But the formula did not stay with Ott & Brewer any more than it did with Ireland. Other companies soon produced Belleek-style art porcelains, among them the Ceramic Art Company (which ultimately became Lenox), Greenwood Pottery and China Company, Columbian Art Pottery, and Willets Manufacturing Company, all of Trenton, and University City Pottery, near St. Louis, Missouri. All saw their designs as "fine art"—unlikely and unacknowledged allies of the Japanese in the debate on an issue that the Japanese had raised to high public awareness by pressing their case at the international expositions, where these companies also exhibited and sought prominence. In addition to bestowing cultural prestige, value as "fine art" also validated the cost, as Willets made clear in its aim, "to command extravagant prices because a guarantee is furnished that no exact duplicate of the decoration will ever be sold again."[15] At its peak, American Belleek commanded anywhere from $200 to $500, equivalent to between $4,000 and $9,000 today. Japonesque designs occupied a conspicuous niche in the pursuit of this lofty and lucrative goal.

Belleek porcelains displayed great variety in their idea of "Japan." True to their roots in British Anglo-Japanese designs and sharing a spirit of novelty and charm with America's silver plate, many were stylistic hybrids that placed Japanese-style naturalistic floral and animal motifs and textile patterns in cropped and asymmetrical compositions or appliquéd to forms otherwise entirely Western. Collar and foot bands of textured gold looked to Satsuma and Kutani for inspiration but not necessarily to the style of the vessel to which they were applied or the nature of the motifs employed. Other designs borrowed directly from Japanese metalwork, ivories, lacquerwork, and prints, freely mixing these references in very un-Japanese ways or sometimes mimicking them so precisely that the porcelain's own qualities all but disappeared. In typical Aesthetic fashion, a broadly "oriental" eclecticism paired Japanese ornamental motifs of luxurious metallic and colored glazes with Persian-form ewers and vases in much the same fashion as Gorham's experiments with silver and mixed-metal appliqués on copper bodies of Islamic derivation.

Ceramic Art Company was among the first American Belleek manufacturers to recognize, as the Japanese had, that one way of transforming an "applied art" into a "fine art" was to present it as the brainchild of one craftsman. Exclusively purveying art porcelains, each often signed by its decorator, helped the firm dominate the market after Ott & Brewer fell into bankruptcy in the early 1890s. As if to emphasize the point of painterly preeminence, it specialized in elaborate embellishment and gilding that all but hid the delicate translucency that had been Belleek's original appeal. They hired talent from all over, including two artists from Japan who went by the names of Tekauchi M. and F. Fouji, the latter of whom a local journalist admiringly wrote, "It is interesting to stand beside him and see him gently stroke a fragile Belleek vase, with a pencil looking as fine as a hair, until the delicate design is completed."[16]

UNIVERSITY CITY, BY FRENCH ÉMIGRÉ TAXILE DOAT, FOR UNIVERSITY CITY. PLATE; PORCELAIN WITH PATE-SUR-PATE DECORATION; 9 INCHES DIAMETER.

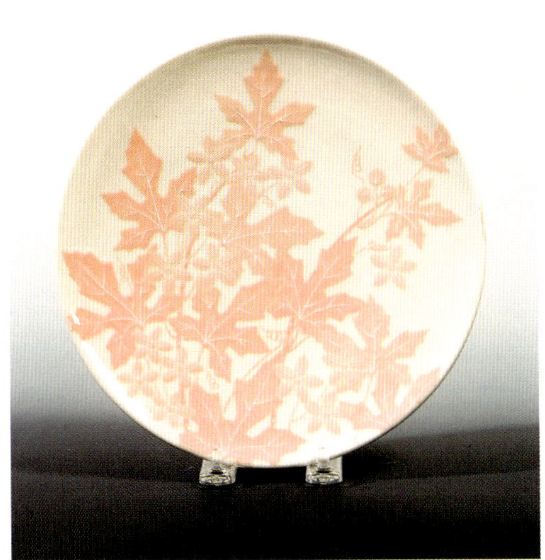

In 1880, even before Ott & Brewer's creative strides with Belleek, one of the era's most influential publications on taste, *The Art Amateur*, informed the American public of a ceramic landmark: a dinner

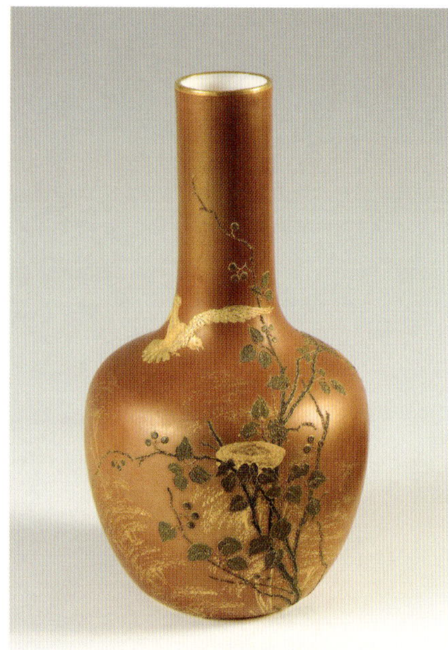

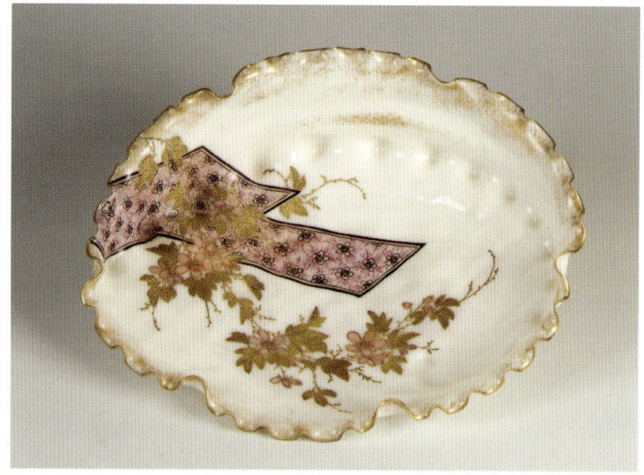

Above, Left: Ott and Brewer. "Bronze Colored Vase with Bird of Prey"; porcelain; 10 inches high. A precise replication in porcelain of Japanese bronze with mixed-metal inlay.

Above, Right: "Shell Dish"; Columbian art pottery; Belleek porcelain; late nineteenth century; 8 inches diameter. Dish in the form of an abalone shell with the motif of a folded *obi* (sash) and floral sprays.

service commissioned by President Rutherford B. Hayes from the Franco-American porcelain manufacturer Haviland. To recoup the huge production expenses, eight duplicate sets were made for sale in the United States, much smaller than the thousand-piece original but bearing the presidential seal; one became the prized possession of railroad magnate Major James H. Dooley of Richmond, Virginia. Such exclusivity showed that the Gilded Age emphasis on "individual character" as reflected in one's possessions extended to the art of dining. Although not Haviland's first presidential commission—the company had already designed china for Abraham Lincoln, Ulysses S. Grant, and would again for Benjamin Harrison—this service perhaps more than any other met the ambitions not only of the American ceramics industry but also of owner David Haviland and his stated personal goal: a ware whose quality and beauty perfectly distilled the distinctiveness of American taste and character—a mandate echoed by the White House itself and duly noted in *Art Amateur*. What the writer did not note was that this American expression, suitable for the home of the nation's leader, owed its look almost entirely to the assimilation of aesthetic principles from Japan. So sophisticated and complete was its absorption that the *Art Amateur* didn't seem to recognize them as Japanese at all.

Ever since the Centennial exhibition, the American art world regarded Japanese art principles an alternative to those of Europe, a beacon out of its condescending shadow. Haviland was uniquely positioned to find a new path, having been established to produce

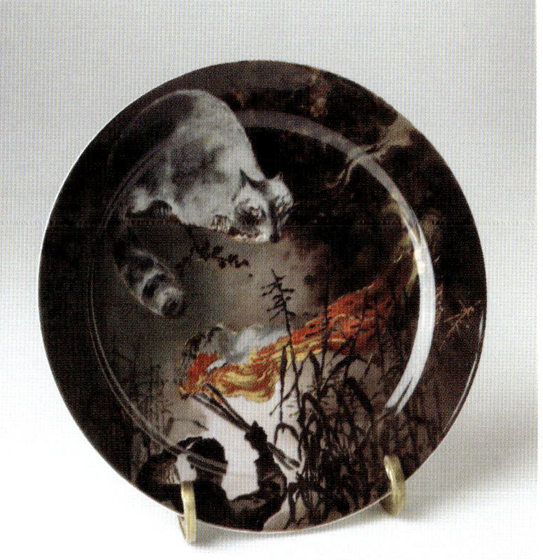

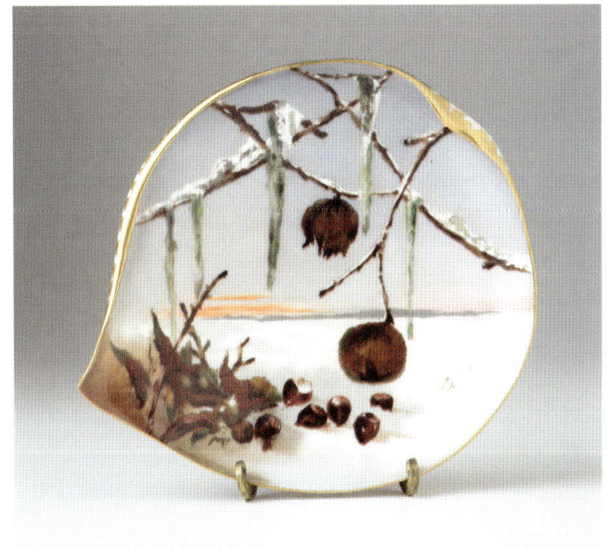

Above, Left: Theodore R. Davis. *On the Plains at Night;* porcelain from the Haviland dinner service commissioned by President Rutherford B. Hayes; 1880; 10.2 inches diameter. Wild things are revealed in the light of a brandished torch.

Above, Right: Theodore R. Davis. *Chincapin Nut;* dessert or fruit plate, modeled on the American wild apple leaf; 9.4 inches wide. Porcelain from the Haviland dinner service commissioned by President Rutherford B. Hayes; 1880.

ceramics of the famous French quality but designed specifically for the American market. Its innovative practices in pursuit of that goal resulted in award-winning design and a preeminent position in the manufacturing world. And it was natural that this prestigious project turned to Japanese ideas, because, paradoxically, it had already had considerable experience with them in the French market. Haviland had hired Félix Bracquemond in the 1860s, resulting in some of the first Japan-inspired dinnerware.

The White House service far surpassed these early experiments, which had adapted manga, *mon* (crest), and other Japanese motifs to standard blanks. For an undeniably American look, Haviland turned away from its highly trained in-house decorators to one of America's most prominent illustrators: Theodore R. Davis, who had acquired a diverse portfolio and a reputation as a swashbuckling man of action over several decades with *Harper's Weekly, Saturday Evening Post,* and other major publications. Haviland boasted that Davis had "fished in the rivers of the East and West and in the sea, hunted fowl and wild game in the forests, the swamps, and the mountains; shot the buffalo on the plains, and visited the historic haunts of the Indians in the East; met the Indians in their wigwams and studied their habits on the prairies of the Far West."[17] Summing him up, *Art Amateur* pronounced him "capable of infusing into the work something of the national spirit."[18]

Davis created one hundred and thirty watercolors of wilderness game and plant life in a virile realistic style. Haviland noted with pride the technical challenge of replicating them on porcelain. Though the crabs, turtles, frogs, smelt, peccaries, snipe, huckleberry, corn, goldenrod, okra, Virginia creeper, and log cabins could not have been more American, the idea of using such informal subjects in highly naturalistic and intimate renditions, and of extending asymmetrical compositions to the rims rather than confining them to the centers of plates, platters, and saucers—all of which took cues from typical Japanese decorative practices—seemed a bit jarring to Americans when placed on something one ate from. As the conventionally minded *Art Amateur* critic observed, not altogether favorably, "we must look at the new White House service chiefly as a collection of ceramic pictures."[19] In the set-making practice of "matching," also popular in silver services, dishes featured different images thematically related in groups according to use. This was understood as a Japanese concept. And, while most shapes were clearly Western, some seemed very unusual to American eyes: fruit plates in the form of the wild apple leaf, or fish dishes based on scallop shells, or (in a nod to the Japanese practice of taking aesthetic advantage of the clay medium) flat rimless serving platters with curled corners, approved by the critic only because this afforded a good surface for decoration. In only one area was the reference to Japan overt and duly noted: coffee

Theodore R. Davis. Platter for serving fish; 1880; porcelain; 24.25 inches long. Porcelain from the Haviland dinner service commissioned by President Rutherford B. Hayes; 1880. Theodore R. Davis's netted catch gracing a fish platter alluded to the custom of presenting the first shad of the season from the Potomac River to the U.S. president, but the motif was well-established in the public consciousness as Japan-derived, thanks to such common sources as stencils, and appeared in many media.

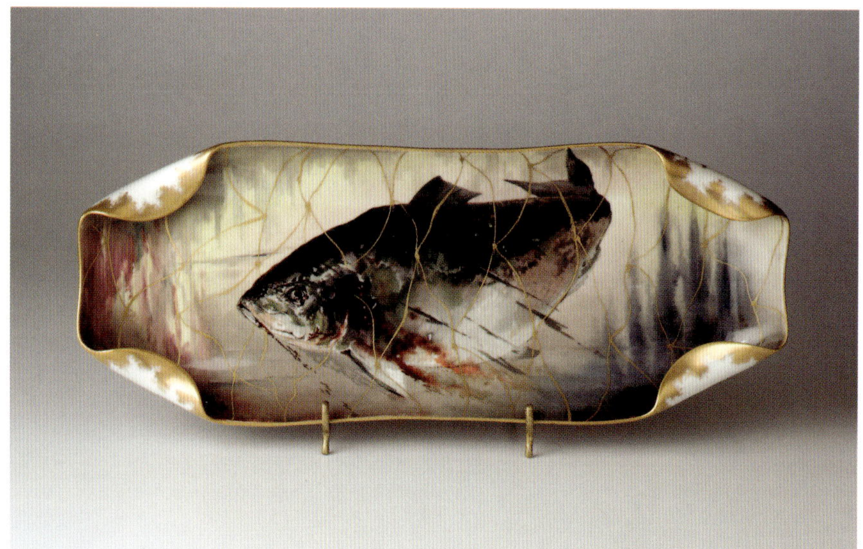

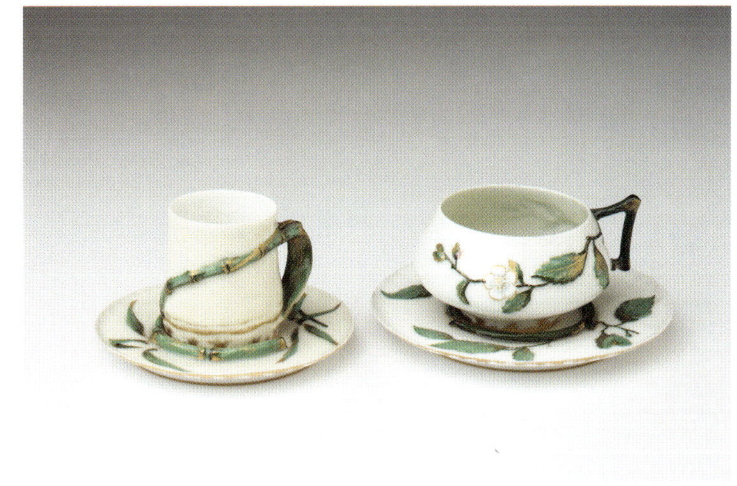

Right, Upper: Theodore R. Davis. Demitasse with relief bamboo motif (left). Teacup with relief cherry blossom motif (right). Porcelain from the Haviland dinner service commissioned by President Rutherford B. Hayes; 1880.

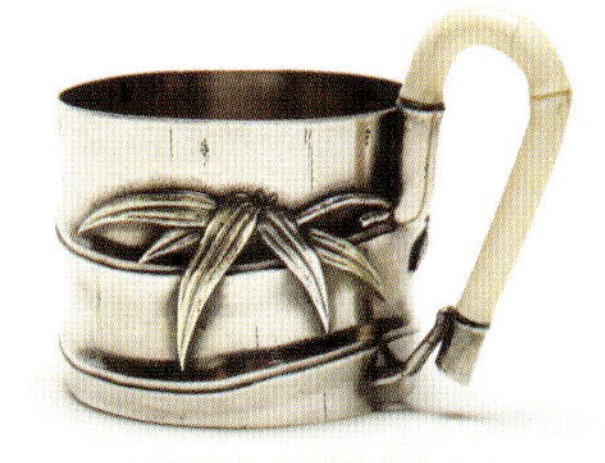

Right, Lower: Western-style teacup, in the form of a section of leafing bamboo; Meiji period, late nineteenth century; silver and ivory; unmarked.

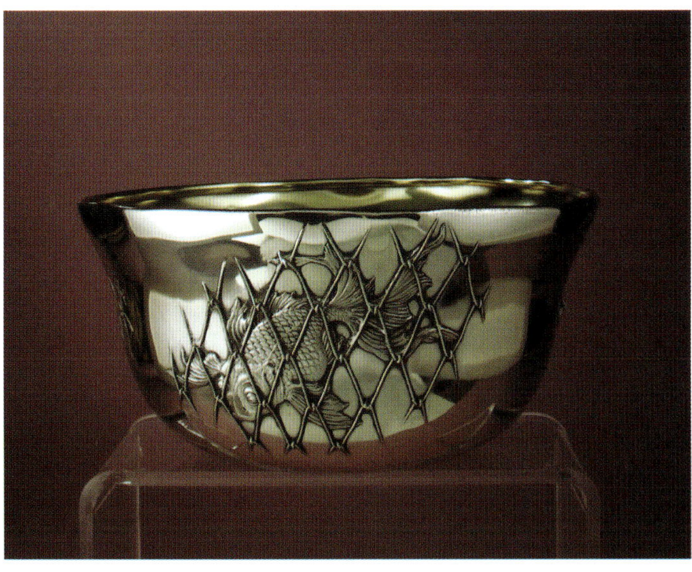

Below: Whiting Silver Company. Fish salad bowl; ca. 1889; silver with gilt interior; 8.2 inches diameter, 4 inches high; engraved on side, cypher of "KS"; marked with Whiting lion and shield, "STERLING / 1872 O."

and teacups of exquisitely thin, translucent porcelain embraced by bamboo and cherry blossom sprigs in relief—in standard Japonesque fashion.

Japan's Centennial exhibition exhibits left yet another imprint upon American ceramics' transformation from humble domestic object to esteemed art craft. Belleek looked to export porcelain styles through Anglo-Japanese taste; Haviland detached design principles and thematic concepts from their Japanese origins in quest of a quintessentially American vision. "Art pottery" went even farther, achieving a look universally seen and admired as "American." American art pottery lessened emphasis on the molded forms and surface decoration characteristic of Aestheticism to

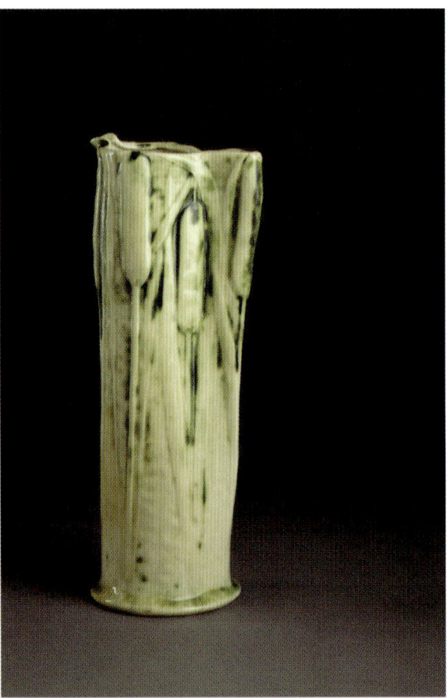

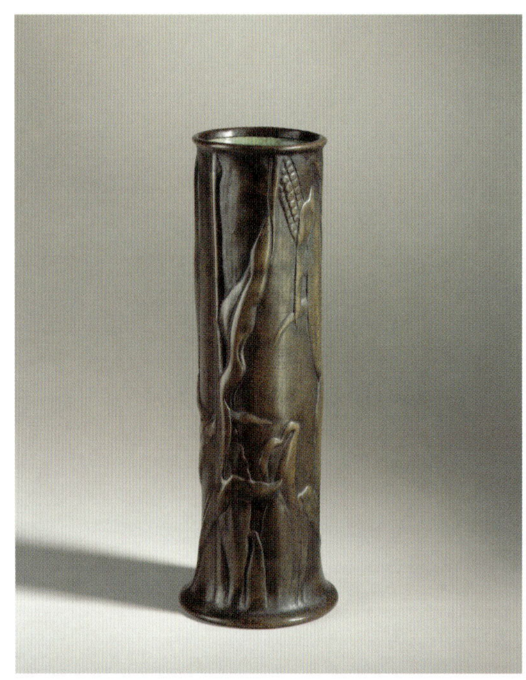

Above, Left: Louis C. Tiffany: Favrile pitcher, with cattail relief; ca. 1904–1914; pottery; 10.4 inches high.

Above, Right: Louis C. Tiffany. Favrile vase; ca. 1904–1914; maize relief of electroformed bronze on white clay; 13 inches high.

stress simplicity and the inherent qualities of material made possible by the more plastic clays of pottery and stoneware and by the technical expertise required to achieve this. And, while porcelain manufacturers emphasized the potential of mass production in attaining "fine art" standards, art pottery makers elevated the Ruskinian ideal of the workshop craftsman. In all of this, the traditional Japanese wares shown for the first time at the 1876 Centennial exhibition presented an epiphany to a few talented individuals among the throngs. By the 1893 Columbian exhibition, it had distilled to a movement of overlapping aesthetics: Art Nouveau (short-lived in the United States) and the more deeply transformational Arts and Crafts, with its associations of beauty in egalitarianism. Art pottery succeeded in its quest to be recognized as "art"; the best was sold in the finest stores, enjoyed international acclaim, was collected avidly, and was acquired by museums.

Despite the umbrella term, art pottery did not pigeonhole neatly in style, in method, or in the nature of its Japan-related adaptations. Tellingly, like Arts and Crafts copper and many art porcelains, some of the best benefited from marketing sleight of hand that sought to attach workshop identity to pieces neither entirely handmade nor actual products of the name associated with them. A case in point was Louis Comfort Tiffany's Favrile ceramics, an early and very sophisticated example of branding. These were debuted at the St. Louis exposition in 1904—the moment when the strict definition of "fine art" was finally done away with, thanks in large measure to the efforts of the Japanese. The association of its name with handwork notwithstanding, Favrile was mold-cast in multiples, and the craftsmen who finished each piece uncredited so that it conformed to few of the usual criteria for "art pottery." It won acceptance as such, thanks to a quality and distinctive look due to intense planning, scrutiny, and identity linked to Tiffany himself. It was among only three American lines deemed *art nouveau* by Siegfried Bing and sold in his elegant Paris establishment.

Tiffany's unsentimentally analytical eye regarding the nature of beauty matched the "art for art's sake" credo of Aesthetic taste that informed Belleek but with much more creative effect. Favrile ceramics melded intimately observed, naturalistic garden and meadow images to form. The root of this distinctive look was Japanese from several perspectives. Tiffany's friend Dresser had already demonstrated that the principles of simplicity, asymmetry, and other features of Japanese aesthetics could be adapted to mold-made, factory-produced wares. Favrile glazes, in their muted greens and yellows and random runniness, looked to Japanese taste. Most significantly, though often linked to Tiffany's long-standing relationship with Emile Gallé, who predated him with similar work, its design origins actually lay in Japan. The elevation of ordinary garden life as a subject worthy of artists was first observed in Japanese prints and decorative art, and, even more directly, Japanese bronzes of identical spirit already occupied a conspicuous niche on the export market. Tiffany directly replicated their look beginning in 1908 with wares that actually wedded metal to a porcelain base. His designs borrowed Japanese forms such as brush pots, in particular those using his own copper-enameled hollowware as molds. His bronze lamp bases made similar use of the Japanese witty sensibility in adapting literal naturalism to function.

Vase, with irises in high relief; Meiji period; bronze; 8.5 inches high; signed "Yoshikiyo."

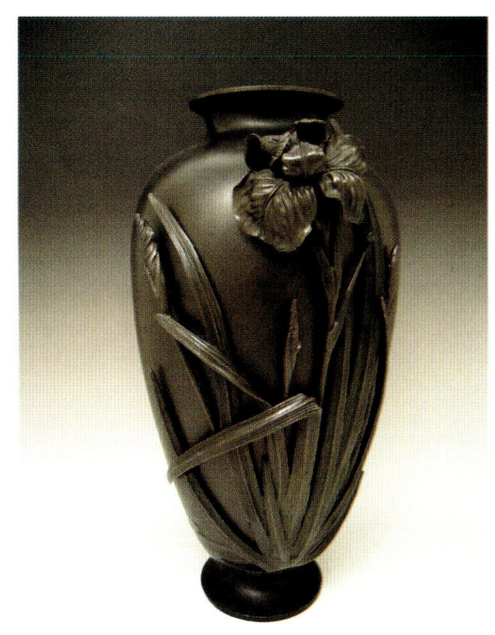

Among the tens of thousands strolling the Japanese exhibits at the Centennial exhibition were Cincinnati society doyenne Maria Longworth Nichols and her equally prominent husband, George Ward Nichols. They had arrived primed with anticipation. An important art educator and critic with a long-standing interest in ceramics, he was an exhibition judge. A recognized china painter with her own work on display, she had already acquired a design book, very likely Hokusai's *Manga.* Both found the encounter landmark. Within a year he wrote the influential *Art Education Applied to Industry,* which advocated Japanese decorative arts as models by which American industry could counter the deleterious effects of mechanization. She established Rookwood Pottery in 1880, the first of its kind in the United States. Rookwood propelled a renaissance in American industrial art and fostered Ohio as a center of art ceramics while becoming the definitive "American" art pottery, its standing confirmed by numerous awards garnered at its international debut at the 1900 Paris exposition, and by Siegfried Bing, who placed it alongside Louis Tiffany's Favrile and Edward C. Moore's silver for Charles Tiffany as the only American decorative arts deserving the designation *art nouveau.* But, despite Rookwood's art pottery being sold at Maison L'Art Nouveau, it is best identified with its formative role in American Arts and Crafts.

MARIA LONGWORTH NICHOLS, FOR ROOKWOOD POTTERY. VASE, WITH FANCIFUL FROGS LEAPING AND SHOOTING DRAGONFLIES; 1882; POTTERY WITH POLYCHROME ENAMEL; 6.5 INCHES HIGH.

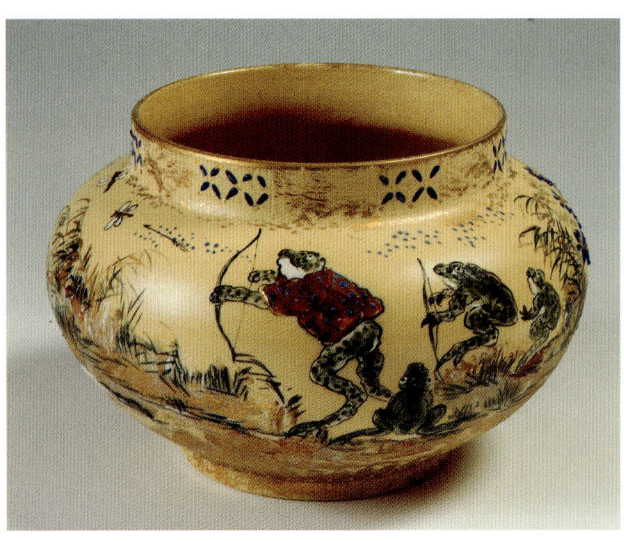

Nichols openly stated that Japan's exhibit had inspired her to found Rookwood and transform her aesthetic vision. In her work and in the earliest offerings by Rookwood's artisans, this revealed itself in an emphasis on surface decoration inspired by such things as Satsuma's ornamental golden bands or, most strikingly, motifs inspired by Hokusai, Japan's master of the intimate and the grotesque. But her expressed aim of creating a "Japanese" pottery in Ohio extended to the philosophy and practical methods of the company, and combined with her intent that her pottery be Ohio "down to the dirt." This meant more than just using the state's superb local clays. In melding Japanese aesthetics to local materials and sensibilities, she

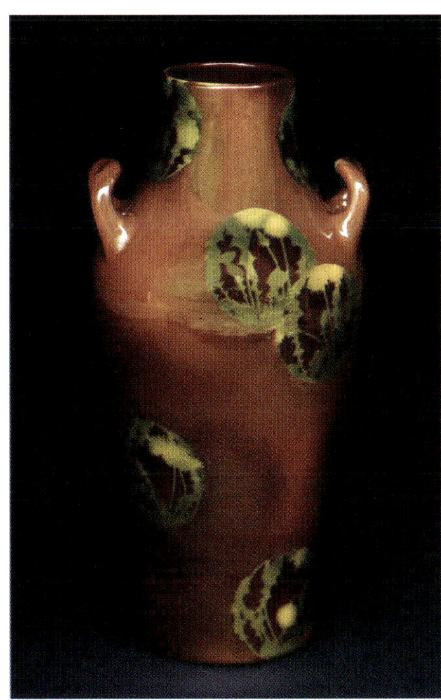

Kataro Shirayamadani, for Rookwood Pottery. Vase, with dandelions in the form of Japanese *mon* (crests); 1898; pottery; 20 inches high. Arrow marks on the underside indicate that the artist saw this vase as an experiment. Because of that and its size, it may have been among those designs considered for Rookwood's display at the Exposition Universelle of 1900 in Paris.

attained what the era's intelligentsia believed Japanese arts could bring: a quintessentially American expression. Yet the ultimate obviousness of her debt made remarkable the critical assertion that Rookwood wares had "nothing" of the Japonesque but were "distinctly American."[20]

To this end, she based Rookwood upon the idea of the inspired artisan as envisioned by Ruskin and idealized by Japanese kilns. She set high standards for decorators, who signed their work as artists. She inspired them: Nichols and her father owned a wide-ranging Japanese art collection, including six hundred ceramics acquired from Edward Morse, who visited her in 1886. She sent potters and decorators to study his collection in Salem, and some to Japan. She sponsored educational events and exhibitions in Cincinnati that featured Japanese art. Her line emphasized handmade, wheel-thrown pieces over mold-made. Expensive complicated initiatives all, she achieved critical acclaim, administrative quagmire, and red ink. To extricate herself she hired W. W. Taylor, who shared her belief that Rookwood produced works of art in the fullest sense and who turned out to be as inspired a manager as she had been a visionary. He brought the company to profitability by, among other things, incorporating limited mass-production methods. Ultimately, Rookwood shared with Tiffany Favrile and even Belleek and, above all, the Japanese export industry from which they took so much inspiration, a gray area between mass-manufacture and studio-made, but succeeded in retaining its artisanal aura.

In 1887 Nichols and Taylor attained a chief goal in bringing a Japanese china painter to Rookwood: Kataro Shirayamadani (1865–1948). He was in the United States with an American-run traveling "Japanese Village" of artisans intended to educate as an example of a model enterprise and had had a stint as employee of an American dealer of Japanese handicrafts. A native of the region around Kutani, his training likely began in the painterly decorative techniques of its export wares. In short, he arrived primed to the nature of American attraction. This he put to effective use: a large 1898 urn in Rookwood's transparent "standard glaze" features roundels of naturalistically observed dandelion plants floating with the seemingly random calm of bubbles—local weeds treated in a classic style of Japanese heraldic crests called *mon;* the matte "vellum"

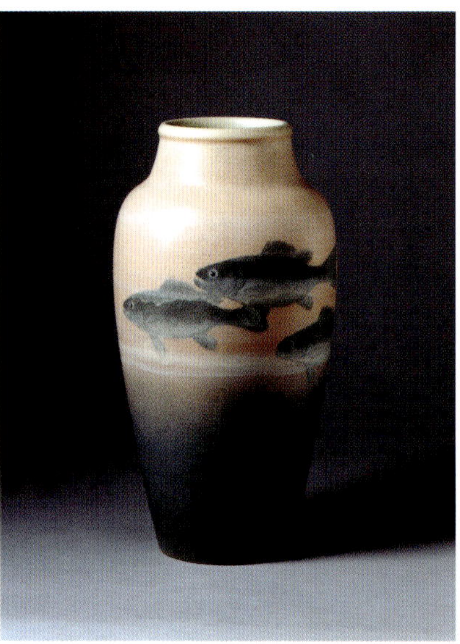

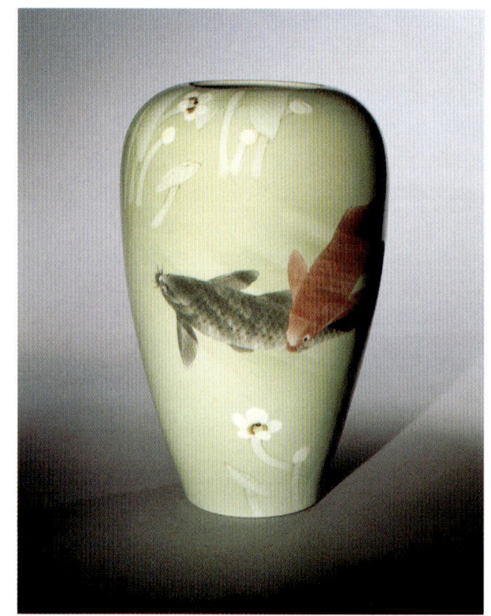

Above, Left: Kataro Shirayamadani, for Rookwood Pottery. Vase, with swimming bass; 1904; 12.25 inches high.

Above, Right: Miyagawa Kozan, for the Makuzu Kiln. Vase, with swimming carp; ca. 1900; porcelain; 11.5 inches high; signed "Makuzu-gama Kozan sei." Many designs of this type appeared in Japanese ceramics, bronzes, and enamels of the later Meiji period. Courtesy of the Nasser D. Khalili Collection of Japanese Art, London, England.

Right: Kataro Shirayamadani, for Rookwood Pottery. Vase, with bas-relief bat; 1899; 5.2 inches high.

glaze surface of another from 1904 serves as a muddy lake bed and water to circulating Ohio small mouth bass; in 1899 he dangled a single bas-relief bat from the rim of a squat vase—all visually dynamic through organic union of sparing yet closely observed motif, glaze quality, and ceramic form—re-creating in an American idiom decorative principles readily observable in the export ceramics of Japan.

Over Shirayamadani's fifty-two years with Rookwood, and with at least one other Japanese decorator, Nichol's original vision that placed Japanese concepts at the center of the kiln's aesthetic was consolidated and inculcated. The tour de force designs of Japan's preeminent art ceramicist and his workshop, Miyagawa Kozan (1842–1916), seemed particularly amenable to Americanization. Rookwood colleagues incorporated these with other inspirations from Native American to the French avant-garde designs of Gallé. Harriet Elizabeth Wilcox (1869–1943),

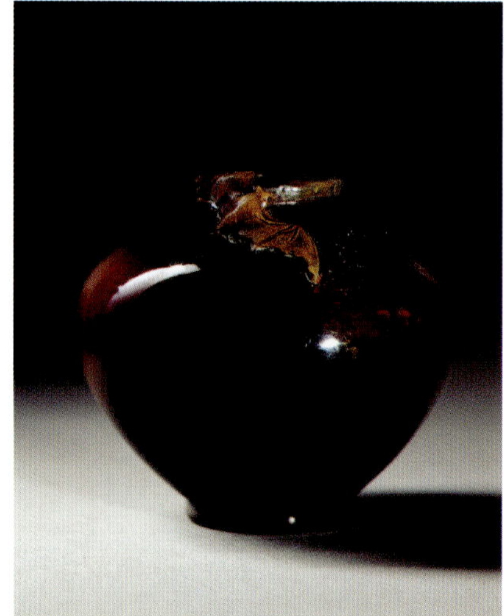

one of Rookwood's most accomplished ceramicists, combined an abiding interest in classical nudes with the Japanese custom of making repairs an aesthetic asset. She made a powerful statement of a simple white vase, where—in a decorative conceit replicating the effect of gold lacquer mend—she balanced its "imperfection" against the perfection of a Grecian figure, highlighting both.

Rookwood was not unique in hiring Shirayamadani and his compatriot; Japanese craftsmen worked in Trenton's Belleek factories and elsewhere. They gave a Japanese cast to a well-established, fruitful industrial practice. Foreign talent on the workshop or factory floor was an important disseminator of the technology and taste that combined to form modern design. The Japanese themselves made brilliant use of the method with Gottfried Wagener, which had much to do with an export art success that became but one "Japanese" avenue in the momentum and eventual look of modern design. Regardless of how people of the time saw them, this begs the question of many decorative arts as specifically any nationality over a general "internationalism," especially as workshop denizens, in addition to their many backgrounds, were not necessarily simple artisans unaware of intellectual trends. The era placed art practice at the foundation of modern education. Crossover from the intellectual community meant that certain individuals were deeply

BELOW, LEFT: WILLIAM ERNST HENTSCHEL, FOR ROOKWOOD POTTERY. VASE, WITH STYLIZED WAVE MOTIF; 1912; VELLUM-GLAZED STONEWARE; 6.25 INCHES HIGH.

BELOW, RIGHT: MIYAGAWA KOZAN, FOR THE MAKUZU KILN. VASE, WITH DRAGON AND WAVE; CA. 1880; 7.68 INCHES HIGH. Courtesy of the Nasser D. Khalili Collection of Japanese Art, London, England.

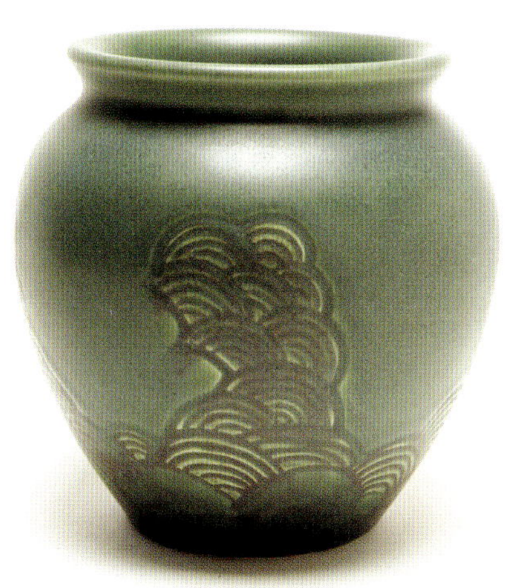

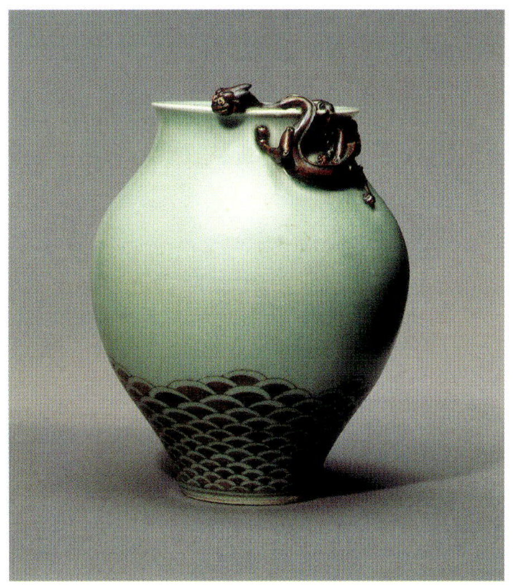

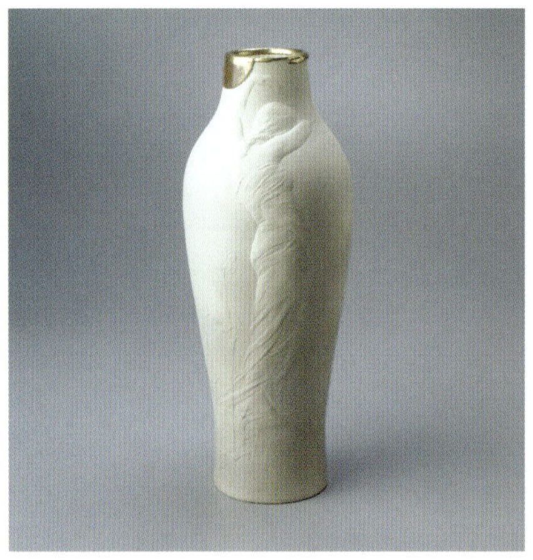

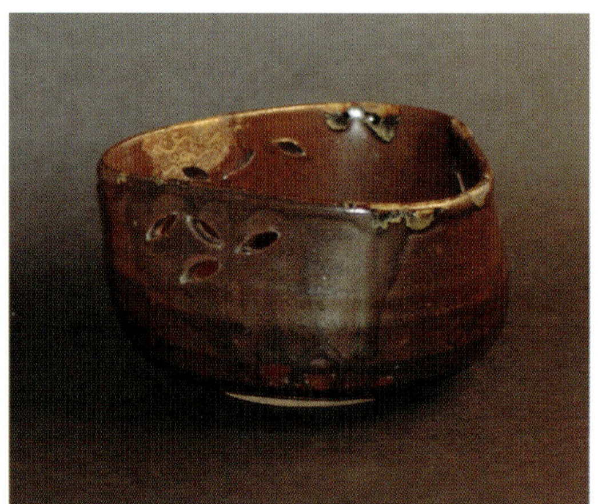

Above, Left: Harriet Elizabeth Wilcox, for Rookwood Pottery. Vase, with bas-relief nude and gold lip; 1899; 10 inches high.

Above, Right: Takatori bowl; Edo period; stoneware with gold lacquer mend; 3 inches high.

influential in both worlds, their impact in one elevating the regard of the other. Such was the case with Arthur Wesley Dow (1857–1922). Dow's concepts looked directly to Japan. In disseminating them as a guiding philosophy rather than limiting them to avenues of personal expression, he arguably achieved the discernibly "American" style that had been sought since the Centennial exhibition.

Dow's theory was born in his exceptional relationship with Ernest Fenollosa, under whom he worked for a time at the Museum of Fine Arts, Boston; Fenollosa had come to a positive view of the Japanese print at last. Dow himself was awakened first by Hokusai, of whom he remarked, "One evening with Hokusai gave me more light on composition and decorative effect than years of studying pictures."[21] The revelation led him to generalize from other ukiyo-e masters the means by which Japanese art distilled any subject to its powerful visual essence—a process Dow called "synthesis." By 1893—the year of change signaled by the great Panic and marked by the Columbian exhibition in Chicago—Dow and Fenollosa were actively advocating its principles in American arts in all media. But while Fenollosa preferred theorizing, Dow sought practice. From bully pulpits at Columbia Teacher's College, the Arts Students League, Ipswich Summer School of Art, and Pratt Institute, his journal *The Lotos,* and in his 1899 book *Composition: A Series of Exercises in Art Structure for the Use of Students and Teachers*—so influential that it went into thirteen editions—Dow transformed art education in the United States.

Synthesis also aligned Dow with those who saw in Japanese tradition the erasing of hierarchical distinctions between fine and applied art. His

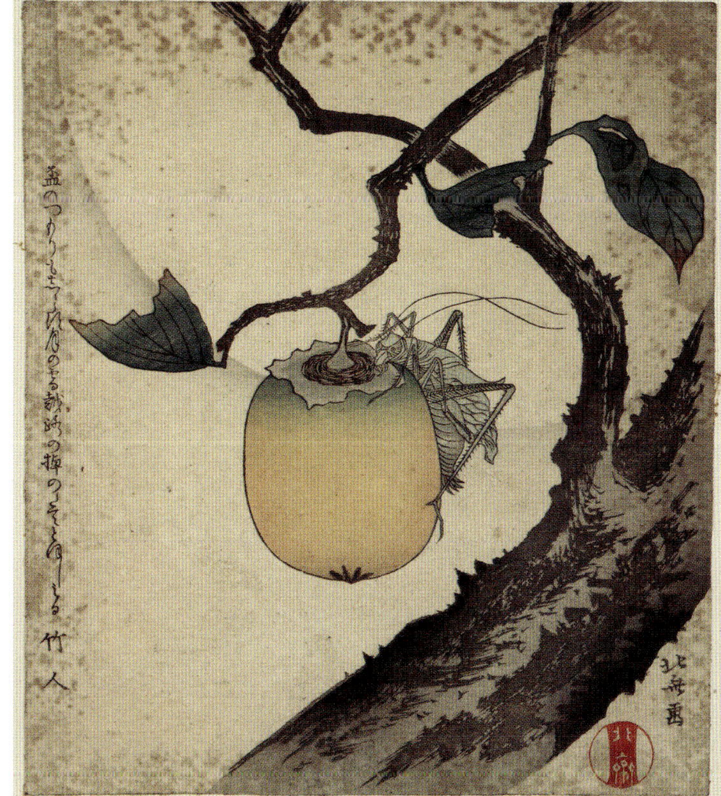

RIGHT: KATSUSHIKA HOKUSAI. *KAKI NI KIRI-GIRISU (GRASSHOPPER EATING A PERSIMMON)*; WOODBLOCK PRINT, REPRINTED AFTER 1850; 8.19 × 7.17 INCHES. The impact of Hokusai was such that, immediately after his death, restrikes (some of very high quality such as this) were produced of many of his prints to meet the demand of Western artists.

BELOW: ARTHUR WESLEY DOW. POSTER FOR *THE LOTOS*; 1896; 24.41 × 17.72 INCHES. Dow's own work looked to that of Hokusai and other ukiyo-e artists, and showed the principle of synthesis among line, light, and shade that he determined was the essence of the concept of *nōtan*.

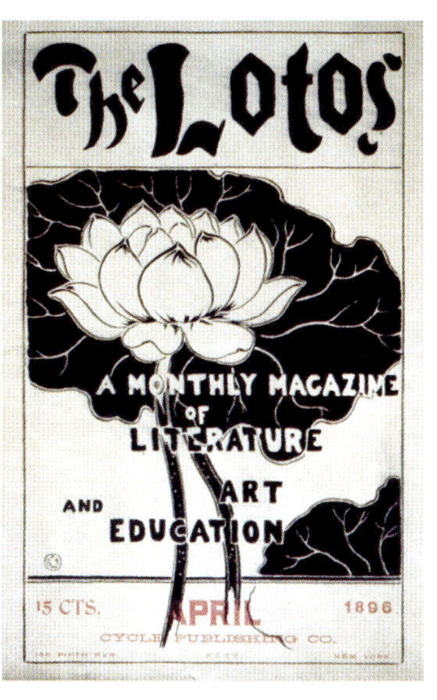

theory found a natural home in the workshop, where it became the guiding light for American Arts and Crafts. Influential in all art pottery, synthesis found fullest expression at Grueby Faience Company of Boston. Its widely imitated style originated with French ceramicist Auguste Delaherche, whose "organic naturalism" took directly from the traditional ceramics of Japan its approach to glazing, sensitivity to material, use of local clays, and wheel-thrown functional forms that did what they chose in the kiln. As redefined at Grueby, these qualities shared sensibilities with work by artists as diverse as Dow's student Georgia O'Keeffe and some of Rookwood's designers. The simple and powerful regular forms; thickly glazed and textured matte finishes in muted ochres, greens and blues; and, above all, emphatically linear carved and sculpted decoration—all produced a textbook example of the system of formal relationships at the heart of Dow's theory: beauty through the union of sensuous line and *nōtan*—a Japanese term referring to compositional

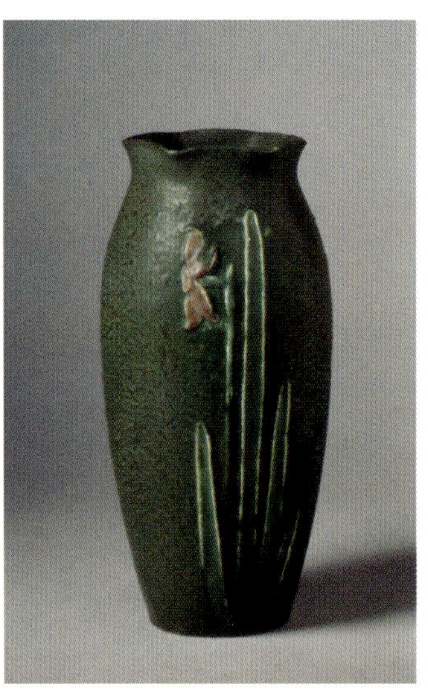

GRUEBY FAIENCE COMPANY OF BOSTON. VASE, WITH NARCISSUS RELIEF AND FLUTED RIM; CA. 1897–1907; GLAZED STONEWARE; 11 INCHES HIGH.

balance that Dow interpreted as the dividing of space into flat fields to form a harmonious whole of pattern, each glorifying the other. Grueby produced these subdued, dignified vases and bowls for fifteen years beginning in 1894, the peak of Dow's proselytizing campaign; when in 1909 it switched to producing decorative tiles, the link to Dow's synthesis theory became even more evident. Dow, like Godwin and Dresser before him, often observed that Japanese artists concerned themselves chiefly with flat relations regardless of the subject; the landscape scenes for which Grueby tile became famous owe their restful quietude to the compositional strength achieved through nōtan, in the interplaying balance of sgraffito delineations of trees, clouds, and sky, and the patterned effects of light and dark color. Pure composition, these are what Dow noted as the universal principles of the surface, resulting in the expression of beauty alone.

Rookwood and Grueby, hybrid operations that combined workshop and factory, attained their reputations by emphasizing studio quality. In this they tapped into the Arts and Crafts ideal of the independent ceramicist as envisioned by Stickley and Dow, both of whom specifically called attention to the traditional Japanese pottery studio as the ideal of the relationship between the artist-craftsman and his medium. Art potters, a vigorous national community, revealed in the variety of their work the general infusion of Japanese aesthetics into the Arts and Crafts movement. Frederick Rhead, a peripatetic Englishman linked to ten different companies from coast to coast, produced bowls, mugs, ewers, and vases that strongly suggested the influence of Dow. Rhead's sculptural clarity resembled Grueby's, as did the sgraffito-like effects of his "squeeze bag" technique. He used the method in a strikingly literal Japonesque interpretation series called "Jap Birdimal" for Weller Pottery,

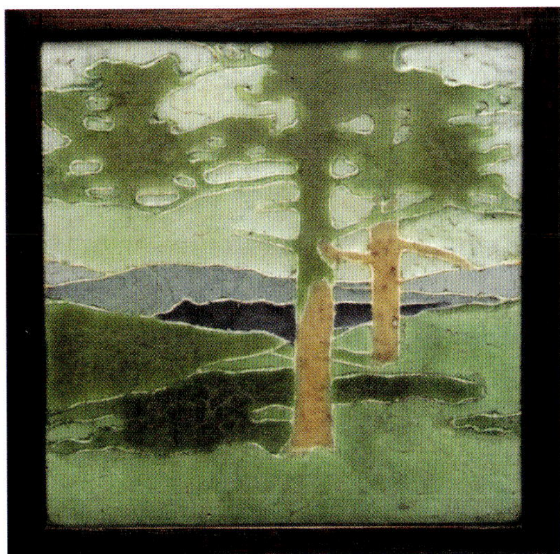

of Zanesville, Ohio, which depicted stereotypical Japanese subjects in a briskly impressionistic style, such as the parading courtesans of classic ukiyo-e, very likely based on the actual prints.

This vase appeared in the March 1905 edition of *Keramic Studio,* the first American publication dedicated to ceramic design and a major force behind the elevation of handcrafted ceramics into the realm of art as advocated by Dow. Adelaide Robineau (1865–1928), the publication's cofounder and editor, became internationally famous for porcelains that included numerous experiments in glaze and form plainly Asian. Robineau's most distinctive included a line of small vases with crystalline glaze,

Above: Grueby Faience Company of Boston. "The Pines"; tile; ca. 1906; glazed stoneware; 6 × 6 inches.

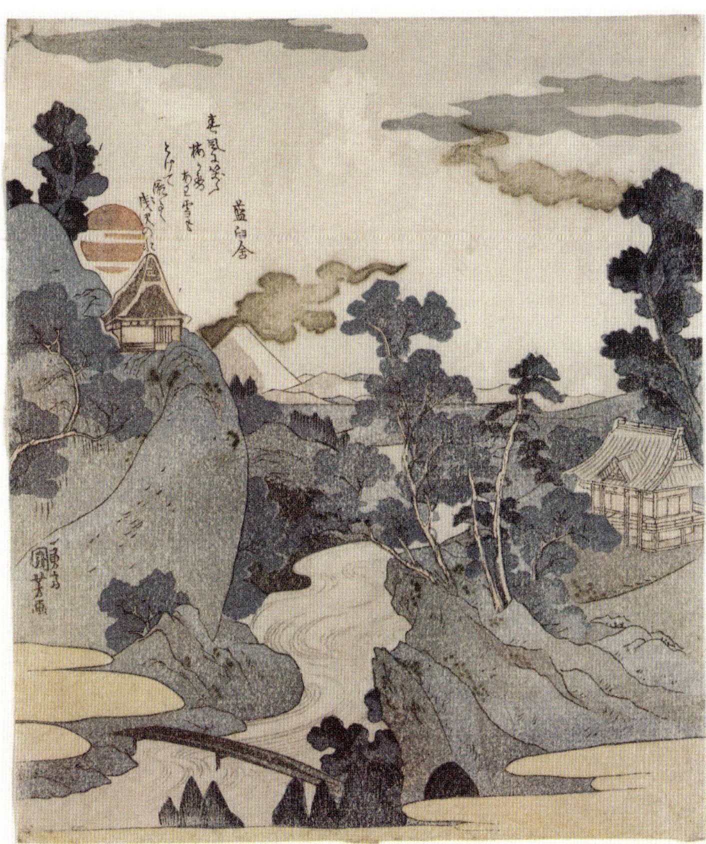

Right: Utagawa Kuniyoshi. *Fuji no Yūke (Evening View of Fuji)*; surimono woodblock print; ca. 1829–1830; 8.35 × 7.28 inches.

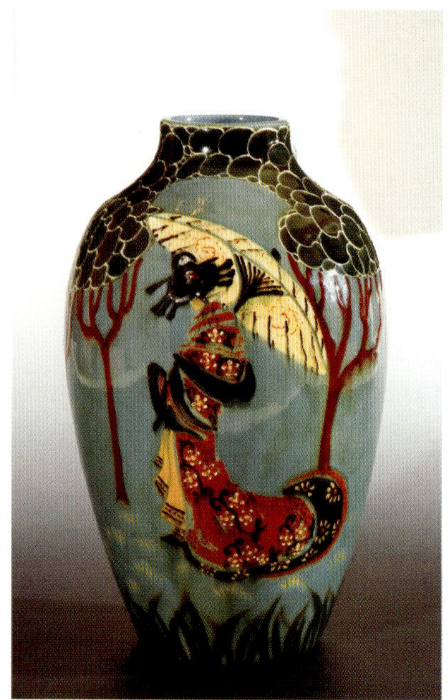

a complex hard-to-control process that produced blossom-like spots scattered randomly over opaline surfaces. She also experimented with classic Japanese tea storage jar forms, called *chaire,* also influential at Rookwood, featuring unctuously thick and sometimes mottled glazes, spherical shapes, and small flat lids in the carved porcelain for which she was famed.

Glazes were also the focus of Detroit ceramicist Mary Chase Perry Stratton (1867–1961). Pewabic, her name for the pottery she established in 1903, came from the Chippewa and referred to copper-colored clay. She associated it with the metallic cast of the iridescent glazes that made her famous, but her aesthetic of thick, random running effects on heavy hand-thrown shapes looked to the irregular forms and textures identified with Japanese tea wares that were among the most ubiquitous of Japanese ceramic influences in Arts and Crafts, especially as increasingly knowledgeable critics declared painted pottery "a travesty"[22] and irregularity a virtue "because ponds and puddles are not symmetrical."[23] Indeed, her close friend Charles Lang Freer noted the affinity between her work and Japanese aesthetics, using Pewabic's tiles for the fireplace surround in the private gallery of his home, whose walls were decorated in imitation gold leaf inspired by his exceptional collection of Japanese screens.

Above: Frederick Rhead, for Weller Pottery. "Jap Birdimal Vase"; 1904; 10.5 inches high. Typical of his early work, Rhead used a squeeze bag technique, much like decorating a cake. Since his name is carved prominently on the side, it is likely that Rhead decorated this vase himself. He submitted this design to Adelaide Robineau for *Keramic Studio,* who published it on page 238 of the March 1905 issue.

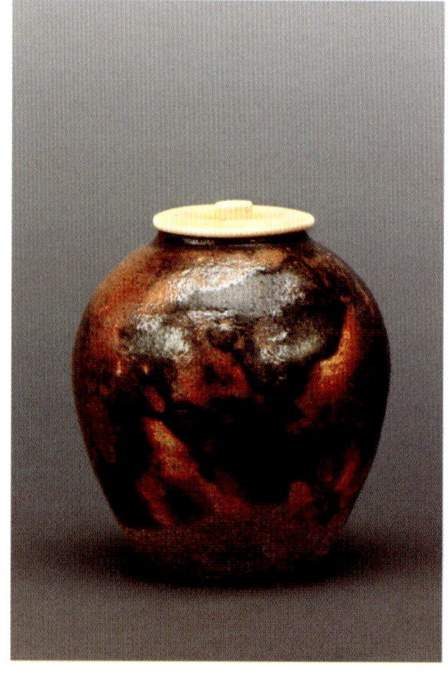

Near Right: Seto ware tea jar; nineteenth century; stoneware; 3.25 inches high. This *chaire* shows the mottled glazes, subtle shape, and simple flat lid that Arts and Crafts ceramists found very compelling; but it is much smaller than the American pieces it inspired.

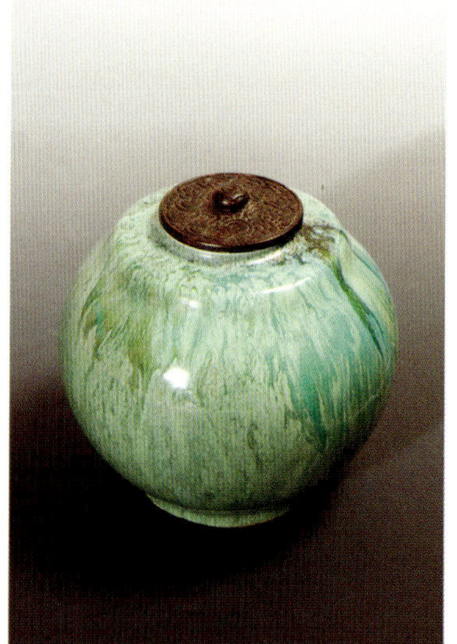

Far Right: Adelaide Robineau. "Green Flambé Covered Jar with Carved Lid"; 1920; 4 inches high. The floral pattern of the ceramic lid is typical of Robineau, who was justly famed for her work in carved porcelain.

The strength of the Arts and Crafts movement assured that its credo of simplicity, utility, respect for materials, and spirit of the artisan expressed through a restrained intellectual aesthetic—all of which assimilated extensively from ideas garnered from Japan—would extend well beyond Rookwood, Grueby, their competitors, and the individual studios of the art pottery movement. The robust yet quiet presence of a molded, low footed basin, ornamented by a snaking vine branch in relief and matte-glazed in a subdued moss-green, shows the presence of Dow's theory in the work of the J. B. Owens Pottery Company, one of many concerns in the orbit of Rookwood in Ohio. Between 1896 and 1907, prolific production combined with Owens' practices of having decorators sign their works and vigorously participating in national competitions testifies to an aim to bring art standards to ordinary people. Many of those who worked there went on to become well known in Arts and Crafts circles.

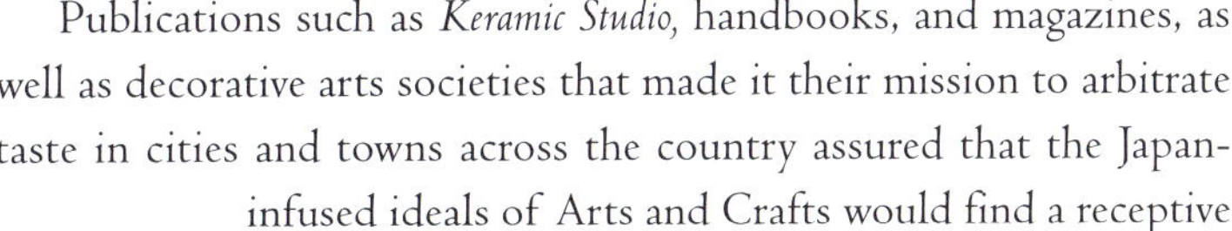

Publications such as *Keramic Studio,* handbooks, and magazines, as well as decorative arts societies that made it their mission to arbitrate taste in cities and towns across the country assured that the Japan-infused ideals of Arts and Crafts would find a receptive clientele anywhere that the bungalow held sway. The plum branch in extreme close-up, rendered with elegant calligraphic assurance in simple hues of white and brown enveloping a solidly potted matte-blue vessel, could not be accidental in its near match to classic Japanese Rimpa-style wares, evidence of the depth to which Japan found its way to unnamed studio kilns to inspire gifted artists, who will remain anonymous.

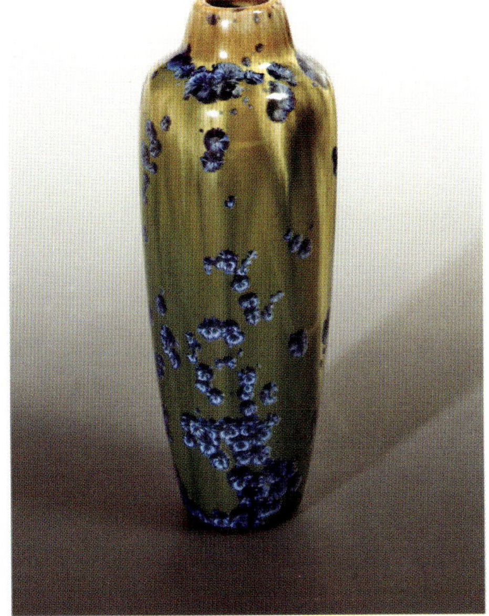

Adelaide Robineau. "Crystalline Vase"; 1905; 6 inches high. The randomness of the crystal blossoms and the streaking of the tiger-eye glaze reflect the influence of Japanese sensibilities, which allowed the interaction of kiln environment and glaze to express itself over human intervention, resulting in a random pattern. Yet, as a mold-made ware, Robineau did not consider its character sufficiently unique.

Stickley, Dow, and others of the Arts and Crafts movement emphasized "uniqueness." Adelaide Robineau ceased making crystalline vases after only five years because, mold-made, they did not meet that standard in her eye despite glaze variations that made each distinct. Western minds linked "uniqueness" to such things as Japanese tea ceramics, where manipulation on the wheel and random interplay of glaze, clay, and kiln under a hand of consummate skill distinguished every ware. The idea that a "unique"

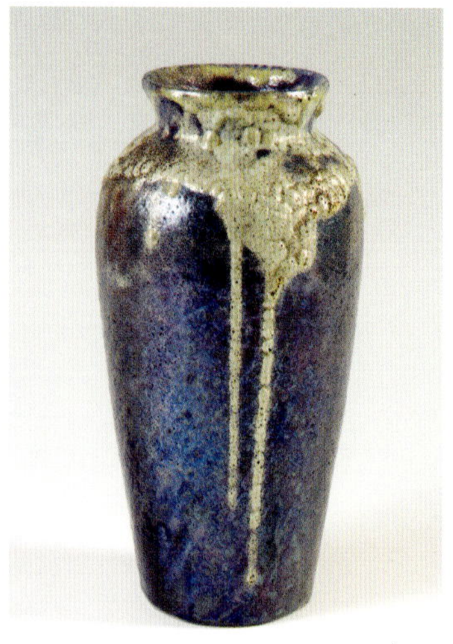

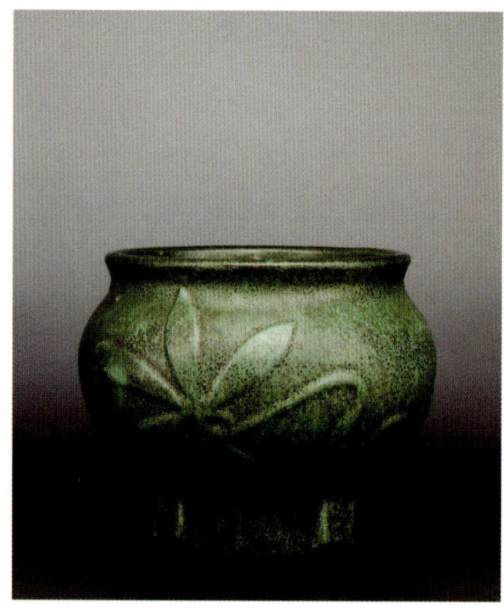

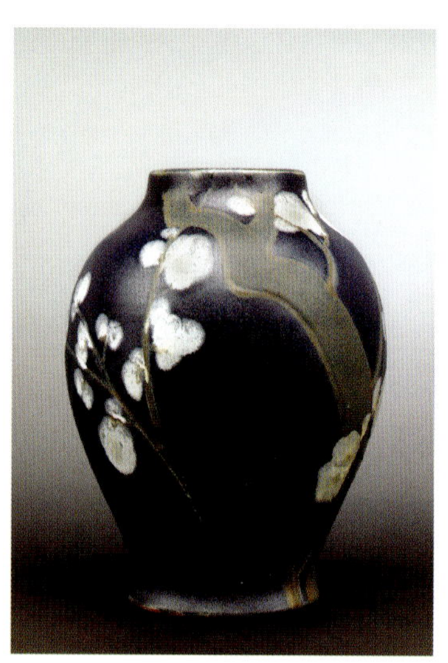

ABOVE, LEFT: MARY CHASE PERRY, FOR PEWABIC POTTERY. "FEATHERED BLUE IRIDESCENT VASE WITH VOLCANIC CELADON DRIP"; CA. 1915; 11 INCHES HIGH.

ABOVE, CENTER: J. B. OWENS POTTERY. POT, WITH BAS-RELIEF LEAFING VINE; CA. 1900; 8 INCHES HIGH.

ABOVE, RIGHT: ANONYMOUS. VASE; CA. 1900; 14 INCHES HIGH. The simple colors and boldly abstracted, expressive execution of the all-over plum design of this American vase strongly suggest Japanese Rimpa motifs as an inspiration.

ceramic identified a "unique" individual—the art revealing an artist in the maker—was a peculiarly Western one. In appropriating Japanese aesthetics and qualities to its own ends, this was a typical pattern. Yet, at the end of the day, the Arts and Crafts community was not unlike the Japanese themselves: a matter of its own conventions. This can be seen in its response to the work of George Ohr.

Ohr met all of Arts and Crafts criteria. Carried to its logical extreme, he arguably attained the ideal they claimed to seek, and it brought him not to simplicity but to a style completely true to a personality flamboyant, irreverent, self-promoting, instinctive rather than intellectual—and emphatically singular. He was a "pure" artistic character in the era's highest sense, wholly dedicated and deeply spiritual in his identification of his wares with the essence of humanity through the biblical metaphor of clay, to such an extent that he rarely could bring himself to sell any. His clay came from local riverbeds; his glazes and forms were inspired by the utilitarian folk wares of rural Mississippi, certain French work, and the Japan-infused experimental elegance of designs by Dresser that he saw at the exhibitions where he entered his own pieces. All came together in pottery of porcelain-like thinness—manipulated, folded, crumpled, and crimped into forms of sometimes baroque complexity—that revealed not just breathtaking skill at throwing but also unmatched sensitivity to material and the processes of firing and glazing. And each was the apotheosis of "unique." Yet Ohr endured a lifetime of rebuff. The tight-knit art pottery community gave him scant critical mention, unable to appreciate such skills in work that did not conform to the restrained aesthetic they espoused. Many, moneyed and educated, perhaps found this largely self-taught, small-town eccentric from the depths of the South—a genuine artisan down to his pores—too coarse for their sensibilities. He did not win a single prize until the more liberal criteria of the exposition in St. Louis in 1904 garnered a silver medal, and even then failed to sell any of the few pieces he could bring himself to part with. He died disappointed in 1918 and immediately slipped into oblivion. At that very moment, the era of the Japan Craze came to a formal close as America entered the cauldron of World War I. Not identifiably "Japonesque" in any way, in his life and work Ohr embodied the assertion of many a pundit of the time that Japanese art had "freed" the artist. Decades later, a transformed world discovered that the self-proclaimed "greatest art potter on earth" had been ahead of his time.

GEORGE E. OHR, FOR BILOXI ART POTTERY, VASE; CA. 1894–1906; GLAZED RED CLAY; APPROXIMATELY 3.5 INCHES HIGH.

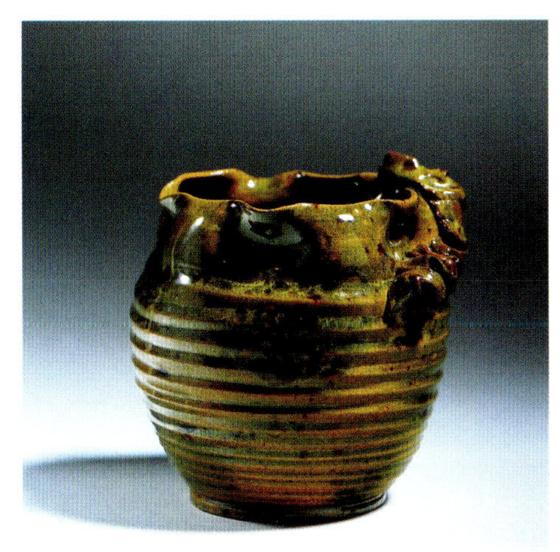

1. Longfellow 1878.
2. *Art Amateur,* February 1880.
3. Jahn 2004, 108.
4. The Japanese Commission 1876, 260.
5. McCabe 1876, 415.
6. Francis 1913, 398.
7. *Art Amateur,* February 1880.
8. Ibid.
9. Jahn 2004, 102.
10. As quoted in Everson Museum of Art 1989, 10.
11. *International Studio,* 1901–1902, 53.
12. *New York Times,* October 28, 1905, 20.
13. As quoted in Frelinghuysen 1989, 43.
14. Ibid., 37.
15. Ibid., 210.
16. As quoted in Frelinghuysen 1989, 242.
17. *Art Amateur,* December 1880.
18. Ibid.
19. Ibid., 17–19.
20. *Art Amateur,* January 1895.
21. As quoted in Hook 1987.
22. *International Studio,* 1901–1902, 53.
23. Ibid., 56.

Epilogue

. . . whether a European goes to Japan for his aesthetic inspiration or a Japanese comes to Europe for his, the result, considered from a point of view of art, is approximately the same.[1]

Sparked by the "pleasing cross in aestheticism" in the watercolors of an artist who Westernized his name as Yoshio Markino (1874–1956) and whose high-profile career embraced San Francisco, New York, and London, as well as Tokyo and his native Toyoda, the above observation noted the new reality that had revealed itself at the junction of two disparate cultures by 1901. Of the events leading up to "the result" to which the writer referred Japan, an ancient culture remaking itself to survive in a strange world and the United States, brand new and without a clear sense of individuality beside its old established European parents, could inarguably lay claim to the most profound experiences, ones that appropriately coupled them. Each exotic to the other, their underlying motives were much the same: economic advancement, international respect, and cultural uniqueness in the modern industrial age. Their transformations, of both underlying attitude and outer image, revealed themselves most deeply not in the "fine art" of painting to which the comment referred, but in the objects, furnishings, and concepts of interior design—the "applied arts" that formed the exterior world and therefore projected people's unselfconscious innermost selves.

Japanese arts and crafts had been, and for at least another decade would continue, indispensable to the emergence of the American image because of their signature roles as a kind of lingua franca in a high-stakes international game of dominance that both nations joined. It was English diplomat Sir Rutherford Alcock who first articulated why Japanese art so suited the West's vision for its domestic environment, distilled to a few short paragraphs in his 1863 landmark book, *The Capital of the Tycoon.* As much as cunning techniques, eye-catching designs, and novel materials, he emphasized economy of means, quality, and perfection as obtainable aims even with the most primitive of tools, the craftsmen's seeming cheerfulness and pleasure in their work, and the lofty moral dimension that all of this imbued. This perspective would persist for the five decades of the Japan Craze, described in almost identical terms by Gustav Stickley. The weaker and newest player of the field, Japan managed to compel rules it had no say in forming to bend but not break, and ultimately found itself imprisoned in artificial amber, placed on a pedestal as the living embodiment of ideals born elsewhere—and expected to remain there. In 1904 the president of the St. Louis exposition lamented, "It is a source of regret to observe a strong tendency, shared by so many of the younger Japanese, to forsake the purity and fine qualities of their native art for characteristics, the outgrowth of a civilization, and educational training opposite to their own."[2] Yet despite a groping relationship rife with mutual misunderstandings and conflicts, the results could not have been more positive. Modern design was born at the point at which the ideals of the West crossed the agenda of the Japanese.

Whether factory floor or artisan's studio, America's creative minds found Japanese arts and crafts vital in crafting a distinctive image for their newly risen culture. Aided and abetted by the Japanese both on an official and independent basis, they enacted a transformation. In the twenty-five years from the Centennial exhibition to 1901, American taste progressed from the charming eclectics of Aestheticism to the elegance of Art Nouveau and restrained beauty of Arts and Crafts, and would shortly proceed to the radicalism of early modernism. Japan took them from fascination with surface to the understanding of refinement and depth revealed in the plain, the commonplace, and even the rough. The example of its craftsmen allowed them to visualize cherished ideals and contributed mightily to the movement away from the idea of beauty as a preserve and reflection of the elite to one as the natural right and expression of the ordinary person. All this made Japan and its arts essential to America's evolution from parochial imitator to cosmopolitan trendsetter possessed of a distinct national image. The windows of Tiffany and La Farge, the ceramics of Rookwood and Grueby, and the architecture of the Greenes and Wright were simultaneously recognized as uniquely theirs, "American," and superb.

But 1915 brought a turning point. Japan and the United States, awkward partners for nearly four decades, found themselves on diverging paths. At the Panama-Pacific International Exposition in San Francisco, Japan once again placed great efforts in its installation and in the export art crafts displayed. At last an entity to be reckoned with, from this point, its art and political worlds were directed increasingly toward the creation of a different image, one suiting what it regarded as its proper place at the helm of the East. The United States, transfixed by a Europe on the brink of World War I, cut short the fair upon the outbreak of hostilities into which it would soon be drawn. Like the entire West, it emerged again transformed, and the domestic arts responded. In this, Japanese taste itself played only a small role, but the spirit and freedom it brought to design, by now completely absorbed, remained in the streamlined geometrical dynamism and elegance of the Style Moderne.

1. *International Studio* 1901–1902, 58.
2. Francis 1913, 359.

Bibliography

The listed periodical sources represent only a few of the virtually hundreds of full articles and passing references about Japan and Japanese arts that appeared regularly in other issues of these publications as well as in almost every newspaper, journal, and magazine of the time, perusal of which were too many to list but proved invaluable in re-creating the atmosphere of the era.

The following historical journals were obtained from online sources:

APS Online:
http://www2.lib.udel.edu/database/apsonline.html

The Art Amateur: A Monthly Journal Devoted to Art in the Household (1879–1903)
Arthur's Home Magazine
Arthur's Illustrated Home Magazine
Godey's Magazine
Hours at Home: A Popular Monthly of Instruction and Recreation
The Ladies' Home Journal
Putnam's Magazine, Original Papers on Literature, Science, Art and National Interests
Saturday Evening Post

Harpweek Online:
http://www.harpweek.com/

Harper's Weekly

Proquest Historical Newspapers:
http://www.proquest.com/products_pq/descriptions/pq-hist-news.shtml

The New York Times
Los Angeles Times

A

Adams, Henry. Kathleen A. Foster, Henry A. La Farge, H. Barbara Weinberg, Linnea H. Wren, and James L. Yarnall. *John La Farge.* New York City: Abbeville Press, 1987.

Allwood, John. *The Great Exhibitions.* London: Cassell & Collier Macmillan, 1977.

The Art Amateur: A Monthly Journal Devoted to Art in the Household—

January 1892, vol. 26, no. 2: "The World's Fair."
January 1895, vol. 32, no. 2: "An English View of American Pottery."
February 1880, vol. 2, no. 3: "Satsuma Faience," by William Elliot Griffis.
February 1883, vol. 8, no. 3: "Genuine and Imitation 'Satsuma.'"
February 1886, vol. 14, no. 3: "Chinese and Japanese Art."
February 1887, vol. 16, no. 3: "Hints for Simple Decoration of Unadorned City Apartments."
February 1889, vol. 20, no. 3: "Hints from Japanese Homes."
March 1880, vol. 2, no. 4: "Piano-Back Decorations."
March 1885, vol. 12, no. 4: "Decoration & Furniture, The Decoration of Our Homes. Preliminary Article," by Christopher Dresser.
March 1894: "Bronze and Wrought Metal, Cameos and Carvings."
March 1894, vol. 30, no. 4: "Interior Decoration at the World's Fair."
March 1901, vol. 44, no. 4: Correspondence.
March 1903, vol. 48, no. 4: "Seen in the Shops."
April 1882, vol. 6, no. 5: "Oscar Wilde on Pottery Decoration."
April 1885.
April 1886, vol. 14, no. 5: "A Japanese Romance."
May 1880, vol. 2, no. 6: "Ceramics: Old Hizen," by William Elliot Griffis.
May 1901, vol. 44, no. 6: "The Note-Book."
May 1903, vol. 48, no. 6: "Seasonal Novelties."
June 1879, vol. 1, no. 1: "Among the Dealers."
June 1889, vol. 21, no. 1: "My Note Book," by Montezuma.
June 1903, vol. 49, no. 1: "Seen in the Shops."
July 1890, vol. 23, no. 2.
July 1896, vol. 35, no. 2: "America's Chief Decorative Artist."
July 1903, vol. 49, no. 2: "Seen in the Shops."
August 1893, vol. 29, no. 3: "Japanese Art at the World's Fair."
September 1, 1879: "The Sweetheart in the Studio," by Edgar Fawcett.
October 1893, vol. 29, no. 5: "The World's Fair."
November 1880, vol. 3, no. 6: "An Artistic Salon in France."
November 1883, vol. 9, no. 6: "Alleged 'Satsuma' in Boston," by Edward S. Morse.
December 1880, vol. 4, no. 1: "The White House Porcelain Service."
December 1885, vol. 14, no. 1: "My Note-book," by Montezuma.
December 1886, vol.16, no. 1: "American Silverware."

December 1893: "Applied Arts at the World's Fair; Ceramics (continued). Germany. England. The United States. Italy. Denmark. Japan."

The Art Bulletin—

December 1962, vol. 44, no. 4: "Tiffany's Fame in Europe," by Herwin Schaefer.

1985, vol. 57, no. 3: "John La Farge's Discover of Japanese Art: A New Perspective on the Origins of *Japonisme*," by Henry Adams.

Arthur's Home Magazine—

February 1866, no. 27: "Queer if True."

May 1892, vol. 62: "The Exposition of 1893," by R. E. A. Dorr.

September 1868.

Arthur's Illustrated Home Magazine—

January 1876, vol. 44, no. 1: "Centennial Notes."

March 1881, vol. 49, no. 3: "Housekeepers' Department."

Arwas , Victor. *Glass: Art Nouveau to Art Deco*, New York City: Harry N. Abrams, 1987.

Audsley, George Ashdown. *Notes on Japanese Art.* Liverpool, 1872.

———*The Ornamental Arts of Japan*, vol. 1. New York City: Charles Scribner's Sons, 1885.

Ayres, Dianne, Timothy Hansen, Beth Ann McPherson, Tommy Arthur McPherson II. *American Arts and Crafts Textiles.* New York City: Harry N. Abrams, 2002.

B

Babbitts, Judith Ann. "'To See Is to Know': Stereographs Educate Americans about East Asia, 1890–1940." PhD dissertation, Yale University, 1987.

Banham, Joanna. "E. W. Godwin and Wallpaper Design," in *E. W. Godwin, Aesthetic Movement Architect and Designer.* Edited by Susan Weber Soros. New York City: Yale University Press, 1999.

Beasley, W. G. *Japan Encounters the Barbarian: Japanese Travellers in America and Europe.* New Haven, Connecticut: Yale University Press, 1995.

Benfey, Christopher. *The Great Wave, Gilded Age Misfits, Japanese Eccentrics and the Opening of Old Japan.* New York City: Random House, 2003.

Bennitt, Mark, and Frank Parker Stockbridge. *History of the Louisiana Purchase Exposition, St. Louis World's Fair of 1904.* St. Louis: Universal Exposition Publishing Company, 1905.

Bing, S. "Artistic America," in *Artistic America, Tiffany Glass, and Art Nouveau.* Translated from the 1895 French version (*La Culture artistique en Amérique*) by Benita Eisler; introduction by Robert Koch. Cambridge: MIT Press, 1970.

Bing. Siegfried. *Artistic Japan, A Monthly Illustrated Journal of Arts and Industries* I (October 1888): 2; published in London by Sampson Low, Martson, Searle and Rivington.

Bird, Isabella L. *Unbeaten Tracks in Japan, An Account of Travels on Horseback in the Interior, Including Visits to the Aborigines of Yezo and the Shrines of Nikko and Ise*, vols. 1, 2. London: J. Murray, 1880.

Blumin, Leonard. *Victorian Decorative Art: A Photographic Study of Ornamental Design in Antique Doorknobs.* Mill Valley, California: Victorian Design Press, 1983.

Brandt, Beverly K. "'Worthy and Carefully Selected': American Arts and Crafts at the Louisiana Purchase Exposition, 1904." *Archives of American Art Journal* 28, no. 1 (1988).

Brown, Jane Converse. "The 'Japanese Taste': Its Role in the Mission of the American Home and in the Family's Presentation of Itself to the Public as expressed in Published Sources—1876–1916." PhD dissertation, The University of Wisconsin, 1987.

Burke, Doreen Bolger. *In Pursuit of Beauty: Americans and the Aesthetic Movement.* New York City: Rizzoli, in association with the Metropolitan Museum of Art, 1986.

C

Carpenter, Charles H., Jr. *Gorham Silver.* San Francisco: Alan Wofsy Fine Arts, 1997.

Checkland, Olive. *Japan and Britain after 1859: Creating Cultural Bridges.* New York City: Routledge Curzon, 2002.

Chisolm, Lawrence W. *Fenollosa: The Far East and American Culture.* Westport, Connecticut: Greenwood press, 1976; reprinted from Yale University Press, 1963.

Clark, Garth, Robert A. Ellison Jr., and Eugene Hecht. *The Mad Potter of Biloxi: The Art and Life of George E. Ohr.* New York City: Abbeville Press, 1989.

Clark, Robert Judson. *The Arts and Crafts Movement in America, 1876–1916.* Princeton, NJ: Princeton University Press, 1972.

Cobbing, Andrew. "The Iwakura Mission in Britain, 1872." Discussion Paper, The Suntory Centre, Suntory and Toyota International Centres for Economics and Related Disciplines London School of Economics and Political Science, 1998.

Cook, Clarence. *The House Beautiful; Essays on Beds and Tables, Stools and Candlesticks.* New York City: Scribner, 1881.

Cox, Kenyon. "Two Specimens of La Farge's Art in Glass." *The Burlington Magazine for Connoisseurs* 13, no. 63 (June 1908).

The Craftsman—

January 1911, vol. 1: "John La Farge, the Craftsman."

January 1912, vol. 1: "A Sheaf of Ramma (Japanese Wood Carving)," by Bunkio Matsuki and Frederick W. Coburn.

February 1910: "How Beauty and Labor Are Interwoven in the Daily Life of Japan," by Curtis M. L. Wakeman.

April 1913, vol. 4: "Japan's Beauty an Inspiration to American Home-Builders," by Kathryn Rucker.

May 1906, vol. 5: "Japanese Architecture and Its Relation to the Coming American Style."

May 1916, vol. 5: "The Influence of the Japanese Print."

August 1906, vol. 8: "Simple Life in Japan—Achieved by Contentment of Spirit and a True Knowledge of Art," by Marguerite Glover.

September 1904, vol. 9: "Japanese Porcelains," by Randolph I. Geare.

October 1903, vol. 10: "Japanese Color Prints and Some of their Makers" by M. Louise Stowell.

November 1903, vol. 11: "A Note of Color," by Harvey Ellis.

Croissant, Doris. 'Fenollosas "Wahre Theorie der Kunst."' *Saeculum* 38, no. 1 (1987).

Cutler, H.G. *The World's Fair: Its Meaning and Scope, Its Old-World Friend, Their Countries, Customs and Religions, What They will Exhibit; The United States at the Fair, the City and the Site, The Colossal Structures.* San Francisco: Star Publishing Company, 1892.

D

D'Ambrosio, Anna Tobin. *A Brass Menagerie: Metalwork of the Aesthetic Movement.* Utica, New York: Munson-Williams-Proctor Arts Institute, 2005.

Decorator and Furnisher—
March 1884.
July 1885.
August 1884, vol. 4, no. 5.
October 1882.
December 1884, vol. 3, no. 4.

Dethier, Kathryn. "The Spirit of Progressive Reform: The 'Ladies Home Journal' House Plans, 1900– 1902." *Journal of Design History* 6, no. 4 (1993).

Dow, Arthur Wesley. "A Course in Fine Arts for Candidates for the Higher Degrees." *The Bulletin of the College Art Association of America* 1, no. 4 (1918).

Duncan, Alastair, Martin Eidelberg, and Neil Harris. *Masterworks of Louis Comfort Tiffany.* New York City: Abradael Press, Harry N. Abrams 1993; reprinted from London: Thames and Hudson, 1989.

Duncan, Alastair, and Georges de Bartha. *Glass by Gallé.* New York City: Harry N. Abrams, 1984.

E

Earl, Joe. *Splendours of Meiji, Treasures of Imperial Japan.* St. Petersburg, Florida: Broughton International, Inc., 1999.

Eastlake, Charles L. *Hints on Household Taste: The Classic Handbook of Victorian Interior Decoration.* New York City: Dover Publications 1969. First issued as *Hints on Household Taste in Furniture, Upholstery and Other Details.* London: Longmans, Green and Company, 1878.

Eberlein, Harold Donaldson, Abbot McClure, and Edward Stratton Holloway. *The Practical Book of Interior Decoration.* Philadelphia: J. B. Lippincott Co., 1919.

"Edward Greey." Virtual American Biologies, Edited Appletons Encyclopedia © 2001. [http://famousamericans.net/edwardgreey/]

Eidelberg, Martin. "American Ceramics and International Styles, 1876–1916." *Record of the Art Museum, Princeton University* 34, no. 2 (n.d.).

Elliott, Brent. *Victorian Gardens.* Portland, Oregon: Timber Press, 1986.

Everson Museum of Art. *Fragile Blossoms, Enduring Earth: The Japanese Influence on American Ceramics.* Syracuse, New York: 1989.

F

Finck, Henry T. *Lotos-time in Japan.* New York City: Charles Scribner's Sons, 1895.

Flinn, John J. *Official Guide to the World's Columbian Exposition in the City of Chicago, State of Illinois, May 1–October 26, 1893.* Chicago: Columbian Guide Company, 1893.

Fowler, Elizabeth J. "The Rookwood Sage: Kitaro Shirayamadani, Japanism, Art Nouveau, and the American Art Pottery Movement, 1885–1912." PhD dissertation, University of Minnesota, 2005.

Foy, Jessica H., and Thomas J. Schlereth, eds. *American Home Life, 1880–1930: A Social History of Spaces and Services.* Knoxville, Tennessee: University of Tennessee Press, 1992.

Foy, Jessica H., and Karal Ann Marling, eds. *The Arts and the American Home, 1890–1930.* Knoxville, TN: University of Tennessee Press, 1994.

Francis, David R. *The Universal Exposition of 1904.* St. Louis: Louisiana Purchase Exposition Co., 1913.

Frelinghuysen, Alice Cooney. *American Art Pottery: Selections from the Charles Hosmer Morse Museum of American Art.* Seattle: University of Washington Press, in association with the Orlando Museum of Art, 1995.

———. *American Porcelain: 1770–1920.* New York City: Harry Abrams, 1989.

———. *Louis Comfort Tiffany and Laurelton Hall.* New Haven, Connecticut: Yale University Press, with The Metropolitan Museum of Art, New York, 2006.

———, Gary Tinterow, Susan Alyson Stein, Gretchen Wold, and Julia Meech. *Splendid Legacy: The Havemeyer Collection.* New York City: The Metropolitan Museum of Art, 1993.

G

Garner, Philippe. *Emile Gallé.* London: Academy Editions, 1976.

Gere, Charlotte. *The House Beautiful: Oscar Wilde and the Aesthetic Interior.* London: Lund Humphries, 2000.

Giberti, Bruno. *Designing the Centennial, a History of the 1876 International Exhibition in Philadelphia.* Lexington, KY: University of Kentucky Press, 2002.

Gibson, Charles Dana. *The Social Ladder.* New York City: R. H. Russell, 1902.

Godey's Magazine (June 1898), vol. 136, no. 816: "Japanese Glimpses" by Mabel Cronise Jones.

Green, Nancy E. *Arthur Wesley Dow and American Arts and Crafts,* New York City: Harry N. Abrams, in association with the American Federation of Arts, 1999.

Greey, Edward. *The Wonderful City of Tokio, or Further Adventures of the Jewet Family and Their Friend Oto Nambo.* Boston: Lee and Shepard, 1883.

Griffis, William Elliot. *The Mikado's Empire.* New York City: Harper & Brothers, 1876.

H

Halstead, Hon. Murat. *Pictorial History of the Louisiana Purchase and the World's Fair at St. Louis,* 1904.

Harper's Weekly—
March 16, 1872: "Our Japanese Visitors."
August 12, 1876: "The Centennial, Bronze and Lacquer Work in the Japanese Department, Main Building."
August 26, 1876: "The Centennial."
November 25, 1876: "The Centennial. Japanese Porcelain."

Holley, Marietta. *Samantha at the World's Fair.* New York City: Funk & Wagnalls Co., 1893.

Hood, William P., Jr., with Roslyn Berlin and Edward Wawrynek. *Tiffany Silver Flatware, 1845–1905, When Dining was an Art.* Woodbridge, England: Antique Collectors' Club, Ltd, 1999; reprinted 2003.

Hook, Dorothy Jean. "Fenollosa and Dow: The Effect of an Eastern and Western Dialogue on American Art Education." PhD dissertation, The Pennsylvania State University, 1987.

Hosley, William. *The Japan Idea.* Hartford, Connecticut: Wadsworth Atheneum, 1990.

Hours at Home: A Popular Monthly of Instruction and Recreation—
October 1867, vol.5, no. 6: "Something about Japan."
November 1867, vol. 6, no. 1: "Something about the Japanese."

The House Beautiful—

April 1900, vol. 7, no. 5: "Japanese Domestic Interiors."

June 1899, vol. 6, no. 1: "A Review of the Recent Exhibitions of the Chicago Arts and Crafts Society."

July 1899, vol. 6 vol. 2: "Individuality in Artistic Furnishing."

December 1904, vol. 17, no. 1: "Japanese Flower Treatment."

Howe, Katherine S., Alice Cooney Frelinghuysen, and Catherine Hoover Voorsanger. *Herter Brothers: Furniture and Interiors for a Gilded Age.* New York City: Harry N. Abrams, in association with The Museum of Fine Arts, Houston. 1994.

I

The International Studio—

1896, vol. 1, no. 1: "A Letter from Japan."

1896, vol. 1. no. 3: "The Lay Figure: 'Kelmscott and Japan.'"

1896, vol. 1, no. 3: "Japanese Drawing."

1897, vols. 2, 3, 8, 11, 13, 16, and 30.

1901–1902, vol. 15: "The Potters Art. Object Lessons from the Far East."

Irvine, Gregory. *Japanese Cloisonné.* London: V&A Publications 2006.

Israel, Fred L. 1897 Sears, Roebuck Catalogue, reprinted with an introduction by S. J. Perelman. Philadelphia: Chelsea House Publishers 1993, a reprint from 1968.

J

Jackson, Anna. "Imagining Japan: The Victorian Perception and Acquisition of Japanese Culture." *Journal of Design History* 5 no. 4 (1992).

———. "Orient and Occident," in *Art Nouveau 1890–1914.* London: V&A Publications, 2000.

Jahn, Gisela. *Meiji Ceramics: The Art of Japanese Export Porcelain and Satsuma Ware 1868–1912.* Stuttgart, Germany: Arnoldsche Art Publishers, 2004.

The Japanese Commission, International Exhibition, 1876. *Official Catalogue of the Japanese Section, and Descriptive Notes on the Industry and Agriculture of Japan.* Philadelphia: W. P. Kildare, 1876.

Johnson, Diane Chalmers. *American Art Nouveau.* New York City: Harry N. Abrams 1979.

Johnson, Marilynn A. *Louis Comfort Tiffany, Artist for the Ages,* London: Scala, 2006.

K

Kakudzo [Kakuzō], Okakura. *The Hōōden (Phoenix Hall).* Tokyo: K. Ogawa, 1893.

Kaplan, Wendy. *"The Art that is Life": The Arts and Crafts Movement in America, 1875–1920.* Boston: Bulfinch Press [Little, Brown and Co.], 1998.

Kardon, Janet, ed. *The Ideal Home 1900–1920: The History of Twentieth Century American Craft.* New York City: Harry N. Abrams, in association with the American Craft Museum, 1993.

Keene, Donald. *Emperor of Japan: Meiji and his World, 1852–1912.* New York City: Columbia University Press, 2002.

Kisluk-Grosheide, Daniëlle O. "The Marquand Mansion." *Metropolitan Museum Journal* 29 (1994).

Knute, Kevin. "Frank Lloyd Wright and Japanese Architecture: A Study in Inspiration." *Journal of Design History* 7, no. 3 (1994).

L

Ladies' Home Journal—

February 1906, vol. 23, number 8: "New Things to Eat; Fruits and Vegetables which are Strange to Most of Us," by John Elfreth Watkins.

March 1903, vol. 20, no. 4: "Some Oriental Ideas," by Florence Pegg Taylor.

March 1905, vol. 22, no. 4: "Bridal Breakfasts and Bridal Luncheons," by Hester Price and Lilian C. Sterrett.

May 1905, vol. 22, no. 6: "A Dragon Bedquilt; An Original Design by the Japanese Artist That Can be Easily Followed by Gazo Foudji.

June 1903, vol. 20, no. 7: "Japanese and Chinese Embroideries for Girls," by Lillian Baynes Griffin.

July 1904, vol. 21, no. 8: "When 'Japanese Tommy' Captured New York."

July 1906, vol. 23, no. 3: "Why Vegetables are so Healthful," by S. T. Rorer.

October 1895, vol. 12, no. 11: "A Japanese Room," by F. Schuyler Mathews.

November 1906, vol. 23, no. 12: "Has Your Church Had Fairs Like These?"

December 1890, vol. 8, no. 1: "Golden Dinner Sets," by Foster Coates.

Laird, Pamela Walker. *Advertising Progress, American Business and the Rise of Consumer Marketing.* Baltimore: Johns Hopkins University Press, 1998.

Lancaster, Clay. *The Japanese Influence in America.* New York City: Abbeville Press, 1983; first issued in 1963 by Walton Rawls.

———. "Synthesis: The Artistic Theory of Fenollosa and Dow." *Art Journal* 28, no. 3 (1969).

Larson, Erik. *Devil in the White City: Murder, Magic and Madness at the Fair that Changed America.* New York City: Random House, 2003.

Lawton, Thomas, and Linda Merrill. *Freer: A Legacy of Art.* New York City: Harry N. Abrams, in association with Freer Gallery of Art, Smithsonian Institution, 1993.

Lockyer, Angus. *Japan at the Exhibition, 1867–1970.* PhD dissertation, Stanford University, 2000.

Longfellow, Henry Wadsworth. *Keramos and Other Poems.* Boston: Houghton, Osgood and Co., 1878. http://www.worldwideschool.org/library/books/lit/poetry/TheCompletePoeticalWorksofHenryWadsworthLongfellow/chap22.html.

Loring, John. *Louis Comfort Tiffany at Tiffany & Co.* New York City: Harry N. Abrams, 2002.

Los Angeles Times, June 8, 1902: "Land of the Japs: Graphic Picture of Life in the Chrysanthemum Country from the Pen of a Lost Angeles Woman."

M

Mackinson, Randell L. *Green and Green, Architecture as a Fine Art: Furniture and Related Designs.* Salt Lake City: Gibbs Smith, Publisher, 2001.

———. *Greene and Greene, the Passion and the Legacy.* Salt Lake City: Gibbs Smith, Publisher, 1998.

Matsuki, Bunkio. *Leathers of Old Japan.* N.p., ca. 1880–1899.

McCabe, James D. *The Illustrated History of the Centennial Exhibition.* Philadelphia: Jones Brothers & Co., 1876.

McConnell, Kevin. *Heintz Art Metal, Silver-on-Bronze Wares.* West Chester, Pennsylvania: Schiffer Art Publishing, 1990.

McKean, Hugh F. *The Lost Treasures of Louis Comfort Tiffany*. Atglen, Pennsylvania: Schiffer Publishing Ltd., 1980. © 1980 Hugh F. McKean; © 2002 Charles Hosmer Morse Foundation.
Meech, Julia. *Frank Lloyd Wright and the Art of Japan.* New York City: Harry N. Abrams, Inc., 2001.
Meech-Pekarik, Julia. "Early Collectors of Japanese Prints and the Metropolitan Museum of Art." *Metropolitan Museum Journal* 17 (1982).
———, Julia, and Gabriel P. Weisberg, *Japonisme Comes to America: The Japanese Impact on the Graphic Arts, 1876–1925.* New York City: Harry Abrams, Inc., 1990.
Merrill, Linda. *The Peacock Room: A Cultural Biography.* New Haven, CT: Yale University Press, 1998.
The Metropolitan Museum of Art Bulletin—
June 1907, vol. 2, no. 6: "The Edward C. Moore Collection," by Conrad Hewitt.
December 1910, vol. 5, no. 12: "John La Farge," by Frank J. Mather; reprinted from *Evening Post,* November 14, 1910.
1962 New Series, vol. 21, no. 3: "'Nature in Her Most Seductive Aspects': Louis Comfort Tiffany's Favrile Glass," by Stuart P. Feld.
Moffatt, Frederick Cambell. *The Life, Art and Times of Arthur Wesley Dow.* PhD dissertation, University of Chicago, 1972.

N

The New York Times—
January 10, 1882: "Oscar Wilde's Lecture."
February 2, 1890: "Art Notes."
February 11, 1906: "Israel's Lost Tribes Again Found."
February 16, 1896: "The Poster," by Robert W. Chambers.
February 29, 1882: "Art Notes."
March 10, 1878: "Japanese Art."
March 12, 1892: "World Fair Plans."
April 11, 1909: "News of the Art World at Home and Abroad."
April 18, 1880: "Fashion's Latest Fancies."
April 23, 1893: "Japanese Art at Chicago."
May 3, 1908: "Art at Home and Abroad."
May 6, 1877: "Japan in New York."
May 11, 1902: "Artist Artisanship Needed" by John Ward Stimson.
May 11, 1902: "Japanese Art," from the London House.
May 27, 1883: "Notes on Art and Artists."
June 10, 1877: "The Furniture Craze."
July 21, 1901: "The Gentle Art of Tattooing."
August 4, 1901: "Decay of Japanese Art," by L. W. Crippen.
August 25, 1881: "The Vanderbilt Palaces."
October 2, 1888: "Suicide of Edward Greey."
October 28, 1905: "Japanese Art."
December 4, 1881: "Making Homes Beautiful, The Growing Taste for Indoor Decorations."
December 5, 1886: "On a Mission of Art."
December 10, 1893: "Art Notes."
December 10, 1898: "John La Farge."
December 11, 1898: "Silver for American Tables."
December 28, 1893: "The Juni-no-taka Bronzes."
Nichols, George Ward. *Pottery, How it is Made, Its Shape and Decorations.* New York City: G.P. Putnam's Sons, 1878.

O

Okakura Kakudzo [Kakuzō]. *The Hōōden (Phoenix Hall), An Illustrated Description of the Buildings Erected by the Japanese Government at the World's Columbian Exposition, Jackson Park, Chicago.* Tokyo: K. Ogawa, 1893.
Okazaki, Akio. "Arthur Wesley Dow's Address in Kyoto, Japan" (1903). *Journal of Aesthetic Education* 37, no. 4 (2003).
Owen, Nancy E. *Rookwood and the Industry of Art, Woman, Culture and Commerce, 1880–1913.* Athens, Ohio: Ohio University Press, 2001.
———. *Rookwood Pottery at the Philadelphia Museum of Art: The Gerald and Virginia Gordon Collection.* Philadelphia, 2003.

P

Peck, Amelia, and Carol Irish. *Candace Wheeler, The Art and Enterprise of American Design, 1875–1900.* New Haven, Connecticut: Yale University Press, with the Metropolitan Museum of Art, 2001.
Peltz, George A. *The Housewife's Library: Many Volumes in One.* Philadelphia: Hubbard Bros., Publishers, 1883.
Pollay, Richard W. "The Subsiding Sizzle: A Descriptive History of Print Advertising, 1900–1980." *Journal of Marketing* 49, no. 3 (1985).
Porter, Glenn. "Cultural Forces and Commercial Constraints: Designing Packaging in the Twentieth-Century United States." *Journal of Design History* 12, no 1 (1999): *Design, Commercial Expansion and Business History.*
Put, Max. *Plunder and Pleasure: Japanese Art in the West, 1860–1930.* Leiden: Hotei Publishing, 2000.
Putnam's Magazine: Original Papers on Literature, Science, Art and National Interests—
April 1868, vol. 1, no. 4: "Life in Great Cities III, Yedo. Industry, Frugality—Then Prosperity, Wealth—Then Art, Power—Then Luxury, Corruption—Then Ruin!"
May 1868, vol. 1, no. 5: "Familiar Letters from Japan I. From San Francisco to Yokohama."
June 1868, vol. 1, no. 6: "A New Yorker in Japan II."

R

Rydell, Robert W. *All the World's a Fair: Visions of Empire at American International Expositions, 1876–1916.* Chicago and London: University of Chicago Press, 1984.
———. *The Books of the Fairs: Materials about World's Fairs, 1834–1916, in the Smithsonian Institution Libraries.* Chicago: American Library Association, 1992.
———. *World of Fairs: The Century-of-Progress Expositions.* Chicago: University of Chicago Press, 1984.

S

Sahr, Robert C. "Consumer Price Index (CPI) Conversion Factors 1800 to estimated 2015 to Convert to Dollars of 1998." Political Science Department, Oregon State University, 2005.
Saturday Evening Post—
January 8, 1881, vol. 60, no. 25: "Sanctum Chat."
July 1, 1876, vol. 55, no. 49: "At the Centennial Exhibition."
July 15, 1876, vol. 55, no. 51: "At the Centennial Exhibition."
July 13, 1878, vol. 57, no. 51: "Sanctum Chat."

Schlereth, Thomas J. *Victorian America: Transformations in Everyday Life 1876–1915.* New York City: Harper Collins, 1991.

Sears, Roebuck Catalogue (1897). Reprinted from 1968, with an introduction by S. J. Perelman; edited by Fred L. Israel. Philadelphia: Chelsea House Publishers, 1993.

Segi Shinich. "Hayashi Tadamasa: Bridge Between the Fine Arts of East and West," in *Japonisme in Art, An International Symposium.* Tokyo: Kodansha International, 1980.

Sharf, Frederick A. *"A Pleasing Novelty": Bunkio Matsuki and the Japan Craze in Victorian Salem.* Salem, Massachusetts: Peabody Essex Museum, 1993.

Sheldon, George William (attributed). *Artistic Houses: Being a Series of Interior Views of a Number of the Most Beautiful and Celebrated Homes in the United States with A Description of the Art Treasures Contained Therin.* New York City: D. Appleton, 1883–1884.

Shinn, Earl. *Mr. Vanderbilt's House and Collection/ described by Edward Strahan [pseudo],* vol. 1. Boston: Geo. Barrie, 1883–84.

Sloan, Julie L., and James L. Yarnall. "Art of an Opaline Mind: The Stained Glass of John La Farge." *American Art Journal* 24, nos. 1 and 2 (1992).

Smith, Walter. *The Masterpieces of the Centennial International Exhibition,* vol. 1: *Industrial Art.* Philadelphia: Gebbie & Barrie, 1875.

Soros, Susan Weber, ed. "E. W. Godwin and Interior Design," in *E. W. Godwin, Aesthetic Movement Architect and Designer.* New Haven, Connecticut: Yale University Press, 1999.

South, Erastus. "Novelties from an Expert's Baggage." *Daily Graphic* (16 April 1877), as found in David A. Taylor, "Dresser in the United States," *Shock of the Old Christopher Dresser's Design Revolution.* Ed. by Michael Whiteway. New York City: Harry N. Abrams, Inc., in conjunction with the Cooper-Hewitt and the Victoria and Albert Museums, 2004.

Stalker, John, and George Parker. *A Treatise of Japanning [sic] and Varnishing.* Oxford: author publication, 1688.

Stankiewicz, Mary Ann. "From the Aesthetic Movement to the Arts and Crafts Movement." *Studies in Art Education* 33, no. 3 (1992).

Strahan, Edward. *The Masterpieces of the Centennial International Exhibition Illustrated,* vol. 2: *Fine Art.* Philadelphia: Gebbie & Barrie, 1876.

T

Thomson, Ellen Mazur. "'The Science of Publicity': An American Advertising Theory, 1900–1920." *Journal of Design History* 9, no. 4 (1996).

Trachtenberg, Alan. *The Incorporation of America: Culture and Society in the Gilded Age.* New York City: Hill and Wang [Farrar, Straus and Giroux], 1982.

V

Venable, Charles L. *Silver in America, 1840–1940: A Century of Splendor.* New York City: Harry N. Abrams, Inc., 1994.

W

Walker, John Brisben. *The Cosmopolitan, September 1904: The World's Fair.* (The editor of *Cosmopolitan* produced articles about his 11 days at the world's fair, providing an overview of the fair, with discussion of state and foreign exhibits, electricity, manufacturing, etc.)

Watanabe, Kaoru. *Influence of Ukiyo-e Woodcuts on Prints of Arthur Wesley Dow.* M.A. thesis, Michigan State University, 1996.

Weisberg, Gabriel P. *Art Nouveau Bing: Paris Style 1900.* New York City: Harry N. Abrams, in association with the Smithsonian Institution Traveling Exhibition Service, 1986.

———. "Japonisme: The Commercialization of an Opportunity," in Julia Meech-Pekarik and Gabriel P. Weisberg, *Japonisme Comes to America: The Japanese Impact on the Graphic Arts, 1876–1925.* New York City: Harry Abrams, Inc., 1990.

———, Phillip, Dennis Cate, Gerald Needham, Martin Eidelberg, and William R. Johnston. *Japonisme: Japanese Influence on French Art 1854–1910.* Clevelend, Ohio: Cleveland Museum of Art, 1975.

Weisberg, Gabriel P., Muriel Rakusin, and Stanley Rakusin. "On Understanding Artistic Japan." *The Journal of Decorative and Propaganda Arts* 1 (Spring 1986): 6–19; Miami, Florida: Wolfson Foundation of Decorative and Propaganda Arts.

Whiteway, Michael, ed. *Shock of the Old: Christopher Dresser's Design Revolution.* New York City: V&A Publications, in association with Cooper-Hewitt, National Design Museum; distributed by Harry N. Abrams, 2004.

Wilde, Oscar. *The Decay of Lying,* from *Intentions.* New York City: Brentano's, 1905. © 1998 by Geoffrey Sauer: http://eserver.org/books/intentions/the-decay-of-lying.html. All rights reserved. Free for educational and non-commercial use.

Wilkinson, Nancy B. "E.W. Godwin and Japonisme in England," in *E. W. Godwin, Aesthetic Movement Architect and Designer,* edited by Susan Weber Soros. New Haven, Connecticut: Yale University Press, 1999.

Wilson, Carol Green. *Gump's Treasure Trade, a Story of San Francisco.* New York City: Thomas Y. Crowell Co., 1949.

Wilson, Joseph M. *The Masterpieces of the Centennial International Exhibition Illustrated,* vol. 3: *History, Mechanics, Science.* Philadelphia: Gebbie & Barrie, 1876.

Winterthur Portfolio—

1975, vol. 10: "Associated Artists and the American Renaissance in Decorative Arts," by Wilson H. Faude.

1979, vol. 13: *American Furniture and Its Makers:* "Mitchell and Rammelsberg: Cincinnati Furniture Manufacturers 1847–1881," by Donald C. Peirce.

1988, vol. 23, no. 4: "Somebody's Aunt and Nobody's Mother: The American China Painter and her Work, 1870–1920," by Cynthia Brandimarte.

1991, vol. 26, no. 1: "Japanese Novelty Stores," by Cynthia A. Brandimarte.

Y

Yamanaka & Co. *Catalogue of Room Decorations and Artistic Furniture.* Osaka, Japan: Yamanaka & Company, 1905.

Credits

Images are courtesy of the following individuals, collections, and organizations:

KEY: upper [u]
lower [l]
left [l]
center [c]
right [r]
upper left [ul]
lower left [ll]
upper center [uc]
lower center [lc]
upper right [ur]
lower right [lr]

Allen Michaan, Auctions by the Bay, Alameda, California: 20, 25, 109, 110, 111, 113 [ul], 113 [ll], 114, 116 a–b [ul], 116 [ur], 117 [ul], 117 [c], 130 [lr], 141 [lr], 142 [ll], 146, 147 [ul], 155 [ur], 166 [ul], 167 [ur], 168 [ll], 168 [lr], 185

Bancroft Library, University of California–Berkeley: 18, 71 [ur]

Berke (Ian) Collection: 164 [lr]

Bain (George Grantham) Collection, Library of Congress, Prints and Photographs Division: 16 [ul] (LC-DIG-ggbain-07799), 16 [ur] (LC-DIG-ggbain-07798), 57 [ll] (LC-DIG-ggbain-20863), 57 [lr] (LC-DIG-ggbain-16803)

Bigelow (William Sturgis) Collection, Museum of Fine Arts, Boston: 77 (11.14676)

Brady-Handy Photograph Collection, Library of Congress, Prints and Photographs Division: 17 [ul] (LC-DIG-cwpbh-00118)

Chadbourne Collection of Japanese Prints, Library of Congress, Prints and Photographs Division: 10 (LC-USZC4-1274), 12 [ul] (LC-USZC4-1314), 14 (LC-USZC4-10386), 23 [ul] (LC-USZC4-10384), 24 [ul] (LC-USZC4-10527)

Chicago Historical Society: 48, 72

Cohen-Bray House, Oakland, California: 88, 109 [ul], 121

Colman (Jacqueline) Collection: 93 [ul], 96 [ur]

DeShong (Alfred O.) Collection, Widener University Art Collection & Gallery, Chester Pennsylvania: 25 [ll], 27, 41, 44 [ll] 115, 150, 182 [lr]

East Asian Library, University of California–Berkeley: 74, 132, 135 [lr] 138 [ur], 155 [ul]

Environmental Design Library, University of California–Berkeley: 17 [ll], 68 [ul], 85, 106 [ul], 109 [ur], 131

Folk (Thomas C.) Collection: 186, 187, 188 a–b, 194, 195, 202 [ul], 202 [lr], 203, 204 [ul]

Free Library of Philadelphia, Print and Picture Collection: 21, 153 [lr] (c021611)

Freer Gallery of Art, Smithsonian Institution, Washington, D.C.:
Charles Lang Freer, Gift of: 78 (F1903.101-F1903.102), 103 (F1904.61), 104 [ul] (F1898.6), 105 (F1907.178)

Gamble (David Berry) House, Pasadena, California: 123 [ul] (I.D.: GGUSC-Gamble-DA-157), 100

Gardner Library, University of California–Berkeley: 81

Grolier Club, New York City: 68 [ll], 69 [lr]

Hood (William P., Jr.) Collection: 138 [ul], 157 [ul], 157 [ur], 158, 160 [ll], 160 [lr], 161 [ul], 161 [ur], 161 [ul], 161 [lr]

Imari Gallery, Sausalito, California: 8, 13 [ul], 108, 123 [lr], 134, 137, 142 [ur], 148 [ur]

Khalili (Nasser D.) Collection of Japanese Art, London, England: 55, 65 [ul], 67 [ll], 67 [lr], 144 [ul], 156, 196 [ur], 197 [lr]

Library of Congress, Prints and Photographs Division: 10 (LC-USZC4-1274), 12 [ul] (LC-USZC4-1314), 12 [ur] (LC-USZC4-8657), 14 (LC-USZC4-10386), 15 (LC-USZC4-8737), 16 [l] (LC-DIG-ggbain-07799), 16 [r] (LC-DIG-ggbain-07798), 17 [ul] (LC-DIG-cwpbh-00118), 23 [ul] (LC-USZC4-10384), 23 [lr] (LC-USZ62-99595), 24 [ul] (LC-USZC4-10527), 28 (LC-DIG-pga-03375), 29 (LC-USZ62-102264), 31 (LC-USZ62-93899), 32 (LC-USZ62-96108), 33 (LC-USZ62-97467), 34, 35 (LC-USZ62-50695), 38 [ll], 38 [ur] (LC-USZ62-125518), 39 (LC-USZ62-96109), 42 [ul] (LC-USZ62-125801), 42 [lr], 43 [uc] (LC-USZ62-112337), 44 [ur], 46, 51 (LOT 13674 (S) [P&P]), 53 (LC-DIG-jpd-00162), 56 [ul] (LOT 4271 (F) [P&P]), 56 [ll] (LC-DIG-jpd-01771), 57 [ll] (LC-DIG-ggbain-20863), 57 [lr] (LC-DIG-ggbain-16803), 58 (LC-USZ62-118752), 59 (LOT 11044 [P&P]), 62 (LC-USZ62-69403), 64 [ul] (LC-DIG-jpd-00222), 64 [ur] (LC-USZC4-9982), 76 [ul] (LC-DIG-jpd-00026), 76 [ur] (LC-DIG-jpd-02711), 92 (LC-USZ62-69512), 95 [ur] (LC-DIG-pga-01236), 96 [ll] (LC-USZC4-

9674), 97 [ul] (LC-USZC2-5739), 97 [uc] (LC-DIG-jpd-01787), 97 [ur] (LC-DIG-jpd-01787), 111 [ur] (LC-USZ62-94017), 120 [l] (LC-DIG-jpd-01796), 120 [r] (LC-DIG-jpd-02394), 135 [u] (LC-USZ62-115996), 138 [l] (LC-USZC2-1767), 139 [ur] (LC-DIG-jpd-02393), 167 [l] (LC-USZC4-8701), 199 [u] (LC-DIG-jpd-00013), 199 [l] (LC-USZC2-410), 201 [l] (LC-DIG-jpd-01764). *See also* Bain (George Grantham) Collection; Brady-Handy Photograph Collection; Chadbourne Collection of Japanese Prints

MACKLOWE GALLERY, New York City: 82, 83, 140 [ll], 143 [ur], 144 [ll]

MARK TWAIN HOUSE & MUSEUM, Hartford, Connecticut:
- Mrs. Horace B. Learned, 1971, Gift of: 148 [ul] (71.16.13)
- Mrs. Francis B. Thurber III, 1972, Gift of: 147 [ll] (72.14.27)

MAYMONT HOUSE MUSEUM, Richmond, Virginia: 111 [ul], 141 [ul], 143 [ul], 153 [ur], 166 [ur], 175, 177, 179, 189 [ul], 189 [ur], 190, 191

MORSE (CHARLES HOSMER) MUSEUM OF AMERICAN ART, Winter Park, Florida: 87, 95 [ll], 112 [ul], 189 [ul], 128, 139 [ll], 140 [lc], 140 [lr], 154, 192 [ul], 192 [ur], 196 [ul], 196 [lr], 198 [ul], 200 [ul], 205

MUSEUM OF FINE ARTS, BOSTON: 70 [ul], 70 [ur], 71 [ul], 77 (11.14676), 80 (21.4430), 125 (21.6756), 139 (21.9497)
- Jack (Edwin E.) Fund and Anonymous Gift of: 133 (69.1224),
- O'Gorman (James F. and Jean Baer), Gift of: 136 (1974.498 a–f)
- *See also* Bigelow (William Sturgis) Collection; Spaulding (William S. and John T.) Collection

NEW YORK PUBLIC LIBRARY, THE BRANCH LIBRARIES, Picture Collection: Astor, Lenox and Tilden Foundations: 93 [l] (ID: 819534)

NEW YORK PUBLIC LIBRARY, PRINTS AND PHOTOGRAPHS: Astor, Lenox and Tilden Foundations, Photography Collection, Miriam and Ira D. Wallach Division of Art, Prints and Photographs: 24 [l], 69 [lr] (Digital ID# 1543220)

NEW YORK PUBLIC LIBRARY, Samuel Putnam Avery Collection, Humanities and Social Sciences Library, Print Collection, Miriam and Ira D. Wallach Division of Art, Prints and Photographs: 75 (Digital ID# 1149389)

NEW YORK PUBLIC LIBRARY FOR THE PERFORMING ARTS, MUSIC DIVISION: Astor, Lenox and Tilden Foundations: 94 [l] (ID: 1165736)

ORIENTAL TREASURE BOX, San Diego, California: 37, 64 [ul], 64 [ur], 65 [l], 89 [l], 89 [u], 104 [l], 107 [u], 107 [l], 153 [ul], 155 [lr], 159 [l], 165, 169, 176 [l], 176 [r], 173, 180 [l], 181, 193

PHOTOGRAPHS BY:
- Borissov, Ognen, "Interfoto": 123 [ul]
- Bye, Randl: 186, 187, 188 a–b, 194, 195, 202 [ul], 202 [lr], 203, 204 [ul]
- Daniel, Jay, "Black Cat Studio": 8, 13 [ul], 108, 123 [lr], 134, 137, 142 [ur], 148 [ur]
- Eckhaus, Orin: 106 [l], 202 [ll], 204 [c], 204 [ur]
- Flynn, Matt: 13, 22
- Konishi, Scott: 37, 64 [ul], 64 [ur], 65 [l], 89 [l], 89 [u], 104 [l], 107 [u], 107 [l], 153 [ul], 155 [lr], 159 [l], 165, 169, 176 [l], 176 [r], 173, 180 [l], 181, 193
- Lee, Jeffrey: 25 [u], 185
- McDonald, Scott: 20 [l], 88, 109, 121
- Sandberg, Douglas: 20, 114, 116, 117 [l], 117 [c], 117 [r], 130 [r], 141 [ll], 141 [ur], 146, 147 [u], 155 [ur], 164 [ll], 164 [lr], 166 [ul], 167 [ur], 168 [ll], 168 [lr], 181, 184 [l], 184 [r], 197, 201 [u]
- Sanders, Sanders: 130 [ll]
- Stanley, Larry: 138 [ul], 157 [ul], 157 [ur], 158, 161 [ur], 160 [ll], 160 [lr], 161 [ul], 161 [lr]
- Street-Porter, Tim: 10
- Welch, Marybeth: 178, 182 [u], 183 [u], 183 [l], 198 [r]

PRIVATE COLLECTION: 36, 98, 119 a–b

REUTLINGER (RICHARD D.) COLLECTION: 194 [u], 91, 117 [ur], 118 a–b, 141 [ur], 153 [ll], 164 [ll], 184 a–b

ROSEBUD GALLERY, Berkeley, California: 20 [l], 43 [l], 152, 159 [u], 191 [c]

SAN FRANCISCO STATE UNIVERSITY, ART DEPARTMENT VISUAL RESOURCES LIBRARY: 19

SMITHSONIAN INSTITUTION, FREER GALLERY OF ART, Washington, D.C.:
- Charles Lang Freer, Gift of: 78 (F1903.101-F1903.102), 103 (F1904.61), 104 [u] (F1898.6), 105 (F1907.178)

SMITHSONIAN INSTITUTION LIBRARIES, COOPER-HEWITT NATIONAL DESIGN MUSEUM BRANCH, New York City: 13, 22

SPAULDING (WILLIAM S. AND JOHN T.) COLLECTION, Museum of Fine Arts, Boston: 80 (21.4430), 125 (21.6756), 139 (21.9497)

STATE UNIVERSITY OF NEW YORK–BUFFALO, UNIVERSITY ARCHIVES: 126 [r]

STEENSMA (KRISTINE) COLLECTION: 170, 180 [r], 197 [l], 201 [u]

TUCK (RICHARD) COLLECTION: 162 [u], 163 [ll], 163 [lr], 191 [l]

UNIVERSITY OF CALIFORNIA–BERKELEY: 17 [l], 18, 68 [u], 71 [l], 74, 81, 85, 106 [u], 131, 132, 135, 138 [ur], 155 [ul]. *See also* Bancroft Library; East Asian Library; Environmental Design Library; Gardner Library

WELCH (MARYBETH) COLLECTION: 178, 182 [u], 183 [u], 183 [l], 198 [r] 202 [ll], 106 [l], 204 [c], 204 [ur]

WIDENER UNIVERSITY ART COLLECTION & GALLERY, Chester Pennsylvania: 25 [l], 41, 27, 44 [l], 115, 150, 182.
- *See also* Deshong (Alfred O.) Collection

WRENN (VIRGINIA) COLLECTION, Richmond, Virginia: 45

Index

Numbers in boldface font indicate the entry subjects are in the captions for the accompanying images.

T

U

V

W

X

Y

Z

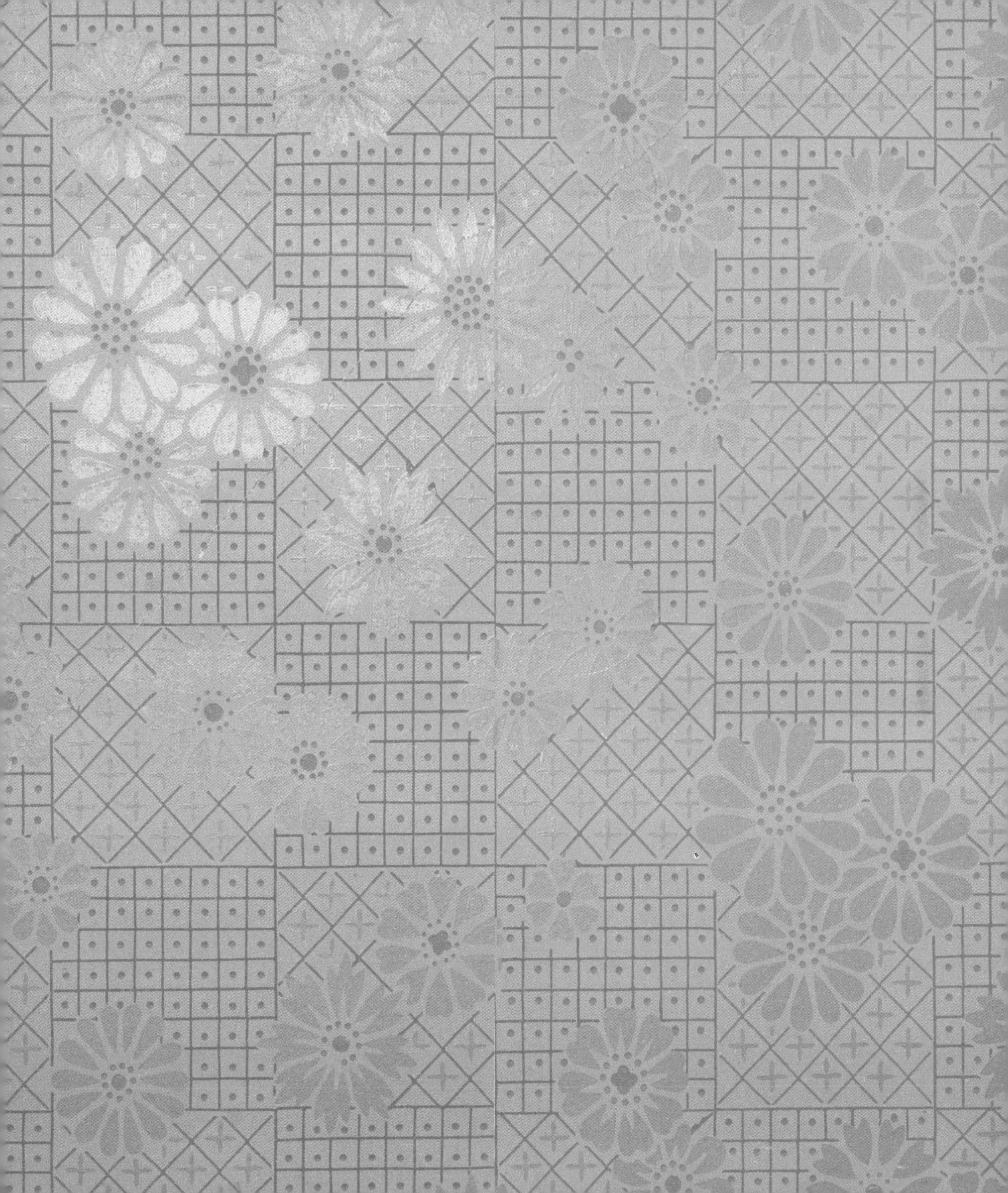

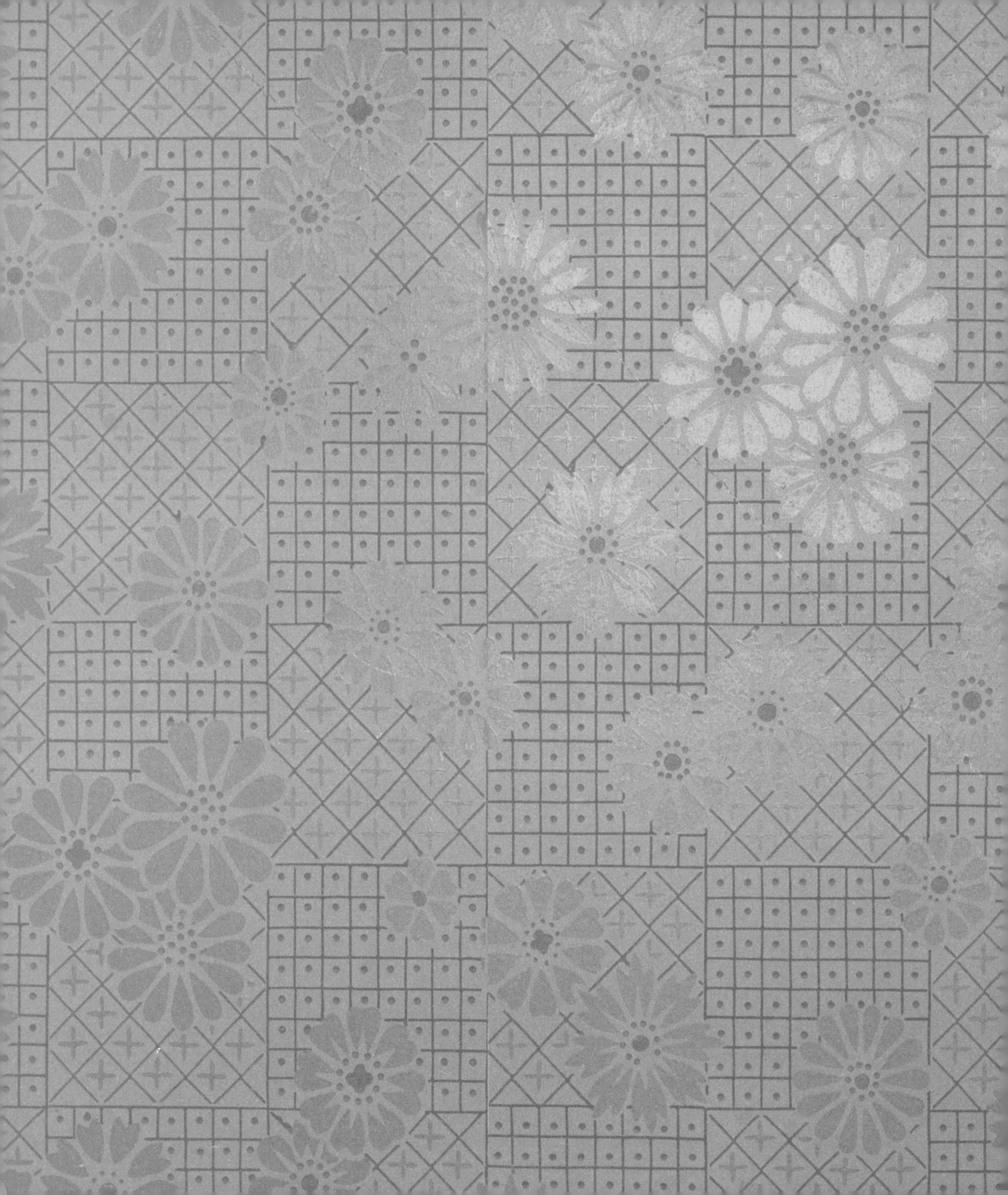